THE BLACK AND TANS

D. M. Leeson is Associate Professor of History at Laurentian University, Ontario, Canada. He received his PhD in History from McMaster University, Hamilton, Canada in 2003.

PRAISE FOR *THE BLACK AND TANS*

'While the Black and Tans served for less than two years, their disastrous deployment has lived long in Irish cultural memory. Through dispassionate research and fastidiously marshalled sources, D. M. Leeson undermines many enduring misapprehensions that still surround this most controversial of police forces.'

Peter Geoghegan, *Times Literary Supplement*

'A fresh, often exciting narrative that convinces the reader that there has indeed been a distortion in the general image of the men in these two forces . . . The Black and Tans will repay close reading by anyone interested in those savage years of the Irish War of Independence, when trust was hard to come by and brotherhood a flexible term for many involved in the horrors. Leeson has convincingly questioned a great deal of received opinion, and probed the way it was received in the first place.'

Stephen Wade, *Times Higher Education*

'. . . lifts the lid on a discreditable episode of recent British history and paves the way for future research.'

Nigel Jones, *History Today*

'. . . careful analysis . . .'

Eunan O'Halpin, *Irish Times*

'It is by far the best book yet written on the subject of the Black & Tans/R.I. C. Auxiliaries and is set to become recommended reading for those studying this period of Irish history and I eagerly look forward to seeing more of his work on the period.'

Padraig Óg Ó Ruairc, author of *Blood on the Banner: The Republican Struggle in Clare*

THE BLACK AND TANS

BRITISH POLICE AND AUXILIARIES IN THE IRISH WAR OF INDEPENDENCE, 1920–1921

D. M. LEESON

OXFORD
UNIVERSITY PRESS

OXFORD
UNIVERSITY PRESS

Great Clarendon Street, Oxford OX2 6DP
United Kingdom

Oxford University Press is a department of the University of Oxford.
It furthers the University's objective of excellence in research, scholarship,
and education by publishing worldwide. Oxford is a registered trade mark of
Oxford University Press in the UK and in certain other countries

First Edition published in 2012
Reprinted 2013

British Library Cataloguing in Publication Data
Data available

Library of Congress Cataloging in Publication Data
Data available

ISBN 978-0-19-965882-4

To the memory of Peter Hart 1963–2010

Contents

Preface

In 1920–1, during the Irish War of Independence, the British government recruited thousands of British ex-servicemen to reinforce the Royal Irish Constabulary (RIC). Ex-soldiers became constables, and were nicknamed 'Black and Tans' for their mixed uniforms of dark police green and military khaki. Ex-officers joined a temporary force, the Auxiliary Division (ADRIC), a special emergency gendarmerie, which was heavily armed, motorised, and organised in military-style companies. Pitted against the guerrillas of the Irish Republican Army (IRA), the Black and Tans and Auxiliaries took numerous reprisals, assassinating Irish republicans and burning their homes and shops. As a consequence, their name became a byword for undisciplined violence, and the spectre of 'black-and-tannery' has haunted Ireland ever since.

This book uses evidence from British and Irish archives and newspapers to study these British police and their behaviour in revolutionary Ireland. According to legend, the Black and Tans were ex-convicts and psychopaths, hardened by prison and crazed by war. In fact, most of them were quite ordinary men, whose violent and even criminal behaviour was a product of circumstance rather than character. The British government insisted on treating insurgents as criminals, and relied on its Irish police force to repress the rebel 'murder gang'. Unsuited for guerrilla warfare, the RIC was already losing its discipline and avenging itself on guerrillas and their supporters even before its British reinforcements arrived. British constables lived and worked alongside Irish constables, and generally followed their example, good or bad. Freed from the sometimes moderating influence of the constabulary's Irish majority, Auxiliaries behaved with even greater licence than Black and Tans. The violence of the British and Irish police was then denied, excused, and even encouraged by higher authorities, including the British government, which was anxious to keep up the pretence that Irish revolutionaries were merely terrorists and gangsters.

This book began as a PhD dissertation at McMaster University in Hamilton, Canada. I would like to thank my supervisor, Richard Rempel, and the original members of my supervisory committee, Virginia Aksan, James Alsop and John Sainsbury: special thanks to Stephen Heathorn, both for joining my committee, and for his subsequent friendship and support. Thanks also to the departmental assistants, Wendy Benedetti and Rita Maxwell, and to my fellow graduate students: Daryl Baswick, Nanci Delayen, Rhonda Hinther, Heather Nelson, Greg Stott, and especially Dan Gorman. Finally, thanks to McMaster University, to the Social Sciences and Humanities Research Council and to the Government of Ontario for their generous financial support.

After completing my doctorate, I had the extraordinary good fortune to obtain a tenure-track position within two years, at Laurentian University in Sudbury, Canada. Thanks to my colleagues and friends, especially Stephen Azzi, Sara Burke, and Janice Liedl, along with the departmental assistant, Rose-May Demore, for their friendship and support.

The staffs of the following libraries and archives were most helpful, and I thank them both for their assistance and for permission to quote from documents in their care: the British Library, the Garda Siochana Museum, the Imperial War Museum, the Military Archives of Ireland, Mills Memorial Library, the National Archives of Ireland, the National Archives of the United Kingdom and the Trinity College Archives. Special thanks to Donal Kivlehan at the Garda Siochana Museum for directing me to the Eye and Ear Hospital in Dublin, and to Joyce Latham at the British Library Newspaper Reading Room for letting me consult a volume of newspapers that had been marked 'unfit for use'.

Thanks to my research assistants, Brendan Power and Gary Haines, for making it possible to continue my research even when I could not travel overseas: thanks also to David Fitzpatrick for his kindness to a stranger. Special thanks to Frank Bouchier-Hayes for his continuing interest, enthusiasm, and assistance.

Thanks to my family for their love and support: to my mother, Barbara Leeson, to my father and his wife, Howard and Ede Leeson, to my older and youngest brothers by birth, Evan and Brian, and to my brother and sister by marriage, Bruce and Dawn. Special thanks to my sister-in-law, Lisa, for her expert proofreading of an early draft, and to my younger brother, Corporal Joseph Leeson, Royal Canadian Mounted Police. *Maintiens le droit.*

Thanks also to my editors, Christopher Wheeler, Stephanie Ireland, and Emma Barber; to my copy-editor, Richard Mason; to my map-maker, Dennis McClendon; to my anonymous reviewers; and to all the staff at Oxford University Press.

Finally, I am grateful to the late Peter Hart, who passed away while this book was nearing completion. Dr Hart's work was an early inspiration for my own, and I was honoured when he agreed to serve as external examiner for my PhD dissertation. In addition, Dr Hart recommended my article on the Croke Park massacre for the *Canadian Journal of History* graduate-student essay prize, and suggested that I submit my revised dissertation to Oxford University Press for publication. I knew him only by correspondence, but I always assumed—wrongly—that I would have a chance to thank him in person some day, for all his assistance at a critical stage of my career. *Vitae summa brevis spem nos vetat incohare longam.*

Portions of this book have been previously published as 'The "Scum of London's Underworld"? British Recruits for the Royal Irish Constabulary, 1920–21', in *Contemporary British History*, vol. 17, no. 1 (Spring 2003), pp. 1–38.

D. L.
Sudbury,
Ontario, Canada

Preface to the Paperback Edition

I have taken advantage of this new edition to make a few small corrections. The most important of these are in Chapter Two, which describes the War of Independence in West Galway. On pages 61 and 63, I mention the shooting of two civilians, Thomas Molloy and Thomas McKeever. As the reader will see, I suspected that Molloy might have been killed by the police, and mentioned my suspicions in a note on pages 242–3. But in the end, I attributed both Molloy and McKeever's deaths to the IRA; what is more, I counted them both as having been executed for spying, on page 67. In his review of my book, however, Padraig Óg Ó Ruairc argues that both men were killed by the Crown forces: see http://theirishwar.com/2011/10/the-black-tans-british-police-and-auxiliaries-in-the-irish-war-of-independence-1920-1921-by-david-m-leeson (accessed 1 May 2012). I have adjusted the figures on page 67 to reflect this new information.

List of Maps

List of Abbreviations

ADRIC	Auxiliary Division, Royal Irish Constabulary
CI	County Inspector
DAG	Deputy Adjutant General
DC	Divisional Commissioner
DCM	Distinguished Conduct Medal
DI	District Inspector
DIG	Deputy Inspector General
DMP	Dublin Metropolitan Police
DSO	Distinguished Service Order
GHQ	General Headquarters
GOC	General Officer Commanding
IG	Inspector General
IPP	Irish Parliamentary Party
IRA	Irish Republican Army
MC	Military Cross
MM	Military Medal
OC	Officer Commanding
RIC	Royal Irish Constabulary
UVF	Ulster Volunteer Force
USC	Ulster Special Constabulary

ARCHIVES

IWM	Imperial War Museum
MA	Military Archives of Ireland
NA	National Archives of Ireland
PRO	Public Record Office

TCD	Trinity College Dublin Archives
TNA	National Archives of the United Kingdom

COLLECTIONS

BMH	Bureau of Military History
CAB	Cabinet Office
CO	Colonial Office
HO	Home Office
WO	War Office
T	Treasury

Note to the Reader

The place names and spellings used in this book are those used by the Royal Irish Constabulary in 1920–1, and as a result will sometimes vary from current usage: Connaught, instead of Connacht; Gormanstown, instead of Gormanston; King's County, instead of County Offaly; Londonderry, instead of Derry; Maryborough, instead of Portlaois; Queen's County, instead of County Laois; and Queenstown, instead of Cobh.

Map 1. Ireland, 1920–1.

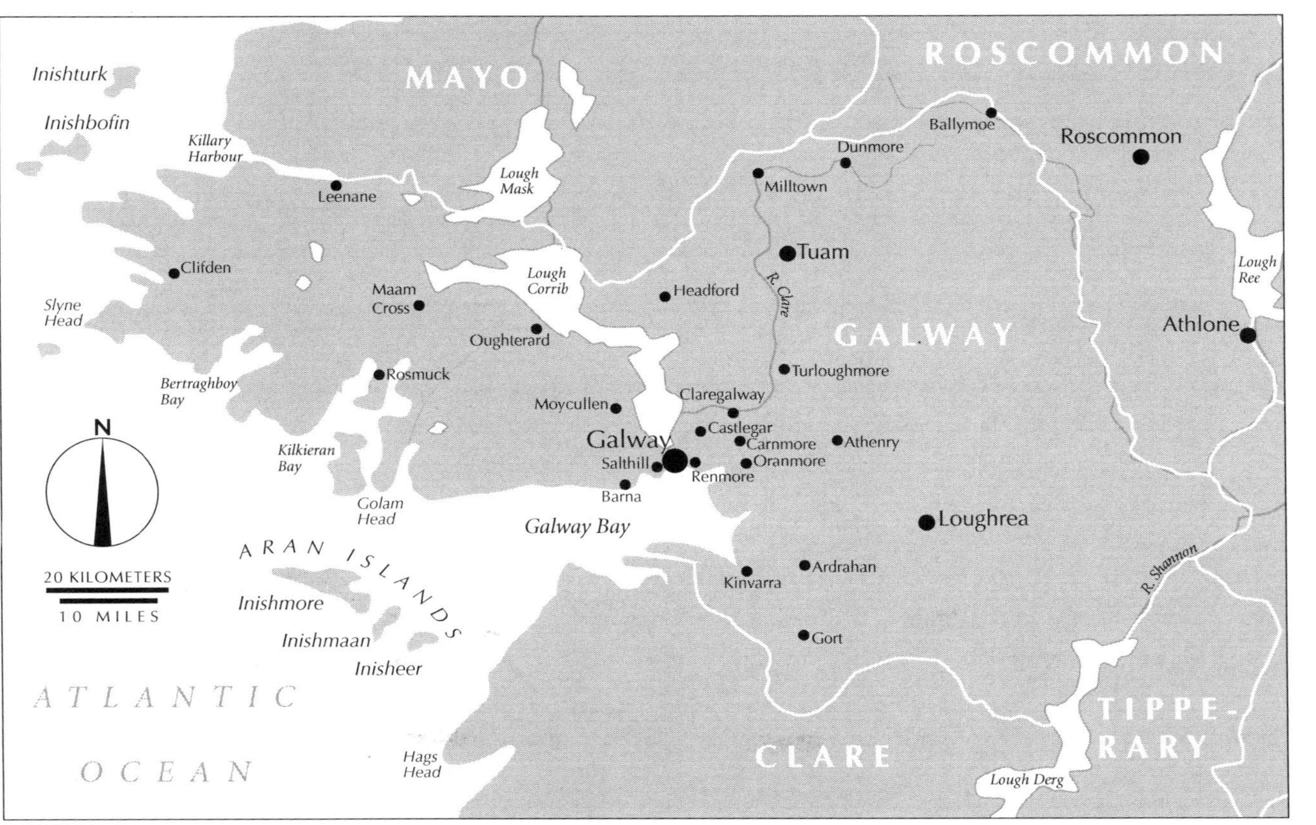

Map 2. County Galway, 1920–1.

Toutes nos qualités sont incertaines et douteuses en bien comme en mal, et elles sont presque toutes à la merci des occasions.

—La Rochefoucauld, *Maximes* (1664)

Introduction

During the Irish War of Independence, between 1920 and 1921, over ten thousand British men enlisted in the United Kingdom's Irish police forces and fought against the Irish Republican Army (IRA). Most of these British police were veterans of the Great War of 1914–18. Ex-soldiers joined the Royal Irish Constabulary (RIC) and quickly became known as 'Black and Tans' for their lack of uniform clothing: in the beginning, they wore a mixture of dark police green and military khaki; some of them had only a cap and belt to identify them as policemen. Ex-officers joined a temporary force, the Auxiliary Division (ADRIC): heavily armed and organised in military-style companies, these 'Auxiliaries' wore mixed uniforms as well, topped with tam-o'-shanter bonnets instead of police caps. During their war year in Ireland, the Black and Tans and Auxiliaries became notorious for their violence and lack of discipline, and especially for taking reprisals against known and suspected revolutionaries: ambushes and assassinations by the IRA were met with extrajudicial killings and property destruction by the police. Demonised by their enemies as a vicious rabble of jailbirds and down-and-outs, and denounced by their critics as paramilitary death squads, the Black and Tans and Auxiliaries have gone down in history as the British equivalent of the Turkish bashi-bazouks or the German Freikorps.

Yet, despite their evil fame, the Black and Tans and Auxiliaries have never been studied closely by historians. In fact, over the past four decades, new research has increased our knowledge of almost every feature of the Irish War of Independence, except the British police forces. Michael Hopkinson has published a general history of the war.[1] William Kautt has produced a military history of the conflict, while Michael Foy has chronicled the secret war between the rival intelligence services in Dublin.[2]

David George Boyce and Charles Townshend have examined the British government's Irish policies, and Tom Bowden has compared and contrasted the Irish insurgency with the Arab Revolt in Palestine.[3] Joost Augusteijn and Peter Hart have written social histories of the Irish Republican Army,[4] while beginning with David Fitzpatrick, a number of scholars have written local histories of the War of Independence period.[5] The Irish police have attracted historians like John Brewer, W. J. Lowe, and Elizabeth Malcolm.[6] William Sheehan has even produced a volume of reminiscences by British soldiers.[7] Yet for some reason, the Black and Tans and Auxiliaries have remained obscure figures—anonymous extras in the revolutionary drama.[8]

Who were these men, and what type of men were they? Were they truly recruited from 'the criminal classes and the dregs of the populations of English cities', as their enemies claimed?[9] What was it like to serve in the police forces and fight the guerrillas? Why did these British police commit 'reprisals' against helpless prisoners and civilians? Do the Black and Tans and Auxiliaries deserve their terrible reputation? This book will try to provide answers for these and other questions using information from a variety of both published and unpublished sources. Although chiefly based on documents in the United Kingdom's National Archives and articles from British newspapers, it also makes use of documents in the National Archives of Ireland, the Irish Military Archives of Ireland, the Trinity College Archives and the Imperial War Museum, along with articles in Irish newspapers, and the United Kingdom Hansard.

The story that emerges from these various documents will be familiar in some ways, but unfamiliar in others. The violence and licence of the British police is no myth, and this book is full of examples of their criminal and brutal behaviour. But the Black and Tans were not ex-convicts; nor had they brought the Great War home, as many historians have supposed. Most of them, as it turns out, were just unemployed British veterans looking for a new start in life as Irish policemen. Social psychologists have come to the counter-intuitive conclusion that, under the right circumstances, 'ordinary, even above-average men and women can harm and degrade totally innocent people', and will even 'behave in ways that violate their preexisting moral and ethical standards'.[10] It was the conditions in which they served, rather than their pre-existing dispositions, that drove many Black and Tans to fight terror, as they saw it, with terror.

As members of a temporary force of ex-officers, Auxiliaries were less ordinary than the Black and Tans: indeed, this 'corps de luxe' had its own staff of temporary constables for servants, allowing its members both to live and fight in their accustomed style. But this elite force was not as elite as it seemed. Most of its temporary cadets had been promoted from the ranks, late in the Great War: their discipline was poor, and their attitude to both public and private property was often casual. The Auxiliary Division itself was improvised quickly, in response to the police manpower crisis in the summer of 1920, and its brief history was characterised by confusion, disorganisation, corruption and waste.

There was a rough division of labour between these two police forces: in military terms, the Black and Tans were static, defensive troops, the garrisons of local strongpoints, whereas Auxiliary companies were mobile, offensive units of raiders. Both forces, however, were fighting blind: their intelligence was poor, and as a result, in their battles with guerrilla bands the police were often caught by surprise, ambushed, and beaten. Their defeats, the casualties they suffered, and the perceived unfairness of this 'one-sided war' all encouraged the police to take reprisals against both guerrillas and civilians.

The reference above to the police in general, rather than the British police in particular, was deliberate, since the evidence makes it clear that Irish police took part in reprisals as well. Though their involvement in these atrocities is not a new discovery, historians have underestimated just how deeply and widely implicated the Irish police really were. And since Irish police were neither hardened criminals nor brutalised ex-soldiers, it follows that if we want to understand the causes of reprisals, we must set aside all dispositional hypotheses and focus on situational factors instead—chiefly, the stresses of counter-revolutionary warfare, compounded by the self-defeating policies of the British government, which sent police to do a job that should have been done either by soldiers or politicians.

I

The Two-Headed Ass

Coalition Policy and Coalition Policing in Ireland

In the political cartoons of David Low, the Lloyd George coalition government of 1918–22 was often depicted as a two-headed ass—a foolish, chimerical creature, 'without pride of ancestry or hope of posterity'.[1] The coalition's conduct of the Irish War of Independence did much to justify Low's caricature. Under the sway of its Conservative and Unionist members, the government pursued a double-headed policy that combined limited repression with limited concessions. This policy's armed implements were hybrids as well. Members of the Cabinet were unable (or unwilling) to view the conflict in military terms. 'The Irish job', in Lloyd George's words, 'was a policeman's job supported by the military and not vice versa.'[2] As a result, the government primarily relied on its Irish police force, the Royal Irish Constabulary (RIC), to defeat what became known as the Irish Republican Army.

Unluckily for the government, the RIC was not up to the job. Though frequently denounced as an army of occupation, it was a mostly civilian force, unfitted for counter-insurgency. This was clear by the autumn of 1919: but instead of replacing the police with soldiers, the government recruited ex-soldiers to work as police. Veterans of the Great War were enlisted to serve as constables in the RIC, and their former officers were enlisted to serve in a special striking force, the Auxiliary Division. These British reinforcements, it was hoped, would give the police the strength and skills they needed to re-establish law and order.

1.1 Policy

1.1.1 The Irish ulcer, 1886–1919

The underlying causes of the Irish War of Independence can be traced back to the Home Rule Crises of 1886 and 1893. In the general election of 1885, Charles Stewart Parnell's Irish Parliamentary Party (IPP) won 85 out of Ireland's 105 constituencies, and its members held the balance of power in the United Kingdom's House of Commons. At first, Parnell threw his party's weight behind Lord Salisbury's Conservatives in exchange for land-reform legislation—but he soon made an alliance with W. E. Gladstone's Liberals when Gladstone offered Ireland Home Rule. Unfortunately for Parnell and his party, Gladstone's Home Rule Bill split their Liberal allies. Liberal Unionists combined with the Conservatives against Irish self-government, and the First Home Rule Bill was defeated. Gladstone then called an election in 1886, and lost.

Six years later, though, Gladstone's Liberals and their Irish allies won the election of 1892, and the Second Home Rule Bill was introduced in 1893. This passed through the Commons, but was defeated in the House of Lords. Gladstone was ready to call another election, but his colleagues were unwilling to fight a constitutional battle with the Lords over Home Rule. As a result, Gladstone resigned, the Liberals were eventually defeated in 1895, and a coalition of Conservatives and Liberal Unionists governed the United Kingdom for the next ten years. In Ireland itself, a new generation of Irish men and women embraced new cultural-nationalist movements like the Gaelic League, the Gaelic Athletic Association, and the Literary Revival. In addition, new nationalist economic and political organisations appeared, such as the United Irish League, the Irish Transport and General Workers' Union, and the separatist Sinn Féin movement.

When the Liberals finally returned to power, in late 1905, they showed little of the Grand Old Man's enthusiasm for Home Rule: and after the general election of 1906, they took advantage of their massive majority to steer clear of the Irish Question; instead of Home Rule, they offered only the Irish Council Bill—a measure so limited that even the Irish rejected it. But in 1910 the Liberals were caught in the constitutional storm they had avoided in 1893. After the House of Lords rejected the 'People's Budget' in

1909, an election was called in January 1910, and another in December, on the single issue of reforming the Upper House. The government, headed by Herbert Asquith, lost its majority in January, and did not win it back in December: Asquith's Liberals won only 275 out of 670 seats, compared to 273 Conservatives and Liberal Unionists. Once again, the IPP, led since 1900 by Parnell's successor John Redmond, held the balance of power in the new Parliament, and the price of their 82 votes was a promise of Home Rule.

The Liberals first neutered 'Mr Balfour's poodle', the House of Lords, by passing the Parliament Act of 1911 and thereby depriving the Lords of their ability to block legislation. The government then kept its promise to the IPP by introducing a Government of Ireland Bill in April 1912. This bill aroused furious opposition from Conservatives and Unionists. Though deprived of their veto, the Lords rejected the bill twice, in January and July 1913, while Northern Irish Protestants organised a private army, the Ulster Volunteer Force (UVF), to resist 'Rome Rule' by force.

By the summer of 1914, the Government of Ireland Bill was completing its third circuit through Parliament, and the Lords could no longer prevent its enactment. Led by Andrew Bonar Law, the Conservatives and Unionist opposition demanded Ulster's exclusion from the bill. Redmond's IPP demanded Ulster's inclusion. The UVF had armed itself and was preparing to fight. Irish nationalists were arming Volunteers of their own. One historian has concluded that 'at the very end of July war in Ulster seemed certain, and only the outbreak of the war in Europe averted it'.[3] But once war broke out in Europe on 28 July with the invasion of Serbia by Austria-Hungary, the British government and the opposition agreed to set Irish Home Rule aside. The Government of Ireland Act was assented on 18 September 1914, but suspended for twelve months, or until 'such later date (not being later than the end of the present War) as may be fixed by His Majesty by Order in Council'.[4]

The Great War, of course, lasted much longer than 12 months—and by the time it was over the Government of Ireland Act had few supporters left in Parliament. From 1914 to 1916 Redmond and his party had stood by the government and encouraged recruitment in Ireland, hoping that her people's loyalty and sacrifice would be rewarded at war's end. This policy split the Irish National Volunteers into two camps: the majority National Volunteers, who supported Redmond, and the minority Irish Volunteers, who swore to resist any move towards partition or conscription, and to work for a 'free National Government of Ireland'. Finally, on Easter Monday, 24 April 1916, the Irish Volunteers rose in rebellion and proclaimed an independent Irish Republic.

The Easter Rising was crushed within a week, and its leaders (including Patrick Pearse and James Connolly) were executed: but Irish public opinion was alienated by the British government's heavy-handed response to the rebellion. This alienation deepened when, in the wake of the rising, negotiations for a new Home Rule settlement ran aground once more on the reef of Ulster: Irish nationalists would not agree to partition, and Unionists would agree to nothing less. This failure finally discredited the IPP. In 1917 the Redmondites lost four by-elections to Sinn Féin, led by Eámon de Valera and Arthur Griffith. Sinn Féin's momentum increased in the spring of 1918. In the midst of Germany's final offensive on the Western Front, the British government announced its intention to extend compulsory military service to Ireland. In response, Irish nationalists pledged themselves 'to resist conscription by the most effective means at our disposal'. Ultimately, the crisis passed, and conscription was not imposed on Ireland, but the political damage was done. When a general election was held in December 1918, a month after the Armistice, Sinn Féin swept Ireland, winning 73 constituencies. Their Unionist opponents won only 25, almost all of them in Ulster and in universities. The IPP won just seven seats.

In the meantime, the political situation in Britain was changing just as radically. Asquith's Liberal government had lasted only until May 1915, when the resignation of the First Sea Lord, Admiral Fisher, over the misconduct of the Dardanelles campaign, along with a scandal over the shortage of artillery shells on the Western Front, led the Prime Minister to form a Liberal-dominated coalition with his Unionist opponents. This coalition fell apart in December 1916, when Asquith resigned, and a second coalition was formed, led by David Lloyd George, author of the 1909 'People's Budget'. Though Lloyd George was a Liberal, he relied heavily on Conservative and Unionist support, in part because Asquith's resignation had once again split the Liberal Party: some Liberals backed Lloyd George and the new coalition, but the majority followed Asquith into opposition. After the Armistice, Lloyd George and the Unionist leader, Bonar Law, agreed to continue their government of national unity in peacetime. In the Coupon Election of December 1918, while Sinn Féin was routing its opponents in Ireland, Lloyd George's coalition was routing its own opponents in Great Britain: the coalition Unionists won 335 seats, and the coalition

Liberals 133; together with 10 Labour MPs, this gave the coalition a crushing majority of 478 seats out of 707 in Parliament. Support for Asquith's Liberals was weak. They won just 28 seats, and as a result, Arthur Henderson's Labour Party became the official opposition, with 63.

Thus, by the end of 1918, Ireland's future was in doubt once again. In theory, the Government of Ireland Act of 1914 would come into force when the war ended. In practice, it was dead. Its enemies dominated the governing coalition. Unionist members outnumbered their Liberal partners five to two, and the Cabinet was full of men who had led the fight against Home Rule between 1912 and 1914: the Lord Chancellor, Viscount Birkenhead; the Lord Privy Seal, Andrew Bonar Law; the Lord President, Arthur Balfour; and the First Lord of the Admiralty, Walter Long. If nothing else, their presence in Cabinet ensured that Ulster's demands for exclusion from any new scheme of Home Rule would be met. In addition, Lloyd George was no Gladstone: his enthusiasm for Home Rule had always been limited, and he was not willing to risk his premiership over Ireland. As a consequence, throughout 1919, while the Prime Minister was preoccupied with peace negotiations in Paris, the Irish Question was left on the back burner. As late as 12 November of that year, in response to a parliamentary question about the Government of Ireland Act, Bonar Law said simply that it would 'come into operation on the ratification of the last of the Peace Treaties'.[5] But by then, the site of the struggle had shifted from Westminster to Ireland itself.

1.1.2 Insurgency: January 1919 to July 1920

An Irish republican insurgency began soon after Sinn Féin's triumph in the general election of 1918. Sinn Féin members did not recognise the United Kingdom of Great Britain and Ireland: instead, they gave their allegiance to the Irish Republic proclaimed by the rebels of 1916. In their view, Ireland's 105 elected representatives were not part of the United Kingdom's House of Commons: they were instead members of Dáil Eireann, an Irish republican parliament. On 21 January 1919 thirty Sinn Féin MPs met at the Mansion House in Dublin and adopted a Declaration of Independence, along with an Address to the Free Nations of the World, which predicted that 'the existing state of war, between Ireland and England, can never be ended until Ireland is definitely evacuated by the armed forces of England'. On that same day a band of rebel Irish Volunteers killed two police constables and stole a shipment of explosives near Soloheadbeg in County Tipperary.

The republican insurgency escalated slowly at first: by the year's end, Irish guerrillas had killed just 15 (Irish) police. But the conflict intensified in the winter of 1919–20. On 19 December 1919 the Volunteers laid an ambush for the Lord Lieutenant of Ireland, Viscount French, outside his official residence in Dublin's Phoenix Park. Though this attack was unsuccessful, it provoked a strong reaction from the Irish government.[6] Beginning on 7 January 1920, the British Army was given special powers to combat the insurgents, and the security forces carried out mass arrests of republican leaders. Not long afterward, the Lloyd George ministry finally started implementing its own plans for the future of Ireland. A new Government of Ireland Bill was introduced on 25 February. Before the Great War, Ulster Unionist opposition had blocked the road to Home Rule. The Fourth Home Rule Bill used partition as a detour. The bill would establish two provincial parliaments: one for a Protestant enclave in the north, and another for the rest of Ireland. In addition, the bill would set up a joint council, appointed by the governments of both north and south. In time (it was hoped), this council would become a single Irish Parliament.

Ireland's revolutionaries were not impressed by this complicated but limited scheme. The guerrillas killed another 12 police in the first three months of 1920, and celebrated Easter by burning hundreds of tax offices and abandoned police barracks; soon afterward, many of their imprisoned leaders began a hunger strike. Dismayed by these developments, Dublin Castle tried to calm the situation by switching from coercion to conciliation. They let the republican hunger strikers out of Dublin's Mountjoy gaol on 14 April, and they took away the military's emergency powers on 3 May.

Instead of appeasing the revolutionaries, these concessions demoralised the men of the Royal Irish Constabulary, who felt abandoned and betrayed. To make matters worse, instead of simmering down, the conflict began to boil in the summer of 1920. The guerrillas, now becoming known as the Irish Republican Army (IRA), escalated their campaign against the RIC by attacking its barracks and ambushing its patrols. Police casualties doubled, and then doubled again: 28 members of the force were killed between April and June; another 55 were killed between July and September. In many districts IRA supporters increased the pressure on the police with a boycott. Railway workers went on strike, refusing to move trains that carried police or troops bearing arms. Merchants refused to serve police customers. The police and their families were shunned and threatened. Police recruits and servants were attacked and intimidated. Women who were friendly with police had their hair cut off. Police property was wrecked and stolen: in some cases police bicycles were snatched while their owners were in church. Meanwhile, the rebels were building their alternative state. Local governments were acknowledging the Dáil's authority. IRA Volunteers were acting as republican police. Republican courts were adjudicating civil and criminal cases. In many parts of Ireland the Republic was becoming a reality.

This full-scale insurgency finally provoked a full-scale counter-insurgency in the midsummer of 1920. In both Britain and Ireland criminal cases were tried quarterly. The summer assizes were held in Ireland in June and July 1920. For the British government, the results were disastrous. In a memorandum dated 24 July the Chief Secretary for Ireland, Sir Hamar Greenwood, told the Cabinet that 'throughout the greater part of Ireland criminal justice can no longer be administered by the ordinary constitutional process of trial by judge and jury':

> At the recent assizes the criminal business of many of the counties of the south and west was left undisposed of owing to the non-attendance of jurors and when a jury can be got together even in the clearest cases a conviction is not assured. This is the result of a campaign of intimidation and violence carefully planned and vigorously executed. If the campaign were confined to the intimidation of jurors a remedy might be found in the suspension of trial by jury and the establishment of special tribunals of two or more judges as was done in 1882 but the violence and intimidation extends to all officers concerned in the administration of justice, Clerks of the Crown, Magistrates, Petty Sessions Clerks, Sheriffs, Process-servers and Bailiffs; Courthouses are burnt down and court records are destroyed. The administrative machinery of the Courts has been brought to a standstill.[7]

Like the release of the hunger strikers in the spring, the failure of the summer assizes further demoralised the Royal Irish Constabulary. Most of the crimes that went unpunished had been committed against the police. When it became clear that the guerrillas were above the law, the number of retirements and resignations from the constabulary went up dramatically: 225 constables had resigned and retired in May and June; 783 resigned and retired in July and August.[8] The men who stayed in the force became increasingly bitter and violent. There had been disturbances in Tipperary during the winter, and police death squads had killed a handful of Irish republicans in the spring: their most prominent victim had been Tomás MacCurtain, Lord Mayor of Cork and Commandant of the IRA's 1st Cork Brigade, who had been shot dead on the night of 19 March. Still, in most areas, the RIC's discipline did not finally crack until July, when the quarter sessions collapsed, and the police began to riot in the streets.

Soon, police reports from the south and west were full of despair and anger. 'Murder and outrage are universal', wrote one official:

> The loss of life inflicted on Government forces cannot but have a disastrous effect on the morale of the men.
>
> The R.I.C. hitherto have been indomitable & have carried on with fearlessness, courage, & initiative, but recent events point to the breaking point being reached.
>
> This is evidenced by the numerous applications to resign made by men who, having no means of livelihood outside the force after resignation, have to face the world again to win bread for themselves & their families.
>
> So far as the R.I.C. are concerned in this Riding, they may be considered to have ceased to function. The most they can do is try to defend themselves and their barracks.
>
> It would seem that the time has arrived for the military to supersede the R.I.C. in this Riding.
>
> If action is not speedily taken the R.I.C. will exist only in name.
>
> Further resignations may be expected daily.
>
> The men consider that that they are merely pawns in a political game.[9]

Dublin Castle's outlook was equally pessimistic. The British government's top civil servants in Ireland attended a Cabinet conference on 23 July 1920, where William Wylie predicted that 'within two months the Irish Police Force as a Police Force would cease to exist'. 'In two month's time,' he said, 'fifty per cent of the Police Force would have resigned through terrorism, and the remainder would have to go about in considerable force committing counter outrages. Am [*sic*] Irish policeman either saw white or he saw red; if he saw white he resigned from the force through terrorism, and if he saw red he committed a counter outrage.'[10] Alfred Cope told the Cabinet that 'he thought that the Sinn Fein courts were doing more harm to the prestige of the British government than the assassinations'.[11] Finally, Sir John Anderson made it clear that in his opinion the government 'had either to give way or to go very much further in repression'. 'The alternatives were, in fact,' he said, 'the declaration of martial law or some kind of agreement with Sinn Fein.'[12]

For their part, Anderson and his colleagues were convinced that the British government had to give way. 'By proclaiming martial law it would be possible to beat the people into insensibility,' said Wylie; 'but when martial law was taken off—and it must end some time—the feelings of hatred and bitterness would be intensified, and there would be a return to the present state of affairs.'[13] The best course of action, they suggested, would be to drop the Government of Ireland Bill in favour of Dominion Home Rule—autonomy for Ireland within the Empire.

1.1.3 The Restoration of Order in Ireland Act, 9 August 1920

A negotiated settlement, however, was anathema to many Cabinet ministers—especially Conservatives and Unionists. On 24 July Arthur Balfour denounced any suggestion of dropping the Government of Ireland Bill. 'The Government cannot abandon a measure so elaborate in its structure and so far advanced in its Parliamentary career as the present Home Rule Bill without some discredit,' he wrote: 'the discredit would amount to disgrace if this course were adopted, not on its merits, but as a concession to those who worked through organised assassination. When it became known as, of course, it would be—that the flag of truce had been sent by the Imperial government to the assassins,—not by the assassins to the Imperial government,—the disgrace would deepen to infamy.' In addition, government faith had been pledged, to Northern Unionists in particular. 'A parliament has been promised to Ulster,' he wrote. 'Whether the promise was originally wise or unwise is quite immaterial; it cannot now be withdrawn.' The bill must be regarded as a final settlement: any other position would just encourage the revolutionaries. 'If then we let it be understood that our Home Rule Bill is no more than an instalment, we invite further agitation: we give the extremists the occasion they seek; and we shall have before us a long perspective of Home Rule Amendment Bills to which no term can be assigned except that of complete separation.'[14]

Balfour's views were seconded by Walter Long. On 25 July the First Lord of the Admiralty warned his Cabinet colleagues that 'any hesitation on the part of the Government to proceed with the measure in its present form would be attended with the gravest consequences in Ulster'.[15] Even so,

Sir John Anderson appealed again for an offer of autonomy within the Empire. 'I believe,' he said, 'that, if what is commonly described as Dominion Home Rule—with protection for Ulster—could be offered immediately sufficient popular support would be obtained in Ireland to enable the suppression of crime and the re-establishment of law, to be effected by means of the ordinary civil machinery temporarily reinforced.'[16]

In the end, the hawks prevailed. Ignoring his Under Secretary's 'profound misgiving' about its prospects, Chief Secretary Greenwood submitted emergency legislation to the Cabinet. The Restoration of Order in Ireland Bill would give Dublin Castle the power to govern by regulation; to replace the criminal courts with courts martial; to replace coroners' inquests with military courts of inquiry; and to punish disaffected local governments by withholding their grants of money.[17] On 29 July the Cabinet's Conservative-dominated Irish Situation Committee recommended 'that no person serving under the Irish government should in any circumstance be permitted to hold communication with Sinn Fein, except on the basis of the Government's expressed policy, viz: the repression of crime and the determination to carry through the Government of Ireland Bill on its present main lines.'[18] The Restoration of Order in Ireland Bill was approved with a few modifications and amendments on 2 August.[19] It was introduced and given a first reading in the House of Commons the same day.

Three days later, at around 4:00 p.m. on Thursday, 5 August, Bonar Law rose to move the first guillotine resolution since the end of the Great War. The second reading debate on the bill would conclude at 11:00 p.m. The committee stage and third reading would begin on the afternoon of Friday, 6 August, and conclude by 6:00 p.m. In his speech the Lord Privy Seal presented the government's official position on the conflict in Ireland. Dublin Castle needed emergency powers, he said, because peace and order had broken down, threatening the 'conditions of civilised society'. The men responsible for this breakdown were common criminals: 'The very fact that an attempt is made to describe murder by another name, and to make excuses for it as if it were political action, must demoralise the whole life of any country where such excuses can be made.' These gangsters, he said, did not represent the people of Ireland: 'The great mass of the Irish people, whatever their political views, however strong their desire for independence, would rejoice if this criminal conspiracy of murder could be put an end to.' The bill would give the police and courts the powers they needed to suppress this 'murderous conspiracy' and allow the government 'to give to the Irish people the widest measure of local government which is compatible with our national safety, our national existence, and fairness to other sections in Ireland'.[20]

The guillotine resolution was passed, and the House proceeded to debate the bill in principle. Opposition members pleaded in vain for a more generous policy. Asquith called on the government to drop its bills for the Restoration of Order and the Government of Ireland, and adopt instead 'a large, liberal, and adequate measure of Home Rule on Dominion lines'.[21] In his reply Lloyd George brushed aside Asquith's arguments. 'I have rarely, in this House, heard a more inadequate or futile contribution towards the solving of a great emergency from a first-rate statesman,' the Prime Minister said.[22] An Irish dominion was out of the question. It would raise its own army and navy. Its parliament would control Ireland's ports. Ulster would never agree to be part of a Dominion of Ireland. Proposals of dominion status would just encourage Irish republicans. 'Supposing you proposed it,' said Lloyd George, 'what would happen? The men who speak on behalf of the majority would repudiate it. They would say, "Here they are on the run, press them on, we will get our independent Republic." No,' said the Prime Minister. It was idle to talk of an Irish dominion while Sinn Féin held out for an Irish republic:

> The authentic representatives of the Irish people demand something which Britain can never concede except as a result of disaster and defeat, and that is secession. We cannot accept it. It would be fatal to the security of the Empire. Until, therefore, Irish opinion accepts the fundamental, indefeasible fact that Britain will never concede those terms, it is futile to attempt to propose alternative schemes for their consideration. They decline to accept the autonomy of Ulster. They decline to accept the authority of the Crown. They decline to accept the defence of the realm. These are three fundamental conditions. What is the use, then, of talking about schemes of self-determination and of Dominion Home Rule until, at any rate, some gleam of sanity is introduced into the minds of those who are responsible for directing the majority of Irish opinion?[23]

The Prime Minister was willing to compromise—but only if the revolutionaries compromised first. 'Britain will make sacrifices,' he promised, but 'Ireland must also sacrifice extravagant demands and too extravagant ideas.' Until Sinn Féin's leaders displayed a 'gleam of sanity' and accepted Lloyd George's fundamental conditions, the government would not change its policies. And for the moment, the Prime Minister was happy to preach to his Conservative and Unionist choir. 'Meanwhile,' he concluded, 'speaking on behalf of this House of Commons, which is responsible for sending these men [i.e. the police] there to protect life, to establish law, and to maintain the authority of the Empire—which is not a thing to sneer at—an Empire in which I hope to see Ireland a proud partner, I say that it is our duty to see that every device, every resource, every protection is used to prevent these people from being massacred in the performance of their duty.'[24]

The guillotine resolution fell at 11 p.m., and the bill was read a second time. A Committee of the Whole House considered the bill for less than six hours on Friday, 6 August. The government accepted a harmless Opposition amendment, requiring Dublin Castle's regulations to be laid before the Commons. At one point an IPP member disrupted the proceedings, refusing to sit down or withdraw from the House, and was finally suspended for disorderly conduct.[25] Finally, at 6 p.m. the committee reported, and the bill was read a third time. It was introduced in the House of Lords later that evening, and was debated briefly on Monday, 9 August. When the Lord Chancellor moved a second reading, a spectator shouted, 'If you pass this Bill, you may kill England, not Ireland.'[26] After this brief interruption, the Restoration of Order in Ireland Act was passed by the Lords, and assented to by King George V.

1.2 Policing

If the Irish insurgency began in earnest on 19 December 1919, when the IRA tried and failed to kill the Lord Lieutenant of Ireland, Viscount French, then the British counter-insurgency truly began in earnest on 9 August 1920, when the Restoration of Order in Ireland Act was passed. The British government insisted almost to the end that it was only 'suppressing disorder and punishing crime in Ireland,' and used its Irish police as window dressing for this dubious position.[27] In fact, the government clung so tightly to this conception of the conflict that it refused even to strike a campaign medal or clasp for its security forces. 'The gallantry and devotion of the troops and police in Ireland are gratefully recognised both by His Majesty's Government and the nation,' said Bonar Law, 'but it is not considered that a special medal, as suggested in the question, is desirable as a mark of that recognition.'[28] But by the Truce of 11 July 1921 the RIC were police in appearance alone. After 11 months of guerrilla warfare, the constabulary had become an irregular military force, bound by neither military law nor military discipline, and its British reinforcements had played an important part in this transformation.

1.2.1 Peelers: The Royal Irish Constabulary

This transformation was more than a little ironic, since, for much of its history, the Royal Irish Constabulary had been a force of police dressed like soldiers. Most of Ireland's police forces had been consolidated in 1836, creating an Irish Constabulary. The new constabulary had absorbed the police forces of Belfast and Londonderry in 1865 and 1870, and was responsible thereafter for the whole island outside of Dublin, which had its own Metropolitan Police. The new constabulary finally became the 'Royal' Irish Constabulary as a reward for its part in the Fenian uprising of 1867.

The RIC's headquarters were in Dublin. Its chief officers were an inspector general, a deputy inspector general, and three assistant inspector generals. Each county had its own force of police (and sometimes two), with a county inspector who reported directly to headquarters. Counties were divided into districts, with district inspectors who lived in the principal towns therein. Districts were divided into sub-districts, each with a sergeant and a small force of constables. The police in each sub-district lived in their stations, which consequently became known as 'barracks': in larger towns these were specially constructed buildings, but in smaller villages they were just modified houses.

Ordinarily, the RIC comprised about ten thousand officers and men, all of them Irish, most of them Catholic. Irish constables were given six months of training at the depot in Phoenix Park: dressed and drilled like soldiers in a Rifle Regiment, they were armed with carbines and bayonets, as well as the more usual truncheons and revolvers. Their discipline was rigorous, and political surveillance was one of their most important responsibilities. The police were expected to know the sympathies and activities of the people in their sub-districts, and county inspectors submitted monthly reports on political factions in their areas. As a consequence, Irish republicans thought of the 'Peelers' as their most dangerous enemies, and republican politicians denounced the RIC as 'England's janissaries'—a force of traitors and spies.[29]

But by 1919 the RIC had become 'a thoroughly domesticated, civil police force', despite its militaristic appearance.[30] Decades of internal peace had left the force unready for internal war. There was not much ordinary crime in Ireland, and as a result the police had been assigned a wide variety of civil-service duties: they acted as inspectors of weights and measures, food and drugs, explosives and agriculture; they collected the census and compiled annual statistics of tillage and livestock; in addition, they sometimes acted as clerks of petty-sessions courts.[31]

Even during periods of widespread unrest like the Ranch War of 1904–08, the Edwardian RIC did most of its work without firearms.[32] One man, Daniel Galvin, joined the constabulary in 1907 and resigned in July 1920. 'When I first joined, it was different then,' he recalled. 'I did not have any arms then. Of course, they had arms then, but at the same time I never took them out with me on duty, the same as I had to do the last seven or eight months. We had the arms, but they were simply for show purposes.'[33]

The arms that the RIC did have were poor. Compared to the British Army's khaki and webbing, the constabulary's rifle-green uniforms and black leather accoutrements looked almost Victorian. Their carbines were obsolescent cast-offs. In 1905 the Army had adopted a new short rifle for both infantry and cavalry, and ten thousand of the cavalry's old six-shot Lee-Enfield carbines had subsequently been handed down to the RIC. After the rebellion of 1916, constables complained that these weapons were more decorative than useful.[34] Lack of practice made them less useful still: police fired only 21 practice rounds each year, using Morris tubes and miniature .22-calibre ammunition.[35] One former constable recalled later that he had never fired a shot out of a rifle during six years of service, between 1912 and 1918: 'I just carried it,' he said. 'It was used for the purpose of training and deportment. We went through the form of loading and unloading the magazine. I cannot recall ever having put a bullet into it.'[36]

Once the guerrilla war began, the force was gradually rearmed with the Army's ten-shot short Lee-Enfield rifles, and with Mills grenades: but its constables needed to be trained in using their new military weapons. Seven decades later, an old RIC constable named Crossett described how he was nearly shot by one of his colleagues in a training accident: the man's weapon had discharged while he was being taught how to load the magazine. 'Jeepers if this fellow, instead of putting the bullet down low enough, and damn it if the bullet didn't just pass me and stick in the wall behind me, chancy enough,' he said. 'Lots of fellows didn't know how to use arms. Some wasn't fit to handle a rifle and go out; they couldn't have protected you, protected themselves.'[37] In fact, the RIC was still being taught firearm safety just four days before the Truce. A circular dated 7 July 1921 started with the basics: 'Fire arms should always be regarded as loaded, and when picked up, should be opened and examined.' It warned police to 'keep the finger off the trigger' when loading their revolvers. It ordered them not to carry a loaded rifle with a round in the chamber: 'this practice is contrary to all orders and highly dangerous to all concerned.' Finally, the circular suggested that mishaps like Crossett's were common. 'All loading and unloading should be carried out in line under the orders and supervision of a Sergeant, Head Constable, or Officer', it said.[38]

'The old police knew very little about armaments,' Crossett remembered. 'In the Barracks I was the only one who really knew much about a revolver or a rifle or anything else, how to load and so on.'[39] To make matters worse, these 'old police' were numerous—at least at first. In 1919 the average RIC man was about 35 years old, and had been serving for 15 years. Married men, who made up almost half of the force, were even older: the typical married man was over 41 years of age, and had been serving for more than 21 years.[40] In military terms the average RIC constable was too old for first-line military service, while the average married constable was too old even for second-line service.

The situation becomes even clearer when we examine the police forces from four of Ireland's 32 counties: Londonderry, Mayo, Tipperary, and Wexford.[41] In January 1920 there were 820 constables in these four counties (see Table 1.1). A little under half of these men (47.4 per cent) had enlisted in the 1910s and had been serving for 10 years or less, while 34.2 per cent of them had enlisted in the 1900s and had been serving for between 11 and 20 years. Another 8.4 per cent had enlisted between 1895 and 1899 and were in sight of a pension by 1920, while fully 9.7 per cent of them had enlisted before 1895.

Their non-commissioned officers were older still. In January 1920 there were 228 sergeants in the counties of Londonderry, Mayo, Tipperary, and Wexford (see Table 1.2). Almost two-thirds of them (66.2 per cent) had enlisted in the 1890s: 18.4 per cent of them had enlisted in the 1880s, and only 15.4 per cent of them had enlisted in the 1900s. The majority of sergeants (59.2 per cent) had enlisted before 1895, and had been serving with the Royal Irish Constabulary for more than 25 years.

Not many middle-aged men like these could bear the mental and physical stresses of counter-guerrilla warfare. In August 1920 one county inspector wrote about clearing out 'the majority of the old useless men who were not

Table 1.1. Enlistment dates of RIC constables in selected county forces, January 1920.

Year of Appointment	Londonderry	Mayo	Tipperary	Wexford	Total	%
1915–19	6	65	64	31	166	20.2
1910–14	33	67	87	36	223	27.2
1905–1909	21	57	74	33	185	22.6
1900–1904	10	40	34	11	95	11.6
1895–99	6	22	35	6	69	8.4
1890–94	9	18	14	5	46	5.6
1885–89	2	8	12	1	23	2.8
1880–84	1	2	6	1	10	1.2
1875–79	—	—	1	—	1	0.1
Unknown	—	1	1	—	2	0.2
Total	88	280	328	124	820	99.9

Source: RIC Returns by County, 1920, TNA: PRO HO 184/61.

Table 1.2. Enlistment dates of RIC sergeants in selected county forces, January 1920.

Year of Appointment	Londonderry	Mayo	Tipperary	Wexford	Total	%
1905–1909	2	3	2	2	9	4.0
1900–1904	4	5	12	5	26	11.4
1895–99	5	17	20	16	58	25.4
1890–94	11	32	31	19	93	40.8
1885–89	4	12	15	1	32	14.0
1880–84	—	1	6	3	10	4.4
Total	26	70	86	46	228	100.0

Source: RIC Returns by County, 1920, TNA: PRO HO 184/61.

pulling their weight against the rebels'.[42] Two months later, in October, another county inspector complained about the 'apathetic, inert condition of the [county] Force, the older members of which are "playing for safety", while the younger men are naturally therefore discouraged, and afraid, not without good reason, that they will be given away'.[43] As a consequence, hundreds of old police were pensioned off during the Irish War of Independence. Constables who completed 25 years of service were entitled to retire on half pay, whereas constables who completed 30 years service were entitled to retire on two-thirds pay.[44] On average, 48 constables retired each week during the summer of 1920.[45] The 'old useless men' mentioned above had probably completed 20–24 years of service, and were hoping simply to stay out of trouble until they retired.

At the Cabinet conference of 23 July 1920, Greenwood said that 'with regard to the police there were many who were just hanging on for the sake of their pensions, and there were about 2,000 of them due to be pensioned during the course of the next six or twelve months'.[46] The nominal returns for Londonderry, Mayo, Tipperary, and Wexford appear to bear this out. For example, in January 1920 there were 82 constables in these four counties who had enlisted before 1895 (see Table 1.1): a year later, there were only 32 (see Table 1.3). On the other hand, in January 1920, there were 69 men who had enlisted between 1895 and 1899: by January 1921, there were still 60 remaining.

While these older men 'played for safety,' hundreds of younger police were quitting their jobs: on average, 52 constables applied to resign each week during the summer of 1920. If we compare the returns for Londonderry, Mayo, Tipperary, and Wexford in 1920 and 1921, we will discover that the number of constables increased by more than 50 per cent, from 820 to 1,241—but that the number of experienced constables went down by

Table 1.3. Enlistment dates of RIC constables in selected county forces, January 1921.

Date of Appointment	Londonderry	Mayo	Tipperary	Wexford	Total	%
1920 Irish	20	8	129	28	185	14.9
1920 British	40	68	339	38	485	39.0
1915–19	13	53	57	17	140	11.3
1910–14	20	51	46	35	152	12.2
1905–1909	13	52	41	10	116	9.3
1900–1904	12	23	22	15	72	5.8
1895–99	6	18	30	6	60	4.8
1890–94	6	7	6	4	23	1.9
1885–89	—	—	7	—	7	0.6
1880–84	—	—	—	1	1	0.1
1875–79	—	—	—	—	—	—
Total	130	280	677	154	1241	99.9
% British	30.8	24.2	50.0	24.7	39.0	

Source: RIC Returns by County, 1921, TNA: PRO HO 184/62.

Table 1.4. Enlistment dates of RIC constables in selected county forces, January 1920 and January 1921, compared.

Date of Appointment	Londonderry	Mayo	Tipperary	Wexford	Total	Percentage Remaining
1915–19	+7	-12	-7	-14	-26	84.3
1910–14	-13	-16	-41	-1	-71	68.2
1905–1909	-8	-5	-33	-23	-69	62.7
1900–1904	+2	-17	-12	+4	-23	75.8
1895–99	—	-4	-5	0	-9	87.0
1890–94	-3	-11	-8	-1	-23	50.0
1885–89	-2	-8	-5	-1	-16	30.4
1880–84	-1	-2	-6	—	-9	10.0
1875–79	—	—	—	—	—	0.0
Unknown	—	-1	—	—	-1	0.0

Source: RIC Returns by County, 1920 and 1921, TNA: PRO HO 184/61–2.

more than 30 per cent, from 820 to 573 (see Table 1.4). The loss of experienced men in 1920–1 was greatest among those who had enlisted between 1910 and 1914: their numbers declined from 223 (in 1920) to 152 (in 1921). But the five county forces lost an almost equal number, and an even greater percentage, of those who had enlisted between 1905 and 1909: their numbers declined from 185 to 116—a loss of close to 40 per cent. The men most likely to resign, it seems, were Edwardians like Daniel Galvin, who had enlisted in 1907: men to whom a pension was a distant prospect, and who were old enough to remember when Irish policemen could perform their duties unarmed, but still young enough to start a new career.

RIC constables quit the force for various reasons. Some were demoralized and frustrated. Some were afraid for their lives, or for their families.[47] Some of them objected to their new, more military duties. Galvin told the American Commission on Conditions in Ireland that he resigned 'simply because I did not like the system they have at the present time'. 'I was simply only a soldier when I left the police force,' he said. 'I had to carry arms and bombs and the like. I had to have my rifle beside me at nights in bed.'[48] Another witness, John Tangney, enlisted in 1918 and resigned in 1920. The police, he said, 'haven't very much of their old jobs left to them. The only thing that you had to do as a policeman since 1918 was to lead the military around and point out the men they wanted to get'.[49] Others were dismayed by the brutal behaviour of their comrades. John Caddan enlisted in February

1920 and resigned in September. 'I couldn't stop in such surroundings,' he said. 'I didn't fancy the way they were treating the people.'[50] Some police even supported the revolutionary cause. Daniel Crowley enlisted in 1917. Later, he told the American Commission that 'I tendered my resignation from the Constabulary because of the misgovernment of the English in Ireland.'[51]

For all these reasons, the RIC began haemorrhaging men in the summer of 1920. On an average week, only 76 recruits enlisted in the force to replace the approximately one hundred police who retired and resigned. As a result, the strength of the constabulary declined by almost 1,300 men from the beginning of July to the end of September.[52]

These losses were disastrous. The RIC was large for a police force,[53] but quite small for an army of occupation. At the beginning of 1920 it included only 9,276 non-commissioned officers and men.[54] Out of this number, 997 were tied up in Belfast, and another 281 at the Phoenix Park depot. Fewer than 8,000 police were left to garrison the rest of Ireland, scattered across the island in about 13,000 small detachments. 'Their duty was primarily the maintenance of law and order in their locality,' one British Army officer later said, 'and it is clear that in these isolated posts, which were often eight or ten miles apart, they were not in a position to carry out offensive operations against the rebels.'[55] To make matters worse, many RIC stations could not even defend themselves. At the end of 1913, 87 per cent of the RIC's barracks held fewer than ten police, while 41 per cent held fewer than five.[56]

On 8 November 1919 the Royal Irish Constabulary was ordered to close as many stations as necessary to bring the remainder up to a minimum of six men.[57] This minimum was later doubled, and more barracks were abandoned to reinforce the rest. Even more barracks were closed by the wastage of men in the summer of 1920: as we have seen, the strength of the RIC declined by thirteen hundred men—enough to man 100 stations. The effect, it seems, was most pronounced in the west, and least pronounced in the north (see Table 1.5). In County Mayo, for example, the police abandoned more than half their barracks: in January 1920 the county force had been distributed among 47 stations; but by January 1921 it was occupying just 23. In County Londonderry, by contrast, not a single station was closed between January 1920 and January 1921. The redeployment of police in the south and east, it seems, fell between these two extremes (see Table 1.5). The police in County Tipperary abandoned 18 of their 61

Table 1.5. Numbers of RIC stations in selected counties, 1920 and 1921.

County	1920	1921	Total Change	Percentage Remaining
Londonderry	16	16	0	100.0
Mayo	47	23	-24	49.0
Tipperary	61	43	-18	70.5
Wexford	23	15	-8	65.2
All	147	97	-50	66.0

Source: RIC Returns by County, 1920 and 1921, TNA: PRO HO 184/61–2.

barracks between January 1920 and January 1921. During the same period, in County Wexford, the number of stations declined from 23 to 15. In total, across the four counties, the number of police barracks went down by 34 per cent, from 147 to 97.[58]

The abandonment of police barracks may have solved one problem, but it aggravated another. The new police outposts were more strongly defended, but also more isolated, and their garrisons were unable to patrol wide areas of Ireland. In July 1920 Mayo's county inspector complained bitterly that 'the closing of Police Stations has proved a most disastrous and dangerous expedient'. 'The countryside left without protection now bows the knee to Sinn Fein,' he said.[59] In one extreme case, all police barracks in the Dungloe district of County Donegal in the north-west were closed after the Army withdrew from the area in October 1920. 'This,' according to Donegal's county inspector, 'has handed over all West Donegal and its coast line to the lawless element'.[60] By March 1921 the Deputy Inspector General noted that Dungloe district still had no police. 'This area comprises about one-sixth of the county and it seems to have become a miniature Republic,' he said.[61] Redistribution alone could not cure the disease that was crippling the RIC in the summer of 1920: the force was just not large enough to fulfil its new paramilitary duties.

More police were needed, but sufficient replacements could not be found in Ireland, where the guerrillas were doing their best to strangle recruiting for the RIC. Some candidates were sent threatening letters. Other candidates were intimidated in person. In part as a result, on average, the RIC recruited only seven Irishmen per week in the summer of 1920.[62] An Ulster Special Constabulary was formed in the autumn, but this was a body of Protestant loyalists, recruited for service in the six counties that would soon become Northern Ireland. There was no chance of raising an equivalent force elsewhere.

1.2.2 The Black and Tans

The Black and Tans were the government's answer to this manpower crisis. There were large numbers of unemployed ex-servicemen in post-war Britain—young men with both military training and combat experience. In June 1920 the Ministry of Labour reported that there were about 167,000 fit ex-servicemen receiving unemployment benefits in Britain, including 52,000 in London alone.[63] Walter Long had suggested using these men to raise the strength of the RIC in a letter to the Lord Lieutenant, Viscount French, as early as 19 May 1919.[64]

This proposal found favour with French, and with General Shaw, commander-in-chief of the Army of Ireland: but the RIC's Inspector General, Sir Joseph Byrne, was against it, out of concern that ex-military men could not be controlled by police discipline.[65] But the government was losing confidence in Byrne: the Inspector General was a Roman Catholic who supported negotiations with Sinn Féin and resisted the militarisation of the constabulary.[66] In his letter of 19 May, Long told French that Byrne had 'lost his nerve' and should be replaced with his deputy, T. J. Smith (an Orangeman). French finally took Long's advice in December, when he relieved Byrne of his duties and replaced him with Smith.[67] On 27 December 1919 the new Inspector General issued an order authorising recruitment in Britain. The first British recruits joined the Royal Irish Constabulary six days later.[68]

These British recruits were nicknamed 'Black and Tans' because of their motley clothing. As already noted, the RIC wore bottle-green uniforms with black leather kit. Black and Tans at first wore military khaki uniforms with a policeman's cap and belt. On 28 February 1920, for example, the *Connacht Tribune* reported that 'English ex-soldier R.I.C. recruits were seen for the first time in Galway on Tuesday evening,' acting as escorts for a prisoner. 'The new police, who were, it is stated, drawn from the depot, were in khaki uniform but wore the policemen's long black coats and black caps.'[69] Similarly, on 17 March 1920 the London *Daily Herald* reported that a 'detachment of police attired in khaki tunics and trousers but wearing constabulary caps and greatcoats' had arrived at a town in County Tipperary. 'Their mixed costumes attracted considerable attention as they marched to the local barracks.'[70]

It seems that a shortage of police clothing was to blame for these makeshift uniforms. On 15 October 1920 a police newspaper, the *Weekly Summary*, reported that the RIC 'has allowed itself to run out of uniforms and cannot clothe its recruits. As even in Ireland a policeman cannot function clad only in a cap and belt, it was necessary to find something to cover his nakedness. As a result, the R.I.C. recruit found himself fearfully and wonderfully attired in a mixture of dark green and khaki, and was promptly dubbed a "Black and Tan" by an astonished Ireland.'[71] Six months later, on 15 April 1921, the same periodical reported that when British recruits first appeared, 'it was found impossible to provide them with R.I.C. uniforms of dark green. All Southern Ireland at the time was boycotting the Crown Forces, and uniforms would not be tailored for the Police. So the recruits went on duty in soldier khaki.'[72]

By the summer and autumn of 1920, many Black and Tans were wearing pieces of police green with pieces of Army khaki—a constable's trousers with a soldier's tunic, or vice versa: one old constable recalled that 'as soon as they got the khaki suit along with the black one they immediately switched the trousers, wore the khaki trousers with the black tunic and vice versa'.[73] When Chief Secretary Greenwood reviewed a group of British recruits on 15 October, the *Manchester Guardian* reported that 'they certainly presented an extraordinary appearance, wearing a mixture of dark green and khaki, with, in some cases, civilian head-gear'.[74] By the winter of 1920–1, however, both Irish and British constables were wearing the RIC's traditional rifle green.[75]

The intake of British recruits was modest at first—about one hundred enlistments per month from January to June 1920.[76] Recruiting in Britain did not pick up until the summer, when the Royal Irish Constabulary was given a substantial pay raise: a new constable's pay more than doubled, from 31s to 70s per week. On average, the force took in 58 British recruits per week in July, and 78 British recruits per week in August.[77] Then, rather suddenly, in the last weeks of September, the weekly intake of British recruits more than tripled: whereas 61 British men enlisted in the week ending 19 September, 222 enlisted in the week ending 26 September (see Table 1.6).[78] The reasons for this abrupt upsurge are not clear, but it may have been connected to the Sack of Balbriggan on 20 September 1920. On that Monday evening, a newly promoted RIC head constable was shot and killed in Balbriggan, just north of Dublin, near the training camp for British RIC recruits at Gormanstown. Later that night, a mob of police including

Table 1.6. Irish and British RIC recruits, summer 1920 to spring 1921.

Season	Irish	British
Summer 1920	92	1,348
Autumn 1920	206	2,944
Winter 1920	237	2,206
Spring 1921	143	1,435
Total	678	7,933

(*Source*: Outrage Reports, TNA: PRO CO 904/148–50)

Black and Tans attacked Balbriggan, killing two men, looting and burning four public houses, destroying a hosiery factory, and damaging or destroying 49 private houses. The Sack of Balbriggan caused a sensation in Britain: it made headlines in the British press, and made reprisals an important topic of debate in Parliament.[79] Ironically, this negative publicity may also have alerted many British ex-servicemen to the prospect of employment in the Royal Irish Constabulary.

In any case, thousands of British recruits flooded into the RIC during the autumn and winter of 1920–1. By the spring of 1921, 39 per cent of the constables in our four selected counties—484 out of 1,241—were Black and Tans (see Table 1.3). The nominal returns for 1921 make it clear that these new British recruits were not evenly distributed across Ireland. Almost 70 per cent of the Black and Tans in our four counties—338 out of 484—were stationed in County Tipperary, where nearly 50 per cent of all constables were British. The next largest contingent—68 British recruits—was stationed in County Mayo, while the counties of Wexford and Londonderry received 38 and 40 recruits, respectively. Thus, it seems that the number of Black and Tans in each region was roughly proportional to the level of violence therein—with a couple of interesting exceptions. There were very few Black and Tans in strife-torn Belfast. 'At no time did the Black and Tans and Auxiliaries operate in Belfast, where I was stationed in the years 1919–21 apart from a few weeks in the country,' said one former constable.[80] In addition, there were very few Black and Tans in the special Reserve Force quartered at Phoenix Park. 'People in the Reserves was mostly from the North,' said one former member.[81]

For the most part, however, the Black and Tans were not a separate force. They were treated as ordinary constables, despite their strange uniforms, and they lived and worked in barracks alongside the Irish police. In January 1921, for example, 36 constables, 5 sergeants, and 1 head constable were stationed in Tipperary (see Table 1.7). Out of these 36 constables, 19 were Irish and 17 were British. The station's Irish constables were a fairly diverse group, though they were mostly young and inexperienced. Twelve of them had joined the force during the reign of King George V. Four of them had joined up during the reign of King Edward VII, and three of them were left over from the reign of Queen Victoria. Only 6 of the 17 Black and Tans had joined the force before the sack of Balbriggan on 20 September 1920: 9 of the remaining 11 had enlisted not long afterward, in October 1920. Thus, in many ways, the men who lived and worked in Tipperary RIC barracks were a microcosm for the two county forces, and indeed, for the RIC as a whole.

Whether Irish or British, a constable's living and working conditions were poor. The police spent much of their time on patrol—walking, cycling, or riding on Crossley tenders.[82] These patrols were not infrequent victims of rebel ambushes, and though most of the Black and Tans had fought in the Great War, their training and experience was of limited worth in their battles with Irish guerrillas. After 11 police (including 7 Black and Tans) were ambushed and killed at Dromkeen, County Limerick, on 3 February 1921, General Macready warned Sir John Anderson, Under Secretary for Ireland, that the police were 'not properly trained for coping with big ambushes':

Table 1.7. Enlistment dates of RIC constables in County Tipperary, January 1921.

Date of Appointment	Tipperary Station	%	County Tipperary	%
1920 Irish	5	14	129	19
1920 British	17	47	339	50
1915–19	4	11	57	8
1910–14	4	11	46	7
1905–1909	3	8	41	6
1900–1904	1	3	22	3
1895–99	1	3	30	4
1890–94	1	3	6	1
1885–89	—	—	7	2
Total	36	100	677	100

Source: RIC Returns by County, 1921, TNA: PRO HO 184/62.

> Although many of your Police recruits and all the Auxiliaries have been soldiers, it by no means follows that they are necessarily experts in this game. If you take the finest soldier who had served in France alone and suddenly put him in the Himalayas to cope with the Afridis you would find that until he had absorbed that particular mode of warfare he would be quite useless, and the same, in my opinion, applies to Police methods here, with the additional disadvantage that people like the D.I.'s [District Inspectors] are quite untrained in anything like Military tactics.[83]

In addition, police patrols were often as tedious as they were dangerous. The longer the war lasted, the more the guerrillas relied on roadblocks to reduce the mobility of the security forces. By May 1921 Kerry's county inspector was reporting that the IRA had 'trenched all roads, blew up bridges, tore up railway lines, felled trees across roads, built up walls across roads, stretched wires across roads, with the intention of making the journeys of Crown Forces by motors impossible. They have made it practically impossible to travel in the dark. Journeys of about 20 miles sometimes take between 4 & 5 hours to accomplish.'[84] That same month a policewoman, Inspector Walton, described a drive to the next county in her diary:

> The journey took four hours, owing to our having to try several ways before we could get through. As so often happens, the rebels had been at work during the night—one road had two huge trees right across, another had a deep trench. At one place, on turning a corner, we were all but precipitated into a deep river. The driver only just pulled up in time to avoid having the car and its occupants thrown into the water below. A wide hole had been hewn right through and across the bridge.[85]

Autumn and winter patrols were often caught in the rain. 'You see,' said one old constable, 'an open tender with a central seat both facing outwards and no cover on you, you sit in the back for a hundred miles and you're soaked through. It runs down you see and goes right through.'[86] The rain let up in the spring and summer of 1921, but sunny weather brought its own discomforts. On 5 June 1921 Inspector Walton wrote: 'The long-continued spell of hot, dry weather makes these rough roads unbearable, the dust covering us all, especially those seated in the second or third Crossleys, who have layers of white on their eyelids, noses and chins, which makes travelling quickly by road none too pleasant, and gives us all a most curious and dirty appearance.'[87]

The police spent most of their off-duty time in their fortified stations, which were generally dark, stuffy, and cramped. In one remarkable case, the police in Tralee, County Kerry lived in a commandeered prison. Tralee prison became Tralee No. 2 Barracks on 5 November 1920. Those police unlucky enough to be stationed there lived in the prison cells. There was no laundry. According to the head constable in charge, 'often after the long heavy marches and runs in very wet Country' the police 'had no other way to dry their uniform except to hang it up in their cells &c.' By the following spring, the sanitary facilities had broken down completely. There was no water supply to the washhouse or its adjoining bath. 'The baths were for this reason never used by the Police, though they would have often wished to do so.' In addition, the lack of water made it impossible to flush the toilets. 'Every morning a party of Police and prisoners had ... to remove the soil from the WCs and carry it out in buckets and bury it in deep holes in the outer grounds of the prison. It was only with the utmost persuasion I was able to get political prisoners to do this work.'[88] On 2 March 1921 Kerry's county inspector noted that there was 'a heavy smell about the premises.'[89]

Conditions in barracks could be tense as well as uncomfortable. Attacks on RIC barracks were almost as frequent as ambushes, and to make matters worse, relations between British and Irish constables were often strained. Some Irish police got along well with the Black and Tans. 'Oh, we got on alright, just the same as ourselves,' said one old Peeler. 'They were alright to work with,' said another. 'I didn't pass much remarks on them, give them their dues they were alright, reasonable enough you know.'[90] It seems, however, that many Irish police did not like their new British colleagues. As we might expect, the four Irish constables who testified to the American Commission had nothing positive to say about the Black and Tans. 'They were the lowest type of humanity,' said John Tangney: 'they were rough-necks.' Irish constables 'had no friendship for them, and had nothing more to do with them than necessary'. John Caddan said the Black and Tans 'were generally very careless fellows, and did not give a hang about what they did'. Many Irish constables did not respect their British reinforcements, and did not associate with them. 'They were not friendly by any means. Only, of course, they had to go together with them on duty.' 'We did not mix with them,' said Daniel Galvin. 'We had as little to do with them as we could.'[91]

Seventy years later, one old RIC veteran took an equally dim view of the Black and Tans, saying they did 'damn all' as police. 'Their atrocities were against [the interests of] the RIC men,' said Constable Gallagher. 'They weren't dependable enough. They were the scum of Britain. We could have done without it.' However, most of John Brewer's interviewees gave the Black and Tans mixed reviews. 'I met one or two of them, there was some right fellows and then there was others who weren't great, weren't good you know,' said one man. 'Some of the Black and Tans were alright,' said another, 'some of them were decent fellows, and some of them were a real damned nuisance, you know. Drink; they were a bit rough, especially when they got drink taken, but you know, there were some fine fellows among them.' Even Constable Gallagher qualified his views: 'There were some of them right good,' he admitted, 'like all men of war and ex-Army, and some of them mixed.'[92]

'Rough' is a word that Irish constables used often to describe the Black and Tans. Policing had been a respectable occupation in Edwardian Ireland: most of the RIC's constables had been farmers, and there were few ex-soldiers among them. As a result, some Irish police felt disdain for the Black and Tans, who were mostly urban working-class war veterans.[93] 'We didn't like them,' said one, 'we would have no place for them, we didn't like them coming along and mixing with us.' 'The regular force didn't have much contact with them at all,' said another, 'we didn't really know them, they were stationed along with us but they were never popular with the regular force.' A third constable named Sterrett was one of 40 police in a large barracks at Abbeyleix, in Queen's County. When interviewed later in life, Sterrett remembered that ten Black and Tans had been stationed at Abbeyleix: out of these ten, just two had been quite respectable: 'But the others were very rough,' he said, 'they were very rough, f-ing and blinding and drinking and booze and all. They'd have shot their mother, oh desperate altogether.'[94]

1.2.3 Major General Tudor and the Auxiliary Division

To make matters worse, it seems there was no love lost between the RIC and its Auxiliary Division either. The ADRIC was a paramilitary force composed of ex-British military and naval officers, dressed in distinctive uniforms and organized in military-style companies. The men of the division were officially 'temporary cadets', but were paid and ranked as RIC sergeants. Some Irish RIC men saw these temporary cadets as upstarts: before the Great War, a constable had served an average of 18.5 years before being promoted to the rank of acting sergeant.[95] One civilian witness told the American Commission that Auxiliaries were being 'brought over from England as Sergeants and put over the RIC. This has made for bad blood in many cases. The old local senior military police resent this, because these English who are brought over are getting more pay and are put over them.'[96] As well, when the Division first appeared in the summer of 1920, some RIC constables were afraid that these temporary cadets would become permanent sergeants. RIC headquarters even issued a special circular to reassure these men: 'I wish to make it clear,' said the Inspector General, 'that the "Temporary cadets" are a temporary service only, inaugurated to assist the constabulary in the present pressure, that they are supernumerary to the establishment, and their appointment as Sergeant will in no way operate adversely in the promotion of Constables to that rank, which will continue under the existing rules of the Service.'[97]

The Auxiliary Division seems to have been Winston Churchill's brainchild. At a conference of ministers on 11 May 1920 'the Secretary of State for War undertook to submit to the Cabinet a scheme for raising a Special Emergency Gendarmerie, which would become a branch of the Royal Irish Constabulary'.[98] The strength of this new corps would not exceed eight thousand men. This proposal was referred to a committee chaired on 19 May by the new commander-in-chief of the forces in Ireland, General Sir Nevil Macready. This committee rejected the scheme, for three reasons: first, because a completely new force could not be raised in a hurry; second, because police discipline was not strict enough to control such a force; and third, because the men of this new force 'would have to be paid at exceptional rates, and this would undoubtedly lead to trouble with the Royal Irish Constabulary regarding their pay'. Instead of a 'Special Emergency Gendarmerie', Macready's committee recommended raising a special military force of eight 'garrison battalions', consisting of war veterans enlisted for one year and paid at a special rate.[99]

Twelve days later, at a Cabinet meeting on 31 May, Churchill seems to have lost his enthusiasm for this idea. The new force would require a public appeal from the government, and Churchill was 'in two minds if it was wise to risk an appeal and get no response'. Lloyd George agreed: 'I read the appeals,' he said, 'and I did not think you would make any young fellow drop his tools and go over to Ireland.' For his part, General Macready was doubtful that the government could find enough officers for the new force: 'I find no great alacrity among the officers to go to Ireland,' said the general.

'You do not want the scallywag.' As a consequence, the Cabinet gave no further attention to these plans.[100] Yet remarkably, two months later, the Irish government went ahead with Churchill's original scheme, and began recruiting a 'special Corps of Gendarmerie', the Auxiliary Division.

The man behind this turn of events was Major General Henry Hugh Tudor. On 11 May 1920 the conference of ministers had also concluded that 'a special officer, with suitable qualifications and experience, should be appointed to supervise the entire organisation of the Irish police, namely the Royal Irish Constabulary and the Dublin Metropolitan Police, who should have at his disposal a small staff, including a first-rate Intelligence Officer to co-ordinate and develop the Intelligence Services'.[101] Major General Tudor was appointed 'Police Adviser' to the Irish government four days later, on Winston Churchill's recommendation.

Tudor was an artilleryman: born in Devonshire in 1871, he enrolled at the Royal Military Academy, Woolwich, in 1888 and was commissioned in the field artillery in 1890. He was stationed in India from 1890 until 1897, when he returned to England. He fought in the South African War, where he was badly wounded at the Battle of Magersfontein (11 December 1899), but recovered. After serving in South Africa, he went back to India for another five years (1905–10), and then was posted to Egypt, where he stayed until the start of the Great War. Tudor then served on the Western Front from December 1914 to the Armistice, rising from the rank of captain in charge of an artillery battery to the rank of major general and the command of the 9th (Scottish) Division. He continued to command this formation after 11 November 1918, as part of the Army of the Rhine, until the 9th Division was disbanded in March 1919. His chief qualification for the position of Police Adviser seems to have been his friendship with the Secretary of State for War. Tudor and Churchill had met at Bangalore in 1895, and became lifelong friends. During the brief period when Churchill had served as an infantry officer on the Western Front, after the formation of the Asquith coalition in 1915, he was posted to the same sector as Tudor, near Ploegsteert.[102]

Tudor's assignment, as he saw it, was to raise police morale, to punish crime, and to restore law and order.[103] At the Cabinet conference of 23 July 1920, Tudor agreed with Wylie that the RIC would soon become ineffective as police, 'but as a military body he thought they might have great effect'. While his civilian colleagues were calling for an offer of Dominion Home Rule, Tudor was confident that 'given the proper support, it would be possible to crush the present campaign of outrage'. The government, he said, should replace the civil courts with military tribunals; introduce identity cards and passports; restrict changes of residence; deport Irish prisoners to Britain; and levy fines and other collective punishments on disturbed districts. Finally, Tudor wanted 'a special penalty of flogging imposed for the cutting of girls' hair and outrages against women.' 'The whole country was intimidated,' he said, 'and would thank God for strong measures.'[104]

One author has recently described Tudor as the leader of a 'war party' within the Irish executive—a faction 'bent on reviving RIC morale, re-equipping it with modern weaponry, rebuilding its intelligence service and then grinding down the IRA, as the British Army had worn down the Germans in a battle of attrition'.[105] Like the Secretary of State for War, the Police Adviser gave senior Irish police appointments to his military friends and acquaintances. Tudor's deputy and head of intelligence, Brigadier General Ormonde Winter, was another old friend from India before the Great War. One of Tudor's divisional commissioners, Lieutenant Colonel Gerard Smyth, had been a battalion commander in the 9th Division, while another, Brigadier General Cyril Prescott-Decie, had become friends with Tudor in April 1916, soon after Prescott-Decie's arrival in France.[106]

In addition, the Police Adviser chose a pair of old colonial fighters to command his new Auxiliary Division: Brigadier General F. P. Crozier and Brigadier General E. A. Wood. The former was an Irishman, and the latter was an Anglo-Indian. Crozier began his career fighting in the South African War from 1899 to 1902 (less four months in 1900, when he fought in the Third Ashanti War). After 1902 he took part in a number of West African campaigns until 1908, when he resigned under a cloud after passing some bad cheques. He spent four years in Canada, then returned to Ireland and became an Ulster Volunteer Force officer in 1912. Wood, on the other hand, spent nine years in the late-Victorian Army before transferring to the British South Africa Police in 1895. He took part in the Jameson Raid (1895) and fought in the Matabele Rebellion (1896–97) before serving in the South African War. From 1903 he continued to serve in various police forces until after 1909, when he retired and became a tin miner.

Both Crozier and Wood had rejoined the Army in 1914, had fought on the Western Front until the Armistice, and been awarded numerous decorations: Wood won the Distinguished Service Order (DSO) three times, and was twice recommended for the Victoria Cross. Crozier was the

Auxiliary Division's first Commandant, and Wood was his assistant. However, Crozier gave up command for two months after he was injured in a road accident on 23 November 1920. He resumed his duties on 17 January 1921, but resigned a month later, on 19 February, after a dispute with Tudor.[107] Wood commanded the Division thereafter, until its demobilisation in the winter of 1922.[108]

In theory, the Auxiliary Division's duties consisted of 'training and co-operating with Police in patrol and defence work'.[109] In practice, it was a completely separate force. One RIC constable who served in County Kerry remembered that 'the Auxiliaries didn't mix up with the police at all'. Another constable who served in County Cork said 'I did meet the Auxiliaries but we never mixed with them.' A third man described them as 'a force unto themselves'. Decades later, one RIC veteran who served in County Tipperary seemed to resent the Auxiliary Division's freedom from ordinary police duties. 'We weren't fond of them, like,' he said. 'We had to stand the brunt, we had to stay there, while they were sailing here and there.' Another man who served in Sligo and Mayo mocked them for their administrative inefficiency. 'They weren't there more than a week,' he said, 'till everything was topsy-turvy, there was nothing right about it. So the RIC had to supply them with a Head Constable and a Constable for office work; there wasn't one of them Auxiliary officers who was a first class scholar. All of them high ranks in the Army and no education. The RIC had to do the whole paperwork.'[110]

The men of the Division spent much of their time conducting raids. Denis Morgan tried to describe their duties to the American Commission: 'It is very hard to place this Auxiliary Corps I spoke of under any head,' he testified. 'It is not a police force. It is more for raiding purposes. It seems to be particularly the duty of the Auxiliary Corps to carry out raids on houses.'[111] One of the Division's units (F Company) was based in Dublin Castle, and raided 181 addresses in Dublin between 13 April and 2 July 1921—sometimes as many as 13 addresses a day, though three raids a day was much more common.[112] Sometimes they were looking for arms, ammunition, and seditious literature. Other times, they were looking for wanted men. On 18 May, for example, they were told: 'PETER KERNAN 8 BLESSINGTON St was seen throwing a bomb in a recent ambush. Arrest him after curfew tomorrow night 19th.' On 20 May the company was ordered to raid a pawnbroker named Mrs Kelly at 48 Fleet Street: 'Two brothers managing this shop are supplying arms & uniform to IRA. They are supposed to have received a consignment of revolvers & uniform a week ago. Information reliable.' Ten days later, on 30 May, they were instructed to raid 50 Seville Place, 'belonging to SHEERAN BROS Dairymen. Search for arms documents etc and arrest SHEERAN who is Captain F Coy 2nd Bn IRA'. More often, however, the company was just given addresses to search: sometimes they were cautioned not to arrest anyone unless incriminating evidence was found; other times they were told to arrest anyone who could not account for themselves.

F Company raided for other reasons as well. In some cases they were looking for incriminating documents: on 22 April they were instructed to raid 45 Munster Street. 'Look out for letters from Liam TOBIN,' they were told. 'The daughter of the house aged 18 is a rabid SF & friend of Tobin. She may have charge of documents &c.' On other occasions the Auxiliaries were looking for bombs and bomb materials: they conducted a number of raids in late May and early June 1921 looking for James Leahy, suspected of being 'the official bomb maker of the IRA'. Their most unusual assignment came on 26 April, when the company commander was given the following orders:

> Send a few plain clothes Cadets to 14–15 Lower SACKVILLE St the buildings in which are the offices of the American Consul. On the first landing of the entrance leading to the second landing (on which second landing the consulate is located) a Dail Eireann notice is said to be posted. This landing is the property of the owner Messrs Donnelly & Son of Westmoreland Street & has no connection with the consulate. Have the poster removed quietly. The consulate is not to be interfered with.

The negative results of many of these raids are noted plainly in the logbook, with a check mark and the word 'NIL' in coloured pencil. This lack of success should not be surprising, given the scraps of information with which the Auxiliaries were working. Their intelligence was so unreliable that in one case F Company's commander was told to 'use discretion as to extent of search as information is not very certain'. On another occasion he was told that 'enquiries should be made before any thorough search as to whether this is the correct address'.

As a consequence, the company sometimes raided the same addresses more than once. On 13 April they were sent to raid 31 Upper Fitzwilliam Street: 'This house was searched on 6.II.21 & now in captured letters MC [Michael Collins] is informed that luckily only the "main building" was searched; it is obvious that there must be some outhouses, cellars or communications with another building which escaped observation.' On 21 April they were ordered to raid the home of Mrs Mitchell at 76 Aughrim Street: 'There was a raid here before for O'Neill who escaped through the back door. She had a son in the Army, and every time she is raided, she pretends to be loyal, and shows her son's discharge papers.' On 20 May they were sent to 51 Denzille Street: 'The roof should be searched for men in hiding,' they were told, 'as after a previous raid there men were seen to leave the building.' About a month later they were told to raid five addresses on Molesworth and Dawson Streets: 'Just to make sure there is nobody there.'[113]

Sometimes, however, the Auxiliaries raided the right address at the right time. On 20 November 1920, the eve of Bloody Sunday, for example, F Company captured Dick McKee and Peadar Clancy, commandant and vice-commandant of the IRA's Dublin Brigade. That same night they also managed to capture William Pilkington, commandant of the Sligo Brigade, in a separate raid on Vaughn's Hotel. Later, in December 1920, IRA headquarters sent another officer, Ernie O'Malley, to County Kilkenny to organise an attack on the local Auxiliary company's barracks at Inistiogue. O'Malley was just beginning to plan this attack when the Auxiliaries raided his house. The guerrilla leader was taken completely by surprise: according to his memoir, O'Malley was reading in his room when a cadet opened the door and walked in. 'He was as unexpected as death,' said O'Malley.[114]

Other Volunteers had a number of close brushes with the Auxiliaries, including Michael Brennan, leader of the IRA's East Clare Flying Column. Auxiliary Company G was headquartered at Killaloe, County Clare, and its men almost caught Brennan on several occasions. The first time, Brennan was having tea with a small party of Volunteers at the house of Michael Gleeson, captain of the IRA's Bodyke Company. 'When tea was about half through,' he recalled, 'one of the Gleesons rushed in to say he thought he heard the squeak of brakes coming down the hill. He said he heard no sound of engines and he was sent back for a further report. Almost immediately he returned and shouted "Auxiliaries!"' The guerrillas got out of the house just as the raiding party was hammering on the front door, and escaped from the back yard as cadets were jumping over the wall. Once the raiders left, Brennan returned and discovered what happened. 'We found that engines and lights had been switched off at the top of the hill outside the village and the lorries had coasted silently down to the very gate of Gleeson's house.'

After a few more close calls, the Clare Volunteers began blocking the roads around G Company's billets and keeping a close watch on the Auxiliaries, using visual signals to warn the flying column if a raiding party was heading in their direction.[115]

On still other occasions, Auxiliaries found the guerrillas by accident. On the morning of Bloody Sunday, 21 November 1920, for example, a team of ten IRA men invaded a house at 22 Lower Mount Street in Dublin. Once inside, they caught a British Army lieutenant named Angliss and shot him to death as he lay in bed. The gunfire alerted another officer across the hall. While this man blocked his bedroom door with furniture, the housekeeper rushed upstairs, leaned out of a window, and screamed for help.

By coincidence, a party of Auxiliaries in plain clothes was driving along Lower Mount Street at that moment. (The men were on their way from their depot at Beggars Bush to the train at Amiens Station.) They noticed the screaming housekeeper, stopped, got out of their vehicles, and surrounded the house. The IRA men were still trying to break down the second British officer's bedroom door when they heard shooting. Two Volunteers managed to escape out the back, but a guerrilla named Frank Teeling was wounded and fell. The remaining seven shot their way out of the front of the house, ran down Grattan Street, and escaped across the Liffey on a commandeered ferryboat.[116]

General Crozier arrived at 22 Lower Mount Street soon afterward, with a platoon of reinforcements. The wounded Frank Teeling had been captured, and the Auxiliaries were threatening to finish him off: when Crozier entered the house, he found a cadet holding Teeling at gunpoint and counting up to ten. Crozier knocked the revolver out of the cadet's hand and ordered his men to take Teeling to King George V Hospital.[117]

The incident described by Crozier was not unusual. The Auxiliaries were sometimes known as 'Tudor's Toughs', and once again, 'rough' was the word that RIC veterans used to describe the behaviour of temporary cadets. 'They were rough chaps indeed,' said one. 'They were rough, no doubt about that,' said another, who served in County Waterford. 'They just got somebody that were doing something wrong, they would lift him and throw him into this van and take him away with them.' A man who served in County Clare described them as 'fairly rough, they done their work in a very rough way. I mean to say, as regards interviewing people who they met on the roads and one thing and another.' 'The Auxiliaries were in a kind of world of their own,' he concluded, 'they raided rough.'[118]

In the end, none of these three forces was truly an effective implement of government policy. The Royal Irish Constabulary was a civil police force. It had neither the numbers nor the training that an army of occupation required, and its Irish constables had not enlisted to fight a guerrilla war. Some retired, and others resigned. Others were playing it safe, or just marking time. Still others began feuding with local republicans, executing known and suspected guerrillas, and burning the homes and shops of boycotters. Their British reinforcements, the Black and Tans, had military training and combat experience, but they were fish out of water in Ireland, where they soon picked up the bad habits of their Irish comrades, and worse. The Auxiliary Division was intended as a mobile police force for service in disturbed areas, but in some of these areas its companies began behaving like bashi-bazouks. When faced with resolute resistance, these forces not infrequently lost all restraint, and committed numerous atrocities, which only hardened insurgent resolve. In the next chapter, we will study the conflict between the police and the guerrillas on the level of a single county, where we can watch closely as the spiral of violence unwinds.

2

'The dark hours are dreaded'

The War of Independence in West Galway

The Irish War of Independence was a complex conflict. Its character varied widely from place to place. Rural guerrilla warfare in the south was quite different from urban guerrilla warfare in Dublin—and both were quite different from the sectarian civil war that erupted in Belfast. As a consequence, one of the most interesting ways to study the War of Independence is by studying the conflict in a single county, stepping back now and then to look at events nationwide. David Fitzpatrick pioneered this approach in the 1970s, with his book on County Clare, and a number of other historians have since followed in his footsteps, with very fruitful (though sometimes controversial) results. Local histories allow the social historian to see the war from the local perspective of the combatants. Since the Royal Irish Constabulary was organised into county forces, with county inspectors who submitted monthly reports on the local progress of the conflict, this approach is especially suitable for a history of the police.

Here we shall follow the War of Independence in County Galway's West Riding—the most violent district in the province of Connaught. The war in west Galway was very well documented, which allows us to build our narrative with a wide range of materials. The level of conflict in the West Riding varied greatly from season to season, and as a result, overall trends were clearer there than elsewhere. Finally, there was violence enough to provide a steady stream of incidents, but not so much that these incidents become a blur.

Once we have chronicled the War of Independence in this district, from the summer of 1920 to the summer of 1921, it will become clear that, from the police perspective, the conflict between the United Kingdom and the Irish Republic went through five roughly seasonal periods. In the winter and spring of 1919–20 Irish republicans were on the offensive, building an alternative state and pushing their chief enemy, the Royal Irish Constabulary, to the brink of collapse. But in the summer and autumn of 1920, armed with emergency powers and reinforced with British recruits and Auxiliaries, the RIC counter-attacked, driving the Irish Republic and its Army underground. The winter of 1920–1 was a period of deadlock and attrition, a 'wearing-out fight' in which casualties rose on both sides. This was followed by a new republican offensive in the spring.

The tipping point came in May 1921, when republican politicians captured almost every seat in the new Home Rule parliament, and republican guerrillas inflicted heavy losses on the Crown forces. After 'Black Whitsun' the British government's Irish policy was in tatters. By the summer of 1921 there were only two choices: military reconquest or a negotiated settlement. The government prepared for the former but offered the latter. Its offer was accepted, an armistice was negotiated, and the fighting ended on 11 July 1921.

2.1 Beaten to the ropes: winter and spring, 1919–20

Early twentieth-century Galway was remarkable in many ways. It was (and still is) the largest county in the province of Connaught, and the second largest county in Ireland: but Galway was also Ireland's most thinly populated county, and one of its poorest. In 1911 roughly 79 per cent of its population lived in poverty, on agricultural holdings valued at £15 or less. The county's population had fallen from 211,227 people in 1891 to 182,224 in 1911—and according to one estimate, more than 50,000 people had emigrated from the county during this twenty-year period. As a result, one writer has described early twentieth-century Galway as a 'barren wilderness'.[1]

But these generalisations disguise a number of important local variations. The waters of Lough Corrib divide County Galway into two distinct regions: a thinly populated western periphery and a densely populated eastern core. The region west of the lake has been described as 'barren, rugged, and mountainous'.[2] The region east of the lake, by contrast, was open country, suitable for grazing and farming—and the unequal division of this region's land, between graziers and farmers, led to chronic social conflict throughout the late nineteenth and early twentieth centuries.

During the Land War, between 1879 and 1882, the RIC reported more than 58 agrarian outrages per thousand people in Galway, compared to a national average of 24 per thousand.

Unrest and violence flared up once again during the Ranch War of 1904–8: as a consequence, Galway became one of the most heavily policed counties in Edwardian Ireland. Its West and East Ridings were treated as two separate counties for policing purposes, each with its own county inspector and county force. By the year 1911, these two county forces together consisted of 900 officers and men, housed in 94 barracks, and there was one constable for every 202 people in Galway, compared to an island-wide average of one constable for every 400 people. By way of comparison, in 1865, when the population of Galway had been larger by tens of thousands, its two county forces together had numbered only 657 men.[3]

Despite this overbearing police presence, radical republicanism flourished in Galway's rocky soil. The nascent Sinn Féin movement attracted many supporters in the county between 1907 and 1910, before the passage of the Birrell Land Act and the prospect of Home Rule made it possible for the Parliamentary Party to reassert itself. Volunteering became quite popular in Galway as well: in fact, during the rebellion of 1916, Galway's Volunteers were some of the few to rise outside of Dublin. The government's heavy-handed response to the rebellion, the failure of the Parliamentary Party to secure Home Rule, the Conscription Crisis of 1918, and Sinn Féin's adoption of a radical agrarian policy all encouraged the growth of the republican movement, until it eclipsed its rival.[4] In the general election of December 1918, Sinn Féin's candidates won decisive victories over their Irish Parliamentary Party opponents in Galway's four parliamentary constituencies.

The conflict between the United Kingdom and the Irish Republic in west Galway built up slowly. The Volunteers concentrated at first on collecting weapons and money. But by the end of 1919, as elsewhere, the situation had become so serious that the Royal Irish Constabulary began consolidating its county force: many stations were abandoned, the remainder were fortified, and the police gave up ordinary patrols.[5] In January 1920, 415 police were spread out among 46 stations in west Galway: by March 1921, 408 police would be crowded into just 19 barracks.[6] The insurgent response was tentative at first. Between the beginning of January and the end of May, they burned a number of unoccupied police barracks and launched assaults on three of the RIC's remaining stations: Castlehacket in January, Castlegrove in March, and Loughgeorge in May. In each case, the attackers were forced to withdraw after two or three hours of severe fighting, but the barracks were so badly damaged that they had to be abandoned.[7]

For the most part, however, Sinn Féin and the IRA concentrated on establishing a republican counter-state and redistributing land. Deprived of police protection, many graziers and landowners fell victim to a renewed upsurge of agrarian agitation. Republican land arbitration courts were set up, and Volunteers began acting as republican police in areas from which the constabulary had withdrawn. Elections for the county, rural, and district councils were held at the beginning of June 1920. 'Probably for the first time in the modern history of Irish elections,' the local press remarked, 'there were no police in attendance at the polling booths. Their places were taken by Volunteers, who performed their duties equitably and creditably.'[8] These elections too were won by Sinn Féin, and at their first meetings these councils pledged allegiance to Dáil Eireann.

The RIC county inspector's report for the month of June 1920 paints a vivid and detailed picture of the 'social war' being waged against the Royal Irish Constabulary at this time. Seen from the police perspective, the situation was already almost hopeless:

> Sinn Fein courts have set aside Petty Sessions courts to a great extent. The Irish Volunteers are in control everywhere and the police are set aside. The Police cannot go on patrol except in considerable force and on the slightest opportunity they are held up. It is difficult for them to get provisions and fuel & light in many places. Their condition of life in barracks with light and air shut out by sand bags, shell boxes and steel shutters is very irksome and disagreeable. At night they cannot sleep during the dark hours apprehending an attack at any time. No one speaks to them in a friendly way. No one will give them any information. Owing to the way mail cars are held up it is getting increasingly difficult to transmit orders and correspondence from County Head Qrs to the Districts of the Riding. Men cannot travel by rail armed, and transfers cannot be carried out by rail, owing to the munition strike. Galway Quarter Sessions is at present sitting and Police cannot attend by rail. Nine police travelling from Galway to Tuam on 23rd June were held up at Athenry and are still there as no train has run to Tuam since then. The old form of police control is practically beaten to the ropes and it is as well to recognise the situation.[9]

2.2 Shoot to kill: summer and autumn, 1920

The breaking point was finally reached when the summer assizes were held in Galway town on Monday and Tuesday, 19 and 20 July. Security was heavy. The judges were escorted from the Railway Hotel to the courthouse by a squadron of mounted Dragoon Guards, an armoured car, and a truckload of armed police. The courthouse was guarded by the military as well, with a machine gun on the roof and dismounted Dragoon Guards with rifles and fixed bayonets at the entrance: the troops presented arms as the judges entered.

But the IRA had initiated a boycott of the proceedings. Messages had been sent to prospective jurors: 'You are requested not to attend as a juror at the coming British assizes at Galway,' they read. 'No decent Irishman can do so without acting traitorously towards the nation.' The roads leading into town were blocked by Volunteers: 'All motor cars approaching were stopped, and jurors requested to leave them.'

As a result, the assizes were a disaster for the government, and a triumph for the revolutionaries. On Monday only 52 out of 480 jurors attended. On Tuesday only 27 jurors attended, despite having been threatened with fines. Most cases were adjourned until the next session, except for a few in which the defendant pleaded guilty. But the overall result was clear: the British government could no longer enforce its laws in west Galway.[10]

Monday, 19 July 1920, marked a turning point in the military struggle in west Galway as well. That evening an RIC sergeant and three constables were returning to their station at Dunmore, after attending the Galway assizes. Around nine o'clock they passed through Tuam. Three miles outside of town they stopped. Guerrillas had blocked the road with a fallen tree, and were waiting in ambush, hidden behind a hedge. When Constable James Burke and Constable Patrick Carey got out of their car to clear the road, the rebels opened fire. Burke and Carey were killed. The other two police fired back until they ran out of ammunition and surrendered. They were taken prisoner, disarmed, blindfolded, and told to walk back to Tuam. Burke and Carey's bodies were recovered later.

Police from Galway and Dragoon Guards from Claremorris hurried to the district and searched the countryside for hours. Finding nothing, they went back to Tuam around three in the morning. Reprisals began shortly before dawn. The police rushed into the streets, shouting, 'Where are the bloody Sinn Feiners? Let the cowards come on!' Soon they were smashing windows, shooting wildly, and throwing grenades. They wrecked shops and public houses, set fires, dragged young men from their beds, threatened to shoot them. They cheered when the town hall went up in flames: a republican court had been held there days before. They burned a drapery warehouse, and the family inside escaped only by climbing onto the roof. Not long after the riot ended, an English reporter came to Tuam and saw the damage. 'As I entered the town this morning,' he wrote, 'it recalled nothing so much as some of the ruined Belgian and French towns, and bore, I thought, a striking resemblance to wrecked Albert.'[11]

The Tuam police riot inspired copycat reprisals across Ireland; police in Caltra, County Longford, even shouted 'Up Tuam!' as they wrecked houses and burned the local Sinn Féin hall three days later.[12] These events, however, did nothing to hearten the police in west Galway: the tone of the county inspector's reports was, if anything, even more pessimistic by month's end. 'The life of the police is scarcely bearable,' he complained at month's end. 'They are shunned and boycotted, and for the most part they cannot get the necessaries of life unless they commandeer them. They are held up and shot at on every opportunity.... Intimidation broods everywhere and the dark hours are dreaded in many places owing to the operations of armed and masked men.'[13]

The West Riding's guerrillas claimed their third victim in August. On the morning of 21 August five policemen were cycling from Oranmore to Galway. Sergeant Healy, Constable Foley, and Constable Brown were carrying despatches: they were armed with revolvers. Sergeant Mulhearn and Constable Doherty were going on leave: they were unarmed. As they were passing a railway bridge they were ambushed. The police dropped their bicycles and ran. Foley was shot four times and later died of his wounds. Sergeant Healy emptied his revolver at the rebels then fled into a nearby wood to escape being surrounded. He and Constable Brown made it to Galway unharmed. Sergeant Mulhearn and Constable Doherty were both wounded, but escaped as well.[14]

The dead constable's comrades took reprisals that night in Oranmore. Their chief suspect was the son of a local woman, Mrs Kane. 'They asked her if her son was home that night,' said a witness to the American Commission. 'Well, he has been shot since. They asked him to come down. They said, "Come down, you coward." So they burned the house—burned the whole place to the ground and tore the house up the same night.'[15]

By the end of the month, the West Riding's county inspector was completely demoralised. 'Sinn Fein has become immensely strong,' he wrote, 'and little short of a Republic will satisfy the leaders now':

> It is recognized that the Police from their local knowledge are a great hindrance, and they are to be removed by murder or threats. They are shunned and hated and rejoicing takes place when they are shot. They have to take the necessaries of life by force. Their wives are miserable and their children suffer in the schools and nobody cares.[16]

On the night of 8 September a Black and Tan, Edward Krumm, and a Volunteer, John Mulvoy, were killed in a shootout at Galway railway station.[17] When news of the shooting reached Eglinton Street barracks, the Galway police rioted again, as they had in Tuam. Constable John Caddan was stationed at Eglinton Street barracks, and was in bed by midnight. 'The next thing I knew,' he said, 'one of the constables came up and gave the alarm, and said one of the constables was shot. And we all had to get up and dress and get our carbines. There were about fifty men in the barracks, and they ran amuck then.'[18]

The Galway police shot up the streets and went hunting for Volunteers, killing Seamus Quirke, adjutant of A Company, 1st (Galway) Battalion. They almost killed the battalion's commandant, John Broderick, but he got away. Caddan watched as his comrades invaded the Broderick family home, abducted their Volunteer son, splashed gasoline around, and set the house on fire. 'They took the son up toward the station,' said Caddan, 'but he got away, and they fired after him, and I think wounded him in the leg, but I am not sure of that. He got away. And then they turned around and saw a crowd of neighbours trying to put out the flames, and they fired into the crowd.'[19] By the time the riot was over, the police had burned another two houses, and had wrecked the machinery of a republican newspaper, the *Galway Express*.[20]

Dublin Castle's new Police Adviser, Major General Tudor, was also in Galway on the night of the riot.[21] The next day he spoke to the police at Eglinton Street. Constable Caddan later described the scene to the American Commission:

> He had two motor lorries of soldiers there to guard him. He had two other officers with him. The County Inspector was there and two District Inspec-

> tors, and all the men in the barracks were there. And he started to talk about this business. He said, 'This country is ruled by gunmen, and they must be put down.' He talked about giving home rule to Ireland, and he said home rule could not be given until all of these gunmen were put down, and he called on the RIC to put them down. He asked them what they required in the barracks, and that whatever they wanted he would give them, and they were also going to get a raise in pay. And he said they needed machine guns, and he said that they would get them, and also tanks and more men—men who had been in the Army during the war and who knew how to shoot to kill; and he said they would be the right men in the right place.[22]

A curfew was imposed on Galway town. Under the terms of the Restoration of Order in Ireland Act, a military court of inquiry was held instead of a coroner's inquest.[23] An independent civilian inquiry into the events of 8 September was suppressed. A woman named Eileen Baker gave evidence to the military court. On the morning of 18 September a gang of Volunteers attacked Baker and cut off her hair. In retaliation, police or soldiers cut off the hair of five Cumann na mBan women that night.[24]

Under cover of darkness, the police began taking revenge on boycotters. By the end of September, at least thirteen homes and shops belonging to well-known republicans had been damaged and looted.[25] In addition, the *Galway Express* was targeted again. The paper had defiantly printed a one-page edition the day after the riot. 'The Murder of Innocent Men' read its headlines: 'People's Admirable Restraint Under Extreme Provocation. *Galway Express* Premises Demolished.' The police soon went back to the paper's offices and wrecked what was left.[26] Later they attacked the editor's home and smashed his furniture.[27] The police report admitted only that 'the damage appears to have been done by anti-Sinn Feiners'.[28]

The men that General Tudor had promised after the Galway police riot began arriving in mid-September. Black and Tans came to reinforce the Riding's police barracks. In addition, a detachment of the Auxiliary Division—D Company—was posted to Galway town. The commander of D Company described his men and their mission to the provincial weekly. 'We are called the "Black and Tans",' he said, 'and a great deal of misrepresentation and exaggeration has got abroad regarding us and our purpose here':

> The 'Black and Tans' are really non-coms. Who have joined the R.I.C. proper; we are the auxiliary force, and act independently. All our men are ex-officers and, I hope, gentlemen. I wish it to be distinctly understood that

> we are not here to shoot people but to restore order. We are obliged to take certain steps to do this. The police were practically confined to their barracks and could not walk abroad in certain districts until we came. Peaceable, law-abiding citizens have nothing to fear from us.[29]

Thereafter, the West Riding's police went on the offensive, with the temporary cadets of D Company leading the way. This police counter-offensive claimed its first victim on the night of 5 October, when Auxiliaries raided the farmhouse of William O'Hanlon near Turloughmore and shot his son John O'Hanlon, secretary of the local Sinn Féin club, when he ran out the back. When the raiders left, William searched outside, but could not find his dead son in the darkness. John O'Hanlon's body was not discovered until the following morning.[30]

Soon, lurid reports of police brutality began to appear in the British and Irish press. For example, on the night of 9 October, a large party of police raided the Deveney home at Maree, near Oranmore. The family had three sons: Thomas, Stephen, and Patrick. Men wearing khaki clothes and black caps pulled the boys out of bed, demanding to know whether they were Sinn Feiners. The three were then dragged out into the road, one in his shirt and trousers, the others in their shirts alone. They were ordered to kneel down and say their prayers, and shots were fired over their heads. Then they were marched down the road a short distance, and finally told to stand still. One of the raiders lit up the boys with a flashlight, and another fired both barrels of a shotgun. Thomas and Stephen were hit in the legs and Patrick was hit in the stomach. The gunmen then told the wounded boys to clear off home.[31]

More attacks took place that same night in the Oranmore district. A man named Albert Cloonan was dragged from his bed and hit in the head with a gun butt. Mrs Anne Cloonan's unoccupied house was burned down, along with the local Sinn Féin hall.[32] 'Motive—anti-Sinn Fein,' says the police report. 'The same party seem to have committed these outrages. Inquiries are proceeding.'[33]

The poet and playwright Lady Isabella Augusta Gregory, a friend and patron of the poet William Butler Yeats, lived at Coole Park in southwest Galway. Lady Gregory heard about the violence at Maree from her doctor. 'He has just been again this evening to see Anne,' she wrote in her journal:

> When he came down he said, 'Those Black-and-Tans that were in Clarenbridge went on to Maree that is a couple of miles further. They dragged three

> men out of their houses there and shot them. They are not dead, they are wounded. I was sent for to attend them. Then they set fire to some of the houses and burned them down.' I asked if anything had happened there, if these were 'reprisals', and he said, 'Nothing, except that a good while ago, last year, a policeman was disarmed there but not hurt.' He said, 'I used not to believe the stories of English savagery whether written or told. I thought they were made up by factions, but now I see that they are true.'[34]

The Auxiliaries became even more savage as the month wore on. On Friday, 16 October 1920, a National School teacher named Patrick Joyce was kidnapped from Barna. Joyce was the county president of the National Teachers' Association, and according to reports was a strong constitutional nationalist.[35] He had also turned informer: the IRA had intercepted his correspondence with the police. After his abduction, Joyce was tried secretly by court martial, found guilty, and executed. His body was never found, and his kidnapping was never publicly explained, but it seems to have enraged the Auxiliaries.[36] On Saturday, 17 October, a notice was posted in Barna, warning that the village would be blown up if Joyce were not returned by that evening. The cadets of D Company scoured the district all weekend, threatening, beating, flogging, and firing shotguns at its inhabitants. Two men wound up in the county hospital after encounters with police and Auxiliaries: Thomas Carr was beaten with a revolver and shot in the leg; William Connolly was first whipped and then wounded by a shotgun blast.[37]

At last, on Monday, 19 October, a mixed force of soldiers and Auxiliaries raided the cooperative society store at Moycullen. The store's manager, Lawrence Tallon, and his four male employees were told to put up their hands, and then were taken outside to stand against the side of a corrugated-iron hut. Tallon described the Auxiliaries as 'several men who were not in any regular uniform, but were a mixed lot. Some had police caps and portions of police uniform, and some had not.' Their leader wore khaki breeches, a blue guernsey, and a knitted blue tam-o'-shanter, held a revolver in one hand, and a whip in the other. Speaking with an English accent, he questioned one of Tallon's assistants, Macdonagh. When Macdonagh said he knew nothing about Joyce's kidnapping, the Auxiliary leader hit him in the face with his revolver.

'On my honour,' cried Macdonagh, 'I know nothing of the man. I have heard of him, that is all.'

'Well,' said the Auxiliary officer, 'we will make you know something.'

The police pulled Macdonagh's trousers down and whipped him. Then they treated a second man, Tim Connor, in the same way. When the manager protested that his assistants were innocent, he was threatened with a bayonet and told to go back inside. As Tallon turned to go back to the store, an Auxiliary pointed a shotgun at him. Tallon got his left hand up before the gun went off, and was wounded in the left arm and the left side of the neck. He stumbled back inside, where he found his female employees kneeling in prayer, terrified. Shortly thereafter, the police outside began shooting at the store, and kept firing their shotguns and rifles until their magazines were empty.[38]

Later that night, in Galway town, five men walked into the public house of Michael Walsh, a republican city councillor. They wore plain clothes and carried revolvers. Walsh and his assistant, Martin Meenaghan, were held up and robbed at gunpoint. Meenaghan told the pressmen what came next:

> Mr Walsh asked me for a drink, and I pointed out a drop of rum. One of the men said: 'It is no good to you, it is going astray; you will be dead within an hour.' Mr Walsh said: 'I should like to see a priest if that is so.' The answer was: 'Your priests are worse than you are yourselves. You will not see a priest, Walsh; you have shot a lot of police.'

The gunmen had English accents and said they were 'English secret service men'. They took Walsh down to the dockside, shot him through the head, and pushed his body into the water. But they let Meenaghan go. When he asked whether the gang was going to shoot him, he was told: 'I don't think so; we have not heard anything about you yet.'[39]

In his report at the end of October 1920 the RIC county inspector's tone was transformed. The pessimism of August was gone. The assistance of the Army and the Auxiliaries, he said, 'is having a very healthy effect on the morale of the force'. He brushed off the bad publicity his men had attracted. 'During the month several Special Correspondents from English newspapers have been in Galway. In no case did they seek information from me or from the C.M.A. [Competent Military Authority]—they were obviously sent over to write up "reprisals".'[40] The RIC's deputy inspector general, Charles Walsh, was optimistic as well. Somewhat remarkably, he concluded his own monthly report on the West Riding with the following words: 'The tone of Galway has never been very bad and it should not be too difficult a task to restore order there.'[41]

Outside of west Galway, the security forces were counter-attacking everywhere in the fall of 1920. As a result, insurgent activity declined, especially in Connaught, where the number of attacks on police dwindled from 42 in the summer to just 14 in the autumn (see Table 2.1). But while the number of attacks on the police declined, the number of police who were killed in these attacks rose, from eight in the summer to 12 in the autumn (see Table 2.2). Five constables were killed in a single battle at Ballinderry, County Mayo, on 12 October; another four were killed when their patrol was ambushed near Moneygold, County Sligo, on 25 October.

These two bloody skirmishes were portentous. All across Ireland, IRA Volunteers were going on the run, to escape arrest, or sometimes to escape summary execution. These fugitives became full-time guerrillas, joining armed bands known as flying columns. These flying columns could be much more dangerous than local units of part-time Volunteers: just how dangerous became startlingly clear on 28 November, when the West Cork flying column, commanded by Tom Barry, massacred a platoon of Auxiliaries at Kilmichael.

Table 2.1. IRA attacks on the police in the province of Connaught, 1920–1.

Season	Galway	Leitrim	Mayo	Roscommon	Sligo
July–September 1920	20	3	8	6	5
October–December 1920	2	—	—	6	6
January–March 1921	4	1	1	9	4
April–June 1921	9	2	15	8	8

Table 2.2. Police deaths from insurgent attacks in the province of Connaught, 1920–1.

Season	Galway	Leitrim	Mayo	Roscommon	Sligo
July–September 1920	4	—	1	3	—
October–December 1920	1	—	—	5	6
January–March 1921	2	—	1	3	1
April–June 1921	4	1	16	1	2

Sources: Outrage Reports, TNA: PRO CO 904/148–50; Richard Abbott, *Police Casualties in Ireland, 1919–1922* (Dublin, 2000). For a more detailed examination of police casualties in the War of Independence, see W. J. Lowe, 'The War against the R.I.C., 1919–21', *Éire-Ireland* 37, nos. 3–4 (Fall/Winter 2002), 79–117 (esp. 88–97).

In the short term, however, the police seemed to be crushing the life out of the IRA in west Galway. On 30 October, however, the Volunteers did manage to ambush an RIC cycle patrol at Castledaly, in east Galway, killing Constable Timothy Horan.[42] This may have kept the West Riding's police force on edge. Police fire discipline was already poor: police travelling in vehicles often fired into the air, to the terror of bystanders. Now police patrols began to reconnoitre by fire, shooting ahead blindly when they came near woods and other likely spots for an ambush.

The results of this reckless procedure were as predictable as they were tragic: on 1 November, while sitting on a wall with a baby in her arms, a pregnant woman named Ellen Quinn was killed by a shot from a police vehicle. When a military court of inquiry was held a few days later, the police testified that they had opened fire as a precaution, when their convoy had approached a dangerous bend in the road. The court returned a verdict of death by misadventure.[43]

Irish public opinion was understandably outraged.[44] The parish priest, Father John Considine, conducted his own investigation, and concluded that Ellen Quinn's death had been manslaughter at best, and murder at worst: 'Either Mrs Quinn was deliberately killed by a bullet aimed directly at her,' he wrote, 'or she was killed by a bullet fired by a policeman, who must have seen her, and did not care whether he hit her or no.'[45]

In its own press release, Dublin Castle soft-pedalled the court's findings, by describing its verdict as 'manslaughter by accidental shooting', and tried to shift the blame onto the guerrillas. 'The case was very sad & most regrettable,' they said, 'but while [the] present state of affairs continues such cases are liable to occur. The police must take precautions to protect their lives & if [the] innocent accidentally suffer at times those who ambush & murder policemen are to blame.'[46] Nonetheless, on the day after Ellen Quinn's death, RIC headquarters issued new orders for 'parties travelling by motor', forbidding indiscriminate firing.[47] A week later, General Tudor must have had the dead woman in mind when he wrote a memorandum on discipline. 'There must be no wild firing', he said. 'It is useless and dangerous to innocent people. Firearms should never be fired except with the intention of hitting the object aimed at.'[48]

Worse was to come. On the night of Sunday, 14 November, Father Michael Griffin left his residence at St Joseph's Church in Galway. His housekeeper heard him talking to someone at the door and thought the priest was going to visit a sick parishioner. Father Griffin never came back that night. His disappearance was reported to the police the next day. On Friday, 19 November, an Irish Parliamentary Party MP, Joseph Devlin, raised the matter in Parliament. Griffin was known to hold strong republican views, and Devlin accused the security forces of kidnapping him.

Chief Secretary Greenwood replied hotly. 'I do not believe for a moment that this priest has been kidnapped by any armed forces of the Crown,' he said. 'It is obviously such a stupid thing that no members of the forces of the Crown would do it.' 'That is why they would do it,' Devlin heckled.[49]

But Devlin was too late. Father Griffin was dead. Like Michael Walsh, he had been shot through the head, execution-style, and buried in a shallow grave in a bog near Barna. His body was found on the night of Saturday, 20 November.[50]

Officially, Father Griffin's murder was never solved, and before long the case was overshadowed by events in Dublin.[51] (The day after Griffin's body was found was Sunday, 21 November—Bloody Sunday.) But the commandant of the Auxiliary Division, Brigadier General Crozier, came to Galway town on Monday, 22 November, where he dismissed the commander of D Company for drinking, and inquired into the Griffin case. Months later, after he resigned, Crozier told the press that Auxiliaries had murdered Father Griffin.[52]

D Company's new commander was Lieutenant Colonel F. H. W. Guard, a highly decorated officer who had served in West Africa, France, and North Russia.[53] Guard seems to have put a stop to his men's worst excesses: at the very least, there were far fewer reports of people being whipped, wounded with shotguns, and forced to crawl after Guard took command. But not long after taking charge, the colonel was at the scene when the first prisoner was shot dead while trying to escape in west Galway. This prisoner was Michael Moran: described in the local press as a 'well-known Irish Volunteer leader' and 'one of the outstanding figures of the Volunteer movement in North Galway', Moran was the commandant of the IRA's Tuam Battalion, and the police held him responsible for the ambush near Tuam in July.

Moran was killed on the evening of 24 November. According to his testimony to the subsequent military court of inquiry, Guard was personally escorting this high-profile prisoner from Eglinton Street to the barracks of the 17th Lancers when Moran tried to flee. The Auxiliaries opened fire, and the insurgent leader fell wounded: the Auxiliaries called an ambulance to take Moran to hospital, but he died on the way. The medical examiner testified, however, that Moran died about three hours after he was wounded—and the court made a point of accepting the medical examiner's testimony.[54]

Despite the growing scandal surrounding killings like these, RIC headquarters was well satisfied with conditions in west Galway. In his report for November, Deputy Inspector General Walsh was sanguine about the Riding's future. 'Much of the moral and material support lent to Sinn Fein is due to fear,' he wrote, 'and with the growth of the realisation that the Government is beginning to get a grip of the situation there are indications of a return to sanity and revulsion against Sinn Fein on the part of the more responsible persons. In Galway Sinn Fein has largely lost its power, matters are well in hand, and the murder gang is on the run.'[55]

The British government was confident as well—and at this point, Galway's local politics may have exercised a decisive influence on the course of the war. According to reports in the local press, on 3 December the clerks of the county's poor-law unions attended a special meeting of the Galway county council, 'to discuss the advisability of submitting the council's accounts to the Local Government Board for audit'. Only six councillors attended, which was not enough to constitute a quorum. But after waiting for two hours, the chairman decided to proceed, and hear 'what the clerks of the different unions had to say about the financial position of each union'.

Two of the six clerks reported that their poor-law unions could not carry on for long without additional funds. The remaining four reported that their unions could not carry on at all. 'Mr Gallagher (Galway union) said they had only £700 to carry on for the current quarter ending on December 31, and a probable expenditure of £5,000 to £6,000.' The union was cutting off outdoor relief, and over seven hundred workhouse inmates were at risk.

In response to this crisis, the six councillors passed the following resolution:

> That we, the members of the Galway County Council, assembled on December 3, 1920, view with sorrow and grief the shootings, burnings, reprisals, and counter-reprisals which are taking place all over England and Ireland by armed forces of the British Empire on one hand and armed forces of the Irish Republic on the other. That we believe this unfortunate state of affairs is detrimental to the interests of both countries in such a crisis in world

> affairs. We therefore, as adherents of Dáil Eireann, request that body to appoint three delegates for the purpose of negotiating a truce.
>
> We further request the British government to appoint three more delegates who will have power to arrange a truce and preliminary terms of peace so that an end may be brought to the unfortunate strife by a peace honourable to both countries. That we consider the initiative lies with the British government who should withdraw the ban on the meeting of Dáil Eireann for the purpose of appointing delegates. That we further consider that if either side refuses to accede to proposals such as these, the world will hold it responsible for any further shootings or burnings that may take place.[56]

Both the Galway county council and the Galway urban council voted to submit their books to the Local Government Board for audit: 'otherwise,' as one elected official put it, 'they will come and take the books forcibly, and some of them might have to go to jail. He considered it a mad and foolish proposal to keep those books, and deprive themselves of the money they were entitled to.'[57]

These resolutions were bitterly criticised by Irish republicans, including Michael Collins.[58] For its part, the British government found these words encouraging. At a meeting of the Cabinet held on 6 December, it was pointed out 'that the first paragraph of the Galway County Council's resolution was the first occasion on which a Sinn Fein county council had condemned the Sinn Fein policy of murder and outrage'.[59] In his speech on the Restoration Order in Ireland Bill, back in August, Lloyd George had warned that no compromise was possible until the 'authentic representatives of the Irish people' showed a 'gleam of sanity', and accepted the British government's fundamental conditions. In the government's eyes, it seems, this uncompromising policy was at last bearing fruit.

The Prime Minister's answer to the Galway county council's resolution was firm. 'The first necessary preliminary to the re-establishment of normal conditions,' he said, 'is that murder and crimes of violence shall cease. It is to that end that the efforts of the Irish executive have been constantly directed, and until it has been attained no progress can be made toward a political settlement.' 'I would add,' he concluded, 'that the Government has learnt with satisfaction of the action of your Council in submitting their accounts to audit by the Local Government Board and that the fullest support can be assured to every local authority which loyally carries out its obligations under the law.'[60]

Lloyd George announced his reply to the Galway county council in a speech to the House of Commons on 10 December. Martial law was proclaimed in four counties of Munster that same day.[61] The Government of Ireland Act was assented to thirteen days later, on 23 December 1920. At a further Cabinet meeting on 29 December, British generals predicted victory by the spring. The Police Adviser (now known as the Chief of Police) agreed. 'General Tudor said he thought that, in his area, in four months' time the terror would be broken if there was no truce. The great hope of the extremists was a change of policy.'[62]

Meanwhile, back in west Galway, the war went on. On the same day that the Galway county council was calling for a truce, people were horrified by the deaths of two young men from Shanaglish. Patrick Loughnane was president of the local Sinn Féin club, and his brother Harry was its secretary. Auxiliaries had arrested the two brothers on Friday, 26 November, but three days later their mother's house was raided, and she was told that her sons had escaped. Lady Gregory made note of these events in her journal: 'The Mason here says the Black-and-Tans have come back to Shanaglish, after two days, looking for the Loughnanes, said they had escaped, and everyone believes they were done away with.'[63]

These suspicions were confirmed on 5 December, when local residents found the bodies of the Loughnane brothers in a pond. A funeral was held for the brothers on 7 December, but before it could proceed a medical officer arrived with an escort of police and soldiers, the coffins were unscrewed, and the bodies were examined. Both corpses were charred from burning, and their skulls had been fractured: the medical officer and another physician concurred that both men had died from their head injuries, and had been dead for about a week.[64] It was widely believed that Auxiliaries had tied the two brothers to the backs of their trucks and dragged them to their deaths.[65]

On the night of 18/19 December a Royal Navy cruiser sailed from Galway to the middle island of Aran, with a force of 250 soldiers and police aboard. This force was divided into two parties that went ashore on opposite sides of the island. The security forces took ten suspects into custody: when Lawrence MacDonagh fled from the second shore party, he was spotted by the first and was shot dead.[66] When the year ended without further incident in the West Riding, the RIC's deputy inspector general thought the war there was almost over. 'The firm manner in which the Crown Forces are performing their duties has subdued the disloyal spirit of the people,' he wrote.[67]

2.3 'You are going to suffer now': winter 1920–1

In fact, the IRA's 'disloyal spirit' was far from subdued. This became clear when the guerrillas resurfaced on 13 January 1921 and shot at a police patrol near Tuam.[68] Then, on 18 January, like their comrades in west Cork, they ambushed a party of Auxiliaries. Eleven cadets in a Crossley tender were on patrol from Galway to Headford that morning. Thirty or forty guerrillas were hiding behind stone fences and trees in the wood at Kilroe, about four miles from Headford. When the Auxiliaries drove into the trap, the rebels threw a bomb and opened fire from both sides of the road.

The fight lasted only a few minutes. The tender's engine was hit by a bullet and stopped. Three cadets were badly wounded, one by a bullet in the right leg, the other two by shot pellets in the head and left arm. Another three suffered slight wounds. The Auxiliaries fired back, and the rebels retreated. When the shooting stopped, an unwounded cadet rode for help on a horse. The remaining Auxiliaries were forced to wait for a passing commercial truck to carry their wounded back to Galway.[69]

A large force of police and Auxiliaries left Galway to search for the ambushers. At Keelkill, Lieutenant Colonel Guard arrested and questioned a young man named Thomas Collins. 'Having got very unsatisfactory answers from him,' said Guard, 'I handed him over to Sergeant Keeney RIC & instructed him to take this man down to the cars which were about 200 yards away':

> Shortly afterwards I heard cries of Halt! & one shot immediately followed by a volley. Sgt Keeney came back & reported to me that the prisoner had attempted to escape, failed to halt when challenged and had been shot dead. I walked over to the body, satisfied myself that the man was dead & ordered that the body should be put in a tender & conveyed back to Renmore Barracks.

At Renmore barracks, an RAMC officer examined the young man and found ten bullet wounds on his body, including one through the head.[70]

The police kept searching, making arrests and taking reprisals. By the end of the day, eight houses and stack-yards had been burned.[71] A few days later, the police killed three men—William Walsh, Michael Hoade, and James Kirwan—in separate incidents near Tuam and Headford.[72] The West Riding's county inspector glossed over much of this violence in his monthly report. The police were fired on during their search, he said, 'and as a result some houses were set on fire':

> As a result of information received the police subsequently searched a large area of country, and arrested 3 men on suspicion of being concerned in a previous ambush. 3 other IRA men were shot dead when attempting to escape from custody. This resolute action on the part of the Crown Forces is having an excellent effect on the peace of the locality.[73]

The county inspector's report made it clear that the Irish Republic was losing ground on the judicial front as well. 'The Petty Sessions Courts are now beginning to again function,' he said. 'At Galway Quarter Sessions on 25th inst there was an exceptionally large attendance of jurors.'[74]

The reprisals continued throughout February. On the night of 13 February, for example, Bridget Quinn's house at Kinvarra was burned, and seven local men were stripped and beaten.[75] The police report on this last incident says that 'a number of armed and disguised men entered the house of Mrs Quinn, farmer, Gort district, where a number of Sinn Feiners were playing cards, and having first taken them outside and flogged them, they set fire to the house. Quinn's house was a meeting place for Sinn Feiners, and two sons are prominent members of the organisation.' Its conclusion is coy: 'There are other people in the locality,' it says, 'who are strongly opposed to this policy.'[76]

More seriously, republican elected officials who had not been arrested and interned became targets for assassination. On 20 February two men in uniform took District Councillor John Geoghegan from his home at Moycullen and killed him.[77] At the subsequent military court of inquiry, Geoghegan's brother, Michael, testified that he had been awakened that night by loud knocking at the door:

> Immediately there was breaking of glass and someone shouting outside, 'Open the door, we want John Geoghegan.' My mother was the first to go down to the door. Two men came into our bedroom. One of them had a black coat and policeman's cap; the other was in khaki, with a tin hat. The man with the overcoat asked where was John Geoghegan? John spoke up and said 'I am here.' 'We want you John; get up at once and dress,' they replied; and at the same time the other man asked me my name and asked my brother his. The

> man with the black coat accused John of being a friend of Michael Collins, and of being friendly with the police and the other side. The man with the black coat said, 'You have been a traitor to Ireland, John, and you are going to suffer now.'

Once Geoghegan was dressed, he was taken out of the house, in his bare feet, and shot to death by the roadside. Eleven empty cartridge cases—five rifle and six revolver—were found at the scene.[78] Six days later bombs were thrown into the houses of two Dunmore county councillors, Michael Finnigan and C. J. Kennedy.[79]

In his monthly report, the county inspector mentioned almost none of this violence—only the killing of 'a man named Geoghegan near Moycullen'. 'This man was a leading IRA officer,' he said. 'A Military Court of Inquiry has been held in this connection.' Otherwise, order was well on its way to being restored. 'Sinn Fein Courts have ceased to exist and the ordinary Petty Sessions are now operating freely.'[80]

On 26 February the IRA had laid an ambush for a small police party on the road from Dunmore to Ballymoe, northeast of Tuam, but their position was given away by local residents; the police went around, and came back with reinforcements, but by then the ambushers had given up and left.[81] On 2 March, perhaps in connection with this failed ambush, Thomas Mullen of Killavoher was arrested, taken away in a police lorry, and later shot dead by the roadside. The official story was that Mullen had tried to escape, but newspaper reporters were sceptical.[82] Houses were set on fire near Dunmore the next day.[83]

For the first two weeks in March, the insurgents confined themselves to small operations, like robbing letter carriers, blocking roads, and enforcing a boycott of Belfast goods. Then, on 14 March, a Galway man, Thomas Whelan of Clifden, was hanged in Dublin's Mountjoy gaol. Two days after the hanging, the IRA's newly formed west Connemara flying column struck for the first time, in Whelan's birthplace. On the evening of 16 March, six guerrillas ambushed four police constables on patrol in Clifden. Opening fire with revolvers, they hit Constable Charles Reynolds in the head, killing him, and wounded Constable Thomas Sweeney in the leg.

The remaining two constables chased the ambushers for a short distance, lost them, and finally reported back to barracks. When reinforcements arrived, the police broke out and took revenge on the town, shooting in the streets and setting fires. Nine buildings were burned, including a hotel, a restaurant, and three shops.

An ex-soldier named John J. McDonnell, son of the hotel owner, was shot dead while 'attempting to evade arrest'. Later, at the court of inquiry into this man's death, a medical officer testified that McDonnell had been shot through the back of the head. Meanwhile, an ex-policeman named Peter Clancy was in his brother's butcher shop when it was set on fire. The police put Clancy up against a wall, forced him to his knees, and shot him too. Additional police reinforcements arrived early the next morning, and both Clancy and Constable Sweeney were taken to hospital in Galway. Sweeney had his leg amputated on 18 March and died the following day. Clancy survived and told the press about the police riot.[84]

The Crown forces had better luck on the morning of 23 March when they caught a rebel officer named Louis D'Arcy at the Oranmore railway station, east of Galway town. D'Arcy was then shot dead the following day, while the police were escorting him from Oranmore to Galway. According to police witnesses at the subsequent court of inquiry, the police convoy had stopped when its leading car suffered a breakdown, and D'Arcy had tried to escape.[85] In his monthly report, the RIC county inspector noted with satisfaction that D'Arcy had been a captain of the IRA.[86]

2.4 Disturbed and restless: spring 1921

General Tudor returned to west Galway for a brief inspection tour at the beginning of April. After visiting Tuam on 1 April, he went to Galway town that night and inspected the local police the following day:

> In his address to the constabulary, the general congratulated them on the fine appearance which they presented. 'In the determined stand you have taken,' he continued, 'in lifting the terror of the reign of the gunmen, I assure you that you have my fullest support.' He emphasized the importance of preserving the magnificent traditions of discipline of the Royal Irish Constabulary.

After visiting a wounded Black and Tan, Constable William Stephens, in the county infirmary, Tudor went on to inspect the Auxiliaries of D Company:

> Having inspected the Auxiliaries, he spoke of the pleasure it gave him to hear from many sources of the excellent discipline of D Company. He congratu-

lated them upon the gallantry a small party of them had shown when ambushed at Kilroe on January 18 last.

Upon leaving the city on Saturday, General Tudor was accorded three cheers by the R.I.C. and the Auxiliaries.[87]

The fighting worsened in April, as the IRA went back on the offensive in west Galway. On 6 April the west Connemara flying column ambushed another police patrol at Screebe, near Rosmuck. The guerrillas wounded a constable and captured a rifle, two revolvers, and ammunition. The security forces retaliated: that same day, five houses in the Screebe district were burned, along with a co-operative store.[88] The wounded man, Constable William Pearson, later died.[89]

Then, on the early morning of 23 April, the IRA struck again, when they ambushed an RIC cycle patrol at Mounterowen, on the road from Maam to Leenane. Fourteen police were on their way to search the house of Patrick O'Malley, TD (Teachta Dála, deputy to Dáil Eireann) for Connemara. The west Connemara flying column was waiting for them, but a nervous Volunteer fired a premature shot. The police scattered for cover, and were quickly pinned down by rifle fire.

A stalemate ensued, which lasted for several hours. The police were on the verge of giving up when a civilian car drove up and blundered into the battle. The police held up the driver at rifle point: jumping on the running board, a constable named Rutledge ordered him to 'drive like hell' for reinforcements.[90] The commandeered car got away, under fire: Constable Rutledge was wounded, but made it back to Maam, where he telephoned for help from Galway. About three hours later, six truckloads of police arrived on the scene, led by an armoured car: the guerrillas, already low on ammunition, prudently withdrew. The police had suffered three casualties: Constable John Boylan had been killed and a Sergeant named Hanley had been wounded, along with Constable Rutledge. Two houses, including O'Malley's, were burned afterwards, as a reprisal.[91]

A week later, on the evening of 30 April, another police party was ambushed on the road from Tuam and Dunmore: this time, however, there were no police casualties. Later that night, the insurgents attacked the RIC barracks at Headford, in the same district. After a ferocious battle lasting two hours, the attackers retreated, once again without causing any police casualties.[92]

Meanwhile, both sides were now attacking civilians. On 2 April the guerrillas used shotguns to kill an ex-soldier and ex-constable named Thomas Morris at Kinvarra.[93] At the subsequent military court of inquiry, a witness testified that she did not know why Morris had been shot, 'if it were not in connection with the burning of Mrs Quinn's house, as it was thought at the time that he was a spy'.[94] The security forces retaliated on 6 April, when masked men took Patrick Cloonan out of his sister's house at Maree and killed him by the seashore.[95] In his monthly report, the county inspector wrote that 'Cloonan was at one time an advanced Sinn Feiner, but latterly it was reported that he was endeavouring to cut away from the movement and go to America. It is believed that some of the Sinn Feiners thought he was about to give them away before he left and therefore, murdered him.'[96]

This was almost certainly a lie. A month later the Army inquired into Cloonan's death. They were told that Cloonan had taken part in the Rebellion of 1916. He was second in command of the Maree Volunteers, and a well-known republican policeman: he was also suspected of taking part in an ambush in May 1920. The Army concluded that 'this man probably was not killed by SF'.[97]

In the meantime, on 27 April, the guerrillas had killed another 'convicted spy', Thomas Hannon of Clonbern, for being friendly with the police.[98] Three nights later, on 30 April, another man, Thomas Molloy, was taken out of his father's house at Kilroe and killed. The testimony of the examining physician at the subsequent military court of inquiry suggested that Molloy had been shot at least ten times.[99]

In response to this upsurge of violence, the tone of the county inspector's monthly report was cautious. 'There is still a strong tendency towards the Sinn Fein movement,' he admitted, 'and this is largely due to the reign of terror exercised by the "murder gang".' Indeed. He went on to say that:

> The majority of the people are afraid to be seen associating with the Crown Forces, and they are also afraid to give the forces of the Crown any information which might lead to the extermination of this band of outlaws. Swift vengeance on the part of the IRA follows those who are even suspected of giving the police any information, and so long as this reign of terror continues the country will be in a disturbed and unsatisfactory condition.

Nonetheless, he said, the war against the republican counter-state was still going well. 'There was no Sinn Fein Arbitration Court held in the Riding during the month. The Petty Sessions Courts in almost every place are now functioning as usual. The Quarter Sessions opened in Galway on 12th April, and there were only two absent jurors.'[100]

The fighting intensified all across Ireland in the spring of 1920. In west Galway the killing peaked in mid-May. A death squad struck again in Galway town. James Folan had been imprisoned for six months for holding a seditious document. He was released on 11 May. That night, armed and masked men came to his house and demanded to see him. When they found he wasn't home, they shot his brothers instead, killing Christopher and wounding Joseph. A short time later the gang went to another house and demanded to see Hubert Tully. When Tully came to the door, they shot him dead.[101] A few days later, on 14 May, the guerrillas ambushed a police patrol at Spiddal: the police got safely back to their barracks and suffered no casualties. That same day five houses were burned and two others raided and damaged in the Spiddal area.[102] Then, that night in Galway, two more men were attacked. A medical student named John Green and an insurance inspector named James Egan were taken from their hotel room, beaten, and shot. This time, however, both men survived and reported the attack to the police. As a result, two Black and Tans (Constable James Murphy and Constable Richard Orford) were arrested the next morning. The two were ultimately tried, convicted, and imprisoned for this crime—a rare event.[103]

Like the murder of Father Griffin, the attempted murder of Egan and Green was overshadowed by what happened the next day. On 15 May District Inspector Cecil Blake drove to Ballyturin House near Gort with his wife Lily. They were accompanied by a pair of Army officers, Captain Cornwallis and Lieutenant McCreery of the 17th Lancers, and by Margaret Gregory, Lady Gregory's daughter-in-law. They spent the afternoon at the house visiting the Bagot family and playing tennis, and left in the early evening. They stopped their car by the gate, and Captain Cornwallis got out to open it. Suddenly, someone shouted 'hands up', shots were fired, and the car's windshield was broken by bullets.

Cornwallis tried to take cover by the gate. The remaining four tried to hide behind the car, but it was too late: they were surrounded. Cornwallis, the Blakes, and McCreery were shot to death. Only Margaret Gregory escaped, unharmed.[104]

The Bagots ran down to the gate when they heard the shooting. John Bagot was held back at gunpoint while the guerrillas came out of cover and searched the bodies of his guests. His daughter May drove off to Gort to warn the police. Her father watched as the rebels ran and cycled away. Someone handed him a note that read: 'Volunteer HQ. Sir, if there is any reprisals after this ambush, your house will be set on fire as a return. By Order IRA.'[105]

May Bagot returned, bringing the police and a doctor. 'We went straight to Captain Cornwallis, who was lying on the further side of the gate between the wall and the road,' she said:

> I then went to see the other 3, but they were all dead. I turned round to the car after getting inside the gate and waited for 2 or 3 minutes. Then a shot was fired and my Father who was present shouted at me 'Take cover'. I ran to the wall and lay down underneath it. There was a good deal of firing and then Constable Kearney who was on the other side of the wall and close to me was hit.[106]

Constable John Kearney died of his wounds on 21 May, raising the body count at Ballyturin House to five.[107]

In the meantime, the police had ignored the IRA's warning to John Bagot. The very next day, on 16 May, nine houses were destroyed or damaged in the vicinity of Ballyturin. A curfew was imposed, and all businesses were ordered to close.[108] Soon afterwards, on the night of 20 May, three armed men took Thomas McKeever from his boarding house in Dunmore and shot him dead by the side of the road. A notice tied around his neck read 'Convicted spy. Traitors beware. Executed by order of I.R.A.'[109]

The RIC county inspector's confidence was clearly shaken by the blood-letting in May. In his report he admitted that the Riding was in 'a disturbed and restless state', and mentioned 'a spirit of restlessness which gives cause for anxiety'. Reinforcements were needed, along with armoured transport. Still, he tried to sound cheerful. 'The morale of all ranks is excellent,' he wrote, 'and search for and pursuit of rebels is energetically kept up. The later [*sic*] dare not come into the open and appear to have a wholesome respect for the Galway Police.' He also continued to blame the IRA for civilian casualties. Christopher and Joseph Folan were shot, he said, because the Sinn Féin party was afraid that James might inform on them. He also said that Tully 'was on good terms with the police and was probably suspected of giving information'.[110]

2.5 Drastic measures: summer 1921

The Ballyturin House ambush was the bloody climax of the war in the West Riding. The fighting continued, but on a smaller scale. On 27 June a police patrol from Milltown was ambushed on the road to Tuam. Sergeant James Murren and a Black and Tan, Constable Edgar Day, were both killed. Murren had been due to retire on pension the week before: for some reason his papers had been delayed. In his monthly report for July the county inspector was pessimistic and bitter. 'There is little prospect of a change for the better,' he wrote, 'until drastic measures are taken to put down Sinn Fein with a strong hand. The great majority of the people would be glad to see this done, but their moral cowardice—coupled with the reign of terror—is so great, that they are afraid to give the least assistance.' In the meantime, more men were needed. 'The morale of all ranks is excellent and while the force available is almost sufficient, I would be glad of a number of recruits to meet wastage, and strengthen stations.' The one bright spot was the purely military nature of the conflict. 'No Sinn Fein Courts were held and the ordinary law is now operating as usual.'[111]

By the end of June, however, the political situation was changing rapidly. The Government of Ireland Act had created two Home Rule parliaments. A general election for the House of Commons of Southern Ireland was held on 13 May 1921. Like the two previous elections, this was a republican triumph, and a disaster for the government. Sinn Féin treated it as an election for a new revolutionary parliament, and won 124 of its 128 seats unopposed. Under the new scheme, County Galway was represented in the Dublin parliament by seven members. In the election of 13 May, the county returned its four sitting TDs, along with three additional candidates: Joseph Whelehan, George Nicolls (imprisoned at Kilmainham), and Patrick Hogan (interned at Ballykinlar).[112]

Once acclaimed, the Sinn Féin MPs declared themselves the second Dáil Eireann and showed every sign of refusing to take their seats in any House of Commons. If that happened, then under the terms of the Act, the southern parliament would be dissolved and the 26 counties would be governed as a Crown colony. In the meantime, the IRA killed 15 police that weekend, on Saturday (14 May) and Whit Sunday (15 May).[113]

Thus, by mid-May 1921 the government's policy—'the repression of crime and the determination to carry through the Government of Ireland Bill'—had failed utterly. Once again, the government 'had either to give way or to go very much further in repression'. At first, it prepared for war: at a meeting on 2 June the Cabinet decided to declare martial law throughout Southern Ireland if its parliament had not assembled by 12 July.[114] The Army of Ireland was reinforced, and in a grim speech to the House of Lords on 21 June, the Lord Chancellor, Birkenhead, at last admitted that the United Kingdom was at war in Ireland—a war that the government was determined to win. Negotiations would be pointless, he said. Ireland's revolutionaries would accept 'nothing less than that which they have repeatedly and publicly avowed that they require—namely, open independence and a Republic of Ireland'. This the British never would concede. 'I profoundly hope,' he concluded, 'that even at this eleventh hour wiser councils will prevail, but should we be forced to the melancholy conclusion that by force and by force alone can these mischiefs be extirpated, it is a conclusion which, however sorrowfully, we shall accept, and upon which we shall not hesitate logically and completely to act.'[115]

Twenty-four hours later, though, the two-headed ass was pulling in the opposite direction. A second election had been held on 24 May, for the House of Commons of Northern Ireland, and the Ulster Unionists had won a strong majority. On 22 June, King George V was in Belfast for the opening session of the northern parliament. The speech His Majesty gave was nothing like Birkenhead's.[116] In his address, the king called on 'all Irishmen to pause, to stretch out the hand of forbearance and conciliation, to forgive and to forget, and to join in making for the land that they love a new era of peace, contentment, and good will'.[117] The Irish War of Independence was not popular in Britain, and the King's appeal was welcomed by British public opinion. It was also well received in the Irish nationalist press, and this, along with some indications that republican leader Eámon de Valera might finally be willing to compromise, appears to have persuaded Lloyd George to try for a negotiated settlement.

At a meeting on 24 June the Cabinet agreed to propose talks with the leaders of Sinn Féin. This agreement was made easier by changes in the Cabinet itself. Walter Long had retired in February 1921, and Bonar Law had retired in March. Austen Chamberlain was the new leader of the Conservative and Unionist Party, and apparently had not inherited his father Joseph Chamberlain's passion for the Union: he agreed that 'the

King's speech ought to be followed up by a last attempt at peace before we go to full martial law'.[118] If nothing else, an offer to negotiate would strengthen the government's moral position, should the revolutionaries refuse.[119] In the end, however, the government's offer was not refused—though De Valera would not negotiate unless a truce was called first. As a result, a truce was arranged in Dublin on 8 July 1921, and came into force three days later, at noon. The Irish War of Independence was over.

Five months later, the Anglo-Irish Treaty of 6 December 1921 conceded dominion status to the 26 counties of Southern Ireland—the very concession that the British government had strenuously rejected in the summer of 1920. But the government did succeed in imposing its three fundamental conditions on the peace treaty—the autonomy of Ulster, the authority of the Crown, and the defence of the realm. Both sides accepted this compromise only after a year and a half of bloody guerrilla fighting, in which about fourteen hundred people were killed.[120] At least 41 people had been killed in County Galway's West Riding: 12 police, 2 soldiers, and 27 Volunteers and civilians, including 2 women, Ellen Quinn and Lily Blake. Three of the dead police were Black and Tans.

In *The I.R.A. and Its Enemies* Peter Hart painted a grim picture of the war in County Cork. It was, he says, 'not primarily an affair of ambushes and round-ups. It was terror and counter-terror, murder after murder, death squad against death squad, fed by both sides' desire for revenge. Each new atrocity demanded a reply and so set off a new round of reprisals.'[121]

The paradigm for these 'interlocking sequences of reprisals' was the violence that followed the killing of an unarmed RIC Sergeant, James O'Donoghue in Cork city on 17 November 1920. Sergeant O'Donoghue's comrades took revenge that same night, killing three equally unarmed men and wounding two others in reprisals. The swiftness of the constabulary's retaliation raised suspicions of betrayal among the revolutionaries: eventually, three other men were executed by the IRA for having informed on O'Donoghue's killers. 'This little cycle of killings reveals the runaway tit-for-tat logic of the guerrilla war in Cork, driven by fear and the overwhelming need to respond,' Hart concludes. 'All of the victims were unarmed and helpless when shot and all were killed or kidnapped near home. The revolution produced many skirmishes and casualties by combat, but many more people died without a gun in their hands, at their doors, in quarries or empty fields, shot in the back by masked men. Murder was more common than battle.'[122]

Clearly, some of the violence in west Galway followed this 'tit-for-tat logic' as well: the IRA's execution of Patrick Joyce, for example, led to at least two extrajudicial killings by the Auxiliaries, including the murder of a Roman Catholic priest. But overall the War of Independence in west Galway seems to have followed a rather different pattern. Between July 1920 and July 1921 the west Galway IRA killed 12 police and at least 4 civilians. Out of these 12 police, 10 were on duty when they were killed: the eleventh and twelfth, Constable Edward Krumm and District Inspector Cecil Blake, were not on duty, but were both armed; as a consequence, every one of them can legitimately be described as having been killed in action. Out of four civilians three were executed for spying: the fourth, Lily Blake, was apparently killed while trying to shield her husband during the Ballyturin House ambush. As cold as it may sound, this must be counted as a death by misadventure.

By way of comparison, out of at least 21 Volunteers and civilians killed by the security forces, just one was definitely killed in action, while another was lynched: these were John Mulvoy and Seamus Quirke, both of whom lost their lives on the night of 8 September 1920. Out of the remaining 19, some 8 were assassinated, including the Loughnane brothers, who may have been tortured to death; 6 were killed for failing to halt; and 4 were killed while trying to escape. Ellen Quinn was most likely killed by a stray bullet, and this puts her in a category of her own, much like Lily Blake.

To be fair, this second set of figures is not as clear-cut as it might appear. The insurgents did not wear uniforms or carry arms openly, and indeed, would often pretend to be non-combatants: as a consequence, the police were given comparatively few chances to kill their enemies in action, and they viewed the killing of fellow police not as an act of war, but as murder. In addition, it seems likely that at least some of the ten Volunteers and civilians who are counted as having been shot for failing to halt or for trying to escape, really did fail to halt and try to escape. But even so, the asymmetric nature of the violence in west Galway is rather striking. The killing of unarmed and helpless men *was* more common than battle—but not *that* much more common: and what is more, most of these unarmed and helpless victims were killed by the police.

3

Constabulary in Khaki

The Black and Tans

The Black and Tans may be the most notorious police in the history of the British Isles—yet in spite of their notoriety, we know very little about these men, and even less about what caused their behaviour in Ireland. Most historians agree that frustration was the chief cause of 'black-and-tannery', and a few have argued that alienation played an important part as well. Most historians also agree, however, that the Black and Tans were somehow predisposed to violence and crime, even before they arrived in Ireland. Many people have believed, and still believe, that the ranks of the Black and Tans were filled with criminals and ex-convicts. In 1926 Piaras Béaslai wrote that 'the Black and Tans were largely drawn from the criminal classes, and authentic cases were discovered where they had been released by a beneficent Government from penal servitude, incurred through revolting crimes, to enable them to bring the lights of English law and order to Ireland. They were, in short, dirty tools for a dirty job.'[1] Others believe the Black and Tans must have been brutalised and demoralised by their experiences in the Great War. In 1937 Dorothy Macardle wrote that 'the despatch of this new force to Ireland helped to relieve England of a very dangerous type of unemployable—men of low mentality whose more primitive instincts had been aroused by the war and who were now difficult to control.'[2]

Neither of these claims will stand up to scrutiny. Instead, the evidence will show that British recruits for the Royal Irish Constabulary were fairly ordinary men. The typical Black and Tan was in his early twenties and relatively short in stature. He was an unmarried Protestant from London or the Home Counties who had fought in the British Army during the Great War. He was a working-class man with few skills who joined the RIC because the pay was good. A few of his comrades might have spent a few days in gaol, but the typical Black and Tan had no criminal record and a good reference from the Army. He was posted to a police station after only two or three weeks of training, and served with the force until it was disbanded, unless he resigned first. He likely stayed out of trouble in Ireland, though he would have known men who were fined or even dismissed; interestingly, many of these would have been older men who had served with the pre-war regular Army. He was certainly not an ex-convict, and there is no evidence that his war experience affected his mental balance. In fact, there is nothing at all in his background that would explain his conduct in Ireland. It was not character but circumstance that explains why he took the law into his own hands.

3.1 'Ex-servicemen of good character and physique'

The single best source of additional information about the Black and Tans is the general register of the Royal Irish Constabulary, which includes the names and several particulars of every man who joined the force during the Irish War of Independence. Let's consider a cluster sample consisting of the single largest monthly intake of British recruits: the 1,153 who joined up in October 1920, close to midway through the conflict.[3] David Fitzpatrick has written that the Black and Tans were 'shorter and feebler' than Irish recruits for the RIC, and our sample confirms this impression.[4] Only 55 per cent of the men who enlisted in October could meet the RIC's minimum height of 5 feet 8 inches.[5] Only one in three could have met the pre-war standard of 5 feet 9 inches.

In practice, it seems the minimum height for British recruits was 5 feet 6 inches: only 26 men in the sample fell below this standard.[6] One man, twenty-year-old Walter Louis of London, stood only 5 feet 2 inches tall—shorter even than the Army's minimum height. Louis had not served in the armed forces during the war, but this may have been due to his youth as well as his size.[7] And the presence of short men like Louis reflects how desperate the constabulary's need for new recruits had become: like the British Army in 1914–18, the RIC had to lower its physical standards to meet the crisis of war. The short stature of many Black and Tans also reflects how recruiting shifted from rural, agricultural Ireland to urban, industrial Britain: in October 1920 the average Irish recruit stood two inches taller than his British counterpart.

The majority of the men in the sample were quite young, between eighteen and twenty-four years of age (see Table 3.1). A little more than half of them had been born between 1897 and 1902, and would have been too young to enlist in the Army when the Great War broke out in 1914. Eleven per cent of them had been born in 1901 and 1902, and would still have been too young to enlist when the war ended in 1918. Men between the ages of twenty-five and twenty-nine made up only 22 per cent of the sample. Less than 20 per cent of them were more than twenty-nine years old. The oldest recruit among them was Benjamin Ebdon of Warwick, a fitter and former Royal Engineer, who turned forty-eight soon after he joined the force.[8] The youth of the RIC's British recruits was noted at the time. 'They were most all young men,' said former Constable John Caddan, though some of them 'were up to forty.'[9]

Ninety per cent of these young men were ex-servicemen, a fact that incidentally suggests how many underaged recruits joined the British armed forces during the war. Interestingly, two Irish 'Black and Tans' interviewed by oral historian John Brewer had both been underage when they enlisted in the British Army: one man named Fails joined in early 1917 at the age of seventeen, and another man named Thompson in late 1917 at the age of sixteen.[10] Eighty per cent of the men who enlisted in October 1920 were ex-soldiers like Fails and Thompson. Eight per cent of them had served in the Navy, and 2 per cent had been Marines. Either the remaining 10 per cent did not serve in the military or their service was not recorded. The register does not mention the arms and regiments of ex-soldiers, but there is

Table 3.1. Birth dates of British RIC recruits, October 1920 (%).

1901–1902	11
1896–1900	48
1891–95	22
1886–90	13
1881–85	5
1871–80	1

Source: Constables 73602 to 75027, RIC General Register, TNA: PRO HO 184/38–9.

evidence that they were predominantly infantrymen. Seventy-three men had their names and regiments recorded in an allocation book preserved at the Garda Siochana museum in Dublin, and out of these 73, 49 had served in the infantry and 13 in the artillery.[11]

The men in the sample were disproportionately English: only 10 per cent of them came from Scotland and Wales, despite the fact that over 16 per cent of Britain's population were Welsh and Scottish (see Table 3.2). Moreover, almost half of these Englishmen came from London and the Home Counties, in spite of the fact that this area made up less than a quarter of Great Britain's population (see Table 3.3). The only other region of Britain that was over-represented in the sample was the south. Every other region of the island was under-represented, especially the north and the midlands: only 27 per cent of the men in the sample came from the northern and central counties, which made up 48 per cent of Britain's population. The proportion of Scotsmen was also low, but as we shall see this was in line with the proportion of Scottish soldiers in the British Army. Moreover, there were very few Welshmen in the sample: only 16 recruits out of 1,153.

The regional nature of British recruiting for the Royal Irish Constabulary becomes even clearer when we consider where men enlisted. The majority of the men in the sample—55 per cent—enlisted in London. The next largest group—19 per cent—enlisted in Liverpool, while another 8 per cent enlisted in Glasgow. The remaining 18 per cent of the men in the sample enlisted in 46 different communities, most of them Army and Navy recruiting centres in

Table 3.2. Nationalities of British RIC recruits, October 1920, compared to the population of Great Britain, 1921, and nationalities of British soldiers, 1920–1 (%).

Nationality	British RIC Recruits October 1920	1921 Census	British Soldiers 1920–1
English	89.0	83.4	87.0
Welsh	1.0	5.2	3.0
Scottish	8.0	11.4	8.0
Empire & Commonwealth	2.0	—	2.0

Source: Constables 73602 to 75027, RIC General Register, TNA: PRO HO 184/38–9; 1921 Census of England and Wales (Preliminary Report), Cmd. 1485 (1921), 63; *General Annual Report on the British Army for the Year Ending 30th September 1921*, Cmd. 1941 (1923), 81. (Note: Irish soldiers have been discounted.)

Table 3.3. Native regions and recruiting offices of British RIC recruits, October 1920 compared to the 1921 Census (%).

Region	RIC Recruits Native Regions	1921 Census	RIC Recruits Recruiting Offices
Central England	12	20	5
Northern England	15	28	20
London and Vicinity	47	23	59
Southern England	12	9	7
Eastern England	3	4	1
Scotland	8	11	8
Wales	1	5	—
Other	2	—	—

Source: Constables 73602 to 75027, RIC General Register, TNA: PRO HO 184/38–9; 1921 Census of England and Wales (Preliminary Report), Cmd. 1485 (1921), xi.

southern and eastern England. These British RIC recruits applied to enlist in the force at their local Army recruiting offices, and as a result the constabulary was competing with the Army for recruits. The RIC's chief recruiting officer in Great Britain, District Inspector Charles Fleming, even worked in the Army's recruiting office at Great Scotland Yard in London.[12] 'The necessity for recruiting large numbers of men for service in the Royal Irish Constabulary, in which body the conditions as to pay, etc., were more attractive than in the Army', was one of three factors the War Office blamed for the unusually small numbers of recruits it raised in 1920–1.[13]

Nonetheless, the regional distribution of RIC recruits in October 1920 was very different from the regional distribution of Army recruits in 1920–1 (see Table 3.4). Whereas only 19 per cent of the Army's recruits enlisted in the London recruiting area, 55 per cent of the RIC's recruits joined the force in the metropolis. Even more surprisingly, though 21 per cent of the Army's recruits enlisted in the Northern Command, only 5 out of the RIC's 1,153 recruits joined the force in this area.[14]

The proportions of Catholics and Protestants among RIC recruits in October 1920 were also somewhat different from those in the British Army (see Table 3.5). Eighty per cent of October's recruits were members of the Church of England. Of the remaining 20 per cent, 8 per cent were

Table 3.4. British Army recruiting, 1920–1, compared to RIC recruiting in Britain, October 1920 (%).

Area	Army Recruits	RIC Recruits
Eastern Command	17	6
London Zone	19	55
Northern Command	21	—
Scottish Command	9	8
Southern Command	18	11
Western Command	16	20

Source: Constables 73602 to 75027, RIC General Register, TNA: PRO HO 184/38–9; *General Annual Report on the British Army for the Year Ending 30th September 1921*, Cmd. 1941 (1923), 5–7.

Table 3.5. Religious denominations of British RIC recruits, October 1920, compared to British soldiers, 1920–1 (%).

Denomination	British RIC Recruits October 1920	British Soldiers 1920–1
Church of England	80	72
Roman Catholic	8	14
Presbyterian	6	7
Nonconformist	6	7

Source: Constables 73602 to 75027, RIC General Register, TNA: PRO HO 184/38–9; *General Annual Report on the British Army for the Year Ending 30th September 1921*, Cmd. 1941 (1923), 83. (Note: Irish soldiers have not been discounted.)

Roman Catholics, 6 per cent were Presbyterians, and 6 per cent were Nonconformists. As we might expect, 90 per cent of the Presbyterians were Scottish. Interestingly, seven of the Anglicans in the sample converted to Catholicism while they were in the force, and one Roman Catholic, Frederick Wilkinson of Lancashire, joined the Church of England.[15] The sample also included five Jews. In 1920–1, by comparison, only 72 per cent of the Army's warrant officers, non-commissioned officers, and soldiers were Anglicans, and 14 per cent were Roman Catholics; the proportions of Presbyterians and Nonconformists were also somewhat higher.[16] This might indicate some reluctance among Roman Catholics to join the RIC, but there is probably a simpler explanation. In 1920–1 there were still over nineteen thousand Irish soldiers in the British Army. Four of the Army's six Irish regiments were disbanded in 1922, and the number of Irish soldiers fell from nineteen to eleven thousand; during the same period, the number of Roman Catholics in the Army fell from thirty-three to twenty-four thousand, or from 14 per cent to 10 per cent.[17]

Most of the RIC recruits in the sample (71 per cent) were single men. However, 25 per cent of them were married when they enlisted. Another 4 per cent married after they enlisted, even though this was against RIC regulations: ordinarily, constables had to serve for seven years before they could marry. Once again, it seems, the RIC was compelled to bend its rules to accommodate its British reinforcements.

Married British recruits were older than average (see Table 3.6). Most of them had been married for less than six years, but there were some exceptions: three men had been married for 17 years, and Scott Arthur of Chester had been married for 20 years.[18] Fifty-three per cent of these men married women from London and its neighbouring counties, which reflects how they tended to marry women from their native regions: the majority of them (52 per cent) married women from their counties of origin. Once again, however, there were exceptions. Fifteen men in the sample married Irishwomen. Fred Warburton of Lancashire was married to a Frenchwoman, and Charles Houlston of Shropshire had married a German woman in September 1920.[19]

More than 90 per cent of the recruits came from the urban working class: fewer than one hundred of the men in the sample were not manual workers, and the majority of these 'middle-class' men were clerks and shop assistants; most of the 'professionals' among them were actors and musicians (see Table 3.7). The majority of them were either unskilled or semi-skilled. About 64 per cent of them worked in just three economic sectors: metal

Table 3.6. Birth and marriage dates of married British RIC recruits, October 1920 (%).

Birth Date		Marriage Date	
1901–1902	2	Enlistment–1922	17
1896–1900	32	1918–Enlistment	40
1891–95	31	1915–17	19
1886–90	23	1912–14	10
1881–85	10	1909–11	7
1871–80	2	1900–1908	7

Source: Constables 73602 to 75027, RIC General Register, TNA: PRO HO 184/38–9.

Table 3.7. Occupations of British RIC recruits, October 1920, compared to occupations of IRA Volunteers from provincial Ireland and Dublin, 1920–1 (%).

Sample . . .	Black & Tans 1,153	IRA Volunteers Provincial 1,985	IRA Volunteers Dublin 507
Farmer/son	0.7	29	—
Farm labourer	1.4	12	—
Unskilled/semi-skilled	52.0	15	46
Skilled	35.0	19	23
Shop assisant/clerk	6.0	14	18
Professional	2.0	4	2
Merchant/son	0.6	5	3
Student	0.2	1	3
Other	0.5	2	5
None given/ indecipherable	1.6	—	—

Sources: Constables 73602 to 75027, RIC General Register, TNA: PRO HO 184/38–9; Peter Hart, 'The Social Structure of the Irish Republican Army, 1916–1923', *Historical Journal* 42, no. 1 (1999), 211, 215; also, Peter Hart, 'The Geography of Revolution in Ireland 1917–23', *Past and Present* no. 155 (May 1997), 161.

manufacturing, transportation, and general labour (see Table 3.8). This fact is reflected in the three most common occupations among recruits, which were labourer, motor driver, and fitter. As Fitzpatrick has noted, British recruits for the RIC 'came of stock strikingly unlike that of the traditional recruit'.[20] The proportion of labourers and skilled workers among Irish recruits for the RIC was only 26 per cent in the spring of 1913, and 19 per cent in the autumn of 1916: the majority of Irish recruits in both cases had been farmers.[21] The social and occupational backgrounds of Black and Tans were also quite different from those of their opponents in the IRA. Peter Hart found that working-class men made up only 34 per cent of a sample of provincial Irish Volunteers, and only 69 per cent of a sample of Volunteers from Dublin, compared to 87 per cent of our sample of Black and Tans. In addition, 23 per cent of the IRA men in both samples came from middle-class occupations, compared to less than 10 per cent of the Black and Tans.

There are numerous indications that British recruits for the RIC were simply ex-servicemen looking for work. According to a memorandum from the Ministry of Labour, in June 1920 the cities of London, Liverpool, and Glasgow were home to the greatest numbers of ex-servicemen drawing

Table 3.8. Common occupational classes and occupations for British RIC recruits, October 1920 (%).

Occupational Class	%	Occupation	%
Metals, Machines, Implements and Conveyances	23.5	Labourer	15.8
Conveyance of Men, Goods, and Messages	22.4	Motor Driver	8.5
Other, General, and Undefined Workers	18.4	Fitter	4.0
Commercial Occupations	5.9	Clerk	3.9
Mines and Quarries	3.9	Motor Mechanic	3.8
Defence of the Country	3.3	Mechanic	3.3
Building and Works of Construction	3.0	Ex-Soldier	3.0
Domestic Offices or Services	2.9	Miner	2.9
Agriculture	2.5	Engineer	2.0
Food, Tobacco, Drink, and Lodging	2.3	Carman	1.9
Professional Occupations	1.8	Painter	1.5
Dress	1.6	Porter	1.5
Total	91.5		52.1

Source: Constables 73602 to 75027, RIC General Register, TNA: PRO HO 184/38–9. (Note: occupational classes follow those in the 1911 Census.)

out-of-work donations in the United Kingdom. As we have seen, these three cities produced 83 per cent of the RIC's British recruits in October 1920.[22] According to the same source, the occupational classes with the highest numbers of ex-servicemen receiving unemployment relief were general labour, transportation, and metal manufacturing.[23] Again, as we have seen, these occupational classes also produced the highest numbers of recruits for the RIC in October 1920, and the most common occupations among recruits fell into these classes. Finally, the testimony of Irishmen who joined the force in 1920 seems to confirm that unemployment was an important factor for many British recruits. John Caddan was a nineteen-year-old Irishman who went to England looking for work; finding none, he joined the RIC in London in February 1920.[24] Seventy-five years later the Irish ex-serviceman Fails recalled that 'there was great unemployment in England, everybody was on short comings and they'd come up in the morning on the boat from Dublin. Some of them only had the suit they stood in.'[25]

In fact, the British economy was imploding during the period of the Irish War of Independence: in the summer of 1920 Britain's brief post-war boom ended and its long inter-war depression began. According to trade union statistics, the percentage of unemployed went up from 2.4 per cent in 1920 to 14.8 per cent in 1921; according to unemployment insurance statistics, the percentage went up from 3.9 per cent in 1920 to 16.9 per cent in 1921.[26] The number of British recruits for the Royal Irish Constabulary increased apace. The *Manchester Guardian*'s correspondent visited Gormanstown camp on 12 October 1920. After interviewing the men, he concluded that 'unemployment has been the pinch that has driven most of them to this hazardous job', and he expected the 'slackening in trade' to provide the government with as many recruits as it wanted.[27]

The constabulary offered such men competitive wages, a chance for promotion, and the prospect of a pension. More than anything else, the pay seems to have drawn British recruits to the RIC. By October 1920, new constables were earning three pounds ten shillings a week, and were eligible for a number of allowances and bonuses besides, including a disturbance allowance of two shillings a day, along with six shillings a week as a cost-of-living bonus.[28] This was good money in 1920. One Irish recruit later recalled that a constable's base pay was 'more than a tradesman had at that time'.[29] Nevil Macready wrote in his memoirs that British recruits 'were only too glad to avail themselves of the high rates of pay which were offered'.[30] One Black and Tan who was dismissed from the force lamented that he had lost 'what is termed an excellent berth with a good rate of pay & good prospects for promotion & in addition a pensionable job'.[31]

In addition, there was no long period of apprenticeship for policemen in Ireland. In his book *Sword for Hire* Douglas Duff described his passage to Ireland as a police recruit. 'In the early grey of the February morning' Duff sailed from Holyhead to Dublin with about 30 other men. As they disembarked at the North Wall, the new recruits found Crossley tenders waiting to carry them to the depot. Duff and the others were handed rifles and ammunition and told to climb aboard. 'First two men keep an eye ahead,' they were told; 'next two on the second floor windows; next couple on the pavements and the rear pair looking astern.' Sitting back to back in the open boxes of the Crossleys, the nervous recruits were driven across Dublin at top speed, first west along the Liffey past the Four Courts, and then north into Phoenix Park and the Royal Irish Constabulary Depot.[32]

After spending an hour at Phoenix Park, Duff and his companions were again armed, loaded onto tenders, and rushed off to the sub-depot at Gormanstown. Once they arrived, they were issued with bedding, uniforms, arms, and equipment. 'At eleven o'clock,' writes Duff, 'we were again paraded, this time in uniform and under arms, upon the drill square and addressed by the Head Constable Major', who told them that the training course would last three days for infantrymen, and three to four weeks for everyone else.[33] Duff pretended to have served in the infantry. His training at Gormanstown, he says, lasted only a day and half, consisting of a brief lecture on hand grenades followed by one practice throw, a bit of target shooting with rifle and revolver, and a single class of instruction on police duties. 'As far as I remember,' he writes, 'the schoolmaster was lecturing on some point of the Game Laws. We solemnly listened for an hour and were then dismissed to our companies as fully trained policemen, ready for duty with the public.'[34]

Duff's memoirs, however, are not altogether trustworthy. According to the RIC General Register, Douglas Duff enlisted on 2 April 1921, not in February.[35] This is confirmed by the details in Duff's account. Duff mentions another new recruit named Beckett, 'who had crossed from Holyhead with me', and who was killed in County Mayo three weeks later.[36] Constable Harry Beckett was killed in an ambush near Kilmeena, County Mayo, on 19 May 1921—about a month after he enlisted.[37] Duff also claims to have been posted to County Galway's West Riding within less than three weeks—in time to have taken part in the Mounterowen ambush on 23 April—and to have seen the aftermath of the Ballyturin House ambush on 15 May. But according to the General Register, Duff was not allocated to west Galway until 7 June—just a month before the Truce.[38]

One of the Irish policemen interviewed by John Brewer does appear, however, to confirm Duff's account of his very brief training when he recalls that 'the ex-servicemen got no training at all. The ex-servicemen got three or four days and then they were sent out.'[39] But as we have also seen, most of the Black and Tans had probably been infantrymen. If such men received only three days' training, and were then sent to police stations, then most of the men in our sample should have been allocated to a county police force very shortly after they enlisted. We know when and where 910 of the men in our sample were allocated to county forces: two-thirds of these men spent between fifteen and twenty-eight days in camp before they were allocated (see Table 3.9), and most of the remaining third spent more than four weeks at Gormanstown; only five per cent of them were in camp for less than two weeks.[40] This is confirmed by the observations of the *Manchester Guardian*'s correspondent, who noted in October 1920 that RIC training had formerly lasted six months. 'For the English recruits,' however,

Table 3.9. Number of days between appointment and allocation for British RIC recruits, October 1920 (%).

Days	%
1–14	5
15–21	38
22–28	29
29–35	8
36–42	6
43–56	5
>56	8

Source: Constables 73602 to 75027, RIC General Register, TNA: PRO HO 184/38–9.

'the course is compressed into twelve or fourteen lectures, which along with drill, revolver, musketry, and bombing practice are crowded into a fortnight or three weeks.'[41]

Admittedly, time spent in camp was not necessarily training time. One Irish ex-serviceman remembered spending two weeks at the depot before he was posted to Tullamore, King's County. 'I was put on duty right away,' he said. 'No drill or anything like that', and no instruction in police duties either: 'I had no police training and I didn't know much,' he admitted.[42] And whether they spent three days in camp or three weeks, the Black and Tans were poorly trained. The *Manchester Guardian*'s correspondent had a low opinion of their course of instruction in police duties. 'It is very plain that a man coming absolutely fresh to all ideas of law or criminal procedure will not be a highly trained guardian of the peace after but a fortnight of cramming.'[43] Jeremiah Mee complained in his memoir that the two Black and Tans at his post in Listowel, County Kerry, 'had no police training whatsoever and showed no inclination to settle down to routine police work'.[44] One of the witnesses at the American Commission, former policeman John Tangney, thought the Black and Tans completed their training in six days, and told the following story:

> They absolutely knew nothing about police duties. On one occasion there was a County Inspector whose duty it was to visit the barracks. He was trying to instruct these fellows, and we were all in the barracks, for we had to go to school to him. And he asked this fellow what was his power of arrest, and he said he didn't know. He tried to make it simpler to him. He said, 'If you see a

man on the street, and you ask him to give you his name and address, and he refuses, what would you do?' And the Black-and-Tan said, 'If I met a man on the street and asked him his name and address, and he refused, I would lift him right under the jaw, and the next thing I would use my bayonet. That is what I would do to the man.'[45]

Recruits may have been glad to cut their training short: conditions at Gormanstown were primitive. 'It is obvious,' said the *Guardian*'s correspondent, 'that with a short staff and hastily improvised living arrangements the conditions have been as bad as in any overcrowded Army depot in the first few months of the war.'[46] Months later Duff was quartered in a draughty aircraft hangar and slept on a plank bed with a straw mattress: he impersonated an infantryman to get out of camp as quickly as possible, and he noticed that his fellow recruits were anxious to volunteer for duty.[47] Others were so dissatisfied that they simply quit. Unlike soldiers, Black and Tans were free to resign on a month's notice, and many of them did. One Irish constable recalled later that, having already served in the Army, many British recruits disliked the paramilitary character of their new duties in the RIC, and were unwilling to drill and live in barracks once again.[48] One of the Irish police veterans interviewed by Brewer blamed resignations on the poor living conditions, especially the food. 'The English people wouldn't have that,' he said, 'they weren't going to be like these people from the bogs of Ireland that put up with anything. They wouldn't have that and they were going back as quick as they were coming over.'[49]

Despite these problems, most Black and Tans were able to endure a few weeks of training at Gormanstown, and went on to serve in police stations throughout Ireland (see Table 3.10). There is no record of the reasons for these allocations, but as we might expect, the proportions of men allocated to each province correspond roughly to the amount of violence against the police therein: 38 per cent of them were posted to stations in the province of Munster, while only 14 per cent of them were posted to stations in the province of Connaught.

Some of these recruits excelled at their new jobs, despite their lack of training. None of the men in the sample were awarded the Constabulary Medal, but 78 received a monetary reward for meritorious service, and 16 of them were rewarded on more than one occasion. Thirty-two of them were promoted to temporary sergeant, and six of them were promoted even higher, to temporary head constable. But the rate of attrition among these British recruits was alarmingly high: only half of them were still serving with

Table 3.10. Allocation of British RIC recruits by province, October 1920, compared to IRA attacks on RIC by province, July 1920–July 1921.

Province	Recruits Oct 1920	%	Attacks 1920–1	%
Munster	338	38	450	50
Leinster	256	28	169	19
Ulster	177	20	150	17
Connaught	129	14	129	14

Source: Constables 73602 to 75027, RIC General Register, TNA: PRO HO 184/38–9; Outrage Reports, 1920–1, TNA: PRO CO 904/148–50.

the force when it was disbanded in the winter of 1922 (see Table 3.11). The register does not record what happened to 169 of the men in the sample. Ninety-eight of the men who enlisted in October 1920 resigned from the force before the end of the year, many of them after only a few days or weeks in Ireland. Another 149 resigned in 1921. Again, as we might expect, a disproportionate number of the men who resigned were stationed in the south, where the fighting was heaviest.

Though guerrilla warfare took a heavy toll on men's nerves, it did not claim all that many lives: only 65 of the men in the sample died or were killed, pensioned off, or discharged. The IRA killed only 21 of them: the first was Harry Biggs of London, on 22 October 1920; the last was William Cummings of Hampshire, on 3 March 1922, after most of the force had been demobilised.[50] Four men in the sample died in accidents, including the

Table 3.11. Fates of British RIC recruits, October 1920 (%).

Sample . . .	All recruits 1,153	Recruits whose fates are known 984
Unknown	15	—
Resigned, 1920	8	10
Resigned, 1921	13	15
Dismissed	8	9
Discharged	3	3
Pensioned	1	1
Killed or Died	2	3
Demobilised, 1922	50	59

Source: Constables 73602 to 75027, RIC General Register, TNA: PRO HO 184/38–9.

unfortunate Francis Hayward of Worcestershire, who drowned on 11 July 1921, the day of the Truce. Just 582 members of the sample definitely continued to serve in the Royal Irish Constabulary until its British recruits were sent home. Some remained with the RIC until the spring and even the summer of 1922, but most of them were demobilised in February of that year. As men who had served for more than a year but less than eighteen months, they were each entitled to a pension of fifty pounds fourteen shillings per annum.

3.2 'Jail-birds and down-and-outs'

Not all these Black and Tans served with honour. Ninety of the men who enlisted in October 1920 were subsequently dismissed from the force. This was a very high percentage (7.8 per cent): less than 1 per cent of the men in the RIC had been dismissed each year between 1885 and 1914, and by way of comparison, only 4 per cent of the soldiers in the British Army were punished for crimes and breaches of discipline in the year 1920–1.[51]

Their dismissal rate is bad enough, but the Black and Tans' behaviour looks even worse when we check their disciplinary records. Of the 1,153 men who joined the force in October 1920, 206 (about 18 per cent) have some kind of punishment entered beside their names in the register. Of these men, 3 merely received a warning, but 138 committed an infraction serious enough to warrant a fine, and 65 of them were fined on more than one occasion. The offences for which these men were punished are not recorded, but some indications are provided by the cases of two men listed in the constabulary's disbandment register. By the winter of 1922 Constable William Simpson had been punished on three occasions, losing two days' pay for absence from hospital, four days' pay for absence from his post and disobedience of orders, and one week's pay for leaving his post and absence without leave. Constable James D. Murphy, on the other hand, had lost four days' pay for drunkenness, assaulting a comrade, and absence on one occasion, and been fined six days' pay for absence and drunkenness on another occasion, when he was warned that any further infractions would result in his dismissal.

Constable Murphy seems to have straightened out after his warning, since he continued to serve with the RIC until it was disbanded.[52] It seems reasonable to suppose that most Black and Tans were punished for infractions like absence and drunkenness—but some of them were punished for much worse. At least ten of the men who joined in October 1920 were dismissed for committing criminal offences. Eight of these men were sacked in February 1921, for offences committed in the autumn of 1920. On 17 November 1920, for example, Constable Edward Knights and Constable William Johnson, both stationed at Roscommon, were arrested for a series of robberies in the district. The two men were searched, and 'a large quantity' of stolen goods was recovered. The pair were tried by court martial on 18 February 1921, acquitted of robbery, but convicted of unlawful possession, and dismissed from the force the same day. Johnson had joined the RIC on 12 October, and had been allocated to County Roscommon on 1 November. He had enlisted in London, but may have been an Irish immigrant returning to his native land: he was a Roman Catholic, and though his home county was London, he had family in Westmeath.[53]

Worse was to come. On the night of 28 November 1920 half a dozen houses in County Wexford were invaded and robbed by three men in police and military uniforms. Wexford's district inspector investigated and arrested two constables and a soldier, who confessed their crimes and returned the money and property they had stolen.[54] The two constables—an Irishman, Patrick Myers, and a Black and Tan with an Irish name, James O'Hara—were court martialled, convicted, and dismissed.[55]

Still later, three Black and Tans from County Longford—William Gibson, Edwin Hollins, and Harvey Skinner—were arrested and ultimately court martialled for robbing a bank in neighbouring County Roscommon on 23 December.[56] Constable Edward King, stationed in County Clare, was arrested for burglary on Christmas Day and dismissed on 6 February 1921.[57] Finally, Constable James Roberts was dismissed on 17 February 1921 for larceny.[58]

The bank robbery in County Roscommon is by far the most interesting and instructive of these cases—as well as the strangest. On the morning of 23 December 1920 a party of 15 police from Longford drove into the community of Strokestown and stopped at the local RIC station. While the sergeant in charge of this party was away giving evidence in court, four men in police uniforms and two in civilian clothes walked into the Strokestown branch of the Northern Banking Company and robbed it at gunpoint. The robbers tried to lock the staff and customers inside the bank when they left, but the manager got away and reported the crime to the Strokestown police. The local head constable arrested six of the visiting Black and Tans: the bank staff identified some of them as gang members, and bundles of stolen money were found in the pockets of others. Three of them had been caught drinking in a local pub with stolen banknotes falling out of their pockets. All six were put into military custody and taken back to Longford.

Apparently, the six bank robbers had friends among the Longford police. On 30 December someone wrote to the manager of the bank and threatened to kill him unless he dropped the charges. The letter was posted from Longford, signed by the 'President' of 'Section B, E.S.S.S.' and illustrated with skull and crossbones. The manager reported the letter to the directors of the Northern Banking Company, but assured them that he was unconcerned. Soon after the letter arrived, however, two men in civilian clothes called at the bank and asked to speak to the manager. When he refused to see them in private, they referred to the letter and alternately threatened and pleaded with him to drop the charges. This incident convinced RIC headquarters that the bank manager was in danger from the Black and Tans, and on 6 January the Strokestown and Longford district inspectors were warned that they would be held personally responsible for the manager's safety.

Nothing more was heard from ESSS. The charges against one Black and Tan were eventually dropped: none of the witnesses had identified him, and while stolen money was found in his coat, there was no way to prove who put it there. The remaining five were tried by field general court martial in February 1921. One was acquitted; the rest were convicted and sentenced to five years' penal servitude.[59]

The RIC's General Register tells us only one thing about crimes like these: whereas the majority of the Black and Tans were young men between the ages of eighteen and twenty-four, eight of the ten criminals in our sample were mature men between the ages of twenty-five and thirty.[60] This seems to have been an especially troublesome cohort. Though men born between 1891 and 1895 made up only 22 per cent of the men who joined the RIC in October 1920, they made up 31 per cent of the men who were subsequently dismissed.

Older men like these might have spent years in prison, or in the trenches, and many writers have suggested that the Black and Tans were the product of one or both of these environments. According to Piaras Béaslai, the Black and Tans had been recruited 'from the criminal classes and the dregs of the population of English cities'.[61] Donal O'Kelly agreed wholeheartedly: 'Of the Black and Tans—so called because of their uniform of khaki tunic and black trousers—nothing good can be said,' he wrote. 'They were recruited from the offscourings of English industrial populations; their individual fighting qualities were not remarkable, but they were past masters of the arts of murder, looting, arson and outrage.'[62] Florence O'Donoghue continued in the same vein: 'The Royal Irish Constabulary included the remnant of the original force which had not retired or resigned, and a reinforcement of British jail-birds and down-and-outs who had been hastily recruited into the force in England when candidates had ceased to offer themselves in Ireland,' he said.[63]

Irish republicans, however, could produce little evidence to support these accusations, even at the time. Frank Gallagher wrote in his memoirs that the *Irish Bulletin* had published the names of six Black and Tans, none of whom were a credit to the force. The first had been arrested for felony: the second, dismissed for theft. The third had died from a drug overdose, and the fourth had been certified a dangerous lunatic. The fifth had been allowed to join the force after being convicted of larceny, and the sixth had committed suicide after being caught stealing in a Liverpool hotel. 'Nothing could have illustrated the character of the Black-and-Tans better than this simple list,' he concluded, rather sweepingly: 'every thief, drug addict, madman and murderer could come into this new force.'[64]

The proof given to the American Commission, by contrast, was just hearsay. Francis Hackett related the following story, which he claimed to have heard from an English officer. 'An English detective, he said, came over here to see me this morning. 'I am over here to find a convict, and I went to the depot of the Black-and-Tans to find him,' the detective told me. 'I did not find him there, much to my surprise, but I found a number of other convicts whom I know very well.'[65] Mary MacSwiney told the commission that 'there is a friend of mine who was temporarily the prison physician at Portland prison, and one day he met a man on the street in the Black-and-Tan uniform and stopped him and said, "Where did I meet you?" And the man said, "Oh, doctor, don't you know? I was at Portland prison when you were the prison physician."'[66]

Claims like these have since been contradicted by witnesses like Pat Mahon, an Irish constable who worked as a clerk in the RIC's recruiting office in London. In a letter preserved among the Goulden Papers at Trinity

College, Dublin, Mahon flatly denies that the RIC was deliberately recruiting criminals. Applications, he says, were screened by checking police reports and Army references: moreover, any applicant without at least a 'good' character from the Army was automatically rejected.[67]

One way of testing these competing claims is by examining the attestation papers of eight Black and Tans that are preserved at the Public Record Office (PRO). All of them have either police reports or Army characters appended—but not all of them have both. Police reports are included with only six of the files: four of the candidates are described as respectable men; in the remaining two cases, the police noted only that they knew nothing against them. Army references are included with only five of the files, but all five men were given 'good' characters; of the remaining three, Gilbert Horace Walker had served with the Leeds University Officer Training Corps and came highly recommended by its commanding officer. Though Walker was a university student, John Blacklaw of Aberdeen had left school at age fourteen, and Geoffrey Fisher of Gloucestershire failed a qualifying examination in reading, writing, and simple arithmetic: nonetheless, District Inspector Fleming approved his application, suggesting that Fisher could improve his education in the force. Finally, there are some troubling details in the papers of one candidate, Thomas Arthur Sellars of Yorkshire. The police reported that Sellars came from a very respectable family, but had recently sold his grocery business and moved, leaving his wife with her parents: his wife had not heard from him in six weeks. Sidney B. Gulpin of Gulpin Hall & Co, Electrical Engineers, wrote that Sellars was 'always a conscientious & reliable workman', but noted that, though Sellars described himself as an 'electrician', he was actually employed as a labourer.[68]

It seems that while the RIC did conduct background checks, it was not quite as choosy with its British recruits as Mahon claimed. This becomes even clearer when we consider the case of another October recruit, Thomas Sanson. Sanson had been a London Metropolitan Police constable before the war. He served in the Navy, but was discharged in 1916 for medical reasons. He applied to rejoin the Metropolitan Police, but was rejected as unsuitable: he had been charged with assaulting a man in Pimlico in May 1917, and in November 1917 he had been fined in Lambeth Police Court for being drunk and incapable.[69] The Metropolitan Police must have reported these facts to the recruiting officer when Sanson applied to join the

RIC. Nonetheless, District Inspector Fleming accepted Sanson's application on 29 October 1920. Bizarrely, Sanson resigned the day after his appointment, complaining to an Irish newspaper that he had joined under the misimpression that he was 'going to be on ordinary police duties, walking about the streets unarmed'.[70]

Sanson, however, was untypical: very few Black and Tans, it seems, had criminal records. This becomes clear when we examine the Calendar of Prisoners, the register of every person committed to prison in Great Britain, which has now been opened for this period. Working on the assumption that, unlike Sanson, almost all of the Black and Tans had remained in the service until the end of the war, we can compare the calendars for London in the years 1919 and 1920 with our sample from the RIC register—a tedious, time-consuming, and unrewarding exercise. Out of 337 men from London, just one had been in prison since the war's end—for two days. Samuel William Butcher, a painter, born 1891, was committed for trial and imprisoned on 15 June 1920, and bailed on 16 June. He was again imprisoned on 19 July, and tried the same day on a charge of 'fraudulently converting to his own use and benefit the several sums of thirteen pounds three pence and three pounds nineteen shillings three pence, received by him for and on account of another person'. Butcher pleaded guilty and was sentenced 'to enter into his own recognizance in the sum of twenty pounds for his appearance to hear judgment if called upon'.[71] He joined the RIC less than three months later, on 1 October, and after less than four weeks' training was allocated to County Londonderry, where he served for thirteen months. He was fined four days' pay on 14 December 1921 and was dismissed ten days later, for reasons unknown.[72]

But while the cases of Sanson and Butcher reveal that it was possible for men with criminal records to join the RIC, they hardly prove that the Black and Tans were 'jail-birds and down-and-outs'. Two men out of every 337 are only 0.6 per cent: this would suggest that about fifty or sixty Black and Tans in total had criminal records. Furthermore, neither of these two men could be described as hardened or habitual criminals, and their crimes were hardly revolting. Finally, there is no evidence that these men were the ones who were breaking the law in Ireland. As we have seen, ten of the men who joined the RIC in October 1920 were dismissed for criminal offences. None of them are known to have criminal records before they joined the force.

3.3 'A career of adventure and bloodshed'

Even while Irish republicans were insisting that the Black and Tans were ex-convicts, other more sympathetic observers were concluding that experience of trench warfare must have altered the dispositions of British recruits, turning formerly ordinary men into thieves, arsonists, and murderers. One of the witnesses at the American Commission suggested that 'you cannot switch off a man's moral nature like you would an electric light. You have produced these feelings by what has recently happened. You have brought these men up to use force during six years of war, and then you cannot expect them to switch themselves off in a moment.'[73] Many historians since have followed this line of reasoning. In his book on the Black and Tans, Richard Bennett suggested that 'their only service experience had been in trench warfare which had a brutalizing rather than ennobling effect'. 'Their morale,' he continued, 'had not been improved by months of unemployment. The Army had taught them that the reputation for a good character can be based on undiscovered crime and that scrounging only becomes stealing when it is found out.'[74] More recently, Charles Townshend has suggested that as veterans of the Great War the Black and Tans were 'habituated to excitement and violence', while Martin Seedorf has concluded that 'the brutal impact of the war and "the long merciless ordeal in the trenches affected their mental outlook"'.[75] F. S. L. Lyons provided the classic expression of what we might call the 'brutalization' hypothesis in 1973:

> The Black and Tans were for the most part young men who found it hard to settle down after the war, who had become used to a career of adventure and bloodshed, and who were prepared to try their luck in a new sphere for ten shillings a day and all found. They were the same type, and produced by much the same circumstances, as the Congo mercenaries of our own day. Their ruthlessness and contempt for life and property stemmed partly from the brutalization inseparable from four years of trench warfare, but partly also from the continual and intense strain imposed upon them by service in Ireland.[76]

There are, however, a couple of serious problems with this explanation. On the one hand, it's completely hypothetical. We have almost no information about the service records of the Black and Tans. We know that most of them were ex-servicemen, but we do not know when they enlisted, where they served, and what battles they fought, if any. We also do not know what kind of men they were before the war. Without this information, we can hardly make meaningful statements about the brutalising effect of the Great War on British recruits for the RIC. On the other hand, there is very little evidence to suggest that there were large numbers of criminalised war veterans in post-war Britain. If this were the case, then common sense suggests that there should have been an increase in the crime rate—when in fact, the number of criminal convictions was lower in post-war Britain than it had been in pre-war Britain.[77]

Moreover, the evidence suggests that Black and Tans who had served in the regular Army *before* 1914 were more likely to commit crimes than wartime volunteers and conscripts. At least two of the nine offenders in our sample seem to have served in the regular Army. Patrick Myers, one of the Wexford home invaders, had no registered occupation but ex-soldier. William Gibson, one of the Roscommon bank robbers, had served in the Gloucester Regiment for ten years before he was demobilised in 1919. Interestingly, the fourth Black and Tan who was convicted for the same bank robbery had also been a regular soldier. Thomas Chester had joined the Royal Fusiliers in 1909, served in India before the war, and had been among the first soldiers to land at Gallipoli on 25 April 1915. After the Dardanelles campaign, he served in Egypt, France, and Belgium; he was wounded six times during the war, and when he was demobilised in January 1919, he was given a 'very good' character.

Given the comparatively small size of the Edwardian Army—only a quarter of a million men, compared to the five million who enlisted during the Great War—and the heavy losses it sustained in the campaigns of 1914–15, it is remarkable that three of these ten constables had been regular soldiers.[78] Furthermore, if we widen our search, we can find other references to regular soldiers among the Black and Tans. Thirty-four of the men who joined in October 1920 listed no occupation but ex-soldier; another two had no occupation but ex-marine. Nor were these the only regulars among them: William Gibson was listed in the register as a miner, and Gordon Smith, a man who had served in the Army for 14 years, described himself as a coachman as well as an ex-soldier.[79] Archibald Thompson, one of two Black and Tans at Listowel barracks in County Kerry in the spring of 1920, was also apparently a former regular. One of his Irish colleagues later recalled that 'whatever brought Thompson to

Ireland, it was not any over-developed sense of patriotism. He had an old soldier's dislike for officers and a true old soldier's love for all the beer he could buy or scrounge. Outside his love for beer he showed no interest in anything.'[80]

More disturbingly, another one of the few prosecutions on record involved a former regular soldier. Thirty-one-year-old William Wilton joined the force on 11 January 1921. Ten days later he was on his way to his station in Cork's West Riding when his convoy stopped for the night at Maryborough, Queen's County. After spending some time drinking in a pub, Wilton and three other men (a Black and Tan named Perkins and two soldiers named Smith and McCowett) went looking for someplace to stay the night. Three families told Wilton they had no room. When the fourth family refused to open up, Wilton fired his revolver at their front door, killing the man on the other side, Thomas Lawless—a former Irish Guardsman. A court of inquiry found a verdict of manslaughter against Wilton on 22 January. He was arraigned at the Maryborough spring assizes on 12 March, tried by court martial on 27 May, convicted of manslaughter, and sentenced to ten years' penal servitude. He is listed in the RIC's General Register as both a bricklayer and an ex-soldier, but like Gibson and Chester he enlisted years before the Great War, serving in at least three campaigns between 1910 and 1913.[81]

Wilton showed no remorse for his crime. After he was arrested, he said 'I knocked at this particular door where the trouble occurred & asked for lodgings. The door was not opened & some one shouted "We have no room" or something to that effect. I imagining that we were going to be attacked took my revolver from my holster & the shot was accidentally discharged into the street.'[82] The two soldiers testified that Wilton drew his gun at the start of their search for a billet, and even threatened to shoot Private Smith when he wanted to go back to barracks. They also testified that when Lawless refused to open up, Wilton swore at him and threatened to shoot through the door before he fired; he was prevented from firing a second shot when Smith caught his wrist and tried to disarm him.[83]

Wilton petitioned the Lord Lieutenant from Mountjoy gaol on 28 June 1921. He continued to claim that the shooting was 'a pure accident' and that he 'had not the slightest intention to harm anyone'. In his petition he emphasised that he was 'not out for any unlawful purpose' and that he made no attempt to escape after the shooting. He also emphasised that he had never met Lawless, 'so that I could not have any malice', and that since the bullet had penetrated the door, 'it could not be said that I fired wilfully at the man'. Wilton also mentioned that he was a married man with two children, and an ex-soldier: 'I was in receipt of a Pension and always held a respectfull [*sic*] character when I have my home if I have to undergo this sentence it will mean my home will have to be sold and that my Family and myself branded for nothing more than a most unfortunate accident which I could not possibly help.'[84]

Wilton's petition was rejected on 13 July 1921, two days after the Truce. However, he appealed to the viceroy again on 31 October 1921, and if anything his tone was even less repentant after five months in prison. 'My motive in sending this,' he wrote, 'is not to appeal to the merciful sympathies of your Lordship, but to ask from you justice. Intuition tells me that British justice has been sadly miscarried in my case, that is to emphasize British justice as it is minstrated [*sic*] by his Majesty's judges.' Wilton called his sentence 'brutal' and pointed out that other men convicted of manslaughter had received sentences of a year or less: 'then,' he continued:

> there was the doubt of any intent which was not given to me at my trial as British law intends it should be, and personally I arrive at the conclusion that the law and justice of the British Nation had ridiculously and shamefully administered for the express purpose that it would serve the then political atmosphere indeed I can anticipate no other formula for the ridiculous sentence of 10 years.

Wilton also mentioned that this was the first time he had ever been in trouble, either as a soldier or a civilian, and argued that:

> my services to King and Empire which include Somaliland 1910 Persian Gulf 1910–11 the British intervents [*sic*] in the Balkan war of 1912–13 then the Late war, and at the call of my country for men to serve in Ireland and as I have always shown my loyal support to my King and Empire in grave and critical times this should at least entitle me to justice.

'I do not plead for mercy,' he concluded, 'but simply ask from your Lordship that which I have always gladly given my services for eaven [*sic*] at the cost of my own life and was never found wanting to uphold that cause namely right and justice.'[85] Wilton was transferred from Mountjoy to Liverpool prison on 4 November, and his second petition was rejected twelve days later.

Prisoner petitions have also been preserved in the Strokestown bank robbery case. The two old soldiers, William Gibson and Thomas Chester, were as unrepentant as William Wilton. Chester had been caught with two bundles of stolen banknotes in his pockets, and all three of the bank's employees had identified him as one of the robbers. Nonetheless, he protested his innocence. According to his account, Chester 'remained with the cars for some little time, eventually going down the town'. When the sergeant in charge returned from court, Chester was ordered to get 'the boys' together: he had just located four of them in the pub when the local head constable arrived and ordered them all back to barracks. Chester went on to complain that the identification parade had not been conducted properly: the bank men 'were all talking together in the centre of the half-circle of men, pointing to different men and arguing pretty strongly'. He also complained that charges had been dropped against one Black and Tan, and that another had been tried for receiving stolen money rather than robbery, 'so that there are 4 men here answering for the original six men'. He concluded by mentioning that his wife had been compelled to sell their home. 'As I am now, Sir,' he wrote, 'my wife has no means of support, a boy 14 months old and expecting another in a few months time. She has nowhere to go except the Workhouse, for she had nothing to rely on except my monthly pay.'[86]

Gibson mentioned many of the same points as Chester. He complained that 'only four have to suffer for a deed committed by 6', and that 'the identification parade on which we were arrested was more or less a farce, as it states in the evidence that the witnesses were talking to one another on the parade & deciding whom they should identify'. Like Chester, Gibson was married: he had two young children, and his wife was pregnant. 'Now that I am in this predicament she has no means of sustenance & the only course laying open to her is to enter the workhouse, & of course selling up the home.' Again, like Chester, Gibson had been caught with stolen money in his pockets, and was identified by all three witnesses. His defence was rather startling. 'On the day this crime was committed,' he wrote, 'I was under the influence of drink and therefore contend that I was unaware of the serious nature of what I was doing, in point of fact, I do not remember having any hand in the affair at all.'[87] Not surprisingly, both Chester's and Gibson's petitions were rejected.

The two men who had not served in the regular Army, Edwin Hollins and Harvey Skinner, made similar excuses and appeals, but neither man made any attempt to deny his guilt, and the tone of their petitions is apologetic. Hollins said simply that he was 'badly under the influence of drink' when the robbery occurred and had no memory of what happened. 'I also wish to state that during my four years Army service I never had any offence against me so this fall is very black against my character.' Skinner too mentioned that his character had previously been good. 'On the day,' he wrote mournfully, 'I was very drunk and not capable of my actions if I had been sober this would not have happened.' Like Chester and Gibson, Hollins and Skinner were married with young families. Skinner had served with the Royal Marine Artillery until 1917 and with the merchant marine until he joined the RIC. 'My wife is not very strong,' he wrote. 'My two children are but little babies the eldest being two years old and the youngest 13 months so my wife cannot go to work & consequently my little home will be sold & my wife will have to go to the workhouse. The children I have never seen much of as being away from home & only then after voyages of 6 & 7 months.' Once again, however, the Lord Lieutenant rejected their appeals.[88]

In late 1920 the *Report of the Labour Commission to Ireland* suggested that 'a by no means negligible proportion' of the Royal Irish Constabulary, 'as at present constituted, consists of men of intemperate habits who are utterly unsuited to their duties. It may be that not more than one percent of the RIC are men of really bad character. Nevertheless, this small fraction has discredited the whole force as an instrument of policy by making it an object of general dread and detestation.'[89] We might easily conclude that this 'small fraction' was composed of old soldiers like Wilton, Chester, and Gibson. The pre-war Army had been recruited from 'the least skilled sections of the working-class', and many recruits were failures in civilian life, unemployed and hungry.[90] For such men, military service was a deal with the devil: the Army taught them no useful skills, and as Gareth Stedman Jones has pointed out, 'Army recruitment alleviated the unemployment of young adults only to reproduce it in a more intractable form in early middle age.'[91] Regular soldiers who survived the war were swept out of the Army in the spring of 1919: every man who enlisted before 1 January 1916 was demobilised, with the exception of those who volunteered for a year's service with the armies of occupation.[92] It is easy to see why such men became Black and Tans, and easy to imagine that they were the Labour Commission's 'men of really bad character' or Macardle's 'dangerous type of unemployable'. If nothing else, old soldiers like Wilton, Chester, and Gibson had many more years to learn Richard Bennett's lessons than their wartime comrades.

However, before we blame men like these for police violence in Ireland, we should remember a few important facts. Out of eleven convicted criminals we have examined here, only four of them were definitely regular soldiers. Similarly, out of the six men arrested for the Strokestown bank robbery, only Chester and Gibson were definitely regulars. Harvey Skinner and Edwin Hollins both enlisted during the war, and we know nothing about the military service of the two men who were acquitted.[93] Furthermore, despite their insolence, Wilton, Chester, and Gibson look more like respectable workingmen than criminals. They were homeowners, not vagrants or lodgers, and all three of them were married with children. Nor were they unemployable. Between leaving the Army and entering the RIC, Chester worked in a munitions factory, and Gibson worked in the London Underground. Furthermore, by 23 December 1920 Chester had been serving with the RIC for ten months and was expecting a promotion to temporary sergeant.[94] Admittedly, we have only their word on many of these matters, but this was good enough for the Chief Crown Solicitor when their cases were reviewed in February and March 1922.[95]

Finally, these men committed unusual crimes. Most of the police crime and violence in Ireland was directed against known and suspected rebels. No Black and Tan was ever prosecuted for taking part in a police riot, or for joining a death squad. To understand why, we must remember that the Black and Tans were a minority in the RIC. Only one in three constables was British when the force was disbanded in the spring of 1922.[96] By the end of 1920 the garrison of a typical rural police station consisted of a couple of sergeants and a dozen constables, only three or four of whom were Black and Tans.[97]

As we shall see, the attitude of the RIC's Irish majority could be crucial. Peelers were willing to tolerate men who killed Volunteers and burned the homes of Irish republicans. In fact, they did a fair amount of killing and burning themselves. But these Irish policemen were not willing to tolerate bank robbery, or the shooting of innocent civilians who refused to open their doors at night. Consequently, men responsible for such offences were frequently prosecuted. In the spring of 1921 at least 36 RIC constables were court martialled and 30 of them were convicted. Sixteen of them were imprisoned for theft and ten of them for crimes of violence; the remaining four were sentenced to three months' hard labour for vandalising a church.[98] Hard cases like William Wilton may have been responsible for crimes like these, but such crimes were extraordinary. Ordinary crimes like the shooting of suspects and the burning of homes were the work of ordinary policemen. This will become even clearer when we turn our attention to a force that was almost never accused of recruiting ex-convicts and thugs, but became just as infamous as the Black and Tans: the Auxiliary Division.

4

Dr Tudor's Beast Folk

The Auxiliary Division

The War of Independence was a liminal period in modern Irish history—a period of between-ness, of ambivalence—when everything, it seems, was neither one thing nor another. Neither the British government nor the Irish Republic were fully in control of Ireland, which was no longer truly part of the United Kingdom, nor yet fully independent. The insurgents who fought for independence were neither soldiers in the conventional sense nor civilians—much like their principal opponents and victims, the Royal Irish Constabulary. In fact, this liminality was even more pronounced on the British side of the conflict than it was among the revolutionaries. The British government—David Low's two-headed ass—was a coalition, neither Conservative nor Liberal. Its declared policy was neither to wage war nor to negotiate peace. And over time, by reinforcing its Irish constabulary with British ex-soldiers, it created a force that was neither Irish nor British, and neither military nor civilian.

The Auxiliary Division of the Royal Irish Constabulary was perhaps the most extreme example of this conflict's tendency toward liminality. The members of this force were officially classed as 'temporary cadets'—that is to say, temporary officer candidates. They wore a mixture of police and military uniforms—in fact, strictly speaking, they wore no 'uniforms' at all. In their own commander's words, they were soldiers 'camouflaged' as police. Their mission was to 'restore order'—and yet, as we have seen, in some areas they succeeded only in creating additional disorder.

Indeed, so liminal was this weird little force that its creator, Major General Tudor, might with some justice be described as the Doctor Moreau of the Irish War of Independence. In his 1896 novel *The Island of Doctor*

Moreau, H. G. Wells described how a mad scientist created a race of hybrid 'beast folk'—part animal and part human. In the summer of 1920 Dublin Castle's Police Adviser created his own race of hybrids. Like Moreau, Tudor seems to have conducted his experiments with little thought for the consequences. And like their science-fictional counterparts, 'Tudor's Toughs' quickly escaped from their creator's control and ran amok on their island.

In terms of both money and public support, the Auxiliary Division was a costly failure. The Division wound up being much more expensive than Tudor anticipated, and the crimes of some temporary cadets made it more expensive still; other cadets behaved more like terrorists than policemen, and their undisciplined violence was widely reported in the British press. The ADRIC was supposed to embody the best features of both military and police forces—but in the end, in many ways, it embodied their worst features instead.

4.1 'These ex-officers will be called Temporary Cadets'

On 6 July 1920 the Police Adviser submitted a scheme for an auxiliary police force to the Under Secretary, Sir John Anderson. 'It is essential to reinforce the Royal Irish Constabulary quickly,' he said. 'Recruiting in the ordinary way will take time.' Tudor then asked for permission to recruit up to five hundred ex-officers, under the following conditions of service:

(1) These ex-officers will be called Temporary Cadets.

(2) Terms of enlistment 1 year, terminable on one months notice after the first 4 months, if the Temporary Cadet wishes to resign.

(3) Pay, £7 per week.

(4) To rank as Sergeants for discipline and (subsistence and travelling) allowances.

(5) Uniform Khaki, with R.I.C. badges and buttons, or Sergeant's uniform, R.I.C., at will. When Khaki is worn the letters T.C., for Temporary Cadet will be worn on shoulders, instead of badges of rank or stripes.

(6) These Temporary Cadets will have priority of consideration for permanent appointment as officers of the R.I.C.[1]

This is an interesting document, for a number of reasons. First, the mission of this new force was left undefined. Tudor seems to have seen his temporary cadets merely as a way to reinforce the RIC quickly. If this was their mission, then they failed completely: recruiting for the ADRIC would always be much slower than recruiting for the RIC. Between July 1920 and July 1921, whereas about thirty-two hundred men joined the Auxiliary Division as temporary cadets and temporary constables, about nine thousand men became permanent constables. In October 1920, when 1,153 men became Black and Tans, only 270 men became Auxiliaries. The Division's relative lack of success in attracting recruits is especially interesting when we consider that an Auxiliary's base pay was double the base pay of a Black and Tan. The prospect of a career as a policeman, followed by a pension, may have made the RIC more attractive than the higher wages offered by the temporary forces.

In any case, Tudor appears to have thought more about his new force's uniforms than its mission. He was also responsible for some of its most peculiar characteristics. He seems to have invented the paradoxical status of 'temporary cadet' in order to wedge these reinforcements into the RIC's table of ranks, and to preserve the illusion that these men were civilian police rather than auxiliary troops.[2] He made it clear that temporary cadets would have no standard uniform: they could wear military khaki or constabulary green, as they wished. He also planned to make his irregular temporary cadets into permanent officers, regardless of the fact that regular members of the RIC worked for years to earn such appointments.

Tudor was given verbal approval for his plan, and on 11 July, the deputy police adviser, Ormonde Winter, wrote another letter to the Under Secretary, asking for written authority to proceed.[3] At the conference on 23 July, Tudor told the Cabinet that 'He had just recruited 500 ex-officers and a number of ex-soldiers, which formed a fine body of men, and he felt that, given the proper support, it would be possible to crush the present campaign of outrage.' Apparently, Tudor was still thinking of his temporary cadets as emergency reinforcements (or even replacements) for the RIC: in reply to a question, he stated that 'the recruitment of the Royal Irish Constabulary was only keeping pace with resignations. If it was impossible to get the men, he must develop the idea of Temporary Cadet officers, 500 of whom he had obtained. These officers were drafted from England to strengthen the Royal Irish Constabulary personnel in certain parts of the country and had had a great effect.'[4]

On 28 July Tudor wrote again to Sir John Anderson and provided a somewhat plainer mission statement for his new auxiliaries. Temporary cadets would be formed into military-style companies, to provide 'a mobile police force to send to threatened points and to the worst disturbed areas', working under the direction of divisional commissioners, county inspectors, and district inspectors. However, the Police Adviser's plans were still vague. He justified a paramilitary organisation on the additional grounds that it would help 'maintain a proper control over the Temp. Cadets', and recommended that companies consist of 200 men in 8 platoons of 25.[5] At this time, he seems to have thought of companies as administrative formations, and platoons as tactical formations, operating independently: the new force would have only five companies, and its company commanders would have the rank of district inspectors. In time, however, companies of one hundred men or fewer became the basic tactical formation, which greatly increased their operational independence: since company commanders were equal in rank to the most senior RIC district inspectors, they took orders only from county inspectors, divisional commissioners, and their own commandant.[6]

The decision to reduce the size of companies had been taken by 11 August. In a letter to Alfred Cope, Tudor wrote that each company would require 1 commander, 1 second-in-command, 4 platoon leaders (instead of 8), 12 section leaders, and a company clerk. (Later, in early November, the number of platoons per company was reduced further, from four to three.)[7] In his 11 August letter the Police Adviser also mentioned that the new force would require a small depot staff, consisting of a quartermaster and a mess caterer. 'The latter two will remain at the Sub-depot,' he wrote, 'and assist the Commandant by dealing with the reception and equipping of recruits as they arrive, and the formation of the successive companies.'[8]

Tudor was seriously underestimating the amount of staff work his new force would require. The Commandant in question was the commanding officer of the RIC sub-depot at the Curragh, not of the auxiliary force. Conditions at the sub-depot were poor: one of the first recruits, Brigadier General Crozier, said they were 'appalling'. 'A lot of misery, inconvenience, and hard drinking could have been avoided,' he said, 'had arrangements been made for the reception of these men, for their ordinary comfort—quartering, messing, and discipline—but instead the men were running about the Curragh as they liked. The original members of the Division, which then had no name, had to arrange their own messing and canteens, and there was nobody in command.'[9]

Tudor did not ask for permission to appoint a commanding officer until a week later, and even then his conception of this officer's role was very limited:

> The Cos. [Companies] have to be formed & unless there is a head at the Sub-Depot to decide between the claims of each Co. there is a danger of the Co. going off with many men best suited for Platoon Leaders of the other Cos. forming. 3 Cos. are already practically formed and are only awaiting completion of clothing. I recommend Brig-General T. Cadet Crozier for this post, & that his command pay should be £1 per diem.[10]

Tudor was then forced to add additional officers and staff almost as soon as the auxiliary force took the field. On 3 September 1920 the Police Adviser asked for permission to appoint an intelligence officer and a quartermaster to each company. The force's commanding officer was given an adjutant by 8 September, and by 29 October the force's headquarters had grown from 3 to 12 officers, with the addition of a second-in-command, a quartermaster sergeant, 3 clerks, and 2 storemen (the mess caterer seems to have been dropped). Each company had also acquired an assistant quartermaster.[11]

Even by late October the Police Adviser was still underestimating the number of additional personnel that his temporary cadet companies would require. As part of the inquiry into the burning of Cork on 11 December 1920, the commander of K Company gave the court a description of his unit's organisation. According to this officer, K Company's headquarters consisted of himself, his second-in-command, an intelligence officer, eight cadet motor drivers, and five cadets 'engaged on Administrative duties'. 'In addition,' wrote the company commander, 'there are 17 Temporary constables who act as Batmen, Cooks etc. but have no status as Policemen.' This despite the fact that K was one of the new, smaller companies, with only three platoons instead of four: there were only 72 temporary cadets in the whole company, including those attached to the company headquarters.[12]

The Division itself was growing rapidly. On 10 August, Tudor informed the Under Secretary that the Chief Secretary had given him verbal permission to recruit up to one thousand temporary cadets: 'Will you please confirm this.'[13] Cope assured the Police Adviser that the Castle was seeking formal sanction for this increase, but warned Tudor that temporary cadets 'should not be promised priority of permanent appointment as officers in the Royal Irish Constabulary, seeing that Head Constables, etc., have also to be considered for such posts, but may be informed that their services will be considered in making selections for permanent appointments'.[14]

Treasury sanction was requested on 13 August and granted on 23 August.[15] About two months later, Tudor once again informed the Irish government that he had permission from the Chief Secretary to increase the size of the Auxiliary Division, from one thousand to fifteen hundred temporary cadets.[16] By the spring of 1921, the Division had grown to 19 companies: a Depot Company at Beggars Bush barracks (in Dublin city)[17] and 17 field companies, labelled A to R; a twentieth company, K Company, had been disbanded on 31 March 1921 for its part in the burning of Cork. A Veterans Division of temporary constables was formed as well.[18]

For a time, there were three field companies in Dublin city: F Company at Dublin Castle, C Company at Portobello barracks (now Cathal Brugha barracks), and Q Company at the London and North Western Railway Hotel. There is a great deal of confusion surrounding the disposition of the remaining companies outside of Dublin. Several authors have supplied lists, none of which agree, and the records are fragmentary. To further confound matters, Auxiliary companies were sometimes moved from one county to another. C Company, for example, was originally based at Macroom Castle, County Cork, until most of its No. 2 Platoon was wiped out in the famous ambush at Kilmichael on 28 November 1920. A few weeks thereafter, C Company was transferred to Dublin city and replaced in County Cork with J Company.

There is also some confusion about the uniforms worn by temporary cadets. A number of sources say the men of the Division wore khaki at first, and then switched to dark blue clothing.[19] This is not correct, and the origin of this error is difficult to find.[20] From beginning to end, the Auxiliaries wore either military khaki or the rifle green of the constabulary. 'Uniform of RIC supplied free' say their conditions of service, 'or Service Dress (Officers) may be worn without badges of rank'.[21] Their distinctive caps were either khaki, or blue (like the cap worn by the leader of the raid on the Moycullen co-operative store in October 1920), or green (like the caps worn by the members of K Company in December 1920). However, green caps may have been unusual: a 'Statement of Deficiencies in Stores of Auxiliary Division RIC', prepared in June 1921, lists only green RIC tunics and trousers, along with khaki and blue balmorals.[22]

Clearly, the Auxiliary Division's uniforms were chiefly distinguished by their lack of uniformity. As we have seen, Tudor always intended to allow a mixture of clothing. Photographs show groups of Auxiliaries wearing both police and military uniforms, some with shirt and tie and some without, some with the bottoms of their trousers wrapped with puttees and some without, and some with breeches and leggings. David Neligan worked alongside F Company in Dublin Castle, and later wrote that: 'Generally they wore khaki tunics belonging to their Army service complete with decorations, military riding breeches and a Glengarry woolly cap. I have no idea how they came to wear this curious headgear. I suppose some quarter-master discovered a dump of them in some store or perhaps bought them via a good rake-off from the wholesaler.'[23] Neligan also confirmed that they wore the initials TC on their shoulder straps: 'The Auxiliaries' own interpretation of those letters is unprintable,' he said.[24]

On the other hand, according to a former Auxiliary named Bill Munro, while in County Cork the men of C Company were initially given the peaked caps of the constabulary:

> It was not till some months later that we were given the Balmoral-cum-beret that became the only distinguishing mark between ourselves and the RIC constables. The uniforms we got were the usual RIC, that is to say dark green jackets and trousers, and at no time was the official uniform breeches and leggings. Really there were no uniform regulations and we could turn out in a mixture of Army, RAF and Naval uniforms provided we wore the regulation cap.[25]

Munro also mentioned that the government could not always keep its promise to supply constabulary clothing free. Since the average height in the RIC had until recently been over 5 feet 10 inches, there were no police uniforms available for shorter men.[26] One witness to the American Commission thought the Auxiliaries had no uniform at all. 'They dress in civilian clothes and in soldier's clothes,' said Denis Morgan. 'They dress in every way. You can never tell them.'[27] Indeed, the only time they seem to have dressed alike was on parade.

The Auxiliary Division's uniforms are of more than antiquarian interest, for a couple of reasons. First, their haphazard clothing sometimes made it difficult to distinguish friend from enemy, especially at night. During a night raid on Kilrush, County Clare, in April 1921, men of the RIC twice mistook IRA Commandant Michael Brennan for an Auxiliary.[28] 'I had never seen an Auxiliary up to this time except at night,' he later recalled, 'and a description of their dress on service made the RIC error in my identification at least understandable.' As a consequence, after Brennan and his men mistakenly shot up a convent instead of the RIC barracks, the Auxiliaries were blamed instead of the IRA.[29] Later, in June 1921 an Irish ex-soldier mistook the members of the IRA's North Tipperary flying column for Auxiliaries and condemned himself as a spy by giving the 'police' information about the local IRA. The Volunteers took the man prisoner and were going to shoot him, but he escaped in the confusion following the ambush at Kallegbeg Cross.[30]

Second, the Division's uniforms were apparently designed to advertise its elite status, and the toughness of its members. The balmoral cap and the leather bandolier were the accessories of the Army's glamorous and prestigious Highland and Cavalry regiments, respectively. Instead of wearing their revolvers on their belts, like police and military officers, some Auxiliaries wore them in open thigh holsters, like the gunfighters of the American West—though this last affectation did not always impress onlookers. An RIC veteran later recalled that 'We thought it laughable to see them with the gun strapped to the thigh.'[31] It could also be hazardous: Munro wrote that 'some of us were influenced by Western films and wore our revolvers in holsters low slung on the thigh which looked very dashing but which were the cause of quite a number of shot-off toes—as the enthusiasts attempted to emulate the cowboys of Texas.'[32] Thus, we can learn something about early twentieth-century British masculinity by examining the Auxiliary Division's clothing. In the words of Henry Smart, Roddy Doyle's fictional Irish revolutionary, the Auxiliaries did their best to look like 'nut-hard bastards'.[33]

4.2 Who were the Auxiliaries, really?

What kind of men wore these uniforms? In 1992 English historian A. D. Harvey published some tentative answers to this question, in the form of a communication based on a survey of the ADRIC's registers, along with their accompanying journals.[34] Unfortunately, the Division's record-keeping was just as haphazard as everything else connected therewith.[35] Both the registers and the journals are amateurish, incomplete, and uninformative compared to their RIC counterparts—but Harvey nonetheless came to three interesting conclusions based on the information contained in these documents. First, while studying the decorations they had received, he realised that a significant number of Auxiliaries must have been promoted from the ranks. During the Great War the British Army awarded different decorations to officers and soldiers: officers received the Military Cross and the Distinguished Service Order, while other ranks received the Military Medal and the Distinguished Conduct Medal. Harvey noted that 281 temporary cadets had been decorated for gallantry, and 101 had received medals like the MM and the DCM, in addition to those reserved for officers.[36] Similarly, Harvey concluded that 'the Auxiliaries were, by the standards of the time, far from socially exclusive' because of the regiments they served with during the war: few temporary cadets had served with elite regiments like the Guards, while the register showed that some had served with the merchant marine, the Chinese Labour Corps, and the Burma Police.[37] Finally, Harvey concluded that 'the predominant element in the Auxiliaries comprised men ignorant of Ireland and the Irish people', because he found few men who had either served with Irish regiments or had Irish surnames.[38]

In an effort both to test these conclusions and to build on Harvey's research, I took another cluster sample from the ADRIC's registers: just as before, this consisted of every man who had enlisted in October 1920, when recruiting was at its peak and 270 men joined the Division as temporary cadets.[39] I then attempted to match each of these 270 entries to their corresponding entries in the RIC's general register. In the process, I discovered to my dismay that not every temporary cadet had been recorded in the general register: only 228 of the 270 men who joined the Division in October 1920 are listed in both documents. To make matters worse, the entries for Auxiliaries included few details, compared to the entries for Black and Tans: only the birth dates, native counties, and religions of temporary cadets are recorded in the RIC's general register; the only previous occupation listed for each man is 'ex-officer', and most of the remaining columns were left blank. But, armed with this additional information, I then searched the War Office papers for as many of their service records as I could find. The results were disappointing, to say the least: in the end, I managed to locate the service records for just 36 of my 270 Auxiliaries.

Nonetheless, it is possible to make some generalisations about this group of men, and to compare them in some ways to our sample of British recruits for the RIC. First, Auxiliaries were generally older than Black and Tans (see Table 4.1): 39 per cent of the Auxiliaries were born before 1891, compared

Table 4.1. Birth dates of temporary cadets and temporary constables compared to birth dates of Black and Tans, October 1920 (%).

Sample . . .	Temporary Cadets 211	Temporary Constables 149	Black and Tans 1153
1901–1902	1	—	11
1896–1900	29	7	48
1891–95	30	2	22
1886–90	17	11	13
1881–85	11	23	5
1876–80	10	31	1
1871–75	2	22	—
1861–70	—	4	—

Sources: Temporary Cadets 647 to 920, ADRIC Register No. 1, PRO, HO 184/50 and corresponding numbers in RIC General Register (There was no birth date recorded for one Temporary Cadet); Constables and Temporary Constables 73602 to 75027, RIC General Register, PRO, HO 184/38–9.

to just 19 per cent of the Black and Tans. The majority of the Black and Tans were born after 1895; the majority of the Auxiliaries were born before 1896. Some Auxiliaries were older than any Black and Tan: Captain G. P. T. Dean was born in 1875, while Lieutenant T. Mitchell, Lieutenant J. Munn, and Second Lieutenant G. L. Shaw were all born in 1874, and were old enough to have served in the South African War.[40] Of course, some Auxiliaries were very young: Midshipman P. M. E. Hall and Second Lieutenant G. C. M. Timline were both born in 1902, and three others were born in 1900; all five must have been quite underage if they had served in the Great War.[41] But overall, the average Auxiliary was about five years older than the average Black and Tan.

The men recruited in October 1920 included ex-officers of all ranks from midshipman (of which there were two) to brigadier (of which there was one, Brigadier General E. A. Wood). The sample also included 4 lieutenant colonels, 6 majors, and 39 captains (including 2 Navy captains). However, the majority of the men in the group (139 out of 270) were lieutenants, and of the remainder, 49 were 2nd lieutenants; another 4 were Navy sub-lieutenants. On average, senior officers were seven years older than their immediate juniors: lieutenants and 2nd lieutenants were about twenty-six years old, captains about thirty-three, and majors about forty—though there were some exceptions, like the rather elderly lieutenants mentioned earlier.

No ranks were listed for two dozen men, but what this means is unclear. It probably does not mean that they were not ex-servicemen: two of them had in fact been decorated for gallantry—A. J. Andrews received the Military Cross and the Distinguished Service Order, while J. H. Rogers received the Distinguished Conduct Medal—and a third had served with the 3rd Battalion, Leinster Regiment.[42] It might mean that some of them were not commissioned officers. This was Harvey's explanation, and he was not alone in this suspicion: Frank Pakenham, for example, referred to the men of the Auxiliary Division as 'supposed ex-officers'.[43] However, these blanks are probably evidence of nothing more than bad bookkeeping: for example, one man with no recorded rank, A. J. Andrews, turns out to have been a lieutenant colonel.[44]

The men who joined the Division in October 1920 came overwhelmingly from the Army. A branch of service was recorded for 247 men: out of these 247, only 17 served in the Navy and 3 in the Marines. Once again, the absence of information for the remaining men probably means nothing: in four cases, men who had been decorated for bravery have no regiment beside their names. But the sample does confirm one of Harvey's observations. 'The organization to which the largest single group of officers had belonged,' he said, 'was the Royal Air Force; about one in ten of Cadets whose previous service was listed were from the R.A.F.'[45] This was certainly true in October 1920: 33 out of our 270 temporary cadets had served with the RAF or its predecessor, the Royal Flying Corps—more than any other single regiment or corps in the Army.

This batch of recruits also confirms that a significant number of temporary cadets had been commissioned from the ranks during the Great War. Out of the 270 men in the sample, 48 had been decorated for bravery, though not always for bravery in battle: three men in the sample had won medals for saving life at sea.[46] Fifteen of these 48 men had received medals reserved for non-commissioned officers and other ranks: either the Military Medal or the Distinguished Conduct Medal, including Lieutenant C. A. Burnett of the Black Watch, who won the DCM twice. A sixteenth man, Second Lieutenant E. Handcock of the Royal Engineers, had been awarded the Meritorious Service Medal, which was awarded only to non-commissioned officers of the rank of sergeant or above, for long, efficient, and meritorious service. Six of these 16 men went on to win medals as officers, including Major J. A. Mackinnon MC DCM MM, Captain E. S. Garrod DSO MC DCM, and Captain W. L. King MC & Bar DCM. Mackinnon and King both became company commanders in the ADRIC, and Garrod became a platoon commander. It seems that Harvey was correct when he wrote that men commissioned from the ranks were both a 'significant element in the Auxiliary Division as a whole, and probably included most of the more active and intrepid spirits'.[47]

But on the other hand Harvey's conclusions about the Auxiliary Division's lack of social exclusiveness may have been a bit hasty. If we compare the proportions of temporary cadets from the various Army corps to the proportions of officers in the various corps of the wartime Army, we will find that officers of the Guards were actually *over*-represented among the men who joined the ADRIC in October 1920, while the percentage of cavalry officers was equal to the percentage of cavalry officers in the Army; the socially lowly service corps, by comparison, were greatly *under*-represented among the temporary cadets.[48] (See Table 4.2) In addition, while it is probably true that 'the predominant element in the Auxiliaries comprised men ignorant of Ireland and the Irish people', Harvey was not likely to learn much about the geographical backgrounds of temporary cadets from their surnames, or from the regiments listed in the ADRIC register. The RIC's general register, for example, makes it clear that 16 of the 228 temporary cadets who joined the Division in October 1920 were Irishmen. None of these men's names had the Irish prefixes that Harvey was looking for, and only five of them had served with Irish infantry regiments; it should also be

Table 4.2. Proportions of officers in the various corps of the British Army, 1 January 1918, compared to proportions of temporary cadets from the various corps of the British Army, October 1920 (%).

Corps	Army, Jan 1918	ADRIC, Oct 1920
Guards	0.9	1.4
Cavalry	2.7	2.7
Artillery	12.9	10.5
Engineers	8.9	0.5
Air Force	8.8	15.0
Infantry	43.6	60.9
Cyclists, Machine-Guns, Tanks	5.4	5.9
Service	17.8	3.2

Sources: Temporary Cadets 647 to 920, ADRIC Register No. 1, PRO, HO 184/50; *Army Report (1921)*, 21. (Note: cadets whose corps is unknown have been excluded.)

noted that an equal number of men from outside Ireland (five) had served as officers in Irish regiments.[49]

One thing we can be sure about is from where the men in our sample came (see Table 4.3). Once again, like the Black and Tans, a disproportionate number of temporary cadets came from London and the Home Counties, though the imbalance between north and south was not as extreme as it was with the Black and Tans. But a much greater number of Auxiliaries came from outside the British Isles: 22 out of 212, or more than 10 per cent. Eighteen of these men came from the Empire and Commonwealth: seven from South Africa, four from India, two apiece from Canada, British Guiana, and Jamaica, and one from Australia. The remaining four were foreigners, including one man who claimed to come from southern Russia.[50] Add the 16 men who have been excluded from the sample for being Irish, and it seems that temporary cadets were a somewhat more diverse group than the Black and Tans. The information in the RIC register also confirms, once again, that Harvey's attempt to discern their geographical origins from their former regiments was ill-advised: less than 20 per cent of the men listed in the RIC register (41 out of 228) had served in their local infantry regiments.

Interestingly, Harvey's neglect of the RIC's general register as a source of information also led him to neglect the temporary constables who served

Table 4.3. Native regions of temporary cadets and temporary constables compared to native regions of Black and Tans, October 1920 (%).

Sample...	Temporary Cadets 212	Temporary Constables 149	Black and Tans 1,153
Central England	15	9	12
Northern England	19	6	15
London and Vicinity	34	60	47
Southern England	8	7	12
Eastern England	2	5	3
Scotland	4	6	8
Wales	8	2	1
Other	10	5	2

Sources: Cadets 647 to 920, ADRIC Register No. 1, PRO, HO 184/50 and corresponding numbers in RIC General Register; Constables and Temporary Constables 73602 to 75027, RIC General Register, PRO, HO 184/38-9.

alongside the temporary cadets in the ADRIC. In the House of Commons these 'Temporaries' were described as 'veteran ex-soldiers of 35 years of age and upwards', 'recruited for a year's service' and 'paid 10s. a day and a gratuity of £25 on completion of a year' service'.[51] There is a register for these men, but this tells us little besides their names, their companies, and the total number of enlistments: 997, about one-third of the men who enlisted in the ADRIC overall. However, unlike temporary cadets, temporary constables were given full records in the RIC's general register, which gives us another cluster of 149 temporary constables who enlisted in October 1920.

This group of men was quite distinctive in many ways. Temporary constables were much older than either Black and Tans or temporary cadets (see Table 4.1). Whereas 81 per cent of Black and Tans and 60 per cent of Auxiliaries were born after 1890, this was true of only 9 per cent of temporary constables. The majority of temporary constables were at least forty years old in 1920. Temporary constables were comparable to Black and Tans in height, but they were even more likely than Black and Tans to come from the London area (see Table 4.3). A clear majority (60 per cent) of temporary constables were Londoners, and the remaining 40 per cent came more or less equally from the rest of Britain. In addition, 82 per cent of them joined the force in London, while almost all of the remainder signed up in Glasgow, Liverpool, and Portsmouth. A much greater percentage of them (30 per cent) were married, and almost half of the married men had married before the Great War.

Like Black and Tans and temporary cadets, temporary constables were mostly ex-servicemen: in fact, only one man in the sample has no military service listed in his record. Interestingly, almost one in five temporary constables listed no previous occupation except ex-soldier, suggesting once again that the police forces in Ireland were attracting former members of the pre-war regular Army. But the apparent number of former regulars among them may have been exaggerated by sloppy record-keeping: at one point in the register, there is a batch of temporary constables listed simply as ex-soldiers, in much the same way as temporary cadets were listed simply as ex-officers. Overall, temporary constables were even more proletarian than Black and Tans: 65 per cent of them were unskilled or semi-skilled workers, and another 25 per cent of them were skilled workers (see Table 4.4). Their two most common previous occupations were ex-soldier and labourer, with clerks and cooks a distant third and fourth, and painters fifth. Their

Table 4.4. Occupational backgrounds of temporary constables and Black and Tans, October 1920 (%).

Sample . . .	Temporary Constables 149	Black and Tans 1,153
Unskilled/semi-skilled	65	52
Skilled	24	35
Shop assistant/clerk	7	6
Other	4	7

Source: Constables and Temporary Constables 73602 to 75027, RIC General Register, PRO, HO 184/38–9.

working-class character is confirmed by their religious profile: 124 of the 149 men in the sample were Anglicans, and only two were Dissenters: a Wesleyan and a Baptist.

There is very little record of what these temporary constables did in Ireland. Only 10 of the 149 men in the sample have any sort of note beside their names: five resigned, two were discharged, and three were dismissed, one for taking out a Crossley tender without authority and damaging it, and another for discharging his rifle—the circumstances of this latter case are not clear. Fortunately, we are on much firmer ground with the temporary cadets, whose fates were recorded in the ADRIC register (see Table 4.5). Once again, as with the Black and Tans, though casualties were low, attrition was high. Less than 50 per cent of the Auxiliaries who enlisted in

Table 4.5. Fates of Temporary Cadets, October 1920.

Sample . . .	270	%
Re-engaged	135	49
Resigned	46	17
Did not re-engage	26	10
Discharged (medically unfit)	16	6
Joined Royal Irish Constabulary	16	6
Struck off or dismissed	15	6
Killed or died	14	5
Joined Ulster Special Constabulary	2	1

Source: Cadets 647 to 920, ADRIC Register No. 1, PRO, HO 184/50. (Note: two men in the sample transferred to the Royal Irish Constabulary, but returned to the ADRIC, and are not counted as having joined the RIC.)

October 1920 re-engaged for another year's service in the Division in August and September 1921. Out of the remainder, 17 per cent resigned and a further 10 per cent did not re-engage for another year's service. Proportionately fewer Auxiliaries than Black and Tans were struck off or dismissed from the Division, but a higher percentage was discharged on medical grounds. The Auxiliaries also suffered numerous losses in the form of transfers. Eighteen of the men in the sample transferred from the ADRIC to another police force. Twelve temporary cadets became permanent cadets, and all but one of these men eventually became officers of the Royal Irish Constabulary, though only three of them saw much service before the Truce.[52] Another six men transferred to the RIC's Transport Division. One man from each group wound up rejoining the Auxiliary Division. The remaining two men went to the Ulster Special Constabulary, including Captain J. .C Abraham MC, Welch Regiment, who was appointed second-in-command of the USC training camp at Newtownards, county Antrim, in the spring of 1921.[53]

In terms of casualties, our sample is clearly not representative. Thirty-nine temporary cadets were killed or died in the Irish War of Independence: 14 of these 39 enlisted in October 1920. The sample includes Frank Garniss and Cecil Morris, who were assassinated in Dublin on Bloody Sunday, 21 November 1920. It also includes 4 of the 18 men who were rubbed out at Kilmichael a week later. The sample is also unrepresentative when it comes to promotions: it includes one of the Division's two commandants, Brigadier General E. A. Wood, and the two men who became assistant commandants, Brigadier Wood and Lieutenant Colonel F. H. W. Guard.[54] It also includes 79 men who became officers, about 29 per cent of the sample.

The success of these October recruits in winning promotion was probably due to two factors: first, they enlisted relatively early in the conflict, and were in line to replace officers of the first generation who resigned or were demoted; second, the Division more than doubled in size after October 1920, creating a demand for officers at all levels. As a result, 53 men in the sample became section leaders, 14 became platoon commanders, 9 became intelligence officers, 8 became company commanders, and 7 became seconds in command. Advancement was irregular, however: five of the eight men who became company commanders had not served as junior officers, and a number of platoon commanders and intelligence officers had not served as section leaders. Only one man in the sample, Second Lieutenant N. P. Wood, Royal Air Force, was promoted all four steps, from section leader in G Company on 12 February 1921 to commander of Q Company on 2 August 1921. Furthermore, while promotion could be rapid, demotion could be just as rapid: almost one-third of the men who became officers (25 out of 79) reverted to temporary cadets, only occasionally at their own request, and only one of the eight men who became company commanders still held this post when the Division was demobilised.[55]

4.3 Temporary gentlemen

In similar fashion, the scraps of information obtainable from the handful of available service records also partly confirm Harvey's conclusions. A significant number of these men had indeed been promoted from the ranks. Indeed, if anything, Harvey seems to have underestimated the number of 'temporary gentlemen' in the ADRIC. Out of these 36 Auxiliaries, only 3 definitely began their military careers as officers—and none of them had been officers in the pre-war Army. Captain C. de P. D. Swain had been commissioned as a 2nd lieutenant in the 8th Hampshire Regiment of the Territorial Force in February 1912, and had been transferred to the 2nd (Wessex) Brigade, Royal Field Artillery in June 1913.[56] He finally joined the Royal Flying Corps in 1916. By contrast, Lieutenant Colonel F. H. W. Guard (who we have met before, and will meet again) was a civilian when war broke out in 1914 but soon obtained a lieutenant's commission in the Gold Coast Volunteer Corps.[57] Finally, Captain W. F. Russell-Jones joined the Territorial Force the year it was formed: he was a lieutenant in the 1/9th London (Queen Victoria's Rifles), and served with this battalion on the Western Front from the autumn of 1914 to the summer of 1915, when he was sent home suffering from shell shock, and remained there for the rest of the war.[58]

A number of these officers had seen even less active service than Russell-Jones. The career of 2nd Lieutenant Harold Crossley as an observer in the Independent Air Force had been brief: he had enlisted in May 1918, received his commission in July—and then was shot down in September, spending the rest of the war as a POW.[59] One 2nd Lieutenant Albert James Evans, RAF, had enlisted in April 1918 but never even made it off the ground: a tailor in civilian life, he seems to have served as a clerk.[60] Similarly, 2nd Lieutenant Henry Julius Jacoby had enlisted in Royal Army Service Corps in September 1918, and had not received his commission until February 1919: nearsighted enough to need glasses, he had been rejected by the infantry—he could not march far owing to an old leg injury—and had never served overseas.[61]

Another officer who missed most of the war, Lieutenant Frank Fitch, had been a draper's assistant in civilian life before enlisting in the 1st (Royal) Dragoons in 1897. After serving in the South African War, he had extended his service to 12 years in 1903, and then to 21 years in 1909, while stationed in India. He had reached the rank of corporal when the Great War broke out, and in October 1914 Fitch and his unit were sent to Belgium as part of the IV Corps' 3rd Cavalry Division. After less than two weeks on active duty, however, Corporal Fitch was back in England, after having been shot in the elbow during the opening stages of the 1st Battle of Ypres. He spent the next three years at home, serving with the 5th and 6th Reserve Cavalry Regiments, and was finally commissioned as a 2nd lieutenant in the summer of 1917. When he returned to France, he spent a year as an interpreter in the Indian Labour Corps, was promoted to lieutenant, and finished the war serving with the Royal Field Artillery, as part of the 42nd Division's ammunition column.[62]

More than half of the men in this small group would have been entitled either to the 1914 Star or the 1914–15 Star. Five of them had been serving with the Army, or the Reserves, or the Territorial Force in 1914, and had managed to survive the entire war. Thirteen of them had enlisted between August and December 1914, and another three had enlisted in 1915—or four, if we count 2nd Lieutenant A. F. Fletcher. Born in Londonderry in 1899, Fletcher had enlisted in the 2/6th Black Watch in February 1915, and actually served in France for more than a month before he was sent home and discharged in September 1916 for being underage; he re-enlisted later in the 19th Royal Irish Rifles, and ended the war as an officer in the 3rd Leinsters.[63]

Only 4 of these 36 men had definitely enlisted in 1917 and 1918. The majority, then, were experienced soldiers, usually non-commissioned officers who had served for years before receiving their commissions in 1918 or, less commonly, in 1917. Some of their military careers had been quite varied. Lieutenant Cyril Thomas Joslin, a contractor's clerk, had enlisted in the Royal Army Medical Corps in August 1915 and served with distinction in the 103rd Field Ambulance in France between January 1916 and June 1917, during which time he was mentioned in despatches and promoted to sergeant; he was then commissioned as a 2nd lieutenant in the

Machine Gun Corps in January 1918 and promoted to lieutenant in July.[64] Finally, another man who had been a clerk in civilian life, 2nd Lieutenant Cecil Taverner, had enlisted in the 17th Royal Fusiliers in September 1914, transferred to the Cyclist Corps in July 1915, and then transferred to the Machine-Gun Corps in May 1916, before finally receiving a commission in the 4th Durham Light Infantry—a depot/training unit in the United Kingdom. After his time in the ADRIC, he enlisted in the RAF and served for 12 years—as a clerk.[65]

In addition, most of these 36 men seem to have come from the middle classes. At least 15 of them were lower middle-class: most of these had been students, clerks, and shop assistants, though 2nd Lieutenant George Ernest Lissenden had been a traveller,[66] Lieutenant Stanley Dawson had been a schoolteacher,[67] and Lieutenant Jacoby gave his previous occupation as 'clerk in holy orders'. Some of these men may have been at the start of more promising careers when the war intervened: Lieutenant Reginald Brooks Pawle, for example, was the son of a stockbroker and had enlisted in the 10th Royal Fusiliers, nicknamed 'the Stockbrokers'.[68] Lieutenant Robert L. Worsley's father was a priest in the Church of England,[69] and 2nd Lieutenant Bryan Hardcastle Emery's father was a political correspondent for the *Morning Post.*[70] Of the remainder, Captain William Graham Price had been an insurance broker,[71] and Lieutenant Albert Henry Waugh had been a dentist.[72] Lieutenant Colonel Guard's pre-war occupation is unknown, but he styled himself 'F. H. W. Guard, Esquire' on his commission as a lieutenant in the Gold Coast Volunteer Corps; he was appointed to manage the Togoland Military Railways after the conclusion of hostilities in West Africa.

By way of contrast, only 5 of these 36 temporary cadets had come from the skilled working classes, and only one of them had come from the unskilled working class: 2nd Lieutenant Percy George Wiles MM. A labourer in civilian life, Wiles had served in the 1st Gloucestershire Regiment, had been awarded the Military Medal in September 1916, and had been recommended a second time for this medal in 1917.

Unfortunately, it seems that Wiles never successfully readjusted to civilian life. After serving with G Company for six months, Wiles was dismissed from the ADRIC on 18 April 1921—and according to his War Office file, after his six months in Ireland, he seems to have turned to a life of petty crime. In 1922 he was convicted under the Vagrancy Act of 1824 of being a suspected person and given a sentence of two months' hard labour. Five years later, in 1927, he pleaded guilty to two charges of burglary and larceny, and lost his reserve officer's commission as a result. The War Office tried to send a letter to Wiles informing him that he had been removed from the Army, but it was returned undelivered after his wife refused to accept it: 'her husband,' she said, 'did not reside there'. Nine years after that, in 1936, Wiles was again put on trial, for two charges of attempted false pretences. He was convicted, and sentenced to three months' hard labour.

There is much more to the story of Percy George Wiles, however, than just this. Born in 1882, Wiles had, like Nathan, served as a soldier in the pre-war regular Army: he had enlisted in the Gloucestershire regiment in 1900, and had fought in the South African War. He was transferred to the Reserve after eight years' service in 1908 and was discharged in 1912 with a 'very good' character. He then re-enlisted in the Reserves, and was mobilised when war broke out. He served in France for most of 1915, then from February 1916 to January 1918. Having risen to the rank of sergeant, he was transferred to an Officer Cadet Battalion in February 1918 and commissioned as a 2nd lieutenant in the 3rd Essex in August: that is to say, he spent only the last four months of the war as an officer.

Wiles retired a year later with a commission in the Regular Army Reserve of Officers and a gratuity of £1,500. According to press clippings preserved in his file, it seems the lieutenant lost all his money at the track. A report in the *Daily Mail* says that 'Wiles received a gratuity of £1,500 and unfortunately set up in business as a bookmaker. At Epsom he paid everybody except four persons, and these he paid 50 per cent. The charge of welshing was dismissed, and he was convicted as a suspected person.' Wiles then returned to his pre-war occupation as a tobacco cutter. Five years later he was living in a boarding house when he was arrested for burglary along with his accomplice, Harry Cohen. At their trial, according to the *News of the World*, Cohen was sentenced to 18 months' imprisonment. 'Addressing Wiles,' however, 'his lordship said he thought the receipt by him of so large a gratuity seemed to have brought about his ruin. Recently he had had the misfortune to come under the evil influence of Cohen, but taking all the circumstances into consideration the judge decided to give him an opportunity to regain his character.'[73]

Although Wiles was the only one of our temporary cadets who committed a crime serious enough to cost him his reserve commission, he was not the only one who had money problems. Lieutenant Peter James Grundlingh, a British subject from South Africa, passed a bad cheque for

400 francs (7 pounds 11 shillings 10 pence) while serving as a graves registration officer in France in September 1920. He enlisted in the ADRIC on 14 October 1920, but his career as an Auxiliary was brief: he was discharged on 7 December 1920, 'in consequence of complaints in regard to his conduct'. It was then discovered that Grundlingh had been overpaid by the Army: despite having been demobilised in mid-October, when he joined the ADRIC, he had been mistakenly paid to the end of the month. After Grundlingh reneged on repeated promises to repay this money, the War Office eventually wrote off the whole sum.[74]

In another case, 2nd Lieutenant Edison James Shields of the Tank Corps was actually serving in Galway, Ireland, with an armoured-car company in January 1920 when he went AWOL after being granted 48 hours' leave. A month later he surrendered himself to the deputy provost marshal in London. When ordered to explain himself, he replied:

> I unfortunately got into financial difficulties through a person failing to repay a loan.
>
> I wrote to my brother to pay some money into my account, much to my surprise he replied at the time that it was impossible.
>
> My position was such that I thought I had no alternative but to hasten to town and endeavour to straighten my affairs, expecting to be able to do so in a day or two but a month elapsed before I could do so.
>
> I deeply regret absenting myself, my only excuse being that I did not pause sufficiently, owing to being so worried, to realise the gravity of my offence.

Shields was compelled to forfeit his pay for the period of his absence and was demobilised.[75]

The most interesting member of this group, for a variety of reasons, is Lieutenant George Nathan. Nathan had stayed in the Army after the Armistice, and only applied to retire with gratuity in August 1920, after a year in India. He joined the ADRIC on 20 October 1920, but resigned from the Division on 2 May 1921: less than three weeks later, on 22 May 1921, he gave up his reserve commission to re-enlist as a private in the West Yorkshire Regiment. He was discharged from this regiment at his own request in October 1922, but re-enlisted once again, in the ranks of the Royal Fusiliers, on 26 October 1925. This time, he was discharged with ignominy, in May 1926. Nathan's file does not explain why he was drummed out of the Royal Fusiliers, but a former Temporary Cadet who knew Nathan in Ireland later described him as a 'roaring homosexual'—and discharge with ignominy was a traditional military punishment for men who were caught committing homosexual acts.[76]

Nathan then disappears from history until July 1937, when he was killed at the Battle of Brunete in the Spanish Civil War, fighting on the Loyalist side as an officer in the British Battalion of the XV International Brigade. Tellingly, the sometime commander of the British Battalion in Spain, Fred Copeman, described his former comrade in the following terms:

> Another outstanding member of the group was George Nathan, an ex-Army officer, efficient, capable, with loads of courage; above all the typical British officer; fair, yet one who, when giving orders, left those receiving them under no illusions as to what was required. Nathan dressed as one would expect—his riding boots shining like a new pin, every button polished, hat at the right angle and riding crop in hand. At first I thought him a snob, yet I shall never forget that on the third day of the battle of Jarama, among the chaos and slaughter, with his fine boots and his batman he stood out as the most capable officer.[77]

Copeman might have been surprised to learn that, behind his carefully cultivated British officer's persona, Nathan was a Jewish butcher's apprentice from Hackney, who had enlisted in the Duke of Cornwall's Light Infantry in 1913, transferred to the Cyclist Corps in December 1914, and only received his commission in April 1917. Indeed, Nathan may have invented a whole false persona for himself. Richard Bennett, author of *The Black and Tans*, wrote that Nathan had become in 1918 the only Jewish officer in the Brigade of Guards. In fact, once he had been commissioned as a 2nd lieutenant, Nathan had served instead with the 1st Royal Warwicks.[78]

In his 1992 article on the Auxiliaries, Harvey suggested that the ADRIC offered a post-war haven for men like Nathan: 'schoolboys who had become killers instead of going to university, working-class men disorientated by promotion to the status of officers and gentlemen, fractured personalities whose maladjustments found temporary relief in the 1914–18 War and whose outward stability depended on the psychic reassurance of a khaki tunic on their back and a Webley.455 at their hip'.[79] The Division does appear to have attracted a few such men—but like their counterparts among the Black and Tans, it also seems that most men of this type were eventually weeded out. Grundlingh was discharged in December 1920, Wiles was dismissed in April 1921, and Nathan resigned in May. The most common type of Auxiliary—the man who likely formed the hard core of the Division—seems to have been an efficient and experienced soldier—a man from the lower middle classes who had volunteered in 1914 or 1915, become a non-commissioned officer in 1916 and 1917, been commissioned in 1917 or 1918, and finally demobilised in 1919 or 1920. These were very temporary gentlemen indeed.

4.4 Armed bands

We know very little about how these temporary cadets and temporary constables were recruited and trained. Some of the men who joined the Division in October were probably responding to the following advertisement in *The Times*:

> EX-OFFICERS WANTED. Seven pounds a week, free uniform and quarters. Must have first-class records: to join Auxiliary Division, Royal Irish Constabulary; 12 months' guarantee—Apply, with full particulars, service, age, &c. to R.O, R.I.C., Scotland-yard, London, S.W.[80]

Note how this advertisement emphasises the position's high rate of pay. Seven pounds a week was actually more than what the average Auxiliary would have made in the Army. Temporary Cadet Grundlingh, for example, had been paid 16s a day as an Army lieutenant, and was overissued £13 12s for the period from 15 to 31 October.[81] We have already seen how the recession of 1920 affected British recruiting for the Royal Irish Constabulary. To an unemployed ex-officer, in October 1920, an offer of seven pounds a week might indeed have seemed like 'manna from heaven', as Bill Munro suggested in his memoir.[82]

Brigadier General Wood, on the other hand, was invited to join. Wood had been unemployed since March 1920. On 3 June he applied to the War Office for a position with the Persian Army. Lieutenant General Philip Chetwode, the War Office's military secretary, wrote to Sir Nevil Macready about Wood's situation; on 23 September, Macready wrote back to say that 'I have passed on your letter about Brigadier-General Wood to Tudor, and I daresay we may be able to find a job for him in the Cadet Companies of the "Black and Tans."' On 2 October, Chetwode wrote back to Wood, forwarding a letter from Crozier, and inviting Wood to apply to the RIC's recruiting office at Great Scotland Yard.[83] Wood enlisted in the Auxiliary Division on 20 October and became the second-in-command.

Interestingly, it seems also that Wood was not the only temporary cadet who joined the ADRIC as an alternative to a more conventional military career. Bryan Hardcastle Emery, for example, had been a member of the Dulwich College OTC. He enlisted in the Territorial Force in March 1917, and joined an Officer Cadet Battalion in February 1918: he was recommended for a temporary commission in the Indian Army, but was turned down on the grounds that he had no active service experience. After serving in Northern Russia, he was again recommended for the Indian Army, and again rejected—this time, because he had not graduated from Sandhurst. Emery kept his commission in the Territorial Force even while serving in the ADRIC. In December 1920 his former commanding officer in Russia recommended him for promotion: and when he was promoted to lieutenant, in January 1921, Temporary Cadet Emery acknowledged this news from Dublin Castle.[84]

Applicants were given forms to complete, and the recruiting officer checked their military records and police references; if these were satisfactory, the applicants were called in for interviews.[85] Once their applications were approved, the new temporary cadets were sent from London in groups, twice a week, to their depot in Ireland.[86] Like the Black and Tans, temporary cadets were given very little training. Bill Munro joined the Division in late July or August 1920, and described his training in the following terms:

> We spent about six weeks messing about—what little we got of instruction had very remote relationship to the work we had to do in the country. Theoretically, we were put through a shortened police course, having impressed on us the meaning of a misdemeanour and a felony, our powers of arrest, and what we could and could not do. There was a certain amount of arms and bombing practice but all very sketchy, instructors being drawn from our own numbers.[87]

Although the ADRIC was supposed to be a mobile force, few temporary cadets knew how to operate or repair motor vehicles: men from mechanised units and the air force were used as drivers and mechanics, but according to Munro, 'some of the drivers were sitting behind the wheel for the first time and barely knew how to change gears'.[88]

As we might expect after only six weeks in camp, temporary cadets were badly disciplined as well as badly trained. The Labour Commission found that 'a licence is permitted among the "Cadets" (the rank and file of the

Division) which makes their conduct depend more on the personality of local commanders than on instructions from headquarters'.[89] Though he was critical of the Labour Commission's report, Sir Nevil Macready's memoirs confirm its verdict in this case: 'Those companies,' he wrote, 'that had the good fortune to have good commanders, generally ex-Regular officers, who could control their men, performed useful work, but the exploits of certain other companies under weak or inefficient commanders went a long way to discredit the whole force.'[90]

Documents preserved at the National Archives of the UK would seem to confirm this picture of a poorly disciplined force. In its supplementary routine orders for 9 December 1921, Divisional Headquarters published the names and numbers of 63 temporary cadets and 18 temporary constables who had been fined over the past couple of months. The most common offence among both temporary cadets and temporary constables was absence without leave. In one case, three temporary cadets from J Company were fined £3 apiece for sneaking out of barracks and for 'entering Barracks in an irregular manner' the following day. Other Auxiliaries apparently had trouble getting out of bed: many were fined for being absent from morning parades, and one man from N Company was fined 10 shillings for 'Conduct to the prejudice of good order and Police discipline, i.e. Being in bed at 10.30 hours.' 'Conduct to the prejudice of good order and Police discipline' was a common charge that covered a wide variety of offences. For example, two cadets in J Company were fined £3 for creating a disturbance in a cinema, and a third was fined £5 for 'making an improper burlesque of a superior Officer'.

As might be expected, both temporary cadets and temporary constables were fined for drunkenness: in one case, Temporary Constable J. Curley of Depot Company was fined £7 for being drunk in barracks, being in the officers' mess without permission, and refusing to obey an order. In addition, the temporary cadet in charge of one company's canteen was fined £5 for selling liquor to his comrades on credit. However, a few offenders did not fall into any of these categories. Two temporary cadets were fined and ordered to pay for losing their service revolvers, and another was punished for incurring a debt with a civilian. A temporary constable attached to F Company was fined £1 for threatening a temporary cadet, and a temporary cadet belonging to the same unit was fined £3 for 'using abusive and obscene language to a superior Officer'. Commandant Wood dealt personally with the most serious case: Temporary Cadet J. L. Lamb was fined £5 for 'being in illegal possession of a motor car'. Since this was the same fine imposed for 'making an improper burlesque of a superior Officer', the Commandant seems to have taken a lenient view of auto theft.[91]

Other records make it clear that Lamb's case was not an isolated one. In its weekly review for 11 March 1921, Dublin Castle announced that 'Fines of £30 and £15 were inflicted on four members of the Auxiliary Division, RIC who were found guilty of having entered the premises of the Bank of Ireland, Dunmanway, without authority and of having assaulted two civilians.'[92] In his confidential report for the same month, the RIC's county inspector for County Dublin wrote that two temporary cadets had been arrested for breaking into a shop in Balbriggan and stealing goods.[93] On 14 April, a member of our sample, 2nd Lieutenant C. W. Martin, Royal Air Force, was dismissed following a civil conviction. During the week of 28 April a temporary cadet was found guilty of stealing money and jewellery and sentenced to three months' imprisonment with hard labour.[94] During the week of 28 June a temporary cadet and a temporary constable were sentenced to five years' penal servitude for robbery.[95]

These cases did not include a pair of notorious crimes by Auxiliaries during the Irish insurgency: the robbery of a creamery at Kells, County Dublin, on 10 October 1920, and the wrecking and looting of a licensed grocery store belonging to Protestant Unionists at Robinstown, County Meath, on 9 February 1921. The latter incident has been described in detail many times elsewhere, since it led to the resignation of the Division's first commandant. When Brigadier General Crozier was told of the looting, he took immediate (some would say precipitate) steps, dismissing 21 temporary cadets and arresting 5. The Chief of Police at first approved of the commandant's actions, but then reversed himself, and reinstated the 21 cadets pending an official inquiry. Crozier then resigned. Months later the cadets in question were finally tried by court martial: some of them were convicted, but most were acquitted.[96] As we might expect, the Robinstown affair created a sensation and was debated furiously in both press and Parliament. Here, however, we will consider the stranger and lesser-known case of Major Bruce and the raid on the Kells creamery.

Major Evan Cameron Bruce of the Tank Corps seems to have had a colourful military career. He was a native of Gloucestershire, and thirty years old in 1920. He had served in Russia and the Far East, and was awarded the Japanese Order of the Rising Sun and the Russian Cross of St George and Order of Vladimir, as well as the Distinguished Service Order and the

Military Cross, before he lost his left arm to a gunshot wound in France.[97] Despite this obvious disability, he was allowed to enlist in the Auxiliary Division, where he became a platoon commander with A Company in County Kilkenny. He claimed to have 'a private grudge against Sinn Fein', and this (along with his skill with a revolver) may have recommended the one-armed Bruce to Major Fleming at the RIC's recruiting office in London.[98] Unfortunately for Bruce, he seems to have let his private grudge get the better of him: at some point in the autumn of 1920 Brigadier General Crozier dismissed the one-armed major for 'striking an Irishman without cause'.[99]

On 10 October, Major Bruce and his nephew, Temporary Cadet A. E. T. Bruce, tried to borrow a car from the RIC's county inspector at Innistiogue, County Kilkenny. After County Inspector Whyte turned him down, Major Bruce and his nephew hired a private car and drove back to Thomastown, where they picked up two soldiers, Lieutenant Cooper and Sergeant Blake of the Devonshire Regiment. The four then drove through Kilkenny to the creamery at Kells, where two of them went inside, held up the manager, John Power, and robbed the safe. Major Bruce left Ireland for England on 19 October. He was arrested in Cheltenham on 21 October and charged with stealing £75 from the Kells creamery. He was brought back to Ireland, and tried by court martial at Waterford on 22 December.[100]

During the trial, the creamery manager admitted that he used the safe for his own money, made unrecorded cash advances to customers, borrowed money from the till for his own use, and did not know how much was there on the day of the robbery; as a result, the judge advocate called Power an 'unsatisfactory witness'. Lieutenant Cooper and Sergeant Blake testified that they stayed in the car while Bruce and his nephew raided the creamery. Cooper also testified that Bruce had organised the raid, and that he went along because Bruce told him he was in secret service; however, he admitted under cross-examination that Bruce had made no such claim; instead, Cooper had heard it from another officer, Major Macfie.[101] Bruce's nephew was not called to testify, but a statement by the temporary cadet was entered into evidence. Major Macfie was called to testify, but did not appear, because his car broke down three times on the way to Waterford. In the end, Major Bruce was found guilty of robbery and sentenced to a year in prison. His nephew was tried separately, found guilty, and received a sentence of three months' imprisonment. The major was committed to

Mountjoy on 28 December, and ultimately transferred to Liverpool on 8 August 1921, after the Truce.[102]

Bruce, however, did not take his conviction lying down. On 14 February 1921 he petitioned to see a solicitor to take action against the Crown. In his petition Bruce wrote that he had been staying with Lieutenant Cooper in Thomastown, and asked to be included in any raids. Cooper, he said, had organised the raid on the Kells creamery, but had no car, and could only trust his sergeant: could Bruce find another trustworthy man, and borrow a car from the ADRIC at Innistiogue? Bruce also claimed that he and his nephew had found nothing and taken nothing: Cooper and Blake, he said, had entered the creamery afterwards. Bruce also derided Power's testimony, accusing him of embezzling money from the creamery, and said that Major Macfie would have testified that he never told Lieutenant Cooper that Bruce was in secret service. Finally, Bruce pointed to his previous record: during the war he had handled money in Japan and Russia with no losses, and 'although when I was with the A.F.R.I.C.[103] I was described as the "terror of the district" yet no one ever—with the exception of Power—missed anything after I or my men had raided them and during those raids literally hundreds of pounds passed through my hands on more than one occasion.'[104]

Bruce did not wait for a reply to his Valentine's Day petition. On 9 March 1921 he wrote a second petition, complaining again about irregularities at his trial and attacking the credibility of both the creamery manager and Lieutenant Cooper. Bruce also made an extraordinary accusation: he had 'discovered and obtained proof that these proceedings were taken by the authorities because I knew the whole story of the raid on the Kilkenny mails, having myself been on the raid':

> I believe Mr Tottenham[105] had worked upon the fears of the authorities by saying that I had said that 'it seemed a damn dirty game' when I found him writing 'Censored by the IRA' on the envelopes, and his pointing out that I left the force a few days later and was the only person outside the A.F.R.I.C. who knew the story of the raid.
>
> Now it was rumoured that a large sum of money, between £700 & £1100, was missing when the mailbags were returned, and I knew in whose hands they were from the time the seals were broken until they were returned.[106]

Crozier wrote later in his memoirs that the 'raid on the Kilkenny mails' had taken place sometime in the autumn of 1920, without the knowledge or approval of either Crozier or the commander of A Company, Colonel Kirkwood. According to Crozier, 'a highly placed and very senior official' had ordered a party of Auxiliaries to disguise themselves as Volunteers and raid the Kilkenny post office at night. The Auxiliaries bound and gagged the sorters, took the mailbags back to Innistiogue for examination, and publicly blamed the IRA for the raid. An unknown amount of money was stolen and divided by the raiders, and while some of the mail was subsequently returned, some of it was dumped in a river.[107]

Major Bruce's conspiracy theory is, however, difficult to take seriously. His denials are not very convincing, and Crozier himself was convinced that Bruce was guilty.[108] Bruce's credibility is not helped by his claim that he simply 'left the force' when Crozier had dismissed him for assaulting a civilian. Of course, it is possible that everyone else was lying when they testified at Bruce's court martial. Power may have been embezzling money from the creamery, and he may have blamed the soldiers and police after the raid, to conceal his crime. Lieutenant Cooper and Sergeant Blake may have planned the robbery and made the luckless one-armed major their scapegoat: the two soldiers had the chance to get their stories straight before the trial, while the two Bruces apparently did not. It is also possible that the four men planned the robbery together, and fell out afterwards. Whatever the truth, the case of Major Bruce reflects no credit on the Auxiliary Division. How a man was allowed to enlist in the Division with only one arm (and perhaps a wasted leg as well) has never been explained.[109]

Although historians have devoted most of their attention to Auxiliaries who stole from the Irish people, temporary cadets also stole from the British government. In March 1922 the Treasury was supplied with a list of deficiencies in the accounts of the Auxiliary Division's various companies. E Company's accounts showed a deficiency of £61, which was blamed on a Major Dudley, 'who was in command up to November 1920, and is now being prosecuted for defalcations in his accounts as a regular District Inspector'. G Company's accounts were short more than £291. 'Lt.-Col. Andrews, who has been under notice in connection with various irregularities, is responsible.' Depot Company could not account for over £319 in cash: 'the whole amount is due to the defalcations of ex-Cadet Joslyn, who was convicted by court martial and sentenced to six months' imprisonment for false pretences and falsification of accounts in December 1921.' Worst of all, P Company's accounts were short more than £535: its commander, Captain Johnstone, had received this money as a temporary advance from the commander of Depot Company. Although Johnstone told the company paymaster that he repaid this advance, 'it has now been ascertained that this is not the case'. Johnstone had been granted compensation under the terms of the Criminal Injuries Act, and the government was taking steps to stop the payment of the captain's award.[110]

4.5 A corps de luxe

Even when the Auxiliaries were not actually stealing money from their employers, the Division was a heavy financial drain on the government. Major General Tudor had planned to pay temporary cadets £1 per day, or £365 per year. This was much better than the salaries being offered to ex-officers in civilian life: many positions paid only £250, £200, or even £150 or less per year.[111] Temporary cadets were also offered allowances (about which more later) and one month's leave per year on full pay, with a free railway warrant both ways. Nonetheless, as early as 1 October 1920, a temporary cadet's base pay was raised to one guinea (£1 1s.) per day, apparently to make service in the Division more attractive. When the Treasury complained about the cost of the ADRIC in February 1921 and suggested reducing the base pay for new recruits to £6 per week, they were told this would be impossible. 'Recruiting is bad and recruits must be obtained. The pay is not excessive for suitable men considering the risk and long hours.'[112]

The Division was also unexpectedly costly in other ways. Like members of the regular RIC, members of the temporary forces were entitled to allowances in addition to their wages.[113] Since temporary cadets ranked as sergeants in the RIC, they were paid a sergeant's allowances. In his original scheme, Tudor had planned to pay temporary cadets £7 a week, inclusive of all but travelling and subsistence allowances, and this rate of pay was approved by the Treasury. However, the conditions of service offered to prospective recruits in London mistakenly promised them '£1 per diem with allowances'—full stop. As a result, on 28 August 1920 the Irish government asked the Treasury for sanction to pay an RIC sergeant's rent and boot allowances to temporary cadets: failure to do so, they argued, would be a breach of faith.[114] The Treasury's response was predictably frosty: they thought the original terms had been adequate, and they found nothing in the Irish government's request to indicate otherwise. They demanded an assurance that temporary cadets would not be offered terms that were 'materially different' from those the Treasury had approved, but in this case, 'in view of the fact that public faith is pledged', they grudgingly approved the payment of rent and boot allowances.[115]

The mistaken promise of full allowances proved to be a costly one, both in terms of money and of Treasury goodwill. In some cases, the Irish government was compelled to ask the Treasury for additional funds: in October, for example, Cope requested approval for an RIC sergeant's separation allowance of 2s per night for temporary cadets forced to live apart from their families.[116] In other cases, the Castle tried to avoid additional expenditures. When General Crozier requested his RIC uniform allowance of £50, for example, he was told he would have to get along with an ordinary cadet's uniform, 'with suitable badges'.[117]

In one case, the Castle actually resorted to trickery in the name of economy. RIC constables who were stationed in disturbed districts were entitled to a disturbance allowance of 2s per day. On 19 September 1920, Crozier wrote to inform Tudor that the question of disturbance allowances had 'arisen again'. Since the Auxiliaries were promised £1 a day plus allowances, they naturally felt entitled to the disturbance allowance. 'I am sure there will be a lot [of] complaints amongst this force if this is not allowed,' said Crozier, 'and I personally think they are perfectly entitled to it.'[118] Tudor suggested paying the allowance at a reduced rate, but somehow it was decided to pay the men a sergeant's plainclothes allowance of 5s per week instead, 'in view of the work which they are from time to time required to carry out in plain clothes'.[119] The Treasury approved this request, and Dublin Castle may well have congratulated itself on its little deception: the Auxiliaries would be pleased with their additional pay, and the Treasury, if not pleased, would be less displeased with 5s per week than it would have been with 14s per week.

Unfortunately, this little deception came back to haunt the Castle a few months later. On 7 February 1921 Cope wrote to the Treasury to request a pay raise for the Division's new assistant commandant, Lieutenant Colonel Guard.[120] Like every member of the Division, Guard was being paid 5s per week for plainclothes work, and 1s 6d per week as a boot allowance. As a married man, he was also being paid a rent allowance of 11s 6d per week, and a separation allowance of 2s per night. His allowances added up to £83 6s per year. Unfortunately for Guard, and for Cope, the Treasury replied to this minute with three questions, the third of which was: why was the assistant commandant receiving a plainclothes allowance?[121]

Cope's initial reply was disingenuous: 'Command allowances,' he wrote, 'are paid in addition to ordinary allowances. Not to pay the ordinary allowances would result in higher command allowances.'[122] However, the Treasury would not be fobbed off. On 26 February they sent a long minute to Dublin Castle complaining that married cadets were being paid allowances amounting to £83 6s per annum, all because the Irish government had mistakenly offered more generous terms than the Treasury had allowed:

> My Lords are aware that at the time it was necessary to make out a case for extra allowances; recruiting was urgent, and men would not come without financial inducement; the position of the Crown Forces in Ireland, especially with winter coming on, was serious; it was originally hoped to get bachelors only; but when a large part, if not the majority, or recruits proud [sic] to be married men, some extra allowance was clearly called for to meet the liability of separation.
>
> But it appears to Their Lordships very doubtful whether these special reasons still apply. Recruits are coming in freely; unemployment is serious all over the United Kingdom; wages are falling.[123]

The minute concluded with the Treasury's suggestion that the pay of new recruits be reduced to £6 a week with allowances. Furthermore, the Treasury continued to press Cope on the issue of the plainclothes allowance. On 8 March, Waterfield wrote: 'I am to point out that the allowance was originally intended to compensate Temporary Cadets for the wear and tear of plain clothes necessarily worn while on duty under certain conditions involving hard wear of their clothing. I am to enquire to what extent these conditions still continue and for what portion of their service on what occasions plain clothes are now worn by temporary cadets, both officers and other ranks, while on duty.'[124] Since the plainclothes allowance had actually been intended as a substitute for the more generous disturbance allowance, it is perhaps not surprising that Dublin Castle tried to avoid answering these questions.[125]

Pressure from the Treasury over these and other financial problems involving the Auxiliary Division may have prompted Cope's outrage over the *Shannon* affair. On 16 November 1920 Lieutenant Colonel R. J. Andrews, commander of G Company in County Clare, commandeered the *Shannon*, a steamship that was the property of the Board of Public Works. On 2 February 1921, Andrews relinquished command of G Company and was replaced by another officer, Lieutenant Colonel Hemming. Hemming decided that the *Shannon* was 'too slow, old, and expensive' for G Company's purposes, and decided to return the boat to its owners. Before he could do so, however, the *Shannon*'s crew of Auxiliaries ran it aground and damaged its bottom on 9 February 1921. Hemming sent the ship into drydock in Limerick, obtained three estimates for the cost of repairs, and accepted the least expensive estimate. Once repairs were completed, Hemming handed the *Shannon* back to the Board of Works, and billed ADRIC headquarters for £56.[126] However, the Board of Works then submitted a claim for over £2,200 to repair their ship and over £574 for stores consumed or missing, along with other expenses.[127]

When Hemming submitted his report on this affair to Dublin Castle, Cope replied with an angry minute to the RIC's director of personnel services:

> I am afraid I cannot accept Hemming's report as satisfactory. I think it most unsatisfactory for he has not met the charge made by the Bd. of Works that a large quantity of goods of considerable value are missing. The Bd. of Works refers to Blankets, Quilts, Mattresses &c. as missing.
>
> Further: On whose authority did Hemming pay £56 for repairs. The boat was the property of the Bd. of Works—a Government Dept.—& his duty was to hand her over & leave her for the Bd. of Works to get her repaired. He exceeded his duty very considerably & he must be told that he is nothing more than OC of an Auxiliary Company & as such is not empowered to spend Govt. money at his own sweet will. He should put his difficulties up to H.Qrs. & get instructions in matters which need not be decided off hand. I should be grateful if you should so inform him & tell him that if he repeats this kind of thing he will be cleared out. We really can't stand this sort of thing. These fellows have got to understand that we will not tolerate the expenditure of public money without our prior consent. I have had (& so have you) more than enough of Col. Andrews and his ilk. The furnishing of the Lakeside Hotel without the knowledge of H.Qrs. is monstrous.[128] Will you please tell me the date when Andrews resigned from the Division. He should have been sacked & not allowed to resign.[129]

Cope's frustration is easy to understand. By the spring of 1921 the Division had become a scandal. General Crozier had resigned, and like the Opposition was denouncing the government for raising a force of bashi-bazouks. To make matters worse, the Division's accounts were in complete disarray, and Castle officials were forced to clean up numerous other financial messes besides the *Shannon* affair. By 30 June, for example, it was determined that the Division could not account for over four thousand pounds' worth of arms and equipment, including seventy-two bayonets, seventy .45 revolvers, fifty-six .38 revolvers, three 12-gauge repeating shotguns, and two .303 service rifles.[130] Ultimately, the government wrote off the whole amount. 'It is to be regretted,' said Mark Sturgis, 'that the deficiencies are partly due to the fact that no accurate record was kept in the early days of the Division of store accounting transactions or of articles lost either by hostile attack or by members of the Division, in circumstances excusable or otherwise.'[131]

Even small sums were causing nagging problems. In November 1920, for example, the 2nd Battalion of the Manchester Regiment had issued £15 17s 9d worth of rations to an Auxiliary platoon. The regiment was never paid for these rations, and in the spring of 1921 the Army asked the ADRIC to settle this platoon's mess bill. Between 23 March and 7 October 1921 over two dozen letters and minutes went back and forth between the Army, the police, and the Castle as they squabbled over who should pay this minuscule amount. Finally, Alfred Cope settled the matter by paying the bill out of the Auxiliary Division's fines fund.[132]

The temporary cadets in question had not paid their mess bill because almost all of them were dead. The Manchester Regiment had issued rations to No. 2 Platoon of C Company, stationed at Macroom, County Cork. On the afternoon of 28 November 1920 most of the men in this platoon had gone out on patrol in two Crossley tenders, and been ambushed by the IRA's west Cork flying column, led by Tom Barry. The guerrillas were waiting at a bend in the road near the village of Kilmichael. While his men took cover behind stone fences on both sides, Barry stood out in the road, wearing a Volunteer officer's tunic, trench coat, and leggings. When the first Auxiliary vehicle came around the bend, they saw Barry waving, mistook him for a British officer, and slowed up. Barry threw a grenade, and his men opened fire.

Within a few minutes, all of the cadets in the leading Crossley were dead and wounded. The following vehicle tried to turn around and get away, but got stuck, and then came under fire itself. The remaining Auxiliaries fought back, but were soon overwhelmed. When it was all over, 16 of the 20 men in No. 2 Platoon had been killed, along with 3 men of the west Cork flying column.[133] We will now turn our attention to battles like the Kilmichael ambush, and see how other Black and Tans and the Auxiliaries fared in combat with their enemies in the Irish Republican Army.

5

One-Sided War

Police and Auxiliaries in Combat

What was it like to fight in the Irish War of Independence? This question has been answered many times, but only by members and supporters of the Irish Republican Army.[1] We know what it was like to fight as a guerrilla; we do not know what it was like to fight as a policeman. Unlike their opponents, the Irish and British men of the Royal Irish Constabulary and its Auxiliary Division have left almost no memoirs. However, they did give evidence to military courts of inquiry into the deaths of their comrades, and their depositions paint a vivid picture of guerrilla warfare from the police perspective. This picture is quite different from the battle pieces of republican memoirists and popular historians. There are no carefully laid plans, and no tense periods of waiting for the enemy to appear; the police are the victims, not the attackers; there are few victories, but many casualties. From the police perspective, the Irish insurgency was a one-sided war. The guerrillas did most of the killing, and the police did most of the dying. When we appreciate this, we can better understand why the police began to take the reprisals that did so much to blacken their name and discredit their cause.

5.1 'A volley of shots rang out'

The best way to start is with a close look at a single battle. On the morning of 13 November 1920 seven constables drove away from Tipperary RIC barracks in a Crossley tender, heading out of town. Constable Derwent Wallace was at the wheel, and Constable Patrick Mackessy was in the passenger seat. The remaining five constables rode in the box: Charles

Buntrock, William Buntrock, Patrick Fardy, John Miller, and Jeremiah O'Leary. The patrol was a mixed group; some of the men were veterans, and some were new recruits. Some of them were Peelers, and some were Black and Tans. O'Leary was a Cork man who had served in the RIC for ten years. Mackessy, from County Kerry, had been a constable for nine years. Miller was an Irishman from County Wicklow but had only served with the force for six months. The Buntrock brothers were Black and Tans from England. Both of them had joined the RIC less than a month before, on 15 October, and had been allocated to the South Riding of County Tipperary on 7 November. There was no sergeant with the group. As the senior constable, O'Leary was probably in charge.

There is no record of the patrol's orders, but their mission seems to have been to reconnoitre the roads to the west and south of Tipperary. The patrol drove northwest to Limerick Junction, where it turned left and proceeded west to Emly. After calling at Emly they turned left again and drove south to Galbally. At Galbally they made another left turn and headed east, through the Glen of Aherlow in the shadow of the Galty Mountains, to Lisvernane. Beyond Lisvernane their penultimate destination was Bansha, where a final left turn would put them on the road back to Tipperary.

The patrol's route must have been too well travelled by the RIC. At about 12:45 in the afternoon the seven constables drove into an ambush at Inches Cross, two or three miles between Lisvernane and Bansha. Dozens of Irish Volunteers armed with rifles, shotguns, and revolvers were waiting for them behind a fence on the right side of the road. Only three policemen survived the battle that followed: Wallace, Fardy, and William Buntrock. Two days later, on 15 November, the three gave evidence at a court of inquiry into the death of Constable Miller. Later, Buntrock and Fardy gave evidence against a number of men who were arrested in connection with the ambush. The following account is based on these depositions.[2]

The police were taken completely by surprise. None of the survivors reported seeing or hearing anything until the rebels opened fire, though some of the ambushers may have fired prematurely. At the court of inquiry William Buntrock testified that 'a few shots rang out, and shortly afterwards a volley', but later he said simply that 'without warning, a volley of rifle shots was fired at us'. None of the other police reported hearing any premature shots. Fardy testified at first that 'shots rang out along the road behind the ditch', and later simply that 'a volley of shots rang out from the right hand side of the road'. The driver, Wallace, said simply that 'a volley rang out'.

Remarkably, none of the police were killed or even wounded by this initial volley. However, a bullet or a slug hit the Crossley's steering gear and disabled it. The tender continued down the road for another 10 to 30 yards before it swerved into the ditch on the left side of the road, hit the fence, and stopped. Fardy later stated that 'I got up and jumped out and told some of the others that it would be better to get down on the ground.' His testimony at the court of inquiry did a better job of conveying the urgency of the situation: 'I jumped out and said to the tothers [*sic*] "Get on the ground."' William Buntrock said that 'all of the men tumbled out except myself'. For some reason, he remained in the car. The remainder of the patrol got down in the ditch, and all of them started to return fire with their service rifles.

The situation was hopeless. The police were exposed, without any cover but their tender, and they were heavily outnumbered. Nonetheless, the battle continued for between 25 and 30 minutes. The survivors could supply few details of the engagement. Wallace said only that 'I with the others got down by the side of the car and returned the fire.' Buntrock said that 'I lay down by the driver's seat and fired several shots through the body of the car at the men inside the fence. I lay there for about half an hour and with the others of my party kept firing away for that time.' At the court of inquiry he mentioned that 'The enemy fired at us with rifles and shot guns and threw five bombs.' Fardy provided the greatest number of details. 'I got down on my knee at the side of the lorry,' he said, 'and opened fire around the end of the lorry between the lorry and the ditch. Constable O'Leary was at my side and one or two more immediately behind me. I remember firing until Const. O'Leary was hit by a bullet, and just after my arm was broken by a bullet; we were then firing for about twenty minutes.' At the court of inquiry Fardy mentioned that, after O'Leary had been wounded, 'He kept on saying "Keep on firing." He fell over on my heels against the ditch.'

By this time, at least five of the seven constables had been killed or wounded. Buntrock said that, after half an hour 'I then heard some of our men groaning painfully and asking us to surrender as they, owing to wounds, could not put up any further defence, and they were being shot at without being able to reply.' Fardy recalled that 'shortly after my being wounded the firing of the police ceased, but the attackers kept on firing for some time. All this time one of the police, whom I believe to be Const. [Charles] Buntrock, was under the car and evidently in great pain. I heard someone of the police say "surrender", but this had no effect on the attackers, who kept on firing.' The police stopped firing, and William Buntrock put up his hands, but the ambushers kept shooting for another 15 minutes. According to the Black and Tan, the Volunteer leader shouted for his party to cease fire, 'but his men took no notice of it, but kept firing away for about a quarter of an hour afterwards, and I saw the leader come out on the road before his men obeyed his order'. Fardy agreed that the shooting continued until 'the leaders of the civilians told them to come out and cease fire'. At this point, between 20 and 30 Volunteers emerged from cover and advanced on the defeated police.

The surviving constables noted that the Volunteers seemed very young, between eighteen and twenty years old, and were dressed like farmers' sons. Fardy was handled roughly, and admitted afterwards that he was afraid for his life:

> When all the firing had ceased a man came up, caught me by the broken arm, lifted me to my feet, and searched me, going through my pockets. I had nothing but some money and an empty pocket book. The man asked the leader something about the money and the leader said, 'don't touch it'. The man who searched me then told me to make an act of contrition and to prepare to die; he had a Webley pattern revolver in his hand. I was fully expecting that he would shoot me, and was then saying my prayers. This man took away my rifle and ammunition and also my belt and then left me.

Once the Volunteers had disarmed the police, they splashed gasoline on the Crossley tender and set it on fire. Buntrock recalled that:

> Const. O'Leary was then lying dead under the motorcar, and I asked them to let me pull him from under it: they gave me permission, and I then pulled him a short distance away from the car. A bullet seemed to have gone through the petrol tank, as a stream of petrol was around Const. Mackessy, so that when the car took fire this petrol also went on fire, and as it was setting fire to Const. Mackessy I ran and dragged him away. He was then alive and his hair was lighting but I quenched it with my hands. He lived for a short time after that but didn't speak.

'I have no doubt,' he concluded bitterly, 'but that the attackers would have left Constables O'Leary and Mackessy to be burnt under the car only I pulled them away.'

The ambush party went away through the fields, and William Buntrock, who seems to have been the sole unwounded survivor, went ahead to

Bansha to get help from the police barracks there. Fardy recalled that once the ambush party had retreated:

> I and another of the wounded Constables then went to look for help and found one house empty. At the next house there were three men inside who refused to let us in. I told them of one man dying above and the others dead but they refused to go. I then went to another house about 100 yards further on the road. The woman there was very kind, and when Const. Miller arrived badly wounded about an hour later she put him to bed.

Mackessy and O'Leary died at the scene. Charles Buntrock and Miller were rescued and taken to Tipperary military hospital, but Buntrock died of his wounds later that afternoon, and Miller died the following day. According to a report published in the *Daily Telegraph* on Monday, 15 November, 'when news of the occurrence reached Tipperary four lorries packed with soldiers and police proceeded to the scene and scoured the country around. It is reported that a cottage in the neighbourhood was set on fire, on the allegation that the wounded police had been refused shelter.'[3]

5.2 Assassinations and ambushes

Throughout the Irish War of Independence, the RIC and ADRIC took part in four types of combat: ambushes, assassinations, barracks battles, and encounter battles. Ambushes occurred when the guerrillas attacked a group of three or more police. Assassinations occurred when the guerrillas attacked one or two police. Barracks battles occurred when the guerrillas attacked a police barracks. In each of these cases, the guerrillas were on the strategic offensive: they chose when and where to fight, and often took the police by surprise. Furthermore, when they laid ambushes for police patrols, the guerrillas were on the tactical defensive: they were under cover, with weapons at the ready, while the police were caught in the open and unprepared. In a barracks battle, the situation was partly reversed: though the rebels were still on the strategic offensive, the police were on the tactical defensive. Encounter battles occurred when the police went on the strategic offensive and encountered guerrillas who were not prepared for combat.

At least 39 Black and Tans and Auxiliaries were assassinated in the Irish War of Independence. Not many of these 39 were killed in the line of duty, and the circumstances of their deaths can only loosely be described as combat. Some of them were simply executed, like temporary cadets Frank Garniss and Cecil Morris. The two cadets were members of the group that stumbled across the raid on 22 Lower Mount Street in Dublin on Bloody Sunday, 21 November 1920. Garniss and Morris were sent back to Beggars Bush barracks for help, but another group of Volunteers caught them on the way, took them around the back of No. 16 Lower Mount Street, and shot them dead.

A resident at No. 16 heard what happened. Earlier, he was in his bedroom with his brother, stropping his razor, when the door was opened and someone told him to put his hands up. The command was followed by a shot from a revolver. The bullet missed the witness and hit the wall, but was fired so close that the flash blinded him. Four men came into the room and questioned him. Who was he? Where did he come from? Where did he work? Were there any other men in the house? Once they were satisfied, they ordered the witness and his brother to stay where they were, and left.

About two minutes later, the witness heard noises in his backyard: voices, then shouted commands, followed by six or seven quick shots. He risked a look out the window, and saw five men escaping through the paddock out back. Then, according to the official report, he went out into the garden, 'and saw the dead bodies of the two Cadets against the side of the house. One was in a sitting posture against the wall, & the other was lying on his right side with his head on the legs of the first body.' Both men had been shot in the head.[4] Garniss and Morris had joined the ADRIC in September. They were the third and fourth members of the Division to die.

Many of the remaining 37 men were killed just as suddenly. Constables George Cuthberton and Walter Shaw, for example, were shot down in a country lane on the afternoon of Sunday, 1 May 1921. The two Black and Tans left their barracks at Arvagh, County Cavan, at about 11.30 a.m. to go for a walk. Gunfire was heard about one o'clock in the afternoon. Since the two constables had not come back, a search party went out along the Longford road at 5.30 p.m. Their bodies were found on the road in the township of Fihora, stripped of their revolvers, ammunition, and handcuffs.

According to the official report, both men had been killed hours before their bodies were found. Shaw had been shot three times. Cuthberton had been shot six times. Around the time the two constables left their barracks, six armed Volunteers had occupied a farmer's house in Fihora. They told the women of the house not to be frightened, and took up firing positions both upstairs and downstairs. Some time after noon, the gunmen opened fire from the windows of the house and left immediately afterwards. Apparently, the farmer found the bodies of the two constables dead in the road when he returned to his house later that afternoon, but left them where they lay.[5]

As these cases indicate, most assassinations are not well documented. Since the victims were alone, there were no police witnesses. Civilian witnesses were few, and had little to say. Captured rebels were understandably reluctant to tell their side of the story to military courts of inquiry. In one case, however, two Black and Tans named Hubbard and McKibbin fought their attackers hand-to-hand and escaped to tell the tale. On 10 April 1921 the pair was picnicking with two Irish women near Athlone, County Roscommon, when two Volunteers held them up. McKibbin said:

> I grabbed my revolver which I had on the grass beside me & aiming it at the man I pulled the trigger it snapped but didn't go off. Immediately I made to jump to my feet & as I did so he fired and hit me in the hip. I staggered to my feet & as I did so he fired at me again. I then tried to fire back at him but as I did so my lady friend got between us so I couldn't fire in case I hit her.

Constable Hubbard was also shot and stunned by a bullet that grazed his head. 'On gathering myself up,' he said, 'I found the lady I was with struggling with this man. I then rushed him a hand to hand fight followed in which I got my man to the ground there I succeeded in taking his revolver from him also my own.' The Volunteer who shot Constable McKibbin rushed off to help his comrade. McKibbin said that:

> I got to the spot as soon as I could and I saw [Constable Hubbard] on the ground in grips with a man, and one of the young ladies was trying to take the revolver of another man he being the one that had attacked me. He had me partly covered with his revolver and I couldn't fire for fear of hitting the young lady. The next thing I noticed was [Constable Hubbard] putting three rounds into the man who he was struggling with.

Hubbard was shot again in the back, before the Volunteers retreated under fire from McKibbin. At that point, however, the two Black and Tans noticed another group of men nearby, and in McKibbin's words, they 'thought it best to get away'. They ran to the police barracks in Athlone, where they reported the incident and handed over the automatic pistol that Hubbard had taken from his attacker. Both men were hospitalized. Their women friends were not injured in the incident, but apparently suffered a reprisal for walking out with policemen. According to the local district inspector, 'the two ladies who accompanied the two Police on this occasion are employed in Mr Burgess's drapery establishment Athlone':

> A few days after this occurrence they were both discharged by Mr. Burgess in consequence, it is alleged, of his having received a threatening letter. I inquired into the matter, and no threatening letter could be produced. It is also alleged that the 'Black and Tans' visited him and asked to have the two girls taken back. This has been done and the girls are now back in Mr. Burgess's shop.

To the researcher's dismay, the district inspector concluded that 'I have taken no written statements from these girls, and I do not intend to bring them as witnesses in the case, as I consider there is sufficient evidence without them.'[6]

Most of the police testimony preserved at the PRO concerns ambushes, and their evidence makes it plain that the battle at Inches Cross was fairly typical. For the police, ambushes began suddenly and unexpectedly, when the guerrillas opened fire. 'Without warning,' said Buntrock, 'a volley of rifle shots was fired at us.' 'A volley of shots rang out from the right hand side of the road,' said Fardy. Words like these recur again and again in the testimony of ambush survivors. After he was ambushed in County Cork, a Peeler named Flaherty reported hearing a shot behind him, 'and then a burst of about fifteen shots'.[7] After he was ambushed in County Kerry, Constable Bergin reported hearing 'a single shot followed immediately by a volley'.[8]

In other cases, battles opened with sudden explosions. On 1 February 1921 a convoy of Auxiliaries was on patrol near Clonfin Bridge in County Longford when the IRA detonated a road mine in front of their lead vehicle, killing the driver instantly. One of the ambushers later described the scene:

> In a brief space of time two lorries of Auxies approached. The mine on being exploded blew the front part off the first lorry up, bringing it to a standstill and throwing out the occupants. The second lorry pulled up behind this and concentrated rifle fire was brought to bear on it. Its occupants jumped, and dived for cover, a good many of them knocked out as they did so. Cover at this point was scarce. They got their Lewis gun into operation immediately, but after a few bursts, the gunner was knocked out and the guns did not get into action any more.[9]

One Auxiliary, Cadet Wilford, later said that 'as soon as we recovered from the shock of the explosion, we jumped out of the Tender, some of us running into a ditch on the inside of the road, and some on the off side'.

Cadet Wase 'fired a few shots from the Tender and then jumped out and took cover near a ditch on the left hand side of the road upon which we were travelling'. Other cadets described how they 'vacated our Tenders at once' and 'dashed to the sides of the road'. However, like the RIC at Inches Cross, the Auxiliaries at Clonfin were almost completely exposed. Cadet Wase said that they had 'practically no cover', Cadet Williamson stated that the cover was 'very poor', while Cadet Maddox noted that they 'took what cover there was alongside the road, this was found to be inadequate, and so we laid in the open'. One cadet, Keeble, stated that 'I tumbled out of the Tender, crawled underneath for cover, and commenced firing in the direction from where I could see spurts of flame coming from the attackers rifles.' However, he soon regretted this move: 'Whilst under the Tender, a shot from the ambushers burst the tyre of the rear wheel which I was firing through. I saw fit to change my position,' he said. After a ferocious battle lasting 30 minutes, the Auxiliaries ran out of ammunition and were forced to surrender: two of them had been killed, and two later died of their wounds; another seven were wounded but survived.[10]

Quite often, the police could not see their enemies clearly. On the night of 8 September 1920 four police were patrolling on foot in the town of Tullow, County Carlow, when 10 or 15 Volunteers appeared out of nowhere, shouted 'hands up' and started shooting. Later, Sergeant Warrington said: 'I returned fire and one of two men who had me covered turned on the roads and ran towards the right hand side of the road; during the firing I saw a man fall face downwards on the road and remain motionless, the firing was then very rapid, and I could not say at the time if it was a policeman or civilian.' The two survivors later admitted that they could not identify the men who attacked them in the dark, even though some of the guerrillas were unmasked.[11]

Even by day, the insurgents were frequently invisible. On 4 April 1920 three constables named Finn, McCarthy, and Byrne were ambushed in County Tipperary. The trio were cycling from Rearcross to Newport when they came under fire in Lackamore Wood. Constable Byrne was wounded in the right shoulder and knocked into a fence on the side of the road. He said: 'I saw Finn and McCarthy lying on the road, and I scrambled over the fence. I heard McCarthy saying, "Oh stop! Stop!!" I took cover behind the fence and drew my revolver and fired into the wood, from where I saw the flashes.'[12] Ten months later, Auxiliaries who survived the ambush at Clonfin Bridge also talked about shooting at the 'flashes' and 'spurts of flame' from the guerrillas' rifles. Two days after Clonfin Bridge, on 3 February 1921 a group of four constables were ambushed while cycling back to their barracks in Ballinhassig, County Cork. One of the two survivors, Constable Flaherty, said: 'I dismounted and without looking back I made for cover on the river side of the road. Thence I fired six shots from my revolver into a clump of small trees about 50 yards from me, where I thought the attackers might be.' Flaherty fired another 14 shots before he escaped, but admitted afterwards that he never caught sight of any of the ambushers.[13]

In some cases, however, the police could see their attackers plainly. A large cycle patrol, for example, was ambushed near Castlemaine, County Kerry, on 1 June 1921. Two constables named Bergin and Cooney were close to the front of the column. They were jumping off their bicycles when Cooney was hit: 'He fell on his face,' said Bergin, 'and I never saw him move afterwards.'

> I knelt down and opened fire. After firing two shots I was myself wounded in the left leg. I fell on my face. I regained a kneeling position and I saw a man in civilian clothes firing at Constable Cooney. He had a rifle. I had a clear view of his head and shoulders. He was the width of the road from me—about 7 or 8 yards. He was dressed in a rain coat and a cap pulled down on one side of his face. I fired at him with my revolver and he ducked down behind the hedge and I saw him no more. I threw a Mill's [*sic*] bomb in his direction and then ran down the road towards the rear of the patrol, where I saw some of the patrol putting up a fight.

Back at the rear of the patrol, two constables named Bowles and Foley were fighting a desperate close-range battle with the guerrillas. 'I saw two men in civilian clothes behind the bank on the other side of the road,' said Constable Bowles. 'Each of them fired point blank at me with rifles.' When Bergin arrived on the scene, he saw 'Constable Bowles firing at a civilian who was behind a bank on the other side of the road. About 8 yards away on the right of Constable Bowles I saw Constable Foley who was standing in the road. I saw him throw a bomb in the direction of the civilian.' When the grenade exploded, both Bergin and Bowles climbed up onto the bank and shot at the Volunteers, who ran away. Bowles said afterwards that 'I had a good view of the two civilians for about 2 minutes when I was wounded in the back.' Bergin said that 'I fired at the two civilians as they ran, with no effect.' The battle had lasted between 30 and

45 minutes. Five of the 12 police in the patrol had been killed, and another 5 had been wounded.[14]

In other cases the police not only saw their attackers but also knew them by name. On 22 March 1921 a Sergeant named Reilly was leading a small cycle patrol from Keadue to Ballyfarnon in County Roscommon when it was ambushed. One of Reilly's men, Constable Tully, said:

> I saw Constable Devereux look over the wall on the left hand side of the road, into the laurel trees, as he did, I heard a shot ring out from the laurels, and saw the smoke blow by near him. I saw him then put up his hands and heard him shout ah! Immediately a shot rang out behind me, and several shots fired in quick succession.

Sergeant Reilly dropped his bicycle and ran for the gate of a nearby Protestant church. As he ran he was shot and wounded in the head, and was knocked down. Once he got up and was through the gate, he ran into a local man he recognized, named Dockery. 'I said "Dockery you scoundrel is this the work you are at", he said "Don't shoot me" and retreated a few yards. A man behind me jumped on my back, gripped my two arms, and Dockery returned, caught the lanyard of my revolver and pulled at it until he succeeded in bursting my shoulder strap and took the revolver.' Reilly fought free of Dockery and the second man, saw more Volunteers armed with shotguns in the churchyard, and fled to the Rectory, pursued by his attackers. 'I managed to get into the Rev. Mr Boyd's house which was only a few yards from me,' he said, 'the attackers followed me near the door, I closed the door and got a bomb ready, I opened the door again and got throwing the bomb between them, immediately after they fired at the door which was followed by the explosion of the bomb.' The Volunteers retreated after Reilly's grenade exploded, and both Reilly and Constable Tully got away.[15]

A policeman was lucky if he escaped unhurt from such an ambush. Police casualties in the Irish War of Independence were not heavy overall. According to the figures provided by Dublin Castle to the British government, 890 policemen were killed and wounded between July 1920 and July 1921 (see Table 5.1).[16] This was less than 10 per cent of a force of ten to twelve thousand. However, combat was extremely dangerous for the police, and casualties among those police who were *involved* in combat were high. Only 34 per cent of police who were attacked by the IRA escaped unharmed; 42 per cent were wounded, and 24 per cent were killed. In some cases,

Table 5.1. Proportions of dead, wounded, and unharmed among RIC and ADRIC engaged in combat with IRA, July 1920–July 1921.

	Unharmed	Wounded	Killed	Total
All police	455	566	324	1,345
	34%	42%	24%	100%
Wounded and killed police	—	566	324	890
	—	64%	36%	100%

Source: Outrages, 4 July 1920–17 July 1921, PRO, CO 904/148–50. These proportions correspond closely to the figures provided by C. J. C. Street: Unharmed 326 (33%), Wounded 428 (44%), Killed 326 (23%); C. J. C. Street, *Ireland in 1921* (London, Philip Alan & Co., 1922), 7.

almost all of the police engaged were killed or wounded, like the six out of seven at Inches Cross. In addition, the proportion of dead to wounded among police casualties was high—almost 1:2. The proportion of dead to wounded among British soldiers in the Great War, by comparison, had been 1:3.[17] In Cork, the most violent county in Ireland, the proportion of dead to wounded among police casualties was almost 1:1.[18]

These high proportions were caused by a number of factors. As we have seen, the police were usually outnumbered and caught by surprise. Most battles began with a volley from the guerrillas, and many police were killed and wounded before they could take cover and return fire. Another important factor was the type of weapons used by both sides. The Great War was mostly fought at long range, with artillery. Shrapnel balls and shell splinters caused the majority of wounds suffered by British soldiers on the Western Front, and most British casualties in the Great War were wounded and killed at random. The Irish War of Independence, on the other hand, was mostly fought at close range, with handguns and grenades. Police casualties in Ireland usually suffered from deadlier bullet wounds, and the police were deliberately shot, sometimes execution-style, especially if they were alone or in pairs.

5.3 Barracks and encounter battles

Casualties were much lower in barracks battles, when the police were defending fortified positions—heavily fortified, if they followed instructions from RIC headquarters in the spring of 1920. Bombing holes were opened in gable walls without windows, to allow police to throw grenades at attackers outside.[19] Later, barbed-wire obstacles were placed at the bases of these walls, and trip wires were laid all around barracks. Doors were plated with steel, and blocked with barricades of sandbags or shell boxes filled with gravel, to prevent more than one man from entering the station at a time. Windows were protected by steel shutters or sandbags, with loopholes for firing, and covered with wire netting to prevent attackers from throwing grenades inside.[20] Further improvements were added in the autumn. Peepholes or periscopes were used to keep raiders from rushing the station doors by surprise. Holes were cut into roofs and protected with sandbags or steel, to let the police bomb and shoot guerrillas attacking from the roofs of adjoining houses.[21] Hollyford RIC barracks, one of the first to be attacked by the IRA in Tipperary, embodied most of these improvements—and more. According to Dan Breen's memoir, 'its ground floor level was about six feet higher than the ground outside, and this ruled out all possibility of a break-in through the walls', while 'the rear gable-end was fortified by a long lean-to building. On the whole,' he concluded, 'it looked a tough nut to crack.'[22]

Not all police barracks, however, were so formidable. Instructions from headquarters make it clear that their commands were not always followed. The March circular noted that in many cases where windows had been covered with steel shutters, 'the loop-holes are placed opposite the iron bars outside, or opposite a wooden sash of the window. Care should be taken in the fitting of steel shutters in the future that this defect does not occur, as it is calculated to interfere with accurate shooting.' The same circular noted that 'sandbag work, though much improved is still defective in some stations. The bags are often filled too full and not beaten or built in regular courses. They should be filled with gravel or sand instead of clay, and built in double instead of single formation. The latter is no defence as it is not bullet proof.'[23] The November circular noted that 'in some cases lately, e.g. at Schull, one of the doors was not properly fortified by shell boxes'.[24] It also complained that police did not fully realise the importance of barbed-wire entanglements and trip wires, and directed them to improve these defences 'in every way possible'.[25]

Other sources confirm this haphazard state of affairs. Kilmallock RIC barracks in County Limerick was attacked and burned on the night of 27/28 May 1920. Afterwards the local district inspector noted that 'the V shaped iron shutters erected in 1867 on this Barrack' had withstood the rifle bullets of the IRA, 'while the flat plates recently erected did not'.[26] Michael Brennan was one of the raiders that night, and saw the light of the fire inside shining through bullet holes in the steel shutters.[27] In County Kerry, Constable Jeremiah Mee discovered that not even the walls of his police hut were bullet proof. In May 1920 the two Black and Tans who had been stationed with him decided to test their defences by shooting at the hut with their carbines. After the men had fired 12 shots apiece, the hut looked undamaged from the outside, but the bullets had gone right through the walls. 'The destruction inside was complete,' said Mee, 'and even the Black and Tans were slightly shocked when they saw it. It was not the state of the hut, however, that annoyed them but the fact that the hut was not "impregnable". What the people of the district thought of the R.I.C. shooting at their own barracks I do not know but I have no doubt that it caused some alarm among those law-abiding citizens.'[28]

Even well-fortified stations were not impregnable. Tom Barry's west Cork flying column attacked Roscarberry barracks in the early hours of 31 March 1921. They began their assault by detonating a large bomb in front of the station's front door. Sergeant Ambrose Shea was asleep in the dayroom, on the ground floor at the front of the station. A Black and Tan, Constable Charles Bowles, was on the first floor, in a room right above the door. A man in the next room later testified that 'when the explosion occurred the occupants of these two upper rooms were thrown onto the ground floor along with the wreckage and furniture of the two rooms and the interior walls of the building':

> With considerable difficulty the witness struggled free from beneath the debris. The bulk of the wreckage including the brick walls fell on the spot where Sergeant Shea was sleeping. The witness heard Constable Bowles calling for help from beneath the wreckage, but they were quite unable to render him assistance owing to the mass of debris, and the continued action of the attackers from a distance of 15 yards.

A fierce battle followed, as both sides fought at close range with rifles, revolvers, and hand grenades. The police were driven upstairs, and the guerrillas occupied the ground floor. The guerrillas fired up through the ceiling, set off more bombs trying to bring down the first floor, and set the barracks on fire. After five hours the police finally surrendered. Out of 22 defenders, 9 were wounded—three seriously. Ambrose and Bowles were killed. A doctor was present when the ruins of Roscarberry RIC barracks were excavated on 1 April and 6 April 1921. 'On the former date,' he reported, 'parts of the flesh and bones of one human body were exhumed and on the latter date charred human bones were found. He had examined both sets of remains, but it was quite impossible to establish any individual identity although he personally knew both of the police officers also who were lost in the debris.'[29]

But not many stations were lost like Roscarberry: in most barracks battles the police emerged victorious. According to Irish Office statistics, 243 occupied police stations were damaged between 1 July 1920 and 11 July 1921, but only 13 were destroyed.[30] A graduate student who checked weekly newspaper reports of about 100 attacks on police stations during this period found that only 11 stations were captured or destroyed.[31] In addition, police losses in barracks battles were low. Indeed, Constable Bowles was the only Black and Tan killed in a barracks battle during the Irish War of Independence.

The police were even more successful when they could seize the initiative and take the offensive, both strategically and tactically. When surprised and faced with superior numbers, most insurgents either surrendered or tried to escape. But the guerrillas were not often surprised. In its brief history of the insurgency in southern Ireland, the general staff of the 6th Division listed 177 attacks on police and mixed forces by the guerrillas, and only 12 attacks on the guerrillas by police and mixed forces.[32]

Still, some encounter battles were fought. The results were mixed. Three weeks before the ambush at Clonfin, on the afternoon of 7 January 1921, District Inspector Thomas McGrath led an RIC party to a cottage near Ballinalee, County Longford. The police were looking for the Commandant of the IRA's Longford Brigade, Seán MacEoin. There was a path about five yards long from the garden gate to the door of the cottage. DI McGrath led the way down the path, accompanied by Sergeant Daniel Ryan. Constable Gilbert and Sergeant Clements came next, and Constables O'Shea and Woods brought up the rear. McGrath and Ryan were almost at the cottage door when MacEoin pulled it open and started shooting at the range of a few feet.

The district inspector fell on his face, shot dead. MacEoin kept firing. Clements and Woods apparently scrambled for cover. Sergeant Ryan returned fire with his rifle, hitting the wall inside the jamb of the door. MacEoin threw a grenade and ducked back in the house. Gilbert got off a single shot before the grenade exploded and wounded him. Ryan shouted to his comrades to surround the house and rushed to the back of the cottage, thinking that the IRA Commandant might try to escape out the back way. MacEoin, however, ran out the front door, in full view of the wounded Gilbert and the unwounded O'Shea, who fired at the rebel leader as he ran. Ryan had just reached the back door when he saw MacEoin escaping across the garden. The sergeant said:

> I fired at him and two other shots were fired by the party and McKeon fell upon his knees but again got on his feet. He then ran directly in front of me and I fired all that was in my magazine at him. He almost stood up on the bogland and exchanged shots with me. He roared at me several times 'Come on you whore' my rifle jammed several times and I was frequently under his fire without being able to return it. Eventually he reached a furzy ditch and we exchanged shots for some minutes and as it was getting dark I lost sight of him and had to withdraw.[33]

Despite the dim light, Sergeant Ryan was sure that the man he was chasing was Seán MacEoin. He said: 'I escorted this man to Sligo prison some months ago and I can identify him as the murderer of DI McGrath without a doubt.'

Two months later, on the evening of 14 March 1921, a section of Auxiliaries in two Crossley tenders escorted by an armoured car went to raid the St Andrew's Catholic Club on Brunswick Street (now Pearse Street) in Dublin. The convoy had just passed through the intersection of Brunswick and Sandwith streets, and the leading tender was just pulling up in front of the club, when the street erupted with gunfire.[34]

Five Auxiliaries in the leading Crossley were quickly shot and wounded. Two fell out of the tender. The remainder fell down in the box. Cadet Dowdall stated that 'I saw the flashes. I fired back ten rounds. The men on either side of me dropped, having been hit. My rifle would not load so I got out to get one of the wounded men's rifles.' However, the night was so dark, and the fighting so sudden and confused, that Cadet Brownrigg did not recall seeing his comrades wounded: 'I saw the flashes,' he said. 'I was in the body of the tender on the left hand side, I fired back at the flashes until I had emptied my gun. I then got out of the car, reloaded and took cover.' An Army officer, Lieutenant Weber, was riding on the back of the armoured car. 'I heard a sudden burst of small arms fire from the direction of the head of the column,' he said:

> My car was then fired on by groups of men standing at the corners of the cross streets immediately in my rear. We all replied to the fire with our pistols. I don't know if we hit anyone. We fired at the points where we saw the flashes. The night was dark and the street was badly lighted. I emptied my pistol.

The shooting lasted for ten minutes. Once it was over, most of the guerrillas had escaped, and five cadets and four civilians lay dead and wounded in the street. Two guerrillas were captured. Lieutenant Weber saw Volunteer Thomas Traynor run past his armoured car. 'I jumped off the car,' said Weber, 'and caught him at the corner of Great Brunswick Street and Upper Sandwith Street. I collared him and brought him down. He was on his back and I was on top of him. I had his right wrist held in my left hand. He had an automatic in his right hand. I called for help.' An Auxiliary officer, District Inspector Crang, came to Weber's aid. 'I heard a shout from a voice I knew round the corner of Sandwith Street,' he said. 'I went to the spot and saw a dark mass in the road. I found this to be an officer, whom I know, kneeling on the chest of a civilian. The civilian was on his back. . . . I saw the officer holding the accused's right arm across his chest and in the accused's hand was a pistol. . . . We got the man on his feet and the officer took the gun from the accused and without examining it put it in his pocket.'

Traynor was a veteran of the Rebellion of 1916: he was thirty-nine years old, married, and the father of ten. His captors put him in the armoured car and took him back to Dublin Castle. On 5 April he was tried by court martial for the murder of Cadet Farrell and found guilty. During the trial District Inspector Crang testified that, while he was on the ground, Traynor had said something like 'For God's sake shoot me now.' Traynor then cross-examined Crang, asking, 'Did not somebody else, when I was down on the ground, say "Shoot him out of hand"?'

'Probably it was me,' said Crang.[35]

Traynor was found guilty and sentenced to death. He was hanged on 25 April. The Tipperary IRA had captured an RIC district inspector named Gilbert Potter a few days before. His captors offered to trade Potter for Traynor, and threatened to kill their prisoner if Traynor was hanged. Their offer was refused, and they shot and buried their hostage on 27 April. On 8 May, Potter's wife received a parcel containing a last letter from her husband, along with his diary, will, gold watch, and signet ring.

5.4 Defeat and surrender

Most of these engagements have one thing in common: they ended in defeat for the police. Some policemen were quicker to accept defeat than others: at Inches Cross, for example, some wounded constables called on their comrades to surrender, while another urged them to keep fighting; one even called out 'surrender' while his comrades were still shooting back at their ambushers. But once it was clear they were beaten, the police had only three choices: they could fight to the death, or they could try to escape, or they could surrender. These are the same options that all defeated fighters face in war, and depending on the circumstances, police in the Irish War of Independence appear to have made the same choices that any defeated fighters would make.

In 1990 Australian historian Roger Noble published an article examining what happened to the more than four thousand Australian soldiers who had been captured by the enemy during the Great War. The first point he makes is that not all of these men surrendered: many were unconscious or badly wounded when they fell into the enemy's hands.[36] This was true of many police in the Irish War of Independence as well. Out of the seven constables ambushed at Inches Cross, for example, only Wallace and William Buntrock surrendered unwounded: another two, Leary and Mackessy, were too badly wounded even to crawl out from under a burning automobile. Another point that Noble makes is that, more often than not, Australian soldiers only gave up the fight when they ran out of ammunition.[37] Once again, this was also true of many police in Ireland: despite their hopeless military situation, pinned down without cover, the Auxiliaries at Clonfin kept on firing until they ran out of cartridges to fire.

Even when it was clear that defeat and quite possibly death were imminent, it seems that most Australian soldiers on the Western Front tried to escape rather than surrender[38]—and this, clearly, was a policeman's first choice in Ireland as well. Again and again, we have seen defeated police running away, even when this meant leaving their dead and wounded comrades behind. Indeed, in one case, constables Hubbard and McKibbin ran away from the hold-up near Athlone, abandoning their women friends in the process. Noble found very few cases where Australian soldiers chose to fight to the death when the situation was hopeless,[39] and it seems that police in Ireland were equally reluctant to choose 'death before dishonour'.

Only one man in this chapter seems to have been ready to fight it out: Sergeant Reilly in County Roscommon—and he only turned at bay when he was cornered in a Protestant church, after trying unsuccessfully to escape.

Like Australian soldiers in the Great War, police in Ireland appear to have surrendered only when it seemed that resistance was futile and escape was impossible. Trapped in a ditch by the side of the road, the constables at Inches Cross finally gave up after five of them had been wounded or killed. In Dublin, on Bloody Sunday, 1920, temporary cadets Garniss and Morris appear to have surrendered when they suddenly found themselves outnumbered and surrounded. Their counterparts at Clonfin, in county Longford, surrendered after they ran out of ammunition. The garrison of Rosscarberry barracks gave up only when they were faced with the choice of either surrendering or burning to death.

Once the police had surrendered, the guerrillas were then faced with choices of their own: they could disarm their opponents and let them go; they could take them prisoner; or they could kill them. In most cases it seems the Volunteers chose the first option. This was especially true after barracks battles, when the surrendered police were numerous, and the insurgent's objectives were not really to kill the police, but simply to drive them out of the district, and hopefully capture some weapons and ammunition in the process.

Indeed, IRA leaders like Sean Treácy and Ernie O'Malley seem to have understood that threats and violence against police who surrendered would only make other police less willing to give up in the future. After the Tipperary Volunteers attacked Hollyford RIC barracks, Treácy criticised his men for shouting threats at the station's defenders.[40] O'Malley wrote later that the guerrillas were yelling they'd have 'roast Peeler for breakfast'. 'Whatever inclination to surrender might have been wedging its way among the garrison,' O'Malley said, 'it was unlikely to gather impetus from this behaviour.'[41] A month later, during an attack on Drangan RIC barracks, the Volunteers kept quiet, and the station was captured. In his memoir O'Malley described how the police came out with their hands up, after he promised them that they wouldn't be shot; in his report Treácy mentioned that, in his opinion, the silence of the Volunteers had encouraged the police to surrender.[42]

Even after successful ambushes, the Volunteers usually chose to simply disarm their prisoners and let them go. The police who survived the ambush at Inches Cross were handled roughly, but their lives were spared. In another case, one of Constable Flaherty's comrades was left wounded and helpless after the ambush near Ballinhassig, County Cork, but the IRA simply took his belt and revolver and left him where he lay. Sometimes, the guerrillas behaved quite chivalrously. After the ambush at Clonfin, the north Longford flying column left the defeated Auxiliaries alone, and burned only one of their two Crossleys, leaving them the other to transport their wounded back to barracks.

The conduct of the IRA commandant in this last-mentioned case made quite an impression on his captives. After he had been disarmed and searched, Cadet Wilford recalled that:

> The 'Shin' leader then came up to me and stated that he was going to leave one Tender, and that we could look after our comrades. He then fired Tender No. 1877. Shook hands with us all, and told us that we had put up a jolly good scrap, and that his name was John McKeown and he would give us our lives and liberty. One of the 'Shinners' urged him to finish us off there and then, but he took no notice of him.[43]

In most cases, however, it could be argued that the guerrillas were simply making a virtue out of necessity. The IRA had few facilities for holding prisoners of war, and even after a victorious battle, the Volunteers were mostly concerned with getting away before police and military reinforcements could arrive on the scene. What is more, as Wilford's account of the aftermath at Clonfin implies, not all Volunteers were as high-minded as Sean MacEoin. A few months earlier, as we have seen, one of the guerrillas threatened to kill Constable Fardy after the ambush at Inches Cross, and was only prevented from robbing his prisoner by the intervention of his commanding officer. After the capture of Rosscarberry RIC barracks, the police were treated well after they surrendered, but only because they had a good reputation: 'the men of this garrison had never run amok,' said Tom Barry. 'Therefore we sought no revenge.'

Other police were not so lucky. A few police were taken as prisoners after battles with the IRA, and when we consider the number of insurgent prisoners who were mistreated and killed by the British, it should come as no surprise that some police prisoners met with a similar fate. On 31 October and 1 November 1920, for example, four police were captured in two separate incidents by the Kerry IRA. Two of these men were set free, but only after suffering at the hands of their captors. One constable had been badly beaten by his captors, and though this man appears to have recovered, another, a Black and Tan named William Muir, was apparently so traumatised by his captivity that he later killed himself by cutting his throat with a razor.[44] The remaining two constables were executed and buried secretly—though rumours went round that their bodies had been burned in a gas furnace, and even that they had been burned alive.[45]

In addition, much like the Crown Forces, the IRA was not above misrepresenting an execution as a failed escape attempt. On 20 January 1922, after the signing of the Anglo-Irish Treaty, Thomas Evans wrote to the provisional government's Ministry of Defence for information about his son, Constable James Evans, RIC, who had gone missing after an ambush at Scramogue, county Roscommon, on 23 March 1921.[46] This letter was passed to the IRA's Adjutant General, Michael Collins, who asked for a report from the officer commanding the 3rd Western Division.[47] This officer replied that Constable James Evans had been captured at Scramogue and shot dead while trying to escape immediately thereafter. The location of his grave was unknown.[48]

This answer was then relayed to the dead constable's father.[49] The truth, however, was more complicated. Shortly before his death, Constable Evans and another policeman, Constable Buchanan, had been arrested for smashing the windows of a church at Elphin. An IRA Volunteer later recalled that:

> Some time about mid-March 1921, I was passing through Elphin on foot. I was on the run for quite a long period at this time. Two of the Tans—Evans and Ross [*sic*]—followed me. I walked briskly and, on reaching the school, I turned in above the school and near the chapel and took across the country. The Tans thought that I had entered the chapel and they entered it and proceed to wreck it. They were arrested for this and taken to the camp at Lancers in Strokestown.[50]

On the morning of 23 March police and soldiers from Strokestown were transporting Evans and Buchanan to Longford in a Crossley tender when they were ambushed by a combined force of Volunteers from both north and south Roscommon. The two constables were in plain clothes and unarmed. They survived the ambush unhurt, surrendered when it was over, and were taken along by the retreating ambushers. The Volunteers later split up, and went back to their brigade areas with one prisoner apiece.

Years later, insurgent eyewitnesses disagreed about when they had realised who their prisoners were. Luke Duffy recalled that 'it was only when we called a halt after some hours trekking that we started to question the prisoners and discovered they were Black and Tans'. In his own account Sean Leavy said the Volunteers discovered their mistake after the ambushers had gone their separate ways. But Martin Fallon said that 'at first when I saw them I thought they were I.R.A. prisoners, that the enemy had on the lorry, but quickly discovered they were Tans'.[51]

Ultimately, the guerrillas decided to get rid of both men: the two Black and Tans had seen their faces and learned some of their names; had either of them escaped or been released, the consequences might have been disastrous.[52] The Volunteers from south Roscommon shot Constable Evans and buried his corpse in secret, in a bog.[53] The Volunteers from north Roscommon took their prisoner, Constable Buchanan, to the bank of the river Shannon, in order to drown him. Their commander, Martin Fallon, described how Buchanan tried to escape:

> We intended taking him out in a boat to mid-river and, having tied a heavy stone to him, put him overboard. The two Volunteers who were with me went off some little distance to get a boat and I stood guard over the Tan with a revolver ready in my hand. We had not bound or gagged him and I started to tell him that he was going to be executed and he should start saying his prayers. He had no religion apparently. He suddenly lunged out with his right fist and hit me on the point of the jaw. The blow put me down on my knees and partly dazed me but I still had the gun in my hand. Had he followed up his attack he could have kicked me on the head while I was partly dazed, but instead, he turned and jumped into the river.

Eventually, Fallon spotted the prisoner climbing out of the water, shot him dead, and disposed of his corpse in the river, as planned.[54]

In a few cases captured police were simply shot on the spot. On 3 February 1921, for example, 11 police were killed in an ambush at Dromkeen, County Limerick. At least one these 11, Constable Samuel Adams of Lanarkshire, was killed after he surrendered.[55] A witness told the subsequent court of inquiry that the Black and Tan was found wounded: 'the Shinners shot me with my hands up,' he said, before he died.[56]

Frustratingly, the proceedings of the military court of inquiry into the Dromkeen ambush have not survived. But the proceedings of the court of inquiry into the Kilmichael ambush are preserved at the National Archives of the UK, and they make for gruesome reading. Doctor Jeremiah Kelleher examined the bodies of the 16 dead police. He concluded that one body had received a 'large gun-shot wound scorched over the heart inflicted after death'. In another case he found 'extensive depressed fractures of the bones of the face and head caused by some heavy blunt instrument and inflicted after death'. A third body had 'a large compound fracture of the skull through which the brains protruded, this wound was inflicted after death by an axe or some similar heavy weapon'.[57] Three other bodies had shotgun wounds inflicted at close or point-blank range, and the court of inquiry concluded that most of the Auxiliaries had been shot and beaten to death after they were wounded.[58]

This brings us, inevitably, to the debate on the Kilmichael ambush. Tom Barry never denied that his men had taken no prisoners at Kilmichael, but he claimed that the Auxiliaries had tried to trick the guerrillas with a false surrender: that, indeed, two Volunteers had been shot and killed after the Auxiliaries had treacherously lured them into breaking cover and exposing themselves.[59] It seems that the traditional version of events was widely accepted (at least in Ireland) until the publication of Peter Hart's *The I.R.A. and Its Enemies* in 1998. In this work Hart argued that there had been no false surrender at Kilmichael: that instead, Barry had decided to take no prisoners from the outset; and having massacred the defeated Auxiliaries, the insurgent commander invented the story of a false surrender in order to justify his own brutality.[60] But Hart's revisionist version of what happened at Kilmichael has been subjected to severe criticism: Meda Ryan, in particular, has defended the traditional version, and her own research has thrown doubt on much of the new evidence that Hart adduced to support his case.[61]

What are we to make of this very bitter controversy? My own impression is that while Hart's critics have succeeded in weakening the case for his revisionist version of what happened at Kilmichael, they have not really succeeded in strengthening the case for the traditional version. That is to say, I now find both versions of this event equally problematic.

One aspect of the traditional version I find particularly troublesome is the fact that it hinges on the perceptions of a single eyewitness—in this case, the insurgent commander, Tom Barry. According to his own account, it was Barry who decided that the Auxiliaries were trying to trick the Volunteers with a false surrender, and Barry who gave the order to show no mercy—or, as he rather nicely puts it in his memoirs, to keep firing until ordered to stop.[62] In a letter to the periodical *History Ireland*, Hart's chief critic, Meda Ryan, admitted that she has not been able to find even one other eyewitness account that mentions a false surrender by the Auxiliaries among the recently opened records of the Bureau of Military History.[63] The best corroborating evidence she could find was a statement by another ambusher, Jack Hennessy, which reads as follows:

> We heard three blasts of the O/C's [Barry's] whistle. I heard the three blasts and got up from my position, shouting 'hands up'. At the same time one of the Auxies about five yards from me drew his revolver. He had thrown down his rifle. I pulled on him and shot him dead. I got back to cover where I remained for a few minutes firing at living and dead Auxies on the road. The column O/C sounded his whistle again. Nearly all the Auxies had been wiped out.

Then, Ryan comments: 'This is a false surrender—after the ceasefire whistle was blown, an Auxie who had thrown down his rifle "drew his revolver".'[64]

These two passages together form what Scottish common-sense philosopher Thomas Reid would have called a 'perception' of what happened at Kilmichael—first sensation, then judgement. Hennessy's account, as quoted, consists entirely of sense impressions—what he remembered seeing and doing that day at Kilmichael. It is Ryan who then passes judgement on these impressions and explains their significance. 'This,' she says, very definitely, 'is a false surrender.'

But is it? It seems to me that 'this' could be any number of things. This could indeed have been a man acting treacherously. But it could also have been a man acting out of confusion, or panic, or despair—none of which would constitute a 'false surrender', as that term is generally understood. Like murder, perfidy requires intent. According to the Geneva Conventions, perfidy consists of 'acts inviting the confidence of an adversary to lead him to believe that he is entitled to, or is obliged to accord, protection under the rules of international law applicable in armed conflict, *with intent to betray that confidence*'—emphasis added.

Thus, Ryan's judgement on this Auxiliary's actions is nothing less than a claim to know this man's thoughts—and in my opinion, her confidence in her own ability to discern this man's intentions from Jack Hennessy's impressions of his actions is remarkable. Among other things, she condemns this Auxiliary for drawing his weapon 'after the ceasefire whistle was blown'. But how was this man to know that three blasts on a whistle were the signal to cease fire—instead of, say, the signal to launch an assault and finish off any survivors?

The prudent thing for the Volunteers to do, under the circumstances, would have been to remain under cover while calling for the Auxiliaries to throw down their weapons and come out with their hands up. This was the procedure adopted by Sean MacEoin a couple of months later, at Clonfin: after one Auxiliary put his hands up, MacEoin ordered his men to cease fire, and went down to accept the surrender:

> I told all the men who were able to stand up, to do so, and put down their arms, which they did. I then called in two of my sections, and ordered them to attend to the wounded, collect arms, ammunition, etc. I then ordered Captain Seán Duffy to search the men who were standing up. Inside their tunics, each man had a .38 Webley revolver concealed. This was a distinct breach of the surrender, and necessitated a search of the remainder of the wounded and the dead.

'They tried to explain that they had forgotten these arms,' MacEoin said.[65] But whether this was true or not, the procedure adopted by the Volunteer commander left no room for mistakes. At Kilmichael, by contrast, according to both Barry and Hennessy's account, once the ceasefire had sounded, the inexperienced Volunteers broke cover and advanced, shouting at their enemies as they came. The potential for misunderstanding and misjudgement in this situation must have been extremely high—and in war, treachery is much less common than misunderstanding and misjudgement.[66]

My own research has uncovered only one incident where police definitely resorted to a feigned surrender—and that was a lone man, who was avenging what looked like the murder of one of his comrades. On 1 September 1920 a small party of police was ambushed near Rathmacross, County Roscommon. A constable named Hopley won a Constabulary Medal for his part in this battle, and his medal citation reads as follows:

> The party was ambushed at a cross roads when cycling in open formation from Ballaghaderreen to Frenchpark Petty Sessions. The Sergeant exhausted his revolver ammunition and was overpowered. One Constable was fatally wounded in the spine. Another was surprised, seized and deprived of his rifle. Constable Murphy lay on the road and opened fire with his rifle. A raider crept up upon him from behind and, disregarding his plea for mercy, shot him dead. Sergeant (at the time Constable) Hopley, with one cartridge remaining in his rifle, employed the ruse of pretending to surrender, emerged from cover at the road side, went right up under the revolver of the murderer of Constable Murphy as if to hand him his rifle, shot him dead and ran towards

> Ballaghaderreen. At the point of the bayonet he commandeered the bicycle of a civilian and brought word of the occurrence to his station.[67]

By way of contrast, there are many well-documented cases of soldiers who have killed prisoners in reprisal for what they thought was a false surrender, only to discover later that they had made a terrible mistake. One of the best-remembered of these cases comes, once again, from the Australian experience in the Great War, during the Battle of Menin Road on 20 September 1917, and is described in a footnote to the Australian official history:

> The mistakes commonly made in hot blood during this murderous pillbox fighting are illustrated by a terrible incident... which has been described by Lieutenant W. D. Joynt of the 8th Battalion, himself afterward a recipient of the Victoria Cross. He states that during this attack he came upon a wide circle of troops of his brigade surrounding a two-story pillbox, and firing at a loophole in the upper story, from which shots were coming. One man, coolly standing close below and firing up at it, was killed, but the Germans in the lower chamber soon afterward surrendered. The circle of Australians at once assumed easy attitudes, and the prisoners were coming out when a shot was fired, killing an Australian. The shot came from the upper story, whose inmates knew nothing of the surrender of the men below; but the surrounding troops were much too heated to realize this. To them the deed appeared to be the vilest treachery, and they forthwith bayonetted the prisoners. One Victorian, about to bayonet a German, found that his own bayonet was not fixed to his rifle. While the wretched prisoner implored him for mercy, he grimly fixed it and then bayonetted the man.

'The Germans in this case were entirely innocent,' the Australian official historian concludes, 'but such incidents are inevitable in the heat of battles, and any blame for them lies with those who make wars, not with those who fight them.'[68] Had Lieutenant Joynt not happened upon the scene of this massacre, it might well have gone down in history as an example of German perfidy, rather than the horrific result of a misunderstanding.

So what really happened at Kilmichael? Did the defeated Auxiliaries somehow conspire to feign surrender in the middle of a firefight, and somehow come to an agreement that some of them would stand up and throw down their rifles, while the rest of them waited for their chance to start firing once again? It seems much more likely to me that, like the Australian soldiers around the pillbox at the Battle of Menin Road, Tom Barry simply misunderstood what was happening. This would have been easy enough to do: Barry was, after all, by his own account, trying to make sense of something he saw while running down a road, under poor light conditions. And if this were the case, it would help explain the confused state of the evidence at present. Peter Hart may have been too quick to conclude that Tom Barry's version of what happened at Kilmichael was 'riddled with lies and evasions'—but Hart's critics may also have been too quick to conclude that Barry's version was the truth.[69]

In any case, it was clearly one thing to fight on the side of the IRA, and quite another to fight on the side of the RIC. For the police, combat began suddenly, with a surprise attack by the guerrillas. Usually, the only warning was a premature shot fired by a nervous Volunteer. The police were often badly outnumbered and caught in the open. Many of them were wounded or killed before their comrades could fight back, shooting blindly in the dark or at well-concealed enemies. Sometimes, the police overcame the odds and defeated the guerrillas, or at least forced them to withdraw. At other times, the police were defeated: some ran for their lives, and others put up their hands. Some police who surrendered were disarmed and released. Others were executed. In most cases, it was left to the police to rescue their wounded and retrieve their dead, and they were infuriated by the real or apparent indifference of civilians. As we have seen, the security forces burned a house near Inches Cross after its occupants had refused to help the survivors of the ambush.

An even clearer example of police frustration can be found earlier in the year. After the small ambush at Lackamore Wood in April 1920, the Tipperary constabulary found the dead bodies of constables Finn and McCarthy sprawled in the road. In his report the local head constable described the scene in bitter terms. 'The house of Thomas Ryan is about 10 or 15 yards away and three other houses are within a radius of 100 yards, but no one came to render any assistance to these murdered Constables, and they were lying there dead when I arrived and no one had done anything for them.' The head constable arrested four men in connection with the ambush, including Thomas Ryan. 'These men,' he concluded, 'were made to kneel down in the blood of our murdered comrades and kiss the road and say "The Lord have mercy on the souls of the men we murdered this morning." They were conveyed to Limerick last night and handed over to the military authority.'[70] These men were lucky that the police took only symbolic revenge. Before long, the RIC and its Auxiliaries would start punishing suspects with fire instead of prayer, and many of their prisoners would not survive to be handed over to the military authorities.

6

'Come out, Sinn Fein!'

Analysing Police Reprisals

Reprisals have always been the most controversial events of the Irish War of Independence: Michael Hopkinson has even written that 'Black and Tan reprisals rival the culpability of the British government for the Great Famine as the most emotive subject in modern Irish history.'[1] In this chapter we will try to study the subject systematically, using both contemporary news reports and official documents. This evidence will show that, in many ways, police violence resembled guerrilla violence. Like the level of guerrilla provocation, the level of police retaliation varied widely from place to place. Like most guerrilla violence, most police violence was petty: large-scale reprisals were as uncommon as large-scale ambushes. Like the guerrillas, the police were waging a low-intensity war of attrition, and in this war, property damage was more common than personal injury. Many guerrillas played it safe by burning abandoned barracks and blocking roads, and many police played it equally safe by burning abandoned homes and looting shops. Nonetheless, just as there were guerrilla bands taking part in ambushes and assassinations, there were police death squads meting out punishment beatings and extrajudicial executions in reprisal. Finally, like the guerrillas, most police did not choose their victims at random. Even during mass reprisals, the police usually singled out well-known republicans for punishment. 'Civilians' who took no part in politics were generally spared, though they suffered indirectly from the consequences of police violence.

6.1 Counting the cost

One of the most interesting available sources of information about reprisals is a very large bound volume preserved at the National Archives of the UK: the Register of Crime for the province of Connaught. As its name indicates, this official document is a chronicle of crimes committed in the western counties of Galway, Leitrim, Mayo, Roscommon, and Sligo during the period from July 1920 to December 1920. The Register is divided into sections by county, with separate sections for each of Galway's two Ridings. Within each section, crimes are listed in chronological order, but by date of report rather than date of occurrence. There are columns for each crime's location, for its nature (agrarian or not), for a brief summary of the case, for details of the accused and his passage through the legal system, and for general remarks. These last are often details of claims for compensation under the Criminal Injuries Act—and these details would seem to be the reason why this register was preserved: it is part of a class of documents devoted to compensation claims. If companion volumes existed for other periods and provinces, their fate is unknown.

Most of the crimes listed in the register are attributed to the IRA, and are marked 'Sinn Fein' or 'S.F.' in red. Some of the remaining entries describe non-political crimes, most of which were agrarian. However, a large number of the crimes described in the register must have been reprisals. In the summaries of these cases, the victims are often identified as 'prominent', 'notorious', 'advanced', 'extreme', or 'violent' Sinn Féiners. In some cases, the victims were on the run when their property was damaged or destroyed. One case—the burning of three houses belonging to Sinn Féiners at Loughrea, in Galway's East Riding on 31 October 1920—is frankly described in the register as a reprisal for the killing of Constable Timothy Horan.[2]

But as we might expect, our anonymous registrar made few admissions of this kind. When a Sinn Féin meeting house was burned in west Galway's Dunmore district on 25 October, the Register says only 'it is believed the fire was caused by some person who suffered through the Sinn Fein movement'.[3] A month after that, when a farmer's turf and hay were burned in Oranmore district, the Register notes that he was an 'extreme' Sinn Féiner, on the run. 'The only motive that can be assigned for the outrage', according to the Register, 'is that his neighbours are so disgusted with his murderous policy, that through spite or revenge, they destroyed his property.'[4]

In a few cases the Register accuses the guerrillas of playing dirty tricks. When a Roscommon publican said that a man in khaki had assaulted and robbed him on 18 October, the Register noted that the publican was a Sinn Féin 'sympathiser' with a brother on the run: 'the police are of the opinion that the larceny never took place and is for the purpose of propaganda'.[5] A month later, on the night of 11 November, hayricks were burned on five farms near the town of Roscommon. One farmer had shots fired through his window before he was taken out of his house and beaten. 'Police believe that these outrages were committed by terrorists with the object of terrorising what they regard as "tame" persons into more extreme measures,' wrote the registrar.[6]

In some cases the Register says nothing at all. There is no mention, for example, of either the Tuam police riot of 19 July or the Galway police riot of 8 September. Thus, the Register of Crime is neither complete nor completely candid. Nevertheless, it still provides a surprising amount of information about reprisals in Connaught in the summer and autumn of 1920.

The first thing we can learn from the Register is that some reprisals were small in scale, and others large. The distinction between small-scale and large-scale reprisals is not always clear, but one useful way to distinguish them is by counting their victims—persons or things or both. A reprisal that had an immediate effect on five persons or things or both will here be defined as large in scale.[7] This definition is not perfect, since a reprisal with a direct effect on just one person might have an indirect effect on many. Reprisals could have widespread economic effects: the burning of co-operative creameries, for example, could affect an entire district. When the Ballymote creamery was burned in County Sligo on 3 November, its destruction affected a co-operative society with 980 members.[8] We should also remember that the indirect, psychological impact of reprisals on the people of a district could far outweigh their direct physical impact. This, after all, was the whole point of reprisals: to deter the few by punishing the many, and at the same time, to deter the many by punishing the few; that is to say, reprisals were intended both to deter the insurgents from attacking the police, and at the same time, to deter civilians from supporting the insurgents. The indirect economic and psychological effects of reprisals are, however, almost impossible to measure. The best we can hope for is an accurate count of the persons and things that were damaged and destroyed.

By this admittedly rough definition (five or more immediate victims), the Register of Crime indicates that there were 11 large-scale reprisals in the province of Connaught in the summer and autumn of 1920 (see Table 6.1). Interestingly, Sligo was the worst county in the province for large-scale reprisals: 82 per cent of the reprisals against property that occurred in this county were taken during three large-scale incidents. After District Inspector James Brady was ambushed and killed at Chaffpool on 30 September, police and soldiers ran amok in the Tubbercurry district, burning and wrecking two co-operative creameries and 17 houses.[9] A month later, after four constables were ambushed and killed at Moneygold on 25 October, nine houses and another creamery were damaged and destroyed.[10] Finally, after Sergeant Patrick Fallon was shot dead at Ballymote Fair on 3 November, the police broke out again, burning and wrecking 15 homes and shops, along with yet another creamery.[11] On the other hand, the province's most violent county, Galway, had the lowest rate of damage and injury resulting from large-scale reprisals: just 24 per cent—though we should remember that the Tuam and Galway police riots went unregistered, and are not counted toward this total.

Table 6.1. Large-scale reprisals on the persons and property of republicans in the province of Connaught, July 1920 to December 1920.

Date	Location	County	Damage and Destruction
23 July	Caltra	Galway ER	6 buildings
2 September	Ballaghdereen	Roscommon	10 buildings
30 September	Tubbercurry	Sligo	17 buildings
8 October	Oranmore district	Galway WR	4 persons, 2 buildings
14 October	Oranmore district	Galway WR	7 persons
27 October	Moneygolden	Sligo	10 buildings
28 October	Ballinrobe district	Mayo	6 buildings, 3 people
3 November	Ballymote	Sligo	15 buildings
25 November	Manorhamilton district	Leitrim	7 buildings
26 November	Strokestown district	Roscommon	11 buildings
29 December	Strokestown district	Roscommon	8 buildings robbed

Source: Register of Crime, TNA: PRO, CO 904/45.

There were five types of reprisals in the province of Connaught in the last half of 1920. Vengeful police were most likely to take reprisals against property. The Register of Crime mentions 226 attacks on Irish republicans: out of this total, property was attacked in 190 cases, and persons in just 36 (see Table 6.2). Arson was the most common type of reprisal against property, and the dwelling house was the most common target: homes were burned in 43 out of 90 cases. After dwelling houses, the most common target for burning was farming stock, especially hay, but also turf, oats, and straw. Stock alone was burned in 19 cases, while in 7 additional cases it was burned along with a farmer's home.[12] Not surprisingly, Sinn Féin halls and meeting houses were also very popular targets: 16 halls were set on fire, along with 2 houses used as halls. In one case, the security forces appear to

Table 6.2. Reports of attacks on the persons and property of republicans in the province of Connaught, July 1920 to December 1920.

	Galway East Riding	Galway West Riding	Leitrim	Mayo	Roscommon	Sligo	Total
JULY							
Property	5	—	—	—	—	—	5
Persons	1	—	—	—	—	—	1
AUGUST							
Property	—	—	—	—	—	—	—
Persons	—	—	—	—	—	—	1
SEPTEMBER							
Property	—	22	1	—	12	20	55
Persons	1	1	—	—	—	—	2
OCTOBER							
Property	4	12	2	7	5	11	41
Persons	1	13	—	3	5	—	22
NOVEMBER							
Property	—	9	18	2	26	19	74
Persons	—	4	1	—	1	—	6
DECEMBER							
Property	1	6	3	1	3	1	15
Persons	—	—	2	—	2	—	4
TOTAL							
Property	10	49	24	10	46	51	190
Persons	3	18	3	3	9	—	36

Source: Register of Crime, TNA: PRO, CO 904/45.

have celebrated Armistice Day by burning four Sinn Féin halls in the Mohill district of County Leitrim.

Only ten cases fell outside these three categories. Reprisals against creameries were widely publicised and condemned in the summer and fall of 1920. The *Report of the Labour Commission* listed 42 cases in which co-operative creameries and other societies were destroyed or damaged by the security forces, including the raid on the Moycullen co-op in Galway's West Riding on 18 October 1920.[13] However, it seems this type of reprisal was not that common in Connaught. Five creameries were burned, and four of these were in just one county, Sligo: Tubbercurry (1 October), Achonry (1 October), Ballintrillick (27 October), and Ballymote (3 November). The fifth creamery was burned on 27 November, in County Roscommon, at Carnadoe. The burning of shops and other businesses was also not common: there are only three registered cases, including the torching of a bakery near Ballymote on 3 November. (As we shall see, shops were generally looted rather than burned.) Finally, there were two cases of miscellaneous damage: a donkey trap destroyed in Galway's East Riding on 25 October, and a nurse's furniture burned at Ballymote on 3 November.

Property was damaged in other ways as well—particularly by gunfire. There are 17 cases in the Register where buildings were 'shot up', including 5 houses in a single night, near Caltra, in Galway's East Riding, on 23 July. (The Caltra Sinn Féin hall was destroyed by fire on the same night.) In another case, in the Manorhamilton district of County Leitrim on the night of 25 November, someone shot out the windows of five houses and shops, and set fire to two hayricks. (The victims' politics are not mentioned, but these crimes were neither described as agrarian, nor blamed on Sinn Féin—an eloquent silence.) There were even two cases of animals being shot and killed—a heifer in Sligo on 27 October and a donkey in Roscommon a month later.

The last and most unusual form of destruction was bombing. There were only two cases listed where property was attacked with grenades: in one, the registrar complains that the female victim 'is a rank Sinn Feiner and will give no information to the Police regarding the outrage'.[14] Since police were seen and heard throwing bombs during mass reprisals like the Tuam police riot, however, this type of destruction was probably more common than the Register indicates.

Of the remaining 79 reprisals on property, 46 were cases of wrecking and looting. This type of reprisal was especially common in Galway city: there were 17 cases where shops were damaged and looted in September and October. In one case, when the grocery store of a 'prominent Sinn Feiner' was damaged and robbed on the night of 2 October, even the registrar conceded 'it may be a reprisal'.[15] Later, Thomas Nolan told the American Commission how his Galway drapery shop had been wrecked and looted on the night of 22 September: 'when they were gone away in the morning at about five o'clock,' he said, 'I came out and went into my shop and found the whole place looted. All the stuff was taken away, and what was not taken away was thrown into the street.' Nolan described himself as a 'Republican Outfitter'. In addition to ready-made clothing, he sold 'habits for dead people, and things that were needed like that'. When he went into his ruined shop that morning, he found the police had laid out a shroud for him, with a card that said 'You are a doomed man.'[16]

The remaining 33 cases involved theft or vandalism, or both. Windows and furniture were smashed in 13 cases. Seven of these incidents took place on the night of 26/27 November, in the Strokestown district of County Roscommon, after a police constable was kidnapped. (Two Sinn Féin halls and the Carnadoe creamery were burned in the same district on the same night.) There were 15 cases of robbery, though some of these cases may not have been reprisals, and 4 were denounced as false reports by the registrars. The house of a farmer was reported robbed in the Strokestown district on 5 December. 'In the opinion of the police', in this case, 'the whole thing is got up for newspaper publication and to enlist the sympathy of Sinn Feiners.'[17] Two days later, after Auxiliaries raided a Sligo creamery, the manager complained that it had been robbed. 'It is believed,' according to the Register, 'that the case was got up for the purpose of enabling the creamery officials to help themselves out of the funds at the expense of the Auxiliary police.'[18] Of course, these counter-accusations may have been lies themselves.

Two motorcars were stolen, one in Sligo (22 November) and one in Galway's West Riding (5 December). In the first case the car was found later, damaged. 'It is alleged that the damage was caused by "Black & Tans" but this is without foundation,' says the Register.[19] The second case involved a former member of the RIC, who had resigned in August, and also said his car had been stolen by Black and Tans. There were another two cases where police took drink without paying. On 25 November in Oranmore, County Galway, the police broke into a pub, drank £50 worth of liquor, and left £1 in payment. 'Local people are anxious to get rid of

Mrs Kane,' the proprietor, 'and her son Joe Howley, leader of the assassin gang,' says the Register.[20] The last case was unique. On 5 December a pair of armed men called on a Catholic priest, Reverend E. Ryan, a resident of the Mohill district in County Leitrim. The reverend was ordered to surrender a shotgun to the police and also to refund £110 to a gentleman in Ballinamore. A republican court had imposed a fine of £110 on the gentleman, for giving information to the constabulary. Ryan had served as the president of this court.

Father Ryan went on the run soon after this visit, in fear perhaps of reprisals on his person: Father Michael Griffin's body had been found in a shallow grave in County Galway two weeks before, and other Catholic priests had been threatened soon afterward. Father John Considine had been bitterly critical of the police. Ellen Quinn had been shot and killed in his parish: 'What Turkish atrocity ever equalled this?' asked Father Considine.[21] Someone replied with an anonymous letter on 24 November. 'Your efforts to stir up the blood lust against the forces of the Crown are duly noted,' it said. 'You will be duly compensated as well as all the friends of the hero Michael Collins.'[22] Remarkably, the Bishop of Galway received a threatening letter the same day. 'If any members of His Majesty's forces are interfered with in Galway, you will meet with Father Griffin's fate—Beware.'[23] This case was investigated personally by the county inspector, and the bishop even received a rather back-handed apology from Divisional Commander Cruise. After saying he was sorry to hear that the bishop had been threatened, Cruise went on to complain that: 'I must say I think it is unfair to attribute every wrong act, such as these and also the shooting of poor Father Griffin, to the Crown Forces. I have striven hard to cntrol [*sic*] the feelings of my men, and unjust charges added to their constant expectation of assassination make the position very difficult.'[24]

Other threats were made public. On the night of 9 November the police had broken into the offices of a republican paper, the *Leitrim Observer*. They held the owner, Patrick Dunne, and his wife at gunpoint as they wrecked his printing presses and then set the building on fire. Later, they visited the jewelry shop of Dunne's brother John, and shot out its window. Afterwards, a skull and crossbones were found chalked on the walls, along with a message: 'Three lives for one of ours. Take heed, Sinn Fein. Up the Black and Tans.'[25]

The police made good on threats like these in many cases. Five murders and 29 assaults are listed among the reprisals recorded in the Register. If they were lucky, victims were simply threatened in person. On the night of 27 October, for example, a Sinn Féin hall near Clonark was burned and three local men were taken from their homes, put on their knees, and made to swear that they would have nothing more to do with Sinn Féin. 'The Black and Tans, at any rate in some places, appear to have taken to themselves the power to administer oaths,' the Labour Commission reported drily.[26]

More often, however, assaults involved beating, wounding, and mock executions. One well-documented case took place on the night of 14/15 October, in Galway's West Riding. Around midnight the Furey family at Oranmore was awakened by two gunshots outside, and shouts of 'Get up! Get up!' Roger Furey, the father, came to the door, but not quick enough to satisfy the raiders. They broke the door open, invaded the house, and demanded to know where Roger's boys were sleeping. Patrick and Michael Furey were still in their bedroom. The invaders lit them up with flashlights, swore at them, accused them of being Sinn Féiners, and ordered them out of bed.

Patrick and Michael were both dragged outside in their shirts and beaten on the head with revolver butts. The raiders took the two young men to the road, pushed them against a wall, and gave them three minutes to say their prayers. While kneeling to pray, they were questioned about the shooting of a police constable in August, and had the barrels of revolvers forced into their mouths.[27] One raider threatened to kill Michael and fired his revolver close to the young man's ear. Then, after the brothers were told to stand up close together, one of the raiders fired a shotgun at them, hitting Michael in the left leg below the knee.

'They shouted to me to keep standing,' Michael said later. 'Two more of the men came up and said, "Captain, you have done enough to these two men, let them go to bed." We were then told to go to bed, and as we were going into the house two revolver shots were fired at the door. "Put out any lights or we will call again in an hour" was shouted at us.' Michael bound himself with strips of bed sheet. An hour later, he said, the raiders returned and threw a grenade in through the kitchen window, damaging the kitchen and shaking the whole house.[28] According to the Register, four other inhabitants of Oranmore complained of being terrorised on the same night. Their raiders told them they were Black and Tans, and one victim said his attacker spoke with an English accent. 'Motive for outrage seems to be agrarian,' says the Register, bravely.[29]

Nor was this the last accusation in the Register of dirty tricks. On the night of 15 December John McGowan was shot dead by masked men in the house of Patrick Dyer, near Boyle, County Roscommon. The Register describes McGowan as an Irish Volunteer captain, and 'in command of the S.F. police'. The death squad spoke with Irish accents. 'Deceased was leader of a gang who terrorised the Country side in the name of the "Black & Tans"', the Register claims.[30]

The remaining four murders pass by with little comment. As we have seen, the Galway police lynched Seamus Quirke on the night of 8 September. According to the Register of Crime, Quirke was merely 'found dead by civilians near where the attack took place'.[31] When Michael Walsh was murdered, on the night of 19 October in Galway town, the registrar noted only that he was a 'prominent' Sinn Féiner, 'and his activities as such was probably the motive for his death'.[32] On the night of 24 October, in Galway's East Riding, Thomas Egan, a publican, farmer, and 'well-known Sinn Feiner', was murdered in his home near Athenry. Mrs Egan said the killers were dressed as police, and one spoke with an English accent. The registrar made no remarks on this case, and was again silent after Father Griffin was killed on the night of 14 November. In cases like these, the Register becomes a wall instead of a window. If we want a glimpse over this wall, we must pile up additional evidence from other sources to stand upon.

6.2 'Hellish laughter and shouts of revenge'

Contemporary newspapers are the best sources of this additional information about reprisals. The sites of large-scale reprisals, in particular, were often visited by British and Irish press correspondents, who saw the damage, interviewed the victims, and reported what they had seen and heard. In some cases these news reports can be checked against others, and against additional sources like the Register of Crime. One such case took place on the night of 30 September 1920, in Tubbercurry, County Sligo. This incident was reported by correspondents of the *Manchester Guardian* and the *Daily News*, and put on record in the Register. In addition, the report of Sligo's RIC county inspector was later made public, and the case was discussed in the House of Commons. As a consequence, the Tubbercurry reprisals are very well documented and can serve as a good example.

The story begins on the late afternoon of 30 September 1920, in Sligo town. Tubbercurry's temporary RIC district inspector, James Brady, had come to Sligo for duty that Thursday, taking the direct route, riding in a truck along with eight other police including Head Constable O'Hara. The district inspector's party stayed in town until 4 p.m., when they left Sligo to go back to Tubbercurry. Instead of taking the same route back, they drove south to Ballymote, and then west. Despite this precaution, at about 5:30 p.m. the group was ambushed on the road between Bunnanadden and Tubbercurry.

The guerrillas opened fire from higher ground, using rifles and shotguns, aiming through loopholes in the walls on both sides of the road. 'The spot was a regular death trap,' says the police report, 'and afforded no chance of success to the police, even if they had been in a position to dismount and attack.' Brady was hit in the body. The head constable was hit in the right leg. Their ambushers, it was claimed, were using dum-dum bullets, and both men suffered gruesome wounds. A third man, Constable Brown, was hit in the face by shotgun pellets. 'The lorry drove on,' says the report, 'under heavy fire to which the police replied as well as they could. They could not see their cowardly assailants, who were safely entrenched in strong numbers behind their loopholed walls.'[33]

The police made it back to Tubbercurry, but they could not call for help: the telegraph wires had been cut. Instead, a second police party drove back to Sligo that evening, arriving at 9:15 p.m. Some time after 11 p.m., Acting County Inspector Russell came to Tubbercurry with reinforcements: a district inspector and 16 men, along with 10 soldiers under the command of an Army lieutenant. There was a fog that night, and the town was almost deserted. Many townspeople had left earlier that evening. Most of the remainder fled when the trucks arrived. The county inspector soon discovered why: District Inspector Brady had died of his wounds at around 8 p.m.

Here the two reports diverge. According to the few civilians who stayed in town, watching through the fog, the police and soldiers drove to Howley's pub and broke down the door. 'They spent half an hour drinking what they could and destroying what they couldn't,' says the *Manchester Guardian*. According to the *Daily News*, the police and soldiers 'helped themselves to as much liquor as they could swallow, smashed the windows, wrecked the interior, and finally set it on fire'.

The county inspector's version was rather different. According to Russell, the police and soldiers drove to Tubbercurry barracks, where they learned of District Inspector Brady's death:

> His naked body was lying on the kitchen floor, being washed by one of his comrades. The three ghastly wounds made by the shots were in full evidence. Head Constable O'Hara was lying in a room near by moaning and suffering intense pain. Police Constable Brown, who had the pellet shots in the face, was wandering about the room in a state of pain.

When the police from Sligo saw this, they became enraged. 'They rushed out,' says the *Guardian*, 'and the next moment the officer [County Inspector Russell] heard shots outside the barracks and the battering of doors.' Russell armed himself with a carbine and the three officers went outside. 'They found the shop next to the barracks broken into and with soldiers and police inside it setting it on fire.' The county inspector and the lieutenant ordered their men to stop and come out. 'The men obeyed the order sullenly and reluctantly', and Russell told them 'that there must be no damage done'. The police and soldiers obeyed at first, 'but there was a good deal of grumbling and murmuring, and after a short interval some of them broke away'. Their comrades followed soon after, ignoring first the orders then the pleas of their officers.

Now the reports converge again. The police and soldiers went on a rampage, firing rifles, throwing grenades, and shouting 'Come out, Sinn Fein! Where are the murderers?' Attacking the shops around the village's three-sided marketplace, they burned three buildings and wrecked several more. The county inspector begged the police to spare the largest store in town. 'The reply of one of his men was an oath.' Meanwhile, the townsfolk shivered in the wet fields nearby, listening to the police rioters curse and rage, and watching the fires glow through the fog. Hugh Martin, the *Daily News* correspondent, saw the ruins a couple of days later. 'Little spires of smoke were twisting up from three jagged stone skeletons,' he wrote, 'and the breeze twirled ashes instead of autumn leaves across the open ground. Many shops—I counted eleven, and there may have been more between and beside the burnt-out buildings—had their fronts battered and broken, so that the whole triangle had the air of having barely survived an earthquake.'

Finally, the county inspector got the police and soldiers from Sligo back under control. Assisted by some of the Tubbercurry police—the ones who had earlier been ambushed—he persuaded his men to get back in their trucks, and at this point the reports diverge again. According to his own statement, Russell went inside the barracks to give instructions to the district inspector, who was remaining in the village. While he was inside, the police trucks drove off without orders, heading for Tubbercurry creamery half a mile away.

The creamery manager, Murricane, was a Sinn Féiner. Awakened by a neighbour, and warned of the reprisals in Tubbercurry, he left his home and hid outside. This was wise, for as the police and soldiers drove past his house they sprayed it with gunfire. While their comrades went on, setting fire to the creamery, four men came back to Murricane's house and fired in through the windows, narrowly missing the manager's wife and children as they cowered in the kitchen. Finally, the gunmen called Mrs Murricane outside. 'They all seemed to me to speak with an Irish accent,' she said. 'The swearing was awful. The men asked me where my husband was, and I asked him what they wanted him for. They replied, "To shoot him." I said I didn't know where he was, and they said, "We'll make you tell," threatening me with their guns.' The four men pushed past her and went through the house, looking for the manager. When they could not find him, they went back to the burning creamery.

So far, the two reports are in agreement. At this point, however, Russell wrote that the raiding party drove back to the village, where he finally persuaded them to return to Sligo. The convoy started back at about five o'clock in the morning, with Russell in the rear. Along the way, the leading truck stopped when it arrived at Achonry co-operative creamery. By the time Russell's vehicle arrived on the scene, his men were setting fire to this establishment as well. 'After a great deal of persuasion,' says the *Guardian*, 'he managed to get the men to resume their journey to Sligo.'

Civilian eyewitnesses remembered things differently. The people of Tubbercurry told reporters that all the police and military trucks left at the same time, two of them heading east, and the remaining two heading north, in the direction of Achonry. Residents of Achonry told reporters that they heard two trucks arrive that night, one after another, at about three o'clock in the morning. Because of the fog, they could not see what the raiders were doing, but they heard the sound of glass breaking, followed by shots and explosions, and then saw the creamery burning. In addition, a glance at a map of the county will raise a few questions about Russell's version of events. Achonry is not on the main road from Tubbercurry to Sligo. Unless the police and military convoy took a detour to lower their chances of being ambushed on the way back, the leading truck would have had to drive about a mile off the main road to reach Achonry.[34]

Mass reprisals like the Tubbercurry police riot generally took place after police had been killed—not just attacked or wounded, but killed. Some followed the killing of officers and non-commissioned officers, like District Inspector Brady. The Templemore town hall and three local creameries in County Tipperary, for example, were burned after District Inspector William Wilson was killed on 16 August 1920.[35] The sack of Balbriggan, County Dublin, on 20 September 1920 followed the killing of Head Constable Peter Burke and the wounding of his brother, a sergeant.[36] Reprisals in Granard, County Longford, followed the killing of District Inspector Philip Kelleher on 31 October.[37] Sergeant Henry Cronin was killed on the same day, leading to reprisals in Tullamore, King's County.[38] The reprisals in the Ballymote district of County Sligo followed the killing of Sergeant Patrick Fallon on 3 November 1920: the Register of Crime says that 'intense excitement prevailed' in the district after the sergeant's death.[39]

In other cases, mass reprisals followed the killing of two or more police constables. The Tuam police riot, for example, followed the killing of two constables on the Tuam-Galway road.[40] Terrible reprisals in County Clare on the night of 22 September 1920 followed the massacre of six constables at Rineen, where the guerrillas were suspected of using dum-dum bullets and finishing off the wounded.[41] The mass reprisals near Moneygold, County Sligo, came after three constables were killed and another three wounded on 25 October 1920.[42] (In this case, most of the damage was done after one of the wounded constables died on 27 October.) The constabulary took widespread reprisals and blockaded the town of Tralee, County Kerry, for a week after 5 police were killed, 11 wounded, and 2 kidnapped in 6 attacks on a single day, 31 October 1920.[43] There was another police riot, in Tipperary town, after the battle at Inches Cross in which four constables were killed.[44]

In most cases, interestingly, the death of a single police constable was not enough to provoke a mass reprisal. The burning of Cork on the night of 11 December 1920 followed the death of a single man, but he was an Auxiliary, Temporary Cadet Spencer Chapman, killed in a grenade attack that wounded ten of his comrades.[45] There was, however, at least one early exception to this rule. After Constable Luke Finegan was fatally wounded in Thurles, County Tipperary, on the night of 20 January 1920, his comrades ran amok, smashing windows and firing in the streets—the first large-scale reprisal by police in the Irish War of Independence.[46] Denis Morgan and his family hid in the basement that night. He later told the American Commission that he first heard 'isolated shots', then 'heavy volleys'. 'We heard the glass going and the plaster falling off the ceiling', when the police mob arrived at his house. In the morning Morgan saw that all the windows in his house had been shot through, along with some of the doors. 'Inside the rooms the ceilings were all torn and the woodwork was all shattered. There was debris lying on the floor all around.' The street 'was littered with plate glass shattered by shots along the side of the large square—both by breaking and by rifle shots'.[47]

In a few cases, large-scale reprisals followed provocation short of killing. Trim, County Meath, suffered a mass reprisal on the night of 27 September 1920, after the police barrack was captured and burned in a daring raid that left a head constable wounded.[48] The police became especially violent when their comrades were kidnapped. The blockade of Tralee in early November 1920 was provoked as much by the kidnapping of 4 constables as it was by the killing and wounding of another 14. Constable Ernest Bright of London and Constable Patrick Waters of Galway were captured by the guerrillas on 31 October 1920 and never seen again.[49] The police posted notices the following day: 'Take notice—Warning—Unless the two Tralee policemen in Sinn Fein custody are returned before ten a.m. on the 2nd inst., reprisals of a nature not yet heard of in Ireland will take place in Tralee and surroundings.'[50]

Word got around the following day that the dead bodies of the missing men had been found, riddled with bullets. The police ordered all businesses to close. When the report was disproved, the police began dragging the local canal and put up more posters: 'Final notice. Take notice, that all business premises, factories, and shops in Tralee must be kept closed and work suspended until such time as the police in Sinn Fein custody are returned. Anyone disobeying this order will be dealt with in a drastic manner.'[51] The blockade was eventually lifted, but its effects lingered. When the Labour Commission visited the town a month later, on 9 December 1920, they were appalled. 'Tralee, more than any other place visited by the Commission, exemplifies the demoralizing effects of coercion, repression and reprisals,' they reported. 'The whole population seems to be sunk in the depths of morbid fear and contagious depression.'[52]

Fortunately, the blockade of Tralee was unusual in many respects. Quite often mass reprisals were not the work of local police forces: instead, the damage was frequently done by reinforcements from larger population centres nearby. The police rioters in Tuam had come from Galway.[53] The police rioters in Tubbercurry had come from Sligo. Apparently, the police who took reprisals at Moneygold in late October came from Sligo too,[54] while those who took reprisals at Ballymote in early November came from Ballaghadereen.[55] Balbriggan was burned by Black and Tans from nearby Gormanstown, and the Auxiliaries who set fire to the commercial centre of Cork were newcomers to the city, stationed on its outskirts.[56] The mass reprisals in County Clare following the Rineen ambush swept across three communities, and the punitive expedition to Granard came from nearby Longford.

It seems that mass reprisals were taken by local police forces only when community relations were especially bitter. Thurles, County Tipperary, was one of the Irish insurgency's first hot zones. By January 1920, when Constable Finegan was killed, the Thurles constabulary had already lost three men: a sergeant and a constable had been killed in the Knocklong railway station ambush of 13 May 1919, and the local district inspector had been assassinated in Thurles on 23 June.[57] As we shall see, the first extrajudicial killings by police took place in this district as well.

Nine months after the sacking of Thurles, in its report on the Tullamore police riot in King's County, the *Manchester Guardian* wrote that 'the police have keenly resented the attempt to boycott them'. The day before Sergeant Cronin was shot, local Sinn Feiners and shopkeepers had received threatening letters with Tullamore postmarks. 'Warning,' they said. 'Beware. You are a doomed man. Clear out.' The letters were signed 'Red hand' or with a skull and crossbones. On the same day a notice was posted on the bridge 'warning traders that if the boycott were not removed within twelve hours they must take the consequences'. After Sergeant Cronin died on the evening of 1 November, the Tullamore police finally went on a rampage, wrecking the local Sinn Féin club, ruining the printing presses of a nationalist paper, the *King's County Independent*, demolishing the Transport and General Workers Union hall, and bombing and burning the town cinema. 'The houses of several prominent Irish Volunteers were also destroyed, and a number of business premises had their windows and exhibits smashed.'[58]

Historians have generally portrayed mass reprisals as blind, idiotic, indiscriminate. After all, the burning of co-operative creameries had a blanket effect on entire districts: according to news reports, the creamery at Achonry, County Sligo, received its milk and cream from eight hundred local smallholders.[59] During the sack of Balbriggan, the police mob destroyed a hosiery factory that was owned by a London firm and managed by an Englishman. Its destruction left at least a hundred people unemployed, and deprived at least another hundred of income from outwork.[60] During the reprisals in Cork on the night of 11 December, over 60 shops were burned and looted, including 4 large department stores, as well as the city hall and the city library.[61] An especially mean spirit seems to have been moving the men of H Company, ADRIC, on the night of 19 April 1921, when they took reprisals once more on Tralee, County Kerry. As well as bombing nine houses and businesses, the cadets vandalised a monument commemorating the Rebellion of 1798: 'The limestone figure of the Croppy Boy was pulled off the pedestal, smashed, and the body of the figure left in the street decapitated. The pike disappeared, as did the arms and legs of the figure. The trunk remains in the street a danger to the passing traffic.'[62]

Clearly, there was no sense in reprisals like these. But a rather different picture emerges from other incidents. In many cases the police chose their victims with care, even in the midst of a riot. John Derham, for example, was a Sinn Féin town commissioner in Balbriggan. On the night of the sack, the police arrested Derham, wrecked and burned his public house, and badly beat his older son Michael, who was left unconscious in the burning building. Derham himself was punched in the face and clubbed on the head with a rifle butt. Months later the town councillor testified at the hearings of the American Commission. 'They did not take everybody,' he said. 'They picked them out like they did me.'[63]

This kind of discrimination is often mentioned in contemporary reports: the police attacked well-known republicans, and left other people alone. In at least one case, prominent local republicans were warned in advance that they would be punished if the police were attacked. An article in the *Manchester Guardian* for 2 November 1920 described how the police had posted threats on shop windows and walls in Buncrana, County Donegal. 'Take warning in good time,' they said, 'that if any harm whatsoever comes to any member of His Majesty's forces or to any person who chooses to associate with them five prominent Sinn Feiners in this locality will be shot. Balbriggan and Trim will be sufficient warning to the sober-minded.' In a letter to General Macready five Buncrana shopkeepers complained that they had been publicly marked as the men to be shot in reprisal. 'Our doors have been numbered,' they said, 'the numerals 1 to 5 being painted on them. The dead walls and concrete footpaths have also been painted with inscriptions: "Buncrana will follow Balbriggan! Up the Black and Tans!"'[64]

When reprisals were taken, it was marked men like these who suffered the most. The houses that were shot up in Thurles, County Tipperary, on 20 January 1920 belonged to men 'known to be associated with the movement for national independence'.[65] When Trim, County Meath, was attacked on 27 September, the police mob 'singled out the shops and business establishments of those residents alleged to be in sympathy with Sinn Fein, and ransacked, pillaged, and burned all'.[66] The same thing happened in Tubbercurry on the night of 30 September. 'The reason these particular houses were attacked,' according to the county inspector, 'appears to have been because either the owner or the shop boys employed by him were active Sinn Feiners.'[67] The *Guardian* summed up the Tullamore police riot of 1 November as 'a tour of Sinn Feiners' houses'.[68]

That same night, in Granard, the column of police and military trucks from Longford stopped at the local police barracks for information before starting their work. 'Houses and shops were selected for destruction according to the politics of their owners and the work of burning carried out expeditiously by the use of petrol.'[69] On the night of 3 November, after military curfew patrols had been withdrawn, the Tralee police went out and 'set fire to business premises of well-known Sinn Feiners'.[70] In at least one case, officers may have actively discouraged purely random destruction. One witness to the mass reprisal at Lahinch, County Clare, on 22 September described how the Black and Tans began to burn the local post office, 'but the officer came running up the street shouting "[Damn] you! Put out that fire at once. Can't you see that is the post office?"'[71]

Mass reprisals were often accompanied by shouting from the men as well as their officers. We have already heard the shouts of the rioters in Tuam and Tubbercurry.[72] John Derham and his family were hiding in the back room of his Balbriggan pub on the night of the sack of the town. 'You could hear them screeching and roaring,' he said, 'and their voices got worse.'[73] 'I was awakened by a sound of shots and the most fiendish yelling imaginable,' wrote the witness from Lahinch. The police were 'yelling for the men to come out now and bring their rifles.' As the reprisals continued, 'above all the din could be heard the hellish laughter and shouts of revenge of the raiders'.[74]

There are some references to cheering as well. The police rioters in Tuam, for example, cheered when they set fire to the town hall.[75] 'The incendiaries seem to have gloated over their evil work for they waved their caps and cheered,' said the *Report of the Labour Commission*, describing the sack of Balbriggan.[76] The police also cheered as they burned buildings at Ennistymon, County Clare,[77] and shouted 'That's the stuff to give them!' as they were preparing to leave Granard in flames.[78]

In some cases the police even called for Sinn Feiners and Volunteers by name. 'Searches were made for young men with Sinn Fein connections whose names were shouted freely by the police' during the reprisals at Milltown Malbay, County Clare.[79] The police also called for the Sinn Féin chairman of the Trim urban council when they burned his mineral-water works on 27 September 1920.[80]

Few men answered these calls, for good reason. Mass reprisals on property were often accompanied by beatings and killings. The police executed Seamus Quirke on the night of the Galway police riot, and wounded another man.[81] The Labour Commission received an affidavit from Michael Derham, describing the beating he was given the night of the sack of Balbriggan. The police invaded his home, arrested his father, and threatened his younger brother. One of them flashed a lamp in his eyes to blind him. 'Another then struck me on the face with his fist,' Derham's affidavit says, 'and releasing the other man's grip I ran to the bed and lay face downwards, with the object of saving my face':

> The men followed me across the room and, raising the butts of their rifles, struck me several times on the back of the head. Then one of them caught me by the arm and turned me over and struck me several times on the top of the head and once on the upper lip also with the butt of his rifle. I implored them to shoot me, but one man answered, 'Shooting is too good for a . . . like you,' using a terrible oath, and accompanying his remark with a blow over the left eye with the butt of his rifle.[82]

There were other cases where the police decided that shooting (or shooting alone) was too good for their victims. Two men were stabbed to death during the sack of Balbriggan. According to the *Guardian*, 'one was the chairman and the other the acting secretary of the Sinn Fein Volunteer movement in the town, and one at least of them was believed by the constabulary to have been implicated in the recent murder of Sergeant Finnerty, of the R.I.C.'[83] Another two men were killed in Ennistymon,

County Clare, two days later. Once again, both of them were 'marked' men—'men believed to have Sinn Fein connections'. One was caught while trying to put out a fire. 'He appears to have been beaten first and shot afterwards.' The second man was Thomas Connole, secretary of the local transport and general workers' union. The police dragged him out of his house, put him up against a wall, and executed him. Then they set fire to his house, dragged his body back, and threw it in the flames.[84]

6.3 'Come out to be shot'

Reprisals, however, were not always the work of police lynch mobs. More commonly, lynch law was enforced by gangs, who dealt out punishment beatings and levied fines in the form of property burned and wrecked. Although there were only nine small-scale reprisals in County Sligo (compared to the widespread damage inflicted during the three police riots already mentioned), the proportions in the rest of the province were very different. In Roscommon there were 27 small-scale reprisals on property (48 per cent of the total). In Leitrim there were 17 small-scale reprisals on property (71 per cent of the total). In Galway 86 per cent of the registered attacks on republican property were small in scale. Moreover, most of the large-scale reprisals in Connaught were the work of small groups moving from place to place. They were spree reprisals by gangs, instead of mass reprisals by mobs.

One such spree reprisal took place on 25 October 1920, near the village of Lixnaw, County Kerry. News reports indicate that republicans had cut off the hair of a village girl about a fortnight before. The young woman, Bridget Brady, was friendly toward the police, and a suspected informer. On the night of the 25th a truck full of police drove into Lixnaw, from the direction of Listowel. The men were in plain clothes. Some had their faces blackened, and some wore motor goggles.

The raiding party stopped first at the Brady home, looking for their son Steve, but the young man had fled out a back window. In Steve's absence, the gang settled for beating another boy, John Nolan. Then they gave Bridget Brady a few minutes to dress before they dragged her outside and cut off her hair. Finally, they told Mrs Brady 'that if her son had not cleared out of the place within 24 hours he would be doomed, and would be shot at sight'. From the Brady home the police went on to burn the local co-operative creamery. The creamery's office and its cheese-room were destroyed, along with its main roof and much of the stock. The damage was later estimated between £10,000 and £12,000.

The burning of the creamery was followed by two more assaults. At the McElligott farmhouse the raiders called for their two sons John and Tom to come out. The young men asked for permission to put on their trousers. This was denied. They were implicated in the cutting of the Lixnaw girl's hair, and the shooting of police, they were told,'There have been no police shot here,' said John McElligott.

'Shut up, you freezing——,' the raiders replied. According to the news report, the noun was 'a familiar Army word'. The two brothers were taken outside in the rain, where they stood in their shirts, faces to the wall, while they were beaten and kicked. The family's two daughters were called out as well. The raiders were going to cut off the older girl's hair, but she ran away.

The raiding party had more success at the Lovett family home, where they found young Maurice in bed. 'This is the——we want,' they said, as they beat him, kicked him, tore his shirt. 'Come out to be shot,' they snarled: then they dragged him outside, knocked him down, and kicked him some more. Maurice's sister Mary was living next door. 'Don't kill him,' she cried, alerting the police to her presence. They went into her house, lit her up with a lamp, and cut off her hair with scissors.

Then, finally, they left the village. A few days later, correspondents for the *Daily News* and the *Guardian* visited Lixnaw, taking statements from victims and witnesses. 'The evidence of these events is perfectly clear,' said Hugh Martin of the *Daily News*, 'and can be obtained on the spot by anyone not a soldier or policeman, even by a member of the Chief Secretary's department, who cares to have it.' 'I saw and spoke to the two girls whose hair had been bobbed,' said the *Guardian*'s correspondent, 'and I can testify to the thoroughness, if not the artistry, with which it was done.'[85]

Episodes like these had at least one feature in common with mass reprisals like the Tubbercurry police riot. Aside from the burning of the creamery, the violence was not indiscriminate: instead, once again, active republicans and their families were singled out for punishment. The McElligott brothers were both Volunteers, as was Maurice Lovett. When the police came to the Lovett home, they found a lodger as well: 'All right, we don't want you,' they told him. Steve Brady was described in the news as a 'leading' Volunteer, and this, along with his flight, and the frustration and threats of the raiding party when it missed him, indicates that he was suspected of leading the men who cut off the suspected informer's hair two weeks before. The raiders also chose their female victims with a certain amount of care. There were two McElligott girls, ages eighteen and fifteen. After the older girl escaped, 'it was decided that her sister was too young to warrant the operation'. Later, they asked Mary Lovett's widowed sister-in-law if she was married. When she said 'yes', they left her alone.[86]

Haircutting was by far the most common form of reprisal against women. We have already seen how five Galway women had their hair cut off after Eileen Baker was attacked in the same way, for giving evidence to a military court of inquiry.[87] Besides the two cases reported by the *Manchester Guardian*, a third case of haircutting in County Kerry was reported in the *Daily News* and the *Cork Examiner*. On their way to Lixnaw the gang stopped at the home of a farmer named O'Sullivan. The farmer's two sons were beaten with rifle butts and his two daughters had their hair cut.[88] The Cork paper mentioned other such incidents as well: on 2 November, for example, it reported that Agnes Daly had been attacked and had her hair cut off in Limerick. Agnes had a sister, Kathleen, who later described this incident in her memoirs. 'They grabbed her, threw her on the ground, and dragged her to the gate on her face, by the hair,' she wrote. 'Then one of them put her foot on his back and stooping over, cut off her hair with a razor.'[89]

Surprisingly, perhaps, reprisals on the persons of women did not often go beyond this type of assault and humiliation. In fact, it seems that not a single woman was ever murdered in a reprisal. In the few documented cases where police and soldiers murdered Irish women, their motives were unrelated to the national struggle. On 24 May 1921, for example, a Black and Tan, Constable William Robinson, shot and killed Anne Dickson in Clones, County Monaghan. Robinson had been stationed in Clones until 13 May, when he was transferred to Ballybay. The constable had been keeping company with Dickson for three months, prior to his transfer, and came back to Clones to visit her on the 24th. In fact, Dickson and Robinson had been thinking of getting married. In a letter from Ballybay dated 14 May, Robinson wrote: 'I wish I could get to know your Mother and Father because I would like to have a talk with them about a certain thing, I suppose you know what that is.' However, the same letter shows that Robinson was a jealous man. 'I don't think you know how I love you,' he wrote, 'but I know that myself and I think you love me in return, if you do darling I can trust you not to walk out with any more boys, because you know I was always jealous of you when I was in Clones, I did not like to see anybody else with you.'[90] On 24 May, Robinson seems to have been angry that another police constable had come to see Dickson the same day.[91]

Robinson said afterward that the shooting was unintentional. 'I started to go towards her & at the same time took the revolver out of my pocket,' he said: 'After I had taken the revolver out of my pocket and was going towards Miss Dickson the revolver went off':

> The revolver is not my own. I exchanged revolvers with Constable McNamee as his was smaller and easier to carry in plain clothes.... I have always used the same revolver, i.e. the one I gave Constable McNamee. The pull-off is much heavier than the one I borrowed. The reason I took my revolver out of my pocket was in case it should go off while I was going upstairs.[92]

The court of inquiry found the constable guilty of 'culpable negligence in so handling his revolver as to allow it to be discharged'.[93] He was tried and acquitted of murder, but found guilty of manslaughter on 15 August 1921.

The finding of manslaughter in this case was probably due to the seeming lack of motive for the shooting. Sarah Kells saw Dickson and Robinson together just moments before Dickson was killed: though Robinson had the revolver in his hand, the two seemed 'very friendly'. 'I heard Miss Dickson laughing,' said Kells.[94] Given his insistence that the revolver's trigger pull was unexpectedly light, and his lame excuse for taking the revolver from his pocket, Robinson may have pointed his weapon at Dickson as an imbecile joke. One interlocutor suggested that Dickson's death might have been the result of 'horseplay'.[95]

There were also surprisingly few reports of sexual assaults on Irish women by members of the security forces. This fact was remarked upon during the hearings of the American Commission. Ellen Wilkinson, for example, was a representative of the British branch of the Women's International League. Wilkinson had investigated conditions in Ireland with her colleague, Annot Erskine Robinson, a Manchester suffragist: the two Englishwomen were the sole British witnesses to give evidence to the commission. Wilkinson told the commission that:

> when we were there, we made very careful investigation, and we found no cases whatever of outrages on women. We have been told since that such cases have occurred. We have been told by Mrs. Sheehy-Skeffington, for instance (she is a prejudiced witness, of course), that outrages have occurred on

> women. But we found no case at all where sexual outrages on women have occurred.[96]

Later, Donal O'Callaghan gave the commission an affidavit from Ellie Lane of Ballinhassig, County Cork, describing how she had suffered an attempted rape during a night raid. This prompted the chairman to ask:

> Is there much of what we call sex crime in connection with these raids? This is the first testimony we have had of that kind. And we were so accustomed to hearing of sex excess in the situation in Belgium that it has been in marked contrast to that. And I am wondering if there had been any charge in this connection in these raids in the treatment of the Irish people.

O'Callaghan replied:

> This is the only case in which I have gotten a definite deposition, and it is the only case of which I know personally in Cork. There have been rumours of such cases throughout the country, but I do not know whether they are correct or not. I have no particulars about them. But I will say that that class of assaults is not very general in connection with raids.[97]

Finally, Caroline Townshend, an officer of the Gaelic League in County Cork, was asked whether she had heard of any sex crimes. 'I have not personally,' she said. 'Except that I have two reports of two cases of court-martials, one of a soldier and the other of a constable, where they were court-martialed for assaults on women; and one was sentenced for two years.'[98]

'Of course,' she concluded, 'it is very difficult to get facts about such cases.' This point was also stressed by the *Report of the Labour Commission*, which says it was 'extremely difficult to obtain direct evidence of incidents affecting females, for the women of Ireland are reticent on such subjects'.[99] Their families could be tight-lipped as well. 'Dr Foley here yesterday,' wrote Lady Gregory, on 20 November 1920. 'He says the family of the girls violated by the Black and Tans wish it hushed up. There has been another case of the same sort in Clare—but there also it is to be kept quiet.'[100] There is no question that some sexual violence took place during the Irish War of Independence. But it seems the rape of women, like the murder of women, was not very common. Even death squads, it seems, had rules. Some types of violence against women were allowed. Other types were not.[101]

This restraint was absent from reprisals against men, who were lucky to get away with a simple beating. As we have seen, the police and Auxiliaries in County Galway seem to have been especially savage, at least in the autumn of 1920. On the night of 16 October 1920, for example, uniformed men wearing 'Scotch caps', some of them with blackened faces, invaded the home of a widow named Mrs Feeney about three miles from Corofin. The house was searched, and Mrs Feeney's four boys were taken outside: her oldest son, Thomas, was caught by the hair on his way out and accused of being a rebel and a Volunteer.

'You have had your day,' said his captor, 'now it is ours.'

Thomas and Martin Feeney were made to lower their trousers and were whipped with a rope on the bare skin. Thomas had a rope or halter put around his neck, by which he was pulled over a wall; his brother William was hit in the head with a gun butt and beaten down, stunned. All three were then kicked as they lay on the ground. Only the youngest brother, Patrick, was left unharmed.[102] A Corofin publican named John Raftery was attacked later that same night. He was accused of being a Sinn Feiner, beaten, and pushed into a wall of loose stones that gave way under his weight.[103]

We have already read about other cases of police cruelty from this county. The Furey brothers were beaten, mock-executed, and wounded with a shotgun. The Deveney brothers were given the same treatment a few nights later. Lawrence Tallon was wounded with shot as well, while his assistants were flogged. Assaults like these take us beyond politically inspired terrorism, into the realm of sadism: the Furey brothers in County Galway were put on their knees and had revolver barrels thrust into their mouths, while other men were whipped after being forced to drop their trousers. To be haltered like an animal, whipped like a naughty schoolboy, or forced into symbolic fellatio was more than just intimidating: it was humiliating, emasculating. One whipping victim told an English reporter that 'the indignity was worse than the pain'.[104] 'To be beaten on the back, and the neck, and to have a prod of a rifle in the head, a man might as well be dead,' a Galway man told Lady Gregory.[105]

Reprisals could scar the mind as well as the body. Nellie Craven told the American Commission that her brother was 'terribly nervous' after being beaten twice in one day by the police. During the first attack two of his teeth were knocked out. During the second attack he had shots fired over his head, and then was undressed and beaten with a belt. Craven testified that her brother was in bed for five days afterward, and now 'the sight of a lorry or a Black-and-Tan is too much for him'.[106] Other instances of apparent post-traumatic stress disorder can be found elsewhere.[107]

Even 'simple' beatings could have terrible consequences. A Limerick teenager, for example, was given 'a prod of a rifle in the head' on New Year's Eve, 1920. A police patrol stopped three young men in the street, including seventeen-year-old John Lawlor. Apparently, Lawlor and the rest made a break for it. Witnesses heard shouts of 'run', then shouts of 'halt'. Lawlor halted, and the Black and Tans caught up with him. 'I saw a policeman strike him in the face with his hand,' said a witness, 'and another hit him on the back of the head with the butt end of his rifle. He fell—A policeman told us to move on and we saw no more.'[108] Some other witnesses testified that Lawlor then got up and ran towards his home. 'We caught him up as he was leaning against a window (Scanlan's) in Market Street, and the other person who was with me asked him how he felt. He said "Oh! my head, Oh! my back." The other person helped him home.'[109] Lawlor lost consciousness later that evening and he died not long before midnight. A post-mortem examination found the cause of death was asphyxia due to compression of the brain's respiratory centre. The compression was the result of a haemorrhage resulting from Lawlor's head injury.[110]

6.4 By persons unknown

There were numerous cases in the War of Independence of men being shot while trying to escape—so many that 'shot while trying to escape' is often interpreted as a euphemism for 'executed'. On the night of 27 February 1921, for example, the police came to Joseph Taylor's house in County Kerry looking for Joseph junior. The young man fled when the police arrived, but he was caught and arrested. While returning to their barracks on foot, the police patrol saw three men run off the road up ahead. They pursued, leaving two constables to guard their prisoner. Taylor took the chance to run, but his guards opened fire, and the young man fell, shot in the right thigh. The police gave their prisoner first aid and went for medical help, but it was too late: Taylor's femoral artery had been severed, and he bled to death.[111]

In his testimony to the court of inquiry, the leader of the patrol admitted that the dead man had not been handcuffed after he was arrested. A similar incident took place a couple of months later. On the night of 30 April 1921, District Inspector Captain Henry Gallogly led a police patrol to search Davis Street, looking for a suspect named Thomas Walsh. Walsh was caught and arrested, and the district inspector handed him over to three constables, with orders to take the prisoner back to barracks.[112] Later, at the court of inquiry, the three constables were identified by letters instead of names—A, B, and C. When Walsh came out of the house, Constable C caught him by the sleeve. 'As senior constable,' said Constable A, 'I looked for my handcuffs when the prisoner was handed over to me, but I found that in the hurry of getting ready to go on this duty I had got the wrong belt on & that there were no handcuffs in the handcuff case. I then turned round & asked the other two constables for handcuffs & when I turned to the prisoner again I saw him running away.'[113] 'I heard Constable "A" ask for handcuffs and was feeling for my own,' said Constable C, 'when the prisoner wrenched himself from my grasp & started to run up Davis Street.'[114] This Keystone-Koppery might have been amusing if the consequences had been less tragic. The constables called on Walsh to halt, and opened fire when he kept running. Walsh fell mortally wounded. He died in the street a few minutes later.[115]

These incidents were not unique. On 24 March 1921 Louis D'Arcy was shot and killed by police in County Galway.[116] D'Arcy was being driven from Oranmore to Galway, guarded by three Auxiliaries, riding in a Crossley tender, with a Ford car in convoy. The Ford broke down along the way, said the Auxiliaries, forcing the Crossley to stop. 'We pulled in to the left side of the road,' said one of D'Arcy's guards, 'and immediately the deceased put his foot on the opposite seat and jumped on to the ground and started running for a gap in the wall. We called out "Halt"; he did not halt and we fired at him. He fell to the ground.'[117]

A court of inquiry was held, and there is a note on the cover of its proceedings: 'Civilian. Attempted escape from custody of RIC. Another case of handcuffs.' Inside the cover General Macready wrote: 'DAG. This would not have occurred if the prisoner had been handcuffed or properly secured.'[118] Another court of inquiry was held in County Kerry on 28 March 1921, after William McCarthy was shot dead while trying to escape. Macready wrote on this file that it was 'quite inexcusable' that McCarthy had not been handcuffed.[119] Two days later Deputy Inspector General Walsh issued the following circular to the RIC: 'In several cases recently prisoners have been shot, others recaptured. In future prisoners must be handcuffed—The police all carry handcuffs, and a very full explanation will be required if any prisoners escaping—do so not handcuffed. Should any prisoner attempt to escape and be shot in the attempt the Senior Police officer present will be held responsible.'[120]

In cases like these the police may simply have been guilty of negligence. But in some other cases the wounds on the dead bodies of escaping prisoners appear to belie the statements of their captors. Thomas Collins, for example, was arrested on 18 January 1921 at Kilkeel, County Galway. According to his captor, Sergeant Keeney:

> Collins was walking in front of us about 5 yards, he looked round suddenly and made a spring for the wall. The wall was quite low & he hopped over it. I ordered him to halt but he did not comply. I fired first with my rifle & ordered the men to fire. He fell at the first shot, a volley being discharged as he fell. I went to him & found him groaning & practically dead.[121]

The medical examiner testified that there were ten gunshot wounds on the corpse. There was an entrance wound over the dead man's right temple, 'with large exit wound in the left side of the head, fractured bone and cerebral matter extruding'. There was another entrance wound in the right groin, 'with large exit wound in right loin with protrusion of the viscera'.[122] A third bullet had entered under the breastbone, injuring the heart and fracturing the spinal column. None of these wounds had been inflicted from behind.[123]

In another case, on 23 December 1920, Auxiliaries in County Kerry found incriminating documents in the house of a forty-three-year-old married farmer, Andrew Moynihan. Moynihan was arrested and put in the back of a Crossley tender under the supervision of Section Leader C. Sutton. Later that evening the Auxiliaries were driving back to Tralee when, according to Sutton, 'the party halted and at the prisoner's request I took him a bit up the road to relieve nature'. Moynihan 'made a dash so as to escape' and Sutton called on him twice to halt: 'as he was trying to get over a wall & the night was dark I ran after him & fired two shots in rapid succession with my revolver. The deceased fell & as far as I know he was killed instantly.'[124] The body was taken back to Tralee military barracks and examined the following day. The medical officer found three wounds, one on the chest and two on the face. 'The two on the face were caused by the same bullet,' he said.[125]

Other cases leave little room for doubt. Michael Tolan, for example, was arrested on 18 April 1921 in County Mayo. He was detained in Ballina barracks until 7 May 1921, when he was handed over to Auxiliaries of D Company ADRIC, for transportation to Galway. The Auxiliaries made it back safely that night—without their prisoner. When a member of Dáil Eireann enquired into Tolan's disappearance after the Truce of 11 July, he was told simply that enquiries were being made. Later, the missing man's comrades learned that a badly decomposed body had been found about a week after Tolan disappeared, in a bog near Ballina. The remains had been taken to nearby League and buried in a plot marked 'unknown'. On 12 October Tolan's brigade adjutant wrote to Michael Collins for permission to disinter and examine this corpse.[126]

Another case of prisoner-killing involved the officer commanding F Company ADRIC, who was actually put on trial for the murder of a Dublin man, James Murphy. Auxiliaries arrested Murphy and his friend Patrick Kennedy in Talbot Street at about 9:30 in the evening of Thursday, 9 February 1921. A couple of hours later, at 11:30 p.m., the two men were discovered in Clonturk Park, Drumcondra, by constables of the Dublin Metropolitan Police. Kennedy had been shot and killed. He was taken to the police barrack, where his father identified his body. Murphy had been shot as well, but he was not dead yet. He was taken to the Mater hospital, where he died on Saturday morning.[127] Murphy spoke to his brother before the end. According to his brother's affidavit, James Murphy and his friend had first been questioned at Dublin Castle, and then driven to Clonturk Park by their Auxiliary captors:

> They halted the motor lorry near a field, where there was unused and derelict ground. They took my brother and Patrick Kennedy out of the motor lorry, brought them into the field, put old tin cans over their heads, put them against the wall, and fired a number of shots at them. I believe Patrick Kennedy was killed almost instantaneously. My brother was hit through the tin can in his mouth on the right cheek, on the left cheek, and through the breast. Having done this the soldiers left them and went away.[128]

Murphy's dying declaration was read out in the House of Commons on 21 February 1921, but the scandal had already broken in Dublin. A court of inquiry had been held, and F Company's commander, Captain W. L. King, had been placed under arrest, along with two of his cadets.[129] But their friends, it seems, were soon at work preparing their defence. In his diary

Mark Sturgis wrote on 13 February that 'Andy tells me that Basil Thomson's man in the Castle, Capt Hardy, has tried to intimidate witnesses against the authors of the Drumcondra affair.'[130] On 15 February General Macready wrote in a letter to Sir John Anderson: 'I am informed that every effort is being made to prove alibis and such like in the case of Major [*sic*] King, but I have every hope that we shall circumvent any efforts in that direction and see that justice is done.'[131]

Macready's hopes were disappointed. Two months later, on 12 April 1921, King and his accomplices were tried by court martial.[132] During these proceedings a Dublin Metropolitan Police officer's evidence was ruled inadmissible: 'A D.M.P. witness who described the finding of the bodies of Kennedy and Murphy shortly after eleven o'clock on the night of the crime said Murphy, who was not then dead, made a statement to him, but after a legal argument the Court ruled that this statement was not admissible as evidence.'[133] Later, two Auxiliaries from F Company testified that King was directing a raid in Leeson Street when Kennedy and Murphy were murdered in Drumcondra.[134] These witnesses were a platoon commander and the company intelligence officer. The platoon commander had signed the report on the Leeson Street raid, and admitted under cross-examination that by signing this report he was indicating that he was the officer in charge, rather than his company commander, Captain King. The intelligence officer, for his part, admitted that his trial testimony contradicted the testimony that he had given at the court of inquiry back in February. Despite these discrepancies, all three defendants had been acquitted of the murder of James Murphy by 15 April.[135] The Kennedy case was never tried.

Other stories were just as horrific as Murphy's dying declaration. James and Patrick Ryan of Knockfune, County Tipperary, were both Volunteers, though neither was a full-time guerrilla. James was limping from a bullet wound: in March 1921 police and soldiers had caught him cutting a road near Tour, chased him, and shot him.[136] At about one o'clock in the morning, on the night of 7 June 1921, the Ryan family was awakened by knocking at the door of their house, and by shouting outside. Patrick answered the door. James and a servant boy were still in bed when two masked men entered their room and told them to get up. 'Paddy was brought out to the yard,' said James:

> I heard voices saying put your face to the wall or something like it. I heard several shots. I cannot say how many. Two or three more came in and

> shouted. All males to get out. I told my mother to ask them for mercy. The house was on fire and we all went outside. About 5 men were outside shouting when they seen me walking down the yard they called me come on here lame fellow what made you lame. I said I was wounded in Tour by the military and am lame since. They were shouting [*illegible*] again when you were not shot in Tour you will be shot now. Two shots were then fired at me but missed me. I turned round & ran & several shots were fired at me. One hit me in the back. I continued to run and after a bit fell.[137]

Patrick was killed. James was wounded but survived. Their home was burned. Their mother, Ellen Ryan, and her daughter Margaret both testified that they saw one man in a black uniform with a peaked cap, a second man in khaki, and a third man in dark plain clothes with a mask.[138]

Often, women like Ellen and Margaret Ryan were the only witnesses left, after their male family members had been killed. James Coleman of Cork, for example, had been murdered in front of his wife seven months before, on the night of 18 November 1920. Knocking and bell ringing awakened Mrs Coleman at about three o'clock. When she asked who it was, she was told 'Military, open quickly please, open quickly please.' Mr Coleman got dressed, went down to the door, and opened it. Someone asked whether he was Coleman. 'Yes,' he said. 'There was then a loud report of shots as if at the door,' his widow testified later:

> During this time I was on my way down the stairs. When I arrived at the foot of the stairs I had a clear view of the door. The candle was still alight in the hall. There was no other light. I saw a very tall man wearing a large grey frieze coat and a cap similar to a policeman's. He fired two shots at my husband as he was falling to the ground. I didn't see his face as he had his cap pulled down and his coat collar turned up. He then left banging the door behind him leaving my husband in a pool of blood.[139]

Four months later fifteen-year-old Mary Horan of Srah, County Mayo, watched as her father Tom Horan was executed right in front of her. On 7 March 1921 she was at home, sitting in the kitchen with her father, when three men came in, dressed in police uniforms. According to Mary, they said 'good day, sir' three times. Tom Horan said 'good day' twice, in reply. Then, Mary said, 'I heared [*sic*] a bang, and he fell into the fire.' One of the men had shot her father in the back of the head with a revolver.[140]

Three months later, on the night of 12 June 1921, in Belfast, Alice Kerr was present when USC special constables led by an Auxiliary came to kill her married brother William. When Alice answered the fatal knock at the door that night, she met a tall man, dressed in a temporary cadet's uniform, and speaking with an English accent, along with two other men. They pushed past her and went upstairs, then came back down, dragging William Kerr along with them:

> It was then I caught hold of the tall man and asked him 'For God's sake to take me in my brother's place.' He just laughed at me and all four went out of the back door. I still held on to the tall man and said 'If anything happens to my brother I can identify you.' He threw me off and said I should never see my brother again.[141]

Alice followed them out into the street, where a Crossley tender was waiting. A man with a handkerchief over his face pointed a revolver at Alice Kerr, telling her in a Belfast accent that if she did not go back he would put a bullet in her.[142] William Kerr was put into the back of the tender, taken away, and killed. Later that morning Alice Kerr said she saw the Auxiliary driving out of the local police barrack. 'I threw up my hand & shouted there he is to the woman who was with me,' she testified. 'The man saw me & turned up the collar of his coat & turned away his head.'[143]

Police and military death squads across Ireland followed similar procedures. They struck first in the city of Cork in the spring of 1920. Their first victim was the city's Lord Mayor, Tomás MacCurtáin. Knocking at their door woke the MacCurtáin household at about one o'clock in the morning on 20 March. Armed men with blackened faces forced a way in past Mrs MacCurtáin, and went upstairs to the Lord Mayor's bedroom door. 'Come out, Curtain,' they said. 'Give me time to dress,' he said. 'I am not ready.' When Mr MacCurtáin opened his door, they shot him twice, wounding him fatally. 'Murder,' a woman screamed as the gang departed. 'Murder, the police are murdering us all!'[144]

Copycat killings followed the next week, in Thurles, County Tipperary. An urban councillor, Michael McCarthy, had been pressing for an inquiry into the January police riot. At about one o'clock in the morning on the night of 27 March, there was a knock at the door of the McCarthy house. When Michael's brother James opened the door, a pair of tall men in black overcoats asked him his name, shot him, and left.[145] The next night a death squad came banging on Thomas Dwyer's door in Ragg, three miles from Thurles. When the door was opened, they pushed inside, went up to Dwyer's room, and shot him down. 'Give him another,' one of the gunmen said, as Dwyer lay wounded.[146]

In some cases the victims of extrajudicial killings had been implicated in the shooting of police. Five men were shot in Cork on the night of 18 November, including James Coleman. The remaining four were suspected of shooting and killing RIC Sergeant James O'Donoghue the previous evening. Eugene O'Connell and Patrick Hanley were killed along with James Coleman. Charles O'Brien and Stephen Coleman were wounded but survived. According to Peter Hart's detailed account of this incident, Charles O'Brien had indeed been one of the three men who shot Sergeant O'Donoghue.[147]

Other men were killed simply for being republicans, or for being part of republican families. Municipal politicians like Lord Mayor MacCurtáin were particularly choice targets for police death squads. We have already read about the murder of an urban councillor, Michael Walsh, in Galway on 19 October 1920, and a district councillor, John Geoghegan, at Moycullen on 20 February 1921. Alderman Thomas Halpin was taken from his home in Drogheda, County Louth, and killed, along with another man, on the night of 8 February 1921.[148] And on the night of 6/7 March 1921 the Mayor of Limerick, George Clancy, was murdered in his home, like Lord Mayor MacCurtáin of Cork—though the Limerick assassins went one better than their counterparts in Cork, by killing a former mayor, Michael O'Callaghan, as well.[149]

British journalist Richard Bennett investigated the killing of Clancy and O'Callaghan forty years later, and found convincing evidence that the two men had been killed by an Auxiliary—an Auxiliary who had, in fact, enlisted in the Division in October 1920, and whom we have encountered before: George Nathan. Bennett interviewed two former Auxiliaries who had served with G Company in County Clare, and who claimed to have known Nathan in Ireland. 'He belonged to an organisation called "The Dublin Castle Murder Gang," who combined the duties of intelligence officers and gunmen,' says Bennett:

> Nathan, I was told, came down to the Auxiliary mess at Killaloe, a few miles from Limerick, and said he had a job to do that night. He then suggested to my old gentleman that they should drive together into Limerick, have dinner at Kidds and then go on from there. In the end it was another officer from the Auxiliary company at Killaloe who went with Nathan. They came back to the mess at six o'clock the next morning, 'boozed up and looking like death'. Nathan told the Auxiliaries at breakfast—to their horror—that he had killed Clancy and O'Callaghan.[150]

Bennett then managed to trace the other Auxiliary, who confirmed this story:

> Nathan had picked him up one night at Kidds to go on a raid, as he said. But they had knocked off a couple of Shinners instead. No, he hadn't shot either of them himself. He had no stomach for that kind of job. Nathan was a bit green about the gills afterward. They went and had a skinful to wash the taste away. There was quite a fuss about it, he seemed to remember.[151]

According to his entry in the Auxiliary Division's register, Nathan himself had served with G Company in County Clare, which would explain a number of things about this story.[152] For example, the two old Auxiliaries appear to have known Nathan quite well. The first said that Nathan 'could be an absolute charmer. An ex-Guards officer. Carried himself with terrific panache. A roaring homosexual. He seemed to be absolutely fearless. He knew he must be a marked man, but it never seemed to bother him.'[153] The second was less impressed. 'All of a sudden, he remembered Nathan—"Typical Jew-boy, but very well-spoken."'[154] Nathan's prior service in G Company would explain both how these men became acquainted with him and why he included them in his plans for the evening—as well as how this particular assignment fell to Nathan.

In many cases retaliation came quickly, tit for tat. The killing of Clancy and O'Callaghan, for example, was apparently triggered by the killing of RIC Sergeant James Maguire on 6 March 1921. In other cases, however, the police waited a long time before settling accounts. Three Black and Tans, for example, had been shot and wounded while on patrol in Limerick city on the evening of 24 July 1920.[155] One of these three, Constable Walter Oakley, later died of his wounds.[156] Five months later, in November, two Limerick men, James O'Neill and Patrick Blake, were put on trial for Oakley's murder, by a military court in Dublin.[157] Both men were acquitted on Friday, 19 November 1920: but this verdict was then set aside—by Judge Lynch. While returning home the following day both O'Neill and Blake were intercepted by armed men on the road from Limerick Junction. The gunmen stopped O'Neill's car and shot him dead: they also fired after Patrick Blake's car as it drove off, killing his brother, Michael.[158] Though sometimes neither swift nor sure, the vengeance of the police was often deadly.

7

The Devil's Work:

Explaining Police Reprisals

Reprisals are easier to describe than explain: but once again, if we study contemporary news reports and official documents, their causes will gradually become clear. During the Irish War of Independence, and especially in the late summer and autumn of 1920, lynch law prevailed in many parts of Ireland. Frustrated by their inability to defeat their enemies in battle, and embittered by their inability to convict them in court; terrorised by the guerrillas, and shunned by the people; enraged by the deaths of their comrades, and inflamed by drink; incited by their officers, and encouraged by faint official censure—the police took to reprisals as a form of rough justice. Police mobs destroyed the homes and shops of republicans, and police death squads executed known and suspected insurgents. These crimes have been widely blamed on the RIC's British recruits, but evidence indicates that Irish police were just as likely to take reprisals as Black and Tans. When British police and Auxiliaries took reprisals, they were following the bad example set by their Irish comrades.

This last point is in many ways the most important. All human behaviour is a product of both character and circumstance. But historians who have tried to explain why the security forces took reprisals in the Irish War of Independence have generally committed what Lee Ross called the 'fundamental attribution error': they have overvalued character-based or dispositional explanations and undervalued circumstance-based or situational explanations. In its earliest and simplest form, this error led historians and memoirists who had lived through the war to blame reprisals on their former enemy's low moral character: the Black and Tans 'were drawn from the criminal classes and the dregs of the population of English cities';

they were 'jail-birds and down-and-outs'—'every thief, drug addict, madman and murderer could come into this new force'. And this belief, it seems, was founded on a deeper, more fundamental belief in the evil nature of 'the English'. Reprisals were 'not only authorized but instigated' by the government, which 'pretended that these were cases of their forces "getting out of hand" under great provocation'. This force of thieves and murderers had been specially selected to 'bring the lights of English law and order to Ireland'—'dirty tools for a dirty job'.

Other historians have rejected this explanation, but have then committed the same fundamental attribution error. Reprisals, they have argued, were committed by violent war veterans. The Black and Tans and Auxiliaries were men degraded and brutalised by years of trench warfare—men 'habituated to excitement and violence'—even, in some cases, 'fractured personalities whose maladjustments found temporary relief in the 1914–18 War and whose outward stability depended on the psychic reassurance of a khaki tunic on their back and a Webley .455 at their hip'. And once again, this view persists today. According to Peter Hart, the brutality of the Black and Tans and Auxiliaries 'was a direct consequence of their alienation and wartime experience'.[1]

But none of these characterisations, it seems, would apply to the Irish constables of the RIC. These men were not the 'off-scourings of English industrial populations': they were recruited, instead, from the Irish countryside. They were not 'jail-birds and down-and-outs', and they were reinforced with British ex-soldiers precisely because so few of them had gone through the allegedly brutalising experience of service in the First World War. If these men, too, were taking reprisals, then we must begin to look beyond character-based explanations, and consider the circumstances in which both British and Irish police found themselves during the Irish War of Independence.

7.1 'A fratricidal vendetta'

So: who took reprisals, and why? After the sack of Balbriggan on 20 September 1920, reprisals were blamed on the Black and Tans and Auxiliaries. This blame came from different quarters, however, and was laid for different reasons, depending on people's perceptions of the Irish War of Independence. Irish republicans understood the conflict of 1920–1 as a war between the British Empire and the Irish Republic, rather than as a civil war within the United Kingdom. In the minds of the revolutionaries, the war was a battle between Ireland and England, us and them, good and evil. But England's Irish collaborators—the 'black-coated rascals' of the Royal Irish Constabulary—did not fit into this republican dichotomy. 'They are Irishmen, with Irish blood in their veins,' said one republican politician. 'They have forsworn the allegiance they owe to their own land, they have sworn allegiance to the enemy of their country, they have degraded their manhood, and, like lost souls who have sold themselves to the devil, they are eager to do the devil's work in Ireland.'[2] Inconceivably, Peelers were both 'we' and 'they'—Irishmen who fought on the side of England. Though described as black, their uniforms were bottle green, and their badge was a harp and crown.

Black and Tans and Auxiliaries may have been hybrids in appearance, but Peelers were hybrids in substance, and it seems that Irish separatists were not entirely happy to be fighting their half-brothers. The coming of the Black and Tans made things much simpler, at least in republican minds. By blaming reprisals on its British recruits, the revolutionaries could bypass the RIC's inconvenient liminality, push its Irish members to the margins of discourse, and think of the conflict in properly binary terms. This desire to simplify the war can be seen in the work of republican propagandist Erskine Childers:

> The main instrument of the executive is—or rather used to be—the Royal Irish Constabulary, a centralised armed force, with a military training, under the direct control of the Castle. This home-bred Irish force, which in quieter times used to perform ordinary civil duties with fair efficiency (though it never bore any resemblance to the locally controlled English civil police), has been ruined by wanton and cruel misuse, and should in common humanity be reorganised, if it is kept at all, as the Royal English Constabulary. Mercifully, it is being recruited mainly from Englishmen now; for, of all expedients for subduing a recalcitrant nation, that of arming it against itself is the most cruel. You set up a fratricidal vendetta in which each side is compelled to regard the other as traitors, and which only becomes clean and chivalrous when conditions permit of open war.[3]

The same urge to marginalise the 'old RIC' can be discerned in the testimony of Mary MacSwiney to the American Commission. On 8 December 1920 MacSwiney denied that IRA gunmen had shot Sergeant James O'Donoghue in Cork on 17 November. 'I know that that was murder,' she said, 'and was not done by any of our people':

> He was an inoffensive old man and within a few months of his pension time. He had not committed a single act of aggression against our people. He was not acting as a spy. He was doing no harm to anybody, and not a single Irish Volunteer would have shot him. And this man was to have his pension and retire from the force in a very short time. He had not taken part in the work of the Black-and-Tans. And he was found shot. The Black-and-Tans have shot several men like that who would not act as spies, in the hope of throwing further odium on Sinn Fein, as they call it.[4]

In fact, as we now know, three Volunteers killed O'Donoghue: one of the sergeant's killers only just escaped execution by a police death squad later that night.[5] MacSwiney might have known this and lied; or she might have been misinformed. Either way, her desire to understand and represent the Irish War of Independence as a conflict between 'our people' and the British—between 'us' and 'them'—is clear.

Progressive British politicians (Labourites, Asquithian Liberals, and Irish Parliamentary Party remnants) also publicised reprisals by the British police forces, but for different reasons. Like Irish separatists, British progressives thought in terms of 'us' and 'them'. But in their case 'we' were the peaceful and parliamentary British, rulers of an empire both civilised and civilising, while 'they' were the militaristic Prussians and barbarous Turks. Progressive politicians were dismayed by the violence of Irish republican guerrillas, but they were doubly dismayed by the violence of British police and Auxiliaries, which reminded them of German atrocities in Belgium or Turkish atrocities in Bulgaria and Armenia—or for that matter, the crimes of the republican 'murder gang' in Ireland. How could British fighters behave like bashi-bazouks? How could 'we' be like 'them'? In a speech on 20 October 1920 the veteran Irish nationalist MP T. P. O'Connor summed up the progressive position:

> Shall we be faithful to the almost unbroken tradition of this great free and constitutional country that law shall be supreme and the protection of the law shall follow even those charged with the most heinous crime, or shall we adopt the opposite principle of Prussianism, that the innocent must suffer for the guilty? It is British justice or Prussian frightfulness: that is the issue.

'That is my complaint,' he concluded, 'that you have the Prussian or the Bolshevik system in Ireland and not the English system.'[6]

In the minds of British progressives, it seems, the system was to blame, not the men. Conservative Junkers were experimenting with Prussian frightfulness in Ireland. These un-British policies had produced un-British atrocities. In its report the Labour Commission to Ireland warned:

> Things are being done in the name of Britain which must make her name stink in the nostrils of the whole world. The honour of our people has been gravely compromised. Not only is there a reign of terror in Ireland which should bring a blush of shame to the cheek of every British citizen, but a nation is being held in subjection by an empire which has proudly boasted that it is the friend of small nations.[7]

However, progressives did not condemn the Black and Tans and Auxiliaries. These men were veterans, even heroes, of the Great War. 'I do not believe,' wrote progressive journalist Hugh Martin, 'that the British "Tommy", when he wears "Black and Tan" in Ireland, becomes a "hired bravo" or delights in bullying peaceable men and women.'[8] By rights, they argued, the blame should fall on the Conservative and Unionist pashas of Whitehall. Pustules of brutality like the sack of Balbriggan were merely symptoms of a poxy government policy. 'Yes,' wrote Robert Lynd, correspondent for the *Daily News*, in his report: 'the White Terror is in full swing, and it is not ignorant Black and Tans, but British Cabinet Ministers and their own advisers that are responsible for it.'[9]

For their different reasons, then, both Irish republicans and progressive Britons agreed that reprisals were the work of British police recruits and auxiliaries. But the evidence makes it clear that the Black and Tans have borne more than their share of the blame for police reprisals. This was noted even at the time. 'As a matter of fact,' said the *Manchester Guardian*'s correspondent, after visiting Gormanstown depot, 'like most popular judgments, the condemnation of the English recruits of the R.I.C., which the Black-and-Tans are, has been much too thorough-going, and they are not responsible for many of the crimes frequently brought against them. They have certainly taken part in a number of reprisals, but an equal number of the participants were Irish members of the R.I.C.'[10]

In some cases the numbers were more than equal. There were no Black and Tans involved in the Tuam police riot of 20 July 1920, and there were no living Black and Tans in Galway when the police rioted on 8 September 1920: Constable Krumm had been the lone Black and Tan at Eglinton Street barracks, and he was dead before the riot began.[11] No Black and Tans, it seems, took part in the Tubbercurry police riot of 30 September 1920.[12] 'Tullamore may stand as a type of reprisal by the old R.I.C.,' says the *Guardian*'s report on the riot of 1 November 1920.[13]

The Irish police also took an active part in many reprisals by Black and Tans. The sack of Balbriggan, for example, was 'organised and countenanced' by the Black and Tans' Irish officers, and led by their non-commissioned officers—Irishmen all.[14] Writing decades later, the Commandant's adjutant at Gormanstown confirmed this: in a letter to J. R. W. Goulden, he denied that any British recruits had broken out of barracks that night, and explained that he had personally sent a detachment of Black and Tans to Balbriggan, to reinforce the local police.[15]

Irish police were implicated in burnings, punishment beatings, and extrajudicial killings as well. After the burning of Tubbercurry creamery, for example, the manager's wife told reporters that her attackers had Irish accents. Later, on the night of 24 October 1920, near Thurles, County Tipperary, a police death squad executed two 'young men members of the Irish Republican Army', Michael Ryan and William Gleeson. Ryan, the registrar of the local republican court, was in bed with pneumonia when he was killed.[16] According to the *Daily News*, the killers 'told Miss Margaret Ryan, a girl of 18 whose word cannot seriously be doubted: "We are secret service men over from England." They spoke, however, with the usual Irish accent.'[17] The police who set fire to the co-operative creamery in Abbeydorney, County Kerry, on 18 November 1920 were 'chiefly men in R.I.C. uniform, and the rest were "Black and Tans" of the usual type—men in khaki with police caps'.[18] About the same time an Irish ex-soldier was telling the Labour Commission that he had been kicked and beaten by police who accused him of training the guerrillas to use machine guns. 'These men were not English,' he said; 'they all spoke with an Irish accent, and one who spoke with a strong brogue served me worst.'[19] Finally, the men who killed John McGowan in a house near Boyle, County Roscommon, on 15 December 1920, also spoke like Irishmen.

In one extraordinary case, both Irish and English police threatened a journalist in Tralee, during the blockade in early November 1920. Their victim in this case was a married man, Thomas Quirke. According to Mrs Quirke, a group of eight police came to their house on 6 November. Some of the men were in RIC uniform, and some of them were in khaki. When they were told that Mr Quirke was not at home, they replied that they had 'a bullet for him for sending lies about the police', then went away. Thomas was home when the police came back on 9 November. The second group apologised for the first and its threats, but insisted that Quirke retract one of his reports that police with fixed bayonets were keeping the Tralee poor away from the bakery. Quirke agreed, under protest, hoping to spare himself and his family further trouble. The following day, however, two more police came to the Quirke house. One of the pair was Irish. His partner was a Black and Tan. They were upset with Thomas Quirke over a different story, which said that police in North Kerry had shot pigs and fowl.

'It is all lies,' the Peeler said. 'We don't kill pigs or any animals. We don't kill swine, but we shoot Kerry swine, and we shall shoot more. The Sinn Feiners have declared war on us, and we are up against them.'

Mrs Quirke asked him whether he was an Irishman and a Catholic, speaking to a woman that way. He said he was, but had no conscience and would not think it necessary to call a priest if he shot a man.

Mrs Quirke then protested that her husband was just earning aliving and had to get his information from a variety of sources.'We know where he gets his information from,'said the Peeler.'He gets it from the Sinn Feiners. Didn't he get a warning from us? Why doesn't he come to us for his information? Why doesn't he get an honest living as we are doing?'

The Black and Tan spoke up at this point. 'He is tarnishing our reputation,' he said. 'He is educating the country into being Sinn Feiners by his writings.' The Peeler then waved his revolver. 'We will give him a dose of this,' he warned, 'and you will be a widow before morning.'[20]

Years later in his memoirs an RIC officer, John Regan, was also convinced that many reprisals were the work of Irish constables rather than their British reinforcements. 'It is a fact,' he said, 'that those police quickest to avenge the death of a comrade were Irishmen and men of an excellent type':

> Black and Tans, having drink taken, might fire out of lorries indiscriminately, loot public houses, or terrorise a village, but the Irishman would avenge his comrade when absolutely stone cold sober and on the right person. It required a great deal of courage to do so as, if detected, he ran a serious risk of being hanged; although it would, of course, have been extraordinary to see a policeman hanged for shooting a member of an organisation which had not only declared war on all police, but shot them whenever the opportunity offered.[21]

It would, indeed, have been extraordinary to see a Peeler go to the gallows: in fact, police were almost never prosecuted for taking part in reprisals—at least partly because they would not give evidence against each other. One observer understood this Irish version of *omertà* very well. On 20 October 1920 Sir J. D. Rees told the House of Commons that while everyone in Westport, County Mayo, knew the person responsible for shooting a resident magistrate the year before, 'not one of them would come forward and give evidence. Is it to be supposed that when similar occurrences occur among those responsible for the maintenance of law and order that anyone is going to inform upon them on their own side.'[22]

It seems to have taken great determination to resist this pressure to keep quiet. Recall that Constable Edward Knights and Constable William Johnson were tried and convicted of unlawful possession after a series of robberies in County Roscommon in early November 1920.[23] According to his own account, the man responsible for the arrest of these two Black and Tans was Constable John Duffy, who overheard Johnson boasting about his crimes. 'There was a sergeant standing at the fireplace,' Duffy recalled, 'so I said: "Come on, sergeant, and we'll put a stop to this thing once and for all." "I will not," replied the sergeant, "they might shoot us." ' Undeterred, Duffy enlisted one of his fellow constables to help him conduct a search, and found the loot in Johnson's bedroom:

> I asked the sergeant to bring out the District Inspector or Head Constable as I wanted to have an end put to this business once and for all. The sergeant replied, no, that we would do it the regulation way. I said: 'I don't care a hang how you do it, but a stop must be put to it.' The sergeant sent the guard to the D.I.s office to ask the Head Constable to come down. I was holding the lighted candle at the foot of the stairs when the head Constable arrived. I used strong language to him and said this must stop. He said, 'what?' So I took him to the bedroom and showed him the loot. He immediately issued orders to have all policemen in the station armed and report to him when the two Tans came in. The Tans duly arrived and seemed surprised when they saw all men under arms. One of their comrades, who had not gone out, told them that they were in for it now.[24]

We have also seen other cases where Black and Tans were tried, found guilty, and put in prison for crimes against Irish people. Constable Wilton was imprisoned for killing Thomas Lawless in Maryborough, Queen's County. Constable Robinson was imprisoned for killing Anne Dickson in Clones, County Monaghan. Four constables—Chester, Gibson, Hollins, and Skinner—were imprisoned for robbing a bank in Strokestown, County Roscommon. Constable Myers and Constable O'Hara were convicted of housebreaking in County Wexford.

What made Irish policemen break the code of silence in these cases? Peter Hart has argued that most of the spies and informers who were executed by the Cork IRA were social deviants and outsiders.[25] 'They were killed,' says Hart, 'not for what they did but for who they were: Protestants, ex-soldiers, tramps and so on down the communal blacklist.'[26] This overstates the case—and, in fact, Hart provides a more nuanced and accurate version of his own analysis a little earlier in his book. 'Almost anyone could be an informer,' he says. 'Almost anyone could be suspected of informing. Whether one was shot (or burned out, or expelled), however, depended upon one's standing in the community.'[27] That is to say: the revolutionaries were more likely to execute known or suspected spies and informers who were social deviants and outsiders. Since one could say virtually the same thing about the treatment of criminals by judicial systems around the world, it would be surprising indeed if this were not true in rebel Cork during the War of Independence as well.

Certainly, one could say the same thing about the treatment of police who broke the law during this conflict. On the whole, Black and Tans who were caught and punished for criminal offences were social deviants and outsiders as well. They committed crimes against 'civilians' (i.e. non-republicans), and committed these crimes in places where they were strangers, unknown to the local police. Wilton killed a former Irish Guardsman in Queen's County, while on his way to a station in County Cork. Robinson killed a woman, while he was away from his barracks in Ballybay. Chester, Gibson, Skinner, and Hollins robbed a bank, in a strange town, in a neighbouring county. Myers and O'Hara broke into houses only nine days after they were stationed in County Wexford. Johnson was caught with stolen goods only two weeks after he was allocated to County Roscommon.

Other cases followed a similar pattern. On 2 February 1921, for example, George Dixon JP was robbed and murdered in Dunlavin, County Wicklow, by 'newly joined English RIC recruits'. Two Black and Tans named Hardie and Mitchell were arrested the same day. In his monthly report the county inspector mentioned that this crime 'aroused intense feeling for a time in Dunlavin neighbourhood against the so-called "Black & Tans" on the part of the loyal & Unionist Section especially as Mr Dixon & his family had been very kind to the police—particularly to the newly joined "strangers"'.[28] Constable Hardie killed himself in Dunlavin barracks on 3 February. Constable Mitchell was tried, found guilty, and hanged on

7 June 1921—the only Black and Tan to hang for murder during the Irish War of Independence.[29]

Though there seem to be few documents relating to this case, another, similar incident had occurred in Queen's County in December 1920, when the county inspector reported that two 'police motor drivers' had been arrested for armed robbery and murder:

> On the morning of the 20th Decr. two masked men gained admittance to the house of a publican in Ballyroan and demanded money. A scuffle ensued and the owner of the house was seriously wounded and his son-in-law killed. Two police motor drivers were arrested on suspicion of being concerned in this affair and were handed over to military custody, from which they escaped on the 27th Decr.[30]

The man who was killed in the robbery was James Whelan. His father-in-law was Patrick McDonnell. The police motor drivers appear to have been temporary constables of the ADRIC: their names were J. H. Cockburn and John Reive. Both temporaries were stationed at Abbeyleix barracks, though neither had been stationed there for long: at the court of inquiry into Whelan's death, Head Constable Michael Flynn testified that Reive had not even been issued a sidearm, 'as he was only here for a couple of days temporarily'.

The two temporaries appear to have hatched a scheme to rob the public house in Ballyroan after it was raided by the police: as Whelan lay dying, his doctor asked him 'if he could say for certain if those two men were in the party that visited his house the night before'.[31] Since Constable Reive had no weapon, they secretly took Head Constable Flynn's. Then, after botching the robbery and shooting Whelan and his father-in-law, they somehow left the head constable's revolver at the scene and tried to replace it with another—apparently hoping that no one would notice.

According to Head Constable Flynn:

> At about 0950 hours on the 20 December 1920 I heard crying and moaning in the kitchen and I went in and found Constable J H Cockburn there suffering from cuts about the head. I questioned him asking how he got injured he stated I got up at 0915 hours went to the Lavatory in the yard but finding someone there I opened the back gate to go out, when I was immediately set on by two men wearing trench coats, they knocked me down & I got stuned [*sic*] they beat me and kicked me while on the ground and I was about 25 minutes there. I shouted but was not heard. I investigated the scene but found no sign of the struggle. I sent for a doctor to dress the constable's

> wounds and I asked the men who were on guard the night before. From whom I learned that Constables J H Coburn [*sic*] and John Reeves [*sic*] had left barracks the night of 19/20 December 1920 without my authority.[32] I then examined the arms but found the exact number produced here. I examined my own revolver. I also examined the records of revolvers kept at this station I found that the revolver in my holster was of the same pattern but had not the number of the revolver served out to me. I produce to the court the revolver found in my holster on the morning of the 20th Dec 1920. I believe it is blood stained. It bears the number R.I.C. 942 while the number of the revolver served out to me is R.I.C. 947.

The revolver left behind after the robbery had borne the number 947. The head constable continued:

> I was present when revolver 947 was handed over to DI Connelly on the 21/12/20 by John Whelan brother of the deceased. It is so injured that it cannot be cocked. It was in my possession up to about 2320 hours on the 19/12/20. I gave no person the authority to remove this revolver 947 from my holster.

When asked where he had left his revolver after 2300 hours, the head constable admitted: 'I thought I brought it into my room, but I am told I left it on the dayroom table.' Perhaps not surprisingly, in light of this admission, a revolver had gone missing from Abbeyleix barracks within the past three months. When asked to whom revolver 942 belonged, Head Constable Flynn said: 'I am unable to say but I can tell you that no record was kept until a revolver was missed from these barracks, and as far as I know revolver 942 was never in this house.'[33]

On the basis of this and other evidence, Cockburn and Reive were both placed under arrest. The military court of inquiry concluded cautiously that Whelan was the victim of wilful murder, 'and that the evidence tends to prove that Constables J H Cockburn and John Reeves of the R.I.C. are implicated in this crime'.[34] In his remarks Major General Jeudwine took a harder line: 'The verdict should be one of wilful murder against Constables Cockburn and Reeves R.I.C.'[35]

Though the county inspector's report mentions that both Reive and Cockburn had escaped from military custody, they were subsequently recaptured: both men were sentenced to death for murder by a general court martial in Dublin on 18 June 1921, but had their sentences commuted to penal servitude for life. In January 1922, while at Dartmoor prison, Reive told the chaplain that the raid on the public house in Ballyroan was not a robbery but a reprisal. According to the chaplain's account:

> The two men were part of an auxilliary [*sic*] force stationed in the neighbourhood of Abbeyleix. Shortly before the occurrence a police barrack had been raided and burned. The men knew that the man, for the murder of whom these two are undergoing sentence, was one of the party who did it, and was seen dancing in the street as the barrack went up in flame. They decided to give him reprisal. There were others to go with them; but at the last moment they did not turn up, and Cockburn and Reive went alone. They protest that they had no intention to commit murder, only to raid and scare him. Cockburn went first into the house, the man resisted, flung Reive down the stair, and tackled Cockburn who fired at him, and killed him.[36]

An equally interesting case comes from Galway's West Riding. In the early hours of 15 May 1921 a gang of police kidnapped a medical student named John Green from his hotel room at Salthill. As Green tried to put on his trousers, he was hit on the head, dragged outside in his nightshirt, and beaten with a truncheon. His kidnappers then took him down to the seaside, where after a brief discussion one of them told Green to say his prayers. 'He then drew his revolver and loaded it,' said Green:

> He then fired and seemed to graze the back of my neck. I stumbled and fell to the left. As I was falling a bullet struck me on the hip, he again fired and struck me on the back. I was still conscious and he said 'Are you dead'? I neither moved nor spoke, he then turned and going towards the road I heard the words 'He is gone.'[37]

The motive for this attack is far from clear. Green was a war veteran and friendly towards the police. Unlike most victims of police and auxiliary death squads, the young medical student survived, and reported the incident to the local constabulary before noon. Both County Inspector Sidley and his superior, Divisional Commissioner Cruise, investigated the case. Green was able to identify two of his attackers, and as a result Constable John Murphy and Constable Richard Orford were arrested, tried, convicted, and sentenced to fifteen years' imprisonment.[38]

This case had a few characteristics in common with other, non-political crimes. Murphy and Orford were not strangers—Green recognised both of them and called Murphy by his nickname, Spud—but they had not been serving long in the West Riding: Murphy had joined the force in late February, and Orford in early March. According to Green and other witnesses, both Murphy and Orford had been drinking. In his report on their arrest, the local district inspector wrote:

> The only motive that can be assigned for the outrage, if committed by the Constables is, that they were under the influence of drink, and while in this state, and owing to very high tension under which the police are living at the present time, and to the fact that on morning of 14th inst. a police patrol was attacked at Spiddal, their nerves being highly strung, they may have committed an act which they would not have attempted while in a calmer temper.[39]

This explanation is very similar to those offered for the Strokestown bank robbery. In one of his petitions Harvey Skinner pleaded that he was not in his right mind when the crime was committed:

> The condition of the country at the time of my arrest was very abnormal & was the indirect cause of my being concerned in the unfortunate affair that led to my arrest later. Through being under the influence of drink that was only too easy of access at the time, this combined with the highly strung condition of my nerves at the time rendering me incapable of my actions.[40]

When the Chief Crown Solicitor recommended clemency for the Strokestown bank robbers in February 1922, he clearly found these arguments convincing. 'The case is difficult to understand if they were in a normal condition,' he wrote.[41]

Whatever their motives, what these men did was illegal—even under lynch law. Crimes like these exceeded what Michel Foucault has called 'the margin of tolerated illegality',[42] and their perpetrators were quickly caught and punished—some of them. Orford and Murphy, for example, were not the only ones who took part in the attack on John Green. They were not even the ones who beat and shot the young medical student. The remaining members of the death squad were never identified.

7.2. No man's land

Why, then, did both Irish and British police take reprisals? In some cases their chief motive was obvious: revenge; revenge for a dead officer; revenge for their dead comrades; revenge on their 'cowardly assailants', guerrillas in overwhelming numbers, attacking by surprise, from ambush, firing from behind cover, giving their victims no chance to fight back; revenge on the communities who sheltered these 'murder gangs'. In a few cases police just went berserk. In his book *Achilles in Vietnam*, psychiatrist Jonathan Shay devotes a chapter to the 'berserk state' among soldiers in war and identifies the death of a 'special comrade' as its leading cause.[43] On 5 June 1921 a police patrol was ambushed in Abbeyfeale, County Limerick, and Robert Jolly, a Black and Tan from Kent, was killed. A republican source describes what happened afterward: 'Head Constable Casey saved the writer from a Black-and-Tan named Nolan, who, seemingly insane, discharged his rifle repeatedly into Jimmy Joy's house before being disarmed by his comrades. He was carried away, still shouting in frenzy that he would have revenge for his chum Jolly.'[44]

A much more disturbing case took place in County Cork on 15 December 1920, just four days after the centre of Cork city was burned. Two trucks full of Auxiliaries were driving from Dunmanway to Cork city for the funeral of Cadet Chapman, who had been killed in the grenade ambush at Dillons Cross on 11 December. Along the way they met a group of three men: an elderly priest, Canon Magner, and the son of a farmer, Timothy Crowley, were helping a resident magistrate fix his car after a breakdown. Cadet Harte was in charge of the rear truck. He stopped his vehicle, got out, and started questioning the priest and the countryman. As the magistrate and the remaining Auxiliaries watched, Harte started abusing the two men, and finally shot both of them dead. 'He was clean off his head then,' said a witness: 'absolutely as mad as a hatter.' At the subsequent military court of inquiry, testimony revealed that Cadet Harte had been 'a particular friend' of Cadet Chapman and had been drinking 'steadily' since Chapman's death.[45] Harte was later put on trial for these two murders and was found guilty, but insane.[46]

There were other, less murderous cases where it seems police went berserk. If we can believe his report, Acting County Inspector Russell's men were uncontrollable after they saw their dead and wounded comrades in Tubbercurry: 'they were simply mad with passion,' he said, 'and all restraints of discipline were thrown to the winds'.[47] But incidents like these were comparatively few. As we know, police who took reprisals were often strangers—reinforcements or marauders from district or county headquarters, with no clear personal connection to the victims of guerrilla violence.

In addition, some reprisals took place after comparatively small provocation. In the early morning of 2 October 1920, for example, a guerrilla band assaulted Frenchpark RIC barracks, midway between the towns of Boyle and Castlereagh in the north of County Roscommon. The battle ended in victory for the police: the barrack was held, and its garrison suffered no casualties. The following night, however, a gang of police and soldiers from Castlereagh went on a reprisal spree. They burned and bombed a pair of shops in the nearby village of Ballinagare; then they drove through the country, setting fire to haystacks and farmhouses.[48] One young man suffered a mock execution along the way. When Patrick Flynn was told he had five minutes to live, he requested a priest. 'You are not going to have any damned priest,' he was told. 'The priests are worse than you are, and we are going to clear them out next.'[49] In his report on these reprisals Hugh Martin laid stress on the fact that no police had been killed or even wounded at Frenchpark. 'The excuse of uncontrollable fury caused by some dastardly outrage is thus altogether absent,' he concluded. 'Intense provocation, at any rate at the moment, must be ruled out.'[50]

The causes of reprisals like these were complex. One element was 'nerves'—the nervous boredom of policing insurgency. Each day police patrols wandered around for hours, looking for the guerrillas, putting themselves in danger. 'We were basically looking for the IRA,' said one old Peeler. 'No still of poteen, no light on your bicycle, no tail lamp, no anything, nobody bothered, the police didn't bother. It was just the police and the IRA.'[51] In many districts lack of information made patrol work almost pointless. The police were merely showing the flag. 'We'd go gawkying down the road and look round and see if anything was suspicious or unusual, and interview somebody who could tell you something,' said another old Peeler. 'It didn't serve much useful purpose as far as I could see, you just were there.'[52] The police had been objectified. Constabulary subdistricts were like the cells of Jeremy Bentham's late eighteenth-century Panopticon, so beloved by Foucault. The guerrillas could see the police. The police could not see the guerrillas. Only their shuttered stations gave them refuge from the rebel gaze.[53]

Lack of rest and recreation was a serious problem as well. In his application for a bonus, dated 13 January 1921, a district inspector in Armagh emphasised how tedious and anxious constabulary life had become, even in one of the safest counties of Ireland. 'I submit that regular warfare would be less trying than the condition of affairs that prevails at present,' he wrote:

> In such warfare officers and men get long periods of rest to recuperate. They are then well looked after, amusements and other luxuries are provided, and their enemies are in front only. They can usually travel free, and everywhere

> are admitted and entertained as honoured guests. In this country there is no rest, the enemy is in front, rear, and flank, no amusements are provided, there is no free travelling or entertainment, friendly people only speak to us by stealth, and we are practically living all the time behind sandbags and steel shutters, peering round corners with alert eyes for assassins when we go abroad, and financially unable to get anywhere for a holiday, or give our wives and families a much needed change.[54]

The whole country was No Man's Land. Police were always in danger, even when they were not on duty. It could be fatal to go for a drink, for example: 19 police were shot and killed in licensed premises, or nearby.[55] Constable Frederick Sterland of Birmingham, for example, was followed out of a Cork city hotel bar and shot dead on 8 May 1921.[56] In another, more bizarre incident on 17 April 1921, three police in plain clothes were drinking while off duty at a hotel in Castleconnell, County Limerick, when it was raided by Auxiliaries, also dressed in plain clothes. The two groups mistook each other for guerrillas and opened fire. By the time the battle was over, a police sergeant, a temporary cadet, and the hotelier had been killed.[57]

Walking out with Irish women could also be dangerous, for both parties. Women who kept company with police were liable to suffer threats or violence or both. On 21 April 1921, for example, two armed and masked men assaulted Rose Logue of Meenacladdy, County Donegal. After accusing her of being friendly to the police, her attackers cut off her hair. 'This was merely a caution as they told her that if she again came unfavourably under notice she would be shot. This lady placed a wreath over the remains of a constable.' Two days later, in Grattanstown, County Louth, three armed and masked men called at the home of John Carroll and cut off the hair of his sister Kate. 'They also threatened to shoot her if she continued keeping company with a policeman from Dunleer.'[58]

Police were always liable to be shot, even in a woman's company. As we have seen, Constable Hubbard and Constable McKibbin were almost assassinated while out on a double date in County Roscommon.[59] Other men fared much worse. On 17 April 1921 Constable John MacDonald of London was out walking with a woman in Cork city when he was attacked, shot, and wounded. His companion helped him to a nearby house, and then hurried to the fire station for an ambulance. When she came back, she met the wounded Black and Tan wandering down the street. 'She helped him to the ambulance outside the fire station and then went with him to the police barracks from which he was conveyed to the military hospital':

> Another constable who was a patient in the same ward as MacDonald stated that the latter told him that he was walking along with a girl friend when two men jumped on his back, pinned his arms behind him and took his revolver away from him.
>
> Another civilian stood by him pointing a revolver but he (the deceased) tried to knock it away and in doing so he was shot in the face. He collapsed on the ground and the civilians fired shots all round his head but none took effect.
>
> Medical evidence was given that the deceased had received a gunshot wound in the face which fractured the lower jaw and the spine at the neck. He died five days later.[60]

Other police were literally dying for a moment's relaxation. The commander of H Company ADRIC, Major John Alister Mackinnon, was assassinated while playing golf.[61] Another temporary cadet, William Hunt, was shot and killed in the dining room of the Mayfair Hotel, Dublin, while having tea with his wife.[62] Constable William Smith and Constable John Webb were killed while fishing near Castlemartyr, County Cork.[63] And as we have seen, Constable George Cuthberton and Constable Walter Shaw were both shot dead while they were taking a walk.[64]

Their more prudent comrades remained in their stations, behind sandbags and steel shutters. In disturbed areas the police were almost imprisoned in their barracks. In Tralee, County Kerry, their barracks were an actual prison: the police lived in the cells. To borrow a phrase from Samuel Johnson, being in the force was like being in a jail, with a chance of being shot. As a result, some reprisals were almost like violent carnivals, in which police enjoyed an escape from house arrest. Rough music was heard in Balbriggan on 21 September 1920, the day after the sack. The *Manchester Guardian*'s correspondent saw three trucks full of Black and Tans drive through Balbriggan, 'shouting and jeering as they passed the ruined buildings and lustily banging tin cans'. A few moments later he heard rifle shots, 'as if, Oriental fashion, they fired a volley into the air for sheer exultation'.[65] During the burning of Granard, County Longford, on 4 November 1920, a few police played melodeons and mouth organs while others burned the town hall, courthouse, and 13 shops and public houses.[66]

Many reprisals were fuelled by alcohol. Sometimes, drinking was a policeman's only recreation: 'there was a lot of these small stations, you know, way out in the country,' said one old Peeler: 'there were only one or two houses near the Barrack—they'd nothing else to do when they were off duty'.[67] The situation was much the same in larger towns, like Galway. John

Caddan told the American Commission that a canteen opened in Eglinton Street barracks in late 1919. There was no limit on the number of drinks police could buy. 'They were up, some of them, most of the night drinking,' he said. Men drank before going on duty, and 'during their idle time. Some of them had only four hours' duty during the day. The rest of the time they usually had liquor in them.'[68] Auxiliary companies had their own canteens as well. According to David Neligan, the cadets of F Company ADRIC were 'hard drinkers and drank all hard liquor. Gin, whiskey and brandy consumed most of their pay.' Night after night, Neligan saw the commander of another company 'being frog-marched to a Crossley tender by two section leaders. He was so drunk that the only thing he could say was that he wanted to "have a crack at the Shinners".'[69] Commandant Crozier took his fateful trip to Galway on 22 November to discipline another drunken company commander. He later estimated that, on average, the Division spent more than 70 per cent of their weekly wages on drinks in their canteens alone. They would extort free drinks from publicans as well.[70]

Police rioters frequently began by looting licensed houses, and those police who were prosecuted were almost always drunk when they broke the law. In one case Dennis O'Donnell was shot and killed by a police patrol in Meadstown, County Cork, on the night of 23 November 1920. Unusually, the three constables involved were cross-examined by a civilian solicitor for the next of kin at the court of inquiry. The results were eye-opening. The police had not only been drinking that day but had also been drinking in public houses during their night patrol, after hours. Constable Wood admitted to having 'one or two' in Lyne's pub and 'about the same' in Welsh's before closing time. He then admitted to having three while on duty, for a total between five and seven. Nonetheless, he testified that he was 'quite sober' that night. When asked whether he knew it was illegal for him to drink in pubs after hours, he said, 'Yes. But there does seem to be any law now.'[71] One of Wood's accomplices, Constable Coe, admitted having a couple of 'small whiskies' on duty that night. Asked whether he knew he was breaking the law by drinking after hours, he said: 'I decline to answer.' Like Wood, Coe began with a couple of drinks at Lyne's before going on duty. 'Q. Were you in any other public houses that day? A. Yes. Q. Which one? A. I decline to answer.'[72] The third constable, Gray, would not answer questions from the solicitor but was cross-examined by the court. 'We understand you visited some public houses just after leaving barracks and had some drinks, did you pay for them,' the court asked.[73] The trio paid for their whiskey that night in Meadstown, but police were known to steal drinks, especially from 'enemy' publicans like Mrs Kane in Oranmore, County Galway.

Police were not confined to barracks by fear alone: in many places they were boycotted as well. Boycotts became especially widespread and severe in the summer of 1920. They began with IRA notices like the following, circulated in the Boyle district of County Roscommon in mid-July 1920:

> Irish Republican Army, Brigade Headquarters, North Roscommon
>
> Notice is hereby given that all intercourse of any kind whatsoever is strictly forbidden between citizens of the Irish Republic and that portion of the Army of Occupation known as the R.I.C.; that a general boycott of the said force is ordered and that you shall cease as from Wednesday, 14th July to transact any business of any nature with said force. All persons infringing this order will be included in the said boycott.
>
> Signed Competent Military Authority.

The police report concludes: 'The boycott has been started and is being rigorously carried out.'[74]

Some police did not blame their communities for shunning them. Boycott orders were enforced with violence and threats. Two cases from County Wexford will serve as examples of how the guerrillas intimidated 'collaborators'. J. Redmond, a motor driver and carpenter in the Gorey district, made the mistake of driving police to the site of a republican court. He suffered a punishment beating for this on the evening of 18 September 1920, when a gang of seven or nine young men attacked him. Redmond fought his attackers and bit one of their fingers in the struggle, but he was badly beaten, his face and clothes were tarred, and he was warned: 'if he ever drove the police or soldiers again he would be shot'.[75] Another Wexford man, Patrick Cullen, was kidnapped on the following evening. A gang of armed and masked men took him from his home, blindfolded him, put him in a car, and then drove him to a churchyard, where his abductors put him on trial and convicted him of informing and 'being friendly' towards the security forces. 'He was told to prepare for death, that his grave was dug, and made to place his hand on the tombstone', but his captors then tied his hands behind his back, took away his coat and vest, hat, boots, and socks, and left him, warning him to remain in the graveyard for an hour. Cullen made his way to a local farmhouse, borrowed some clothes, and returned home by morning.[76]

But in many cases, it seems, police were infuriated by boycotts. Being threatened was one thing. Being despised was quite another. As a result, boycotts were sometimes mentioned in connection with early police reprisals. As we have seen, the police 'keenly resented' the boycott in Tullamore, King's County, before the reprisals on 31 October 1920.[77] After the police riot 'the boycott against them died down considerably'.[78] Earlier, in his first report on the Tubbercurry riot, the *Guardian*'s correspondent wrote: 'It is to be mentioned that in Tubbercurry the police have been rigidly boycotted by the tradespeople, and they have had to fetch their supplies of food from towns at a distance. Mr E. J. Cooke, who was the chief sufferer by the sacking of the town, was accused of playing a part in the boycott.'[79] Boycotting also seems to have provoked reprisals by gangs. The reprisals following the attack on Frenchpark barracks in October 1920 took place in northern Roscommon—the same area covered by the boycott notice mentioned above. By month's end, the county inspector wrote in his report that the boycott of the police 'has been killed by the vigorous action of the police themselves'.[80]

7.3 'Courage wears a uniform'

Another cause of reprisals was the police perception of the conflict. Irish republicans argued that it was not murder to kill police. In their minds the Irish Republic was at war with the United Kingdom, and the RIC was part of the enemy's army of occupation. Its uniformed constables were enemy soldiers, and its plainclothes constables were spies. It was not murder to kill enemy soldiers in battle, and all nations were agreed on the fate of spies in wartime. During her testimony to the American Commission, Mary MacSwiney was questioned about the murder of policemen. 'Here it is called the shooting of policemen,' she said. 'I will simply take the murders of policemen by denying that there ever has been a policeman murdered in Ireland.'[81] Executions of captured guerrillas, on the other hand, were denounced as judicial murder, and condemned along with reprisals as violations of the laws of war. The IRA wore no uniforms and often did not carry arms openly, as the Hague Regulations required, but this was excused on the grounds of necessity.[82]

Some police thought of the conflict as a war as well. 'The Sinn Feiners have declared war on us, and we are up against them,' said the Peeler to

Mrs Quirke in Tralee. And if it was war, then let it be war—on both sides. If the guerrillas could 'shoot' police, then the police could 'shoot' guerrillas. If the guerrillas could execute captured police for 'spying' in plain clothes, then the police could execute guerrillas for doing the same. If the guerrillas could burn the homes and shops of police—i.e., their barracks—then the police could burn the homes and shops of republicans.

This kind of reasoning was encouraged by the police newspaper, the *Weekly Summary*, distributed freely to police barracks by the office of the Chief Secretary for Ireland. In December 1920 the paper published an editorial entitled 'WAR—AS WE LIKE IT. THE REPUBLICAN'S POINT OF VIEW':

> They said—
> 'Let us have War.
> 'Let us have War, as we understand it.
> 'Let us shoot the unsuspecting.
> 'Let us shoot from behind hedges and walls.
> 'Let us shoot policemen when they don't expect us.
> 'Let us ambush soldiers unawares.
> 'Let us murder unarmed men in their beds.
> 'In a word, let us have a one-sided war.'[83]

Clearly, some police were embittered by this 'one-sided war'. News reports of mass reprisals often mention rioters calling for the guerrillas to come out and fight them fairly. In the minds of many police, it seems, guerrilla bands were just 'murder gangs' of cowardly, back-shooting punks. And it is worth noting that 'punk' means both 'a hoodlum or ruffian' and 'a passive male homosexual', since police rhetoric was often highly gendered. The first of the *Weekly Summary*'s rat-a-tat editorials is a good example:

> Courage and cowardice.
> They are in sharp contrast in the Green Isle of Erin to-day.
> Courage does its duty and all the world can see it.
> Courage wears a uniform.
> Cowardice obeys the behests of terrorism—a terrorism without a name.
> Cowardice wears no badge, it is unrecognized, anonymous.
> Courage sticks to its job—twenty-four hours a day out of every twenty-four.
> Cowardice walks disguised for weeks: reveals itself for a moment and then is disguised again.
> Courage is the quality of a man doing a man's job.
> Cowardice is the quality of a skulker; a secret assassin; a marauder by night.

Courage and cowardice.
They are in sharp contrast in the Green Isle of Erin to-day.[84]

This was official propaganda, but there is evidence that many police understood the conflict in similar terms. In their minds the police were masculine—brave and forthright. The guerrillas, by contrast, were effeminate—cowardly and hypocritical. We have already seen how the police dared the IRA to come out and fight during the reprisals at Lahinch, County Clare, on 22 September 1920: the police were 'yelling for the men to come out now and bring their rifles'. In another, even more revealing case, four Volunteers were captured in County Kerry on 4 April 1920. One of them reported later that his captors had pulled him out of his cell and beaten him with the butts of their pistols and rifles: the sergeant in charge had then taken off his tunic, thrown it on the floor, and challenged the captured Volunteer to a fist fight.[85] Later the American Commission received an affidavit in which a young man, James Murphy, described being beaten by 'three British officers', probably Auxiliaries. 'Vengeance is mine,' said one of them, 'and I will repay. These are our Lord's words.' Murphy was knocked down, picked up, and knocked down again. 'If you are a man,' said one of his attackers, 'get up and fight; don't be getting behind ditches and hedges to us. Come on! Come on! Get up and fight!'[86]

Policemen who could not live up to this masculine ideal were scorned. Resigners were seen by some as deserters. The *Weekly Summary* called them 'rats'.[87] 'No men—worthy of the name of men—will desert their posts in the face of gangs of ditch-grovelling, hedge-hidden assassins,' it thundered.[88] Of course, the police themselves often showed 'the quality of a skulker, a secret assassin, a marauder by night'. This contradiction between 'courageous' ideal and 'cowardly' reality was resolved by blaming the guerrillas for police reprisals. Once again, the *Weekly Summary* provides a succinct expression of this view:

Reprisals are wrong.
They are bad for the discipline of the force.
They are bad for Ireland, especially if the wholly innocent suffer.
Reprisals are wrong, but reprisals do not happen wholly by accident.
They are the result of the brutal, cowardly murder of police officers by assassins, who take shelter behind the screen of terrorism and intimidation which they have created.
Police murder produces reprisals.
Stop murdering policemen.[89]

Police violence was defensive and retributive. Reprisals would cease when murder ceased. Arguments like this appeared repeatedly, cut from the pages of Irish and British papers and pasted into the *Weekly Summary*. General Macready's views had already been printed the previous week:

> Formerly, in Ireland, if a police officer were murdered there was no thought of direct reprisals by the R.I.C. They thought only of bringing the murderer to justice, confident that he would be dealt with quickly and adequately by the courts. But now, the machinery of the law having been broken down, they feel there is no certain means of redress and punishment, and it is only human that they should act on their own initiative.[90]

Civilians agreed. 'No body of men could be expected to stand by and see their officers and comrades murdered in cold blood, without being given a chance in most cases to defend their lives, while the population, actively or tacitly, defeated every legitimate attempt to bring the criminals to justice.'[91] 'Is it unnatural that the men, who have a shrewd suspicion of the source of the trouble, but know that the law will be unable to trace or punish the murderers—since the King's writ practically no longer runs in a large part of Ireland—should take the law into their own hands, and administer a rough, blind, and reckless justice?'[92]

Amazingly, in light of the ways in which British propaganda had vilified the 'Hun' during the Great War, the *Weekly Summary* even published approving descriptions of German reprisals against *francs tireurs* during the Franco-Prussian War of 1870–71:

> The honest German soldier was all the more embittered by this behaviour of the francs-tireurs because they were wont at need to hastily assume the appearance of inoffensive peasants by throwing away and hiding their arms and getting rid of every badge indicative of military service. That under such circumstances the Germans gave 'short shrift' to such fellows taken red-handed will be thought only reasonable, even though it is quite possible that at times innocent men may have suffered. The German authorities and troops along the lines of communication had nothing for it but to punish the parishes where outrages against German soldiers or destruction of railways and telegraphs had occurred by levying money contributions or by burning down one or two houses.[93]

To be fair, the *Weekly Summary* also published a number of editorials urging police to show restraint. 'The police exists,' it said, 'for the welfare of Ireland and to lift her from the terror of the pistol. The destruction of

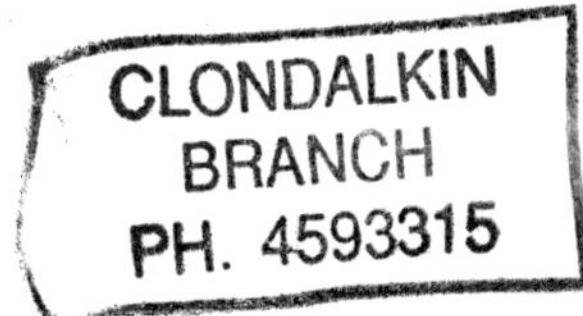

factories, houses, and other buildings only impoverishes Ireland. Do not hurt Ireland. Put out the "murder gang" and free her from the thraldom of terror.'[94] It was 'war to the death' against the guerrillas, but 'every consideration must be shown' to civilians, likewise 'victims of this appalling scourge'. 'Arson, looting and all indiscipline are offences against the people of Ireland. Their persons and their property are sacred.'[95] 'Although the sworn enemy of evil-doers, every constable is the Friend of the Public,' read yet another leader. 'His duty is the protection of their property and persons, just as much as it is his duty to overcome and apprehend those who break the public peace.'[96]

Nonetheless, the message of this 'weekly hate sheet' was clear: guerrilla violence justified or at least excused police violence; reprisals were a poor but necessary substitute for due process.[97] The Royal Irish Constabulary and its Auxiliaries were encouraged to see themselves as both police and soldiers, enforcing the law by waging war on crime. The seeming contradiction between these two missions was obscured by a gendered discourse of masculine defensive violence in which the IRA's guerrillas were both enemies and criminals—unlawful combatants who deserved both defeat and punishment.

7.4 Let the murderers begin

This perception of the conflict brings us to the final few causes of police reprisals in Ireland. In Jonathan Shay's analysis, combat trauma begins with betrayal—the betrayal of 'what's right', a betrayal that produces 'indignant rage' and the shrinkage of moral and social space—that is, a rejection of loyalties and commitments.[98] Twice during the Irish War of Independence the Royal Irish Constabulary suffered a betrayal of 'what's right': when republican hunger strikers were freed in the spring of 1920; and again later, when the summer assizes failed. In the spring the police felt betrayed by the government. In the summer they felt betrayed by the people. The result, it seems, was 'indignant rage' against both, and a narrowing of police moral and social horizons. After the Tuam police riot, for example, jurors were summoned for a coroner's inquest on the two dead constables, Burke and Carey. None of them attended, and without a jury, the inquest fell through. The police response was bitter:

> Head Constable Bowles, who represented the authorities, said from their action in absenting themselves as jurors it might be accepted that the people of Tuam took it to be the right course to murder the police. 'We must take it that that is the general feeling in the town. It looks as if they had no more regard for a policeman's life than a dog's.'[99]

Isolated, alienated, some constables rejected the force itself: they resigned, they retired, or they became passive, 'useless'. Others rejected the government and the people but remained loyal to their fellow police, turning to self-help in place of due process—vengeance in place of justice. The seed of what Peter Hart has called 'a spirit of murderous self-reliance' was planted in the spring, and flourished in the late summer.[100] In mid-April 1920 the *Manchester Guardian*'s correspondent was reporting that there was 'an unofficial vendetta gang in the Royal Irish Constabulary'. 'One can only hope,' he wrote, 'that there will be no attempt at violent reprisals on the "state of war" lines.'[101] The 'violent reprisals' began in earnest that summer, after the legal system fell apart. Hugh Martin of the *Daily News* was clear on this point. The police, he said, 'know that the State is utterly powerless to punish. No one will be, or can be, brought to book for murder or insult so long as the murdered or the insulted is a servant of the Crown.'[102]

Conscious of its own weakness, and fearful that its politically vital Irish constabulary would go to pieces, the State itself connived at police reprisals, especially during the summer and autumn of 1920. During this period the British government, the Irish executive, the British Army, and the constabulary's own officers all tolerated and even encouraged reprisals. Some RIC county inspectors were as alienated as their men. 'There is an underlying hatred amongst the inhabitants against law and order,' one concluded, 'and the rooted desire in the minds of ¾ of the population is to commit crimes against the guardians of law and order, when that can be done with impunity, or at least with small chances of detection.'[103] Their approval of reprisals is clear from their monthly reports in the autumn of 1920. Mayo's county inspector was particularly bloodthirsty:

> I beg to report that the dread of reprisals combined with a more active cooperation of the military in these parts with the Police is exercising a very salutary effect and if quietly and systematically continued will knock the bottom out of the Sinn Fein movement in a short time. People generally are beginning to see whither the Sinn Fein programme is dragging them and to what danger and trouble it exposes them and would for the most part gladly welcome a return to the old status quo with the feeling of safety and security

> that accompanied it. Sinn Fein never counted on it being possible that reprisals would ever overtake them and they have become much exercised in mind and body at the very suggestion of the application to themselves of a little of their own ointment. That it has seriously crippled Sinn Fein prestige and power already there is no room for doubt.[104]

Some officers did more than just write approving reports. On 24 August 1920, for example, Mark Sturgis met the RIC District Inspector for Thurles, County Tipperary. In his diary Sturgis referred to this police officer as 'a professional "Reprisaler"'. 'His explanation of the comparative quiet of his district is that his police have the local blackguards marked—and they know it and know that they personally will pay the price if a policeman is shot.'[105] A couple of months later the discrepancies between official and unofficial versions of the Tubbercurry police riot indicate that the county inspector may have played a more active role in the reprisals than he later admitted: recall the stress that Acting County Inspector Russell's report laid on the sight of the dead and wounded police, which he saw before his men.

Longford's county inspector actually blamed the guerrillas for the burning of Granard on 4 November 1920. 'On night of 3rd and early morning of 4th,' he wrote, 'a large number of persons gathered in Granard. The police were reinforced by military and police from Longford and as long as the extra force remained all was quiet but upon its withdrawal numerous cases of arson and looting occurred.'[106] This rather obvious falsehood was contradicted both by civilian witnesses and by the military officer commanding the soldiers escorting the police punitive column that night.[107] In addition, we have already seen how the county inspector in Galway's West Riding tried to shift the blame for extrajudicial killings onto the insurgents in his monthly reports. Cases like these led some Castle officials to conclude that 'every report of every single policeman *must* be lies from start to finish'.[108]

Higher authorities also permitted, encouraged, and sometimes even ordered reprisals. In March 1921 police reprisals in Clifden, County Galway, and Westport, County Mayo, were 'authorised' by the local divisional commissioner, R. F. R. Cruise. General Tudor approved of these actions, even though the divisional commissioner had exceeded his authority greatly.[109] The Chief of Police himself was notoriously soft on reprisals. His address to the police at Eglinton Street barracks in Galway, the night after the police riot of 8 September 1920, was full of encouragement.[110] Tudor's memorandum on discipline, dated 12 November 1920, was in the same vein. 'The Royal Irish Constabulary has shown unparalleled fortitude in standing up to a diabolical murder campaign,' he wrote. 'Discipline has been maintained at a very high level':

> The R.I.C. will have the fullest support in the most drastic action against that band of assassins, the so-called I.R.A. These murderers must be pursued relentlessly and their organisation ruthlessly suppressed. The initiative must be seized, the ambushers must be ambushed. The leaders and members of the criminal gang are mostly known to us. They must be given no rest. They must be hunted down. But, for the effectual performance of these duties, the highest discipline is essential.

Tudor's memorandum went on to forbid 'wild firing from lorries', 'arson and looting', and assaults on women. 'Just because the cowardly blackguards of the I.R.A. cut women's hair, it is no reason why the R.I.C. should retaliate by similar action,' he said.[111] This was a mild admonition, at best.

The Chief of Police was also quick to defend his men, and slow to believe reports of police misconduct. 'Stories are buzzing about as usual of the almost childlike simplicity of Tudor,' Sturgis noted on 13 January 1921. 'He does not consciously deceive but his belief in all that's good of his Black and Tans and his inability to believe a word against them is super human.'[112] Earlier, in his diary for 19 December 1920, Sturgis had laid some of the blame for the murder of Canon Magner on the Chief of Police: he felt sorry for Cadet Harte, he said, 'as these men have undoubtedly been influenced by what they have taken to be the passive approval of their officers from Tudor downwards to believe they will never be punished for anything'.[113]

However, police officials were not alone responsible. Soldiers were generally sympathetic towards the constabulary, and suspicious of Irish civilians.[114] As a result, military courts of inquiry were often lenient with police, returning verdicts of justifiable homicide, or murder 'by persons unknown', after overlooking implausible or contradictory police testimony.[115] In one case, two Volunteers, John Lean and Maurice Reidy, were shot and killed by Auxiliaries in Ballymacelligott, County Kerry, on the evening of 25 December 1920. In his monthly report the RIC's deputy inspector general described this as a 'murder case'. 'However, it is possible that this case may prove to be, not murder, but justifiable homicide,' he wrote.[116] Sure enough, the police were exonerated by the military court of inquiry, held on 27 December. Major J. A. Mackinnon, commander of H Company ADRIC, gave the following evidence:

> On the December 25th at about 7 P.M. I went with a small party to try and find two or three wanted men whom I thought might come in on Christmas night. On arriving at the house of one Byrne at Ballymacelligott, late manager of the creamery there, I went to the door while the remainder of my party surrounded the house. As I entered I heard a misfire. There were two men in the room. I ordered them at once to put up their hands. Neither of them made any attempt to do so and as I moved across the room I heard a revolver being cocked. I immediately opened fire, hitting Maurice Reidy in the face, who collapsed in his chair, and shooting Lean, who was standing up and firing at me across the table, through the heart. His shot and mine were practically simultaneous, but I think he was hit just before he pulled the trigger. His bullet went past me into the ceiling. Captain Wilkinson then came into the house and took the revolver out of Lean's hand it contained one misfired cartridge one expended round and four unexpended rounds. I then went and fetched the Parish Priest.[117]

Mackinnon's testimony was absurd: standing in a room, facing a man with a cocked revolver, he first shot another, unarmed man sitting in a chair, and then somehow fired again, before his armed enemy could fire. To make matters worse, the men in the major's party that night gave evidence contradicting both Mackinnon and each other.[118] Nonetheless, the court found that Lean and Reidy were to blame for their own deaths: Lean had 'used fire arms against the forces of the Crown in the execution of their duty'; for his part, 'when fire arms were attempted to be used against the forces of the Crown', Reidy 'had refused to hold up his hands when called upon to do so'.[119]

Occasionally, higher authorities told military courts to make further enquiries. A nearby police patrol was not even questioned by the first court of inquiry into the death of Tom Horan, executed in front of his daughter on 7 March 1921 in County Mayo. The court's verdict was murder by persons unknown, dressed in police uniforms. This did not satisfy the high command. The court was ordered to reconvene, and the members of the police patrol were questioned. After the police denied any part in Horan's murder, the court, 'having considered the further evidence', saw 'no reason to alter their original verdict'.[120]

In another case, Volunteer Michael Mulloolly was shot and killed in his farmyard near Strokestown, County Roscommon, on 24 March 1921, the day after the ambush at Scramogue. The shooting took place after Auxiliaries raided Mulloolly's house. According to the testimony of a head constable, Michael 'was suspected of having taken part in the ambush, &

cutting trenches in the road & cutting wires. He was an active Sinn Feiner. His brother was taken into custody the previous day March 23rd charged with being implicated in the ambush.'[121] Once again, however, the court of inquiry did not even question the Auxiliaries involved, concluding that Mulloolly had been killed 'by a member or members unknown belonging to the Crown Forces the motive for it being unknown'.[122]

The Divisional commander, Major General Jeudwine, called these proceedings 'farcical and useless', and ordered the court to reconvene.[123] On 4 April an anonymous Auxiliary testified that, as the raiding party was leaving, he found he had lost a glove, so he jumped out of his Crossley tender and went back alone looking for it. When he got back to the farmyard, he saw Mulloolly, challenged him, and ordered him to put up his hands. 'Instead of which he made a quick movement towards his pocket whereupon I fired,' he said, shooting the Volunteer in the neck. The Auxiliaries then departed the scene, leaving Mulloolly where he lay.[124] These proceedings were sent back to Major General Jeudwine, with the following comments:

> Here is the further evidence in the case of Mulloolly.
>
> Original Court and your remarks flagged.
>
> Not a very convincing story.
>
> The man does not appear to have been searched for arms to see if he was carrying anything, and the Police seem to have pushed off in a light-hearted way without even waiting to see if he was dead.
>
> You will note that the President of the Inquest did not know that these two men would give evidence and apparently therefore the Police made no report until things began to look awkward...
>
> The whole thing looks very bad viewed in cold blood from an office chair![125]

No further action was taken in either case. To be fair, Irish people were sometimes unhelpful, even obstructive, to these military courts of inquiry. Active republicans would not recognise the jurisdiction of these courts. Non-political people were probably just afraid of reprisals.[126] After the assassination of Alderman Thomas Halpin and James Moran in Drogheda, County Louth, on the night of 8 February 1921, witnesses refused to give evidence at a closed court of inquiry. Unwilling either to set a precedent by holding a public hearing or to risk a public relations disaster by prosecuting these witnesses for contempt of court, the military simply let the matter drop.[127]

A few months later, on the night of 15 April 1921, two buildings were burned in Abbeyside, Dungarvan, County Waterford, in reprisal for an attack on the police that evening. Bridget Fahey later swore out an affidavit, claiming that vengeful police had set her public house on fire. She could identify one of the men responsible, and her barmaid, Bridget O'Neill, corroborated her statement. A constable named Cady was arrested and eventually put on trial, but Mrs Fahey refused to testify at the constable's court martial, or even attend a line-up. As a result, Cady was acquitted on 1 July 1921.[128] Anticipating this verdict, a disgusted Major General Strickland complained about Fahey's attitude in a letter to GHQ on 30 June:

> It always seems that such people as these are only too willing to make any kind of statements on paper, but when they are asked to attend in person at a parade of this sort [for identification], they always refuse to do it. This is no help to us, and one would have thought that they would have appreciated the fact that, if only they would do what they are asked on these occasions, cases would be more fully thrashed out to the satisfaction of all parties concerned.
>
> I cannot help thinking that the attitude adopted by civilians, in most of the cases which they bring to notice, is such as to warrant little trouble or action being taken on our part to investigate and bring to justice those against whom allegations are made.[129]

Civil servants and politicians played a part in police reprisals as well. Some members of the Irish executive were not opposed to certain types of retaliation: after the sack of Balbriggan, Sturgis complained only that: 'it is tragic that these men cannot see that indiscriminate burning is idiotic and a little quiet shooting equally effective—and to shoot a known bad man who, if he hasn't just shot your comrade, has no doubt shot somebody else, is morally much more defensible than this stupid blind work.'[130] Members of the Cabinet, including the Prime Minister, took this view as well.[131] In the Sturgis diary for 5 October 1920: 'T. says L.G. is all against burning but not gunning, and told him as much himself.'[132]

In fact, the British government has often been accused of implementing a 'policy of reprisals' in the Irish War of Independence:[133] but its true policy might better be described as 'due process as far as possible; reprisals as far as necessary'. To understand this distinction, we must remember the government's official position: that the Irish rebellion was a criminal conspiracy—an illegal attempt to overthrow the legitimate government of Ireland by terror and intimidation; that by the summer of 1920, the organisation calling itself the 'Irish Republican Army' had grown so violent and powerful that Ireland's criminal justice system had ceased to function; and that this criminal organisation might even be part of an international revolutionary coalition with a common plan to bring down the British Empire. In his speech to the House of Commons on 21 February 1921, Sir Hamar Greenwood described the Irish insurgency in almost hysterical terms:

> For years past and now Sinn Fein extremists and their Soviet colleagues in Ireland—there Sovietism in a marked degree in Ireland—have conspired to smash the Empire. A policy of calculated and brutal arson and murder, with all its ghastly consequences, remains uncondemned by Mr. de Valera and the Sinn Fein leaders. The authors of that policy hope to terrorise into submission the British people and the British government. It is the policy of the assassin that we are fighting, and it is watched by sinister eyes in Great Britain, in Egypt, in India and throughout the world. Its success would mean the break up of the Empire and of our civilization.[134]

It was the criminal and subversive character of the Irish republican movement, in the British government's eyes, that made reprisals tolerable, as a short-term expedient. After all, reprisals are more than just retaliation for enemy attacks: a reprisal is retribution for a war crime. According to the British Manual of Military Law: 'Reprisals between belligerents are retaliation for illegitimate acts of warfare for the purpose of making the enemy comply in future with the recognized laws of war.' 'Reprisals are an extreme measure,' it says, 'because in most cases they inflict suffering on innocent individuals. In this, however, their coercive force exists, and they are indispensable as a last resource.'[135]

We have already seen how the British government characterised Irish insurgents as 'murderers' and insurgent attacks as 'murder'. Lloyd George rejected any comparison between the Irish Republican Army and the Boer guerrillas of the South African War 20 years before: there were no similarities, he said, 'between men who fought openly in the field and men who patrol the streets as civilians under the protection of the law and turn round and shoot their guardians'.[136] Greenwood stressed the illegitimate nature of the IRA's activities as well: 'It cannot be emphasized too clearly,' he said, 'that the Irish Republican Army is not in any sense a belligerent army, carrying on hostilities in accordance with the laws and usages of war, but that its members are, in fact and in law, murderers who have adopted methods of warfare which have never been sanctioned by the laws and customs of war.'[137] Until this murder gang's reign of terror could be broken, and the law could once again take its course, reprisals were excusable, if not exactly desirable: better a rough, blind, and reckless justice than no justice at all.

The problem with this approach, of course, was that Irish republicans were just as convinced of the righteousness of their own cause. Seán MacEoin recalled that, in the aftermath of the Clonfin ambush, he had a chance to explain the IRA's point of view to the commander of the defeated Auxiliaries:

> He informed me that he was Commander Worthington Craven of the Royal Navy. He stated that I was a murderer; otherwise, I would not have shot them down. To this, I replied that, had they remained in the navy or in England, I would not have had any occasion to shoot them down, that this was our country, that we were the Army of the Irish people, acting under proper authority, and that our mission was purely to fight our nation's battle for the independence which was our right. I further stated that, so long as they, an alien force, remained in the country, we would continue to shoot them down, that we were fighting for freedom to govern ourselves only, that the killing by them of any of our people was murder, as they had no right here.[138]

As a consequence, the IRA itself used reprisals to punish what it considered 'illegitimate acts of warfare' by its British enemies. By the spring of 1921 the insurgents were burning the homes of loyalists in retaliation for the burning of republican homes and shops: one Westmeath IRA officer later described how 'the Tans' had burned the homes of seven families as a reprisal for the assassination of a British general; a few days later 'an order was received from G.H.Q. that we were to burn an equal number of houses belonging to supporters of the British regime as a counter reprisal'.[139] The insurgents were also taking hostages, like District Inspector Gilbert Potter, and shooting them in reprisal for British executions of captured Volunteers. An IRA officer from Roscommon later recalled that 'the British had ordered that all I.R.A. men captured under arms were to be shot, and Mick Collins countered this by issuing instructions to the I.R.A. that any member of the British forces captured, armed or otherwise, was likewise to be shot'.[140] And of course, according to his own version of events, Tom Barry ordered his men to take no prisoners at Kilmichael, in reprisal for what he considered a treacherous false surrender.[141]

Clearly, Irish republicans had no objection to reprisals in principle. Reprisals were a necessary last resort—a way of punishing their enemies for waging an illegal war on behalf of an illegitimate regime. On this point, if nothing else, the British government and Irish revolutionaries were in complete agreement.

Conclusion

In light of all these facts, there is no need any longer to speculate about the characters of the Black and Tans and Auxiliaries. The Black and Tans were not the jail-birds and down-and-outs of Irish republican folklore. Most of them were quite ordinary men. The Auxiliaries were somewhat less ordinary than the Black and Tans, and behaved with greater licence, but this was merely the privilege of rank. Some Black and Tans may indeed have been 'men of really bad character'. Many of these men may have been old soldiers who had served in the Army before the Great War. It seems, however, that such men quickly broke the Royal Irish Constabulary's unwritten rules, which allowed violence against republicans but not against civilians. This deviant minority was dismissed and even imprisoned, but most of the Black and Tans continued to serve, often alongside Irish bitter-enders—men who were fighting a vicious political gang war with the IRA. General Tudor's beast folk in the ADRIC were less likely to be punished for exceeding the margins of tolerated illegality—but once again, rank has its privileges. Under the constant stress of guerrilla warfare, relieved only by drinking, many Black and Tans either quit the force or followed the bad example of their alienated Irish comrades. Operating independently, often free from oversight and restraint, and even from the sometimes moderating influence of the RIC's Irish majority, some Auxiliaries behaved with even greater cruelty than the Black and Tans. The violence of both forces was overlooked and even encouraged by the British government, which was anxious to keep up the pretence that the Irish insurgency was a 'policeman's job'. This created a climate of lawlessness, which seems to have encouraged both political and non-political crimes. The results are now legendary: the popular memory of a force of ex-convicts and violent veterans endures to this day.

But even ordinary men would have committed atrocities under circumstances like these. Indeed, researchers who have studied regimes far more brutal than the British regime in Ireland, and conflicts far more atrocious than the Irish War of Independence, have discovered that police violence is usually the work of just such ordinary men. Three researchers who investigated the activities of police death squads and torture units under the military regime in Brazil, between 1964 and 1985, are definite on this point. In the conclusion to their book *Violence Workers*, they write:

> From what we have seen, the violence workers were quite ordinary, showing no evidence of premorbid personalities that would have predisposed them to such a career. Neither anything we have heard from our respondents nor any other evidence we have reviewed about them suggests the existence of sadistic predispositions in these violence workers prior to their immersion in an atrocity unit. Indeed, to the contrary, where torture was concerned, authorities were likely to redirect those with obviously cruel tendencies out of this work. Likewise, the trainers and supervisors of operations teams (i.e. murderers) sought to mold their recruits into 'cool-headed' men who could predictably and dispassionately follow orders. Men who could not be readily controlled by their supervisors—who let their hostile impulses override the detachment necessary for intense field operations or for carrying out prolonged torture sessions—either were not assigned to this work or were transferred to other units.[1]

This last point should remind us at once of police in the Irish War of Independence. Again and again, we have encountered 'men who could not be readily controlled by their supervisors' and 'who let their hostile impulses override the detachment necessary for intense field operations'. Police who attacked loyalists or 'civilians' could be dismissed, prosecuted, and, in some cases, sentenced to death. Those who confined their violence to known or suspected 'enemies', by contrast, were commended and rewarded.

There are other parallels between the Irish and Brazilian experiences as well. The authors of *Violence Workers* identify three types of processes that facilitated the conversion of police officers into torturers and murderers: historical and political; sociological and organisational; and social-psychological. Between 1964 and 1985 'the political foundation supporting violence work in all its myriad forms was rooted in a national security ideology that viewed communists and socialists as subversives that threatened the Brazilian way of life'.[2] Between 1920 and 1921 the British government also justified its Irish counter-insurgency on the grounds of national and imperial security. In the debate on the Restoration of Order in Ireland Act, Lloyd George warned that Irish independence would be 'fatal to the security of the Empire', while Bonar Law argued that the Government of Ireland Act represented 'the widest measure of local government which is compatible with our national safety, our national existence, and fairness to other sections in Ireland'. In the pages of the *Weekly Summary* the government assured its police forces that the Irish Volunteer was *hostis humani generis*—an enemy of all mankind:

> The purpose of the Police in Ireland is to suppress crime and to extirpate criminals.
> The indisputable source of ALL crime in Ireland is that organised gang of assassins which describes itself as the 'Irish Republican Army'.
> Against this bloodstained organisation, which has plunged Ireland in misery and threatens to deluge it with blood, the Royal Irish Constabulary stands arrayed.
> The duty of every member of the force is clear.
> The gang of assassins is a pestilence that must be stamped out at all costs.
> It is the enemy of Ireland and the Empire.
> It is the enemy of civilisation and of all the decencies of social life.
> The Royal Irish Constabulary know their duty.
> It is defined.
> It leaves no shadow of doubt.[3]

In their discussion of institutional and organisational pressures, the writers of *Violence Workers* emphasise both the insulation of the police from the general population and the importance of 'wider social masculinity expectations and performances'. Insularity ensured that 'each man's acts of violence would be indistinguishable from the group's and thus carried out without serious concerns about notoriety, official concern, or censure'.[4] We have seen how the police forces in Ireland became increasingly isolated from the public, mostly because of insurgent violence and popular boycotts. We have also seen how the police were encouraged to see themselves as manly men, standing tall against terror. Only those police and Auxiliaries whose actions exceeded the margin of tolerated illegality needed to fear exposure and punishment—and in many cases, this margin was wide indeed.

Finally, when discussing social-psychological processes, the authors emphasise the ways in which the neutralisation of personal and social responsibility fosters moral disengagement. 'Self – sanctions,' they write, 'can be neutralized by anything that induces a present-oriented focus—alcohol and drugs, intense emotional and physical involvement in the violent act itself, and shared excitement in intense team activities. All of these processes,' they conclude, 'help to deindividuate participants through the sense of anonymity that they help to create.'[5] And all of these processes can be seen at work when police in Ireland broke out and committed large-scale reprisals—looting public houses for drink, firing rifles and throwing grenades, smashing windows and setting fires, and calling for the 'murderers' to come out and fight. Even the simple act of putting on a uniform, it seems, can foster violence: in addition to heightening the sense of anonymity, social-psychological research indicates that uniforms can encourage violence by nurturing a hypermasculine persona.[6] The uniforms of the Auxiliary Division, which combined elements from elite Cavalry and Highlander units with the low-slung holsters of Old-West gunfighters, come to mind at once.

One of the authors of *Violence Workers*, Philip Zimbardo, conducted a famous experiment in the early 1970s to test the relative importance of character and circumstance in human behaviour under abnormal conditions. Zimbardo and his colleagues built a simulated prison in the basement of the psychology building at Stanford University in California; then they chose two dozen carefully screened undergraduates as test subjects. Some of the participants became 'guards'. The rest became 'prisoners'. The experiment was going to last for two weeks, but conditions became so inhumane so quickly that it was ended after just six days. Both groups reacted pathologically to the prison environment. Day by day, the behaviour of the 'guards' grew more tyrannical and brutal. As a result, half the 'prisoners' suffered emotional breakdowns and had to be released early. The researchers were shocked by the impact of the simulated prison environment on their volunteers. 'The inherently pathological characteristics of the prison situation itself,' they concluded, 'were a *sufficient* condition to produce aberrant, anti-social behaviour.'[7] The simulation absorbed both 'guards' and 'prisoners': 90 per cent of the time they spoke of nothing else. 'This excessive concentration on the vicissitudes of their current situation helped to make the prison experience more oppressive for the prisoners because, instead of escaping from it when they had a chance to do so in the privacy of their cells, the prisoners continued to allow it to dominate their thoughts and social relations.'[8]

In the absence of convincing evidence to support character-based explanations, we can only conclude that something similar happened with police forces in Ireland. During the Irish War of Independence, under the malignant influence of Conservative and Unionist ministers who had themselves encouraged both rebellion and mutiny to forestall Home Rule before the Great War, the British government conducted a large-scale version of the Stanford Prison Experiment, in Ireland. Between the passage of the Restoration of Order in Ireland Act in August 1920, and the signing of the Truce in July 1921, police and insurgents fought over the social roles of guard and prisoner, punisher and offender, killer and victim, in a looking-glass world of crimes without criminals, police without laws, trials without judges or juries, and sentences without appeal. For a year during its War of Independence, the Isle of the Saints became Devil's Island.

Notes

INTRODUCTION

1. Michael Hopkinson, *The Irish War of Independence* (Montreal & Kingston, 2002).
2. William H. Kautt, *Ambushes and Armour: The Irish Rebellion, 1919–1921* (Dublin & Portland, 2010); Michael T. Foy, *Michael Collins's Intelligence War: The Struggle between the British and the IRA 1919–1921* (Stroud, Gloucestershire, 2008).
3. D. G. Boyce, *Englishmen and Irish Troubles: British Public Opinion and the Making of Irish Policy 1918–22* (London, 1972); Charles Townshend, *The British Campaign in Ireland, 1919–1921: The Development of Political and Military Policies* (London, 1979); Tom Bowden, *The Breakdown of Public Security: The Case of Ireland 1916–1921 and Palestine 1936–1939* (London, 1977).
4. Joost Augusteijn, *From Public Defiance to Guerrilla Warfare: The Experience of Ordinary Volunteers in the Irish War of Independence 1916–1921* (Dublin, 1996); Peter Hart, *The I.R.A. and Its Enemies: Violence and Community in Cork 1916–1923* (Oxford, 1998).
5. David Fitzpatrick, *Politics and Irish Life 1913–1921: Provincial Experience of War and Revolution* (Dublin, 1977; 2nd edition, Cork, 1998); Oliver Coogan, *Politics and War in Meath, 1913–23* (Dublin, 1983); T. Ryle Dwyer, *Tans, Terror and Troubles: Kerry's Real Fighting Story 1913–1923* (Dublin, 2001); Alan F. Parkinson, *Belfast's Unholy War: The Troubles of the 1920s* (Dublin, 2004); Fergus Campbell, *Land and Revolution: Nationalist Politics in the West of Ireland, 1891–1921* (Oxford, 2005); Marie Coleman, *County Longford and the Irish Revolution 1910–1923* (Dublin & Portland, 2006).
6. John D. Brewer, *The Royal Irish Constabulary: An Oral History* (Belfast, 1990); W. J. Lowe, 'The War against the RIC, 1919–21', *Éire-Ireland* (Fall/Winter 2002); Elizabeth Malcolm, *The Irish Policeman, 1822–1922: A Life* (Dublin, 2006).
7. William Sheehan, *British Voices from the Irish War of Independence 1918–1921* (Cork, 2005).
8. Aside from the present author's own work, see A. D. Harvey, 'Who Were the Auxiliaries?', *Historical Journal* (1992), and W. J. Lowe, 'Who Were the Black-and-Tans?', *History Ireland* (Autumn 2004). As David Fitzpatrick has noted, Richard Bennett's book *The Black and Tans* (London, 1959; new edition, New York, 1995) contains very little information about its titular subject.

9. Piaras Béaslai, 'The Anglo-Irish War', in *With the IRA in the Fight for Freedom: 1919 to the Truce* (Tralee, 1950), 9.
10. Martha K. Huggins, Mika Haritos-Fatouros and Philip G. Zimbardo, *Violence Workers: Police Torturers and Murderers Reconstruct Brazilian Atrocities* (Berkeley, 2002), 263.

CHAPTER I

1. David Low, *Low's Autobiography* (London, 1956), 94–96.
2. Thomas Jones, *Whitehall Diary*, vol. III: *Ireland 1918–1925*, ed. Keith Middlemas (London, 1971), 73.
3. A. T. Q. Stewart, *The Ulster Crisis: Resistance to Home Rule, 1912–1914* (London, 1967), 231.
4. *Parliamentary Debates*, Commons, 5th ser., vol. 65, cols. 991, 1,017.
5. *Parliamentary Debates*, Commons, 5th ser., vol. 121, col. 362.
6. Although part of the United Kingdom, Ireland had a separate administration, known variously as the Irish government, the Irish executive, or simply Dublin Castle. The Lord Lieutenant (a viceroy, in Dublin) and his Chief Secretary (a Cabinet minister, in London) were the heads of this Irish government. The Chief Secretary had a deputy minister, the Under Secretary, who resided in Dublin with his assistant.
7. Memo by the Chief Secretary covering a draft bill providing for the immediate extension of the jurisdiction of Court Martial, 25 July, National Archives of the United Kingdom (henceforward TNA): Public Record Office (henceforward PRO) CAB 24/109, CP 1682, f. 417.
8. Outrage Reports, April–December 1920, TNA: PRO CO 904/148–9.
9. RIC County Inspector's Monthly Report, West Cork, July 1920, TNA: PRO CO 904/112.
10. Cabinet Conference, 23 July 1920, TNA: PRO CAB 24/109, CP 1693, p. 446. Wylie was the Irish Executive's Law Adviser.
11. Cabinet Conference, 23 July 1920, TNA: PRO CAB 24/109, CP 1693, f. 451. Cope was Assistant Under Secretary for Ireland.
12. Cabinet Conference, 23 July 1920, TNA: PRO CAB 24/109, CP 1693, f. 459. Anderson was Under Secretary for Ireland.
13. Cabinet Conference, 23 July 1920, TNA: PRO CAB 24/109, CP 1693, f. 447.
14. The Future of the Home Rule Bill: Memorandum by the Lord President of the Council, 24 July 1920, TNA: PRO CAB 24/109, CP 1683.
15. Irish Situation: Memorandum by Walter Long, 25 July 1920, TNA: PRO CAB 24/109, CP 1688. On this date Belfast was just beginning to recover from three days of sectarian riots that had left 18 dead and over 200 wounded: Parkinson, *Belfast's Unholy War*, 51–54.
16. Irish Situation: Note by Sir John Anderson, 25 July 1920, TNA: PRO CAB 24/109, CP 1689.

17. Draft of the Restoration of Order in Ireland Bill, 25 July 1920, TNA: PRO CAB 24/110, CP 1709.
18. Irish Situation Committee: Note by Mr Long, 29 July 1920, TNA: PRO CAB 24/110, CP 1703.
19. Cabinet Conclusions, 2 August 1920, TNA: PRO CAB 23/22, f. 79.
20. *Parliamentary Debates*, Commons, 5th ser., vol. 132, cols. 2,691–97.
21. *Parliamentary Debates*, Commons, 5th ser., vol. 132, col. 2,743.
22. *Parliamentary Debates*, Commons, 5th ser., vol. 132, col. 2,744.
23. *Parliamentary Debates*, Commons, 5th ser., vol. 132, cols. 2,753–56.
24. *Parliamentary Debates*, Commons, 5th ser., vol. 132, col. 2,756.
25. This was Joseph Devlin, MP for Belfast/Falls. *Parliamentary Debates*, Commons, 5th ser., vol. 132, cols. 2,911–17.
26. *Parliamentary Debates*, Lords, 5th ser., vol. 41, col. 1,026.
27. *Parliamentary Debates*, Lords, 5th ser., vol. 44, col. 125.
28. *Parliamentary Debates*, Commons, 5th ser., vol. 135, col. 199.
29. *Dáil Debates* I (10 April 1919), 67.
30. W. J. Lowe and E. L. Malcolm, 'The Domestication of the Royal Irish Constabulary, 1836–1922', *Irish Economic and Social History* 19 (1992), 32; Brian Griffin, 'The Irish Police, 1836–1914: A Social History' (PhD Dissertation: Loyola University of Chicago, 1991), 502–508.
31. 'The Royal Irish Constabulary', TNA: PRO CO 904/168, 808. This list is not exhaustive: for more, see Malcolm, *The Irish Policeman*, 94–128.
32. Griffin, 'The Irish Police', 51.
33. Testimony of Daniel Galvin, *Evidence on Conditions in Ireland*, 425. Another former constable said his arms were for 'show purposes mainly': Testimony of John Tangney, *Evidence on Conditions in Ireland*, 391.
34. Richard Hawkins, 'Dublin Castle and the Royal Irish Constabulary (1916–1922)', in Desmond Williams (ed.), *The Irish Struggle 1916–1926* (London, 1966), 174.
35. *Committee of Inquiry into the RIC and the DMP*, 189–90; Griffin, 'Irish Police', 505–506.
36. Witness Statement of Liam S. O. Rioghbhardian, National Archives of Ireland [henceforward NA], BMH WS 888, 1.
37. Brewer, *Royal Irish Constabulary*, 75.
38. Precautions in the Use of Fire Arms: RIC Circular D.642/1921, 7 July 1921, TNA: PRO HO 184/127.
39. Brewer, *Royal Irish Constabulary*, 75.
40. Lowe and Malcolm, 'Domestication of the Royal Irish Constabulary', 46–47.
41. These are the same counties that Joost Augusteijn selected for his social history of the Irish Republican Army in *From Public Defiance to Guerrilla Warfare*.
42. RIC County Inspector's Monthly Report, Limerick, August 1920, TNA: PRO CO 904/113.

43. RIC County Inspector's Monthly Report, Meath, October 1920, TNA: PRO CO 904/113.
44. 'The Royal Irish Constabulary,' TNA: PRO CO 904/168, 6.
45. Outrage Reports, April–December 1920, TNA: PRO CO 904/148–9.
46. Jones, *Whitehall Diary*, III, 27; see also Testimony of Daniel Crowley, *Evidence on Conditions in Ireland*, 389.
47. Augusteijn, *From Public Defiance to Guerrilla Warfare*, 208, 222, 226–27; Fitzpatrick, *Politics and Irish Life*, 37; Townshend, *British Campaign in Ireland*, 42, 92.
48. Testimony of Daniel Galvin, *Evidence on Conditions in Ireland*, 424–25.
49. Testimony of John Tangney, *Evidence on Conditions in Ireland*, 424–25. Tangney told the Commission that he enlisted in 1915 and served for five years, but according to the RIC register he enlisted in 1918 and served for two: Constable 69554, RIC General Register, TNA: PRO HO 184/36.
50. Testimony of John Caddan, *Evidence on Conditions in Ireland*, 418; Augusteijn, *From Public Defiance to Guerrilla Warfare*, 215.
51. Testimony of Daniel Crowley, *Evidence on Conditions in Ireland*, 385. Crowley was careful to say that he 'tendered his resignation,' e.g. 'I tendered my resignation on the first day of June last.' (Testimony of Daniel Crowley, *Evidence on Conditions in Ireland*, 376.) This was because Crowley did not resign from the RIC: instead, he was dismissed on 17 June 1920. Constable 68895, RIC General Register, TNA: PRO HO 184/36.
52. Outrage Reports, April–December 1920, TNA: PRO CO 904/148–9.
53. Malcolm, *The Irish Policeman*, 51–52.
54. RIC Returns by County, 1920, TNA: PRO HO 184/61. Commissioned officers are not included in the returns, but on 31 December 1913 there were 36 County Inspectors and 186 District Inspectors: *Appendix to the Report of the Committee of Inquiry into the Royal Irish Constabulary and the Dublin Metropolitan Police* [henceforward *Committee of Inquiry into the RIC and the DMP*], Cmd. 7637 (1914), 341.
55. Lieutenant-General A. E. Percival, quoted in William Sheehan, *British Voices from the Irish War of Independence 1918–1921: The Words of British Servicemen Who Were There* (Cork, 2005), 108.
56. *Committee of Inquiry into the RIC and the DMP*, 346.
57. Safety of Barracks: RIC Circular D.94/1919, 8 November 1919, TNA: PRO HO 184/125.
58. RIC Returns by County, 1920 and 1921, TNA: PRO HO 184/61–2.
59. RIC County Inspector's Monthly Report, Mayo, July 1920, TNA: PRO CO 904/112.
60. RIC County Inspector's Monthly Report, Donegal, October 1920, TNA: PRO CO 904/113.
61. RIC Inspector General's Monthly Report, March 1921, TNA: PRO CO 904/114.

62. Outrage Reports, April–December 1920, TNA: PRO CO 904/148–9. Interestingly, this was not much different from the normal rate of recruitment in peacetime, suggesting that in the absence of IRA intimidation, Irish recruitment might have been higher than normal.
63. The Training and Resettlement of Ex-Servicemen: memorandum by the Minister of Labour, 19 June 1920 [henceforward Training and Resettlement of Ex-Servicemen], TNA: PRO CAB 24/107, CP 1493, ff. 343–44.
64. Eunan O'Halpin, *The Decline of the Union: British Ggovernment in Ireland 1892–1920* (Dublin, 1987), 188; Townshend, *British Campaign in Ireland*, 25.
65. Townshend, *British Campaign in Ireland*, 25, 30, 41, 44; cf. Witness Statement of Peter Folan, NA BMH WS 316, 12–13.
66. O'Halpin, *Decline of the Union*, 188–89, 191–92.
67. Byrne's replacement, Smith, retired on 4 November 1920, and the post of Inspector General was left officially vacant thereafter. In the last year of its existence, the force was headed by the Police Adviser (later Chief of Police), Major General H. H. Tudor, but some of the Inspector General's duties were performed by the Deputy Inspector General, C. A. Walsh: see Royal Irish Constabulary List, July 1921, PRO, HO 184/105, xiv, xxi.
68. Townshend gives 11 November 1919 as the date when British recruitment was authorized, but the RIC's General Register refers to an order dated 27 December 1919: Townshend, *British Campaign in Ireland*, 45–46; RIC General Register, TNA: PRO HO 184/38-9.
69. *Connacht Tribune*, 28 February 1920, 5.
70. Quoted in Shaw Desmond, *The Drama of Sinn Fein* (New York, 1923), 342.
71. *Weekly Summary*, 15 October 1920, 4, TNA: PRO CO 906/38.
72. *Weekly Summary*, 15 April, 1921, 4, TNA: PRO CO 906/38. Cf. Testimony of Denis Morgan, *Evidence on Conditions in Ireland*, 35.
73. Brewer, *Royal Irish Constabulary*, 106–107.
74. C. J. C. Street, *The Administration of Ireland, 1920* (London, 1921), 280.
75. Testimony of John Charles Clarke, *Evidence on Conditions in Ireland*, 713.
76. Townshend, *British Campaign in Ireland*, 209.
77. RIC Constabulary List, January 1920, TNA: PRO HO 184/103; RIC Constabulary List January 1921, TNA: PRO HO 184/104; Fitzpatrick, *Politics and Irish Life*, 20; Outrage Reports, April–December 1920, TNA: PRO CO 904/148–9.
78. Outrage Reports, 19 September and 26 September 1920, TNA: PRO CO 904/149.
79. Boyce, *Englishmen and Irish Troubles*, 51–54.
80. Witness Statement of J. J. McConnell, NA BMH WS 509, 5. In 1913 the RIC's future Inspector General, T. J. Smith, was Commissioner of Police in Belfast, and testified that recruits were not sent there, as a rule. 'We get men in from the country with some little experience of country work after their time in the Depot—generally men from two or three or four years' service' (*Committee of Inquiry into the RIC and the DMP*, 93).

81. Brewer, *Royal Irish Constabulary*, 85. The RIC also seems to have adopted a policy of posting experienced men to County Dublin: in January 1921 only 8.3 per cent (16 out of 192) of the constables stationed in County Dublin were Black and Tans (RIC Returns by County, 1920 and 1921, TNA: PRO HO 184/61–2).
82. Ordinarily, a constable spent about six hours per day out on patrol. Brewer, *Royal Irish Constabulary*, 64, 72, 75, 79, 80, 91–92. Crossley tenders were pick-up trucks built by Britain's Crossley Motors. They had room for 11 men: 3 in front, and 8 on two bench seats in the box. Built originally for the Royal Air Force, they became the RIC's maid-of-all-work in the Irish War of Independence.
83. Macready to Anderson, 5 February 1921, Anderson Papers, TNA, CO 904/188. The Afridis were unruly border tribes in the Indian Empire's North-West Frontier Province.
84. RIC County Inspector's Monthly Report, Kerry, May 1921, TNA: PRO CO 904/115.
85. Quoted in Mary Allen, *The Pioneer Policewoman* (London, 1925), 189.
86. Brewer, *Royal Irish Constabulary*, 85.
87. Quoted in Allen, *Pioneer Policewoman*, 190.
88. 'Tralee prison', 22 April 1922, TNA: PRO HO 351/88.
89. CI Kerry to RIC Office, 2 March 1921, TNA: PRO HO 351/88.
90. Brewer, *Royal Irish Constabulary*, 111, 115–16.
91. *Evidence on Conditions in Ireland*, 400, 402, 414–15, 427.
92. Brewer, *Royal Irish Constabulary*, 112–13, 115.
93. Fitzpatrick, *Politics and Irish Life*, 6, 21, 23.
94. Brewer, *Royal Irish Constabulary*, 112–13, 116.

    Another former constable recalled that one of the Black and Tans at his barracks in Navan, County Meath was a 'decent man,' and another was 'all right.' 'As for the rest,' he says, 'they were a low-down lot of scoundrels, and it was believed that they were mostly jail-birds and men of bad repute.' (Witness Statement of Eugene Bratton, NA BMH WS 467, 5)
95. *Committee of Inquiry into the RIC and the DMP*, 11.
96. Testimony of Francis Hackett, *Evidence on Conditions in Ireland*, 166.
97. Promotion: RIC Circular, 9 August 1920, TNA: PRO HO 184/126. In addition, a special article about the Auxiliary Division was printed in the *Weekly Summary* on 27 August 1920, to reassure the force that temporary cadets 'will not absorb vacancies in the rank of Sergeant, or operate in any way against the promotion of constables'. *Weekly Summary*, 27 August 1920, 1, TNA: PRO CO 906/38.
98. Conclusions of a Conference of Ministers, 11 May 1920, TNA: PRO CAB 23/21, f. 141.
99. Formation of a Special Force for Service in Ireland: Memorandum by the Secretary of State for War, 19 May 1920, TNA: PRO CAB 24/106, ff. 46–47.

100. Jones, *Whitehall Diary*, III, 22.
101. Conclusions of a Conference of Ministers, 11 May 1920, TNA: PRO CAB 23/21, f. 142.
102. Joy Cave, 'A Gallant Gunner General: The Life and Times of Sir H. H. Tudor, KCB, CMG, together with an edited version of his 1914–1918 War Diary, "The Fog of War"', IWM, Misc 175 Item 2658, esp. 92, 97, and 102.
103. Cave, 'Gallant Gunner General,' 308–309. Sir John Anderson later told Tom Jones that 'when Tudor came over to Ireland he was not unfriendly to the Irish cause but that the murdering of his men had embittered him': Jones, *Whitehall Diary*, III, 53.
104. Cabinet Conference, 23 July 1920, TNA: PRO CAB 24/109, CP 1693, ff. 448–51.
105. Foy, *Michael Collins's Intelligence War*, 110.
106. Cave, 'Gallant Gunner General,' 198, 197, 277. These types of patronage appointments had been common in the Edwardian Army: see Tim Travers, *The Killing Ground: The British Army, the Western Front, and the Emergence of Modern Warfare 1900–1918* (London, 1987), 6–12.

    Divisional commissioners were special police officials intermediate between county inspectors and RIC headquarters. There were five divisional commissioners at first (one per province, and one for Dublin city), but by 27 November there were nine. Each divisional commissioner commanded the police forces in an area covering three to six counties: County Inspector R. F. R. Cruise, for example, was in charge of east Galway, west Galway, and Mayo. Their powers and responsibilities were not clearly defined. Townshend, *British Campaign in Ireland*, 56, 91, 165–66; Divisional Commissioners: RIC Circular D.455/1920, 27 November 1920, TNA: PRO HO 184/126.
107. Crozier was a prolific memoirist: see *Impressions and Recollections* (London, 1930); *A Brass Hat in No Man's Land* (London, 1930); *Angels on Horseback* (London, 1932); *Five Years Hard* (London, 1932); and *Ireland For Ever* (London, 1932); see also the documents in TNA: PRO WO 374/16997 and TNA: PRO HO 45/24829. On Wood's career, see the documents in TNA: PRO CAB 134/2803 and Mrs. C. Stuart-Menzies or [pseud.] 'A Woman of No Importance', *As Others See Us* (London, 1924), 116–29.
108. Wood's own second-in-command was an equally adventurous and highly decorated officer, Lieutenant Colonel Frederick Henry Wickham Guard. Born in 1889, Guard had fought in West Africa, France, and North Russia (where he served for a while as General Ironside's Chief of Staff). When he enlisted in the Auxiliary Division in October 1920, the Lieutenant Colonel had already been awarded the CMG, DSO, Croix de Guerre, two mentions in despatches, and the Order of St Vladimir. He remained assistant commandant until the ADRIC was demobilised and was rewarded for his Irish service with a CBE. Apparently not one to rest on his laurels, he then enlisted as a

squadron leader in the RAF, commanded a section of armoured cars in Iraq, and earned his wings as a fighter pilot, before finally succumbing to pneumonia complicated by malaria in 1927. On Guard's career, see http:\\www.artfact.com (accessed 19 February 2009).

109. *Royal Irish Constabulary Auxiliary Division. Outline of Terms on which Cadets were engaged and of Conditions on which at various times it was open to Cadets to re-engage for further Periods of Service* [henceforward *Auxiliary Division: Outline of Terms*], Cmd. 1618 (1922), 7.
110. Brewer, *Royal Irish Constabulary*, 113–16.
111. Testimony of Denis Morgan, *Evidence on Conditions in Ireland*, 49.
112. A British soldier (Private Swindlehurst, Lancashire Fusiliers) describes the men of F Company ADRIC and some of their activities in his diary for January and February 1921: see Sheehan, *British Voices from the Irish War of Independence*, 13, 15–17, 26–27.
113. 'F' Company ADRIC, Raids Completed, April–July 1921, TNA: PRO, WO 351/86B.
114. Ernie O'Malley, *Army Without Banners: Adventures of an Irish Volunteer* (Boston, 1937), 258–59.
115. Michael Brennan, *The War in Clare 1911–1921* (Dublin, 1980), 72–74.
116. Extract from report by Denis Begley, late 'E' Company, 2nd Battalion, Dublin Brigade, IRA, Military Archives of Ireland [henceforward MA], Collins Papers, A/0532/I.
117. Crozier, *Ireland For Ever*, 101–102.
118. Brewer, *Royal Irish Constabulary*, 11, 114, 115. Another RIC veteran who worked in County Mayo described the Auxiliaries as 'wild men' (Brewer, *Royal Irish Constabulary*, 116). Cf. Witness Statement of Peter Folan, NA BMH WS 316, 12.

CHAPTER 2

1. 'Galway', *Encyclopaedia Britannica* (11th ed.), vol. X (Cambridge, 1910), 431–32; *Committee of Inquiry into the RIC and the DMP*, 341; David Fitzpatrick, 'The Geography of Irish Nationalism', *Past & Present* no. 78 (February 1978), 138, 142; Fitzpatrick, *Politics and Irish Life*, xii; Roy Foster, *Modern Ireland 1600–1972* (London, 1989), 352.
2. 'Galway', *Encyclopaedia Britannica*, 431.
3. See the schedule annexed to 28 & 29 Victoria Ch. 70 (29 June 1865).
4. Campbell, *Land and Revolution*, 220–24.
5. *Connacht Tribune*, 3 January 1920, 4.
6. RIC Returns by County, 1920–1, TNA: PRO HO 184/61–2.
7. *Connacht Tribune*, 14 January 1920, 5; *Connacht Tribune*, 27 March 1920, 5; *Connacht Tribune*, 10 April 1920, 5; *Connacht Tribune*, 29 May 1920, 5; Witness Statement of John Conway, NA BMH WS 1201, 4–9.

8. *Connacht Tribune*, 5 June 1920, 5.
9. RIC County Inspector's Monthly Report, West Galway, June 1920, TNA: PRO CO 904/112.
10. *Connacht Tribune*, 24 July 1920, 5.
11. *Manchester Guardian*, 21 July 1920, 7; *Daily News*, 21 July 1920, 1; *The Times*, 21 July 1920, 14; *Morning Post*, 21 July 1920, 7; *Connacht Tribune*, 24 July 1920, 5–8; Richard Abbott, *Police Casualties in Ireland 1919–1922* (Dublin, 2000), 103–104. Pictures of the burned town hall and drapery warehouse were published in the *Connacht Tribune*, 31 July 1920, 6.
12. *The Times*, 24 July 1920, 14; *Connacht Tribune*, 31 July 1920, 8.
13. RIC County Inspector's Monthly Report, West Galway, July 1920, TNA: PRO CO 904/112.
14. *Morning Post*, 23 August 1920, 5–6; *Manchester Guardian*, 23 August 1920, 7; *Connacht Tribune*, 28 August 1920, 6; Abbott, *Police Casualties*, 112.
15. Testimony of Thomas Nolan, *Evidence on Conditions in Ireland*, 852–53; *Connacht Tribune*, 28 August 1920, 6; cf. *Morning Post*, 23 August 1920, 6. Mrs Kane's son's last name was Howley, after her first husband. On 4 December 1920 Michael Joseph Howley of Oranmore was shot dead in Dublin, probably by members of a special police unit known as the Igoe gang: *Connacht Tribune*, 11 December 1920, 5; *Connacht Tribune*, 1 January 1921, 7. On the Igoe gang, see Foy, *Michael Collins's Intelligence War*, 225–29.
16. RIC County Inspector's Monthly Report, West Galway, August 1920, TNA: PRO CO 904/112.
17. Abbott, *Police Casualties*, 120.
18. Testimony of John Joseph Caddan, *Evidence on Conditions in Ireland*, 410.
19. Testimony of John Joseph Caddan, *Evidence on Conditions in Ireland*, 411–12.
20. *Daily Telegraph*, 10 September 1920, 9; *Morning Post*, 10 September 1920, 5; *The Times*, 10 September 1920, 10; *Connacht Tribune*, 11 September 1920, 5; *Manchester Guardian Weekly Edition*, 17 September 1920, 238; Testimony of Francis Hackett, *Evidence on Conditions in Ireland*, 161–62; Testimony of James Cotter, *Evidence on Conditions in Ireland*, 83; Testimony of Agnes King, *Evidence on Conditions in Ireland*, 131–35; Register of Crime, TNA: PRO CO 904/45, 76; Witness Statement of Sean Broderick, NA BMH WS 1677; Witness Statement of Michéal Ó Droighneáin, NA BMH WS 1718, 16–17.
21. Martin Gilbert, *Winston S. Churchill*, vol. IV: *The Stricken World, 1916–1922* (Boston, 1975), 459.
22. Testimony of John Joseph Caddan, *Evidence on Conditions in Ireland*, 413–14.
23. *Connacht Tribune*, 18 September 1920, 5–6.
24. *Daily Mail*, 20 September 1920, 7; *Manchester Guardian*, 20 September 1920, 9; *Connacht Tribune*, 25 September 1920, 2; Testimony of Thomas Nolan, *Evidence on Conditions in Ireland*, 855. The Cumann na mBan was the women's auxiliary of the Irish Republican Army.

25. Register of Crime, TNA: PRO CO 904/45, 78–82; *Connacht Tribune*, 25 September 1920, 5; *Connacht Tribune*, 2 October 1920, 5.
26. *Connacht Tribune*, 2 October 1920, 5; Testimony of Agnes King, *Evidence on Conditions in Ireland*, 134; Testimony of Thomas Nolan, *Evidence on Conditions in Ireland*, 862.
27. Summary of Police Reports, 11 October 1920, TNA: PRO CO 904/143.
28. Register of Crime, TNA: PRO CO 904/45, 82.
29. *Connacht Tribune*, 2 October 1920, 5. Despite my best efforts, I have not been able to identify this officer: see Chapter Four for a discussion of the ADRIC's very shoddy record-keeping.
30. Summary of Police Reports, 5 October 1920, TNA: PRO CO 904/143; Summary of Police Reports, 8 October 1920, TNA: PRO CO 904/143; *Connacht Tribune*, 9 October 1920, 5.
31. *Connacht Tribune*, 16 October 1920, 5; *Manchester Guardian*, 22 October 1920, 9; *The Times*, 22 October 1920, 12.
32. Register of Crime, TNA: PRO CO 904/45, 82.
33. Summary of Police Reports, 12 October 1920, TNA: PRO CO 904/143.
34. Daniel J. Murphy (ed.), *Lady Gregory's Journals*, vol. I (New York, 1978), 192.
35. Summary of Police Reports, 17 October 1920, TNA: PRO CO 904/143; *Connacht Tribune*, 23 October 1920, 5.
36. Witness Statement of Michéal Ó Droighneáin, NA BMH WS 1718, 17–20; Witness Statement of Michael Hynes, NA BMH WS 714, 18–19; Witness Statement of Joseph Togher, NA BMH WS 1729, 4–5; See also Campbell, *Land and Revolution*, 271–73, and the account of Colonel Evelyn Lindsay Young, quoted in Sheehan, *British Voices from the Irish War of Independence*, 161–62.
37. *Manchester Guardian*, 22 October 1920, 9; *The Times*, 22 October 1920, 12; *Connacht Tribune*, 23 October 1920, 5; *Connacht Tribune*, 23 October 1920, 5; *Connacht Tribune*, 23 October 1920, 6. See also Witness Statement of Michéal Ó Droighneáin, NA BMH WS 1718, 20–22.
38. *Manchester Guardian*, 22 October 1920, 9; *The Times*, 22 October 1920, 12; *Connacht Tribune*, 23 October 1920, 5.
39. *Manchester Guardian*, 21 October 1920, 7; Summary of Police Reports, 21 October 1920, TNA: PRO CO 904/143; *Connacht Tribune*, 23 October 1920, 5.
40. RIC County Inspector's Monthly Report, West Galway, October 1920, TNA: PRO CO 904/113.
41. RIC Inspector General's Monthly Report, October 1920, TNA: PRO CO 904/113.
42. Abbott, *Police Casualties*, 139; *Morning Post*, 1 November 1920, 7; *Daily Telegraph*, 1 November 1920, 11; *Connacht Tribune*, 6 November 1920, 5; Witness Statement of Patrick Glynn, NA BMH WS 1033, 10–11; Witness Statement of Peter Howley, NA BMH WS 1379, 28–29. Two local men, Peter Moylan and Michael Callahan, were charged with taking part in the Castledaly ambush and

tried by court martial in Dublin for the murder of Constable Horan on 23–24 March 1921: *Connacht Tribune*, 26 March 1921, 5. Both men were found not guilty: *Connacht Tribune*, 2 April 1921, 5.

43. *Morning Post*, 6 November 1920, 7; *Connacht Tribune*, 13 November 1920, 2.
44. See, for example, *Lady Gregory's Journals*, I, 197–98.
45. *Irish Press*, 4 December 1920, 3.
46. *Manchester Guardian*, 4 November 1920, 7; Statement on shooting of Ellen Quinn, November 1920, TNA: PRO CO 904/168 (1); *Daily News*, 16 November 1920, 3; *Connacht Tribune*, 20 November 1920, 7.
47. Orders for Convoys and Parties Travelling by Motor: RIC Circular D. 436/1920, 2 November 1920, TNA: PRO HO 184/126. The next day, General Macready sent a letter to Sir John Anderson, in which he wrote: 'I have dropped a line to Tudor again asking him to try and put a check on the promiscuous firing in the air of lorry loads of R.I.C. It does not do any good, and is very subversive to discipline, and annoys the Army people extremely.' (Macready to Anderson, 3 November 1920, Anderson Papers, TNA: PRO CO 904/188)
48. Discipline: RIC Circular D. 446/1920, dated 9 November 1920, circulated 12 November 1920, TNA: PRO HO 184/126.
49. *Manchester Guardian*, 20 November 1920, 13.
50. *Manchester Guardian*, 22 November 1920, 7; *Connacht Tribune*, 27 November 1920, 6; Witness Statement of Michéal Ó Droighneáin, NA BMH WS 1718, 24–26.
51. In his monthly report, the county inspector wrote: 'The murder [of Father Griffin] is yet a mystery. At first the Crown Forces were suspected by a large majority of the people, but now opinion is that he was slain by Sinn Feiners, or by some friends of Mr Joyce, NT': RIC County Inspector's Monthly Report, West Galway, November 1920, TNA: PRO CO 904/113. In his own report, the Deputy Inspector General was intriguingly vague on the subject. Walsh wrote only that: 'It is strongly suspected that his murder was the sequel to the kidnapping and presumed murder of Mr Joyce, NT': RIC Inspector General's Monthly Report, November 1920, TNA: PRO CO 904/113.
52. *Daily News*, 24 May 1921, 1. Witness Statements collected by the Bureau of Military History strongly suggest that the killing of Father Griffin was a reprisal for the killing of Patrick Joyce: see Witness Statement of Thomas Hynes, NA BMH WS 714, 19–20; Witness Statement of Joseph J. Togher, NA BMH WS 1729, 8–9; Witness Statement of Mary Leech, NA BMH WS 1034, 2–3.
53. See Chapter One for more details on this officer's career.
54. Police Reports, 25 November 1920, TNA: PRO CO 904/143; Military Court of Inquiry (Michael Moran), TNA: PRO WO 35/155A; *Connacht Tribune*, 27 November 1920, 4; Campbell, *Land and Revolution*, 313. Cf. Witness Statement of John D. Costello, NA BMH WS 1330, 7.

55. RIC Inspector General's Monthly Report, November 1920, TNA: PRO CO 904/113.
56. *Connacht Tribune*, 11 December 1920, 7.
57. *Connacht Tribune*, 11 December 1920, 5.
58. *Connacht Tribune*, 18 December 1920, 3; *Connacht Tribune*, 18 December 1920, 5. See also Witness statement of Alice M. Cashel, NA BMH WS 366, 11; Witness Statement of Thomas Walsh, NA BMH WS 407, 1; Witness Statement of Tomas Bairead, NA BMH WS 408.
59. Cabinet Conclusions, 6 December 1920, TNA: PRO CAB 23/23, ff. 165–66.
60. Cabinet Conclusions, 8 December 1920, TNA: PRO CAB 23/23, ff. 206–7.
61. *Parliamentary Debates*, Commons, 5th ser., vol. 135, cols. 2601–11: the four counties were Cork, Kerry, Limerick, and Tipperary; on 30 December the Cabinet extended martial law to Clare, Kilkenny, Waterford, and Wexford.
62. Minutes of Cabinet Meeting, 29 December 1920, TNA: PRO CAB 23/23, ff. 345–46.
63. *Lady Gregory's Journals*, I, 209–10.
64. *Connacht Tribune*, 11 December 1920, 5.
65. *Lady Gregory's Journals*, I, 209–10; Witness Statement of Patrick Glynn, NA BMH WS 1033, 12; Witness Statement of Joseph Stanford, NA BMH WS 1334, 30–31; Witness Statement of Michael Hynes, NA BMH WS 1173, 7–8.
66. *Connacht Tribune*, 25 December 1920, 5; *Connacht Tribune*, 1 January 1921, 5.
67. RIC Inspector General's Monthly Report, December 1920, TNA: PRO CO 904/113.
68. *Connacht Tribune*, 15 January 1921, 5; *The Times*, 14 January 1921, 12; Witness Statement of John Conway, NA BMH WS 1201, 11–12.
69. RIC District Inspector's Report, Galway district, 18 January 1921, TNA: PRO CO 904/168 (2); *Manchester Guardian*, 19 January 1921, 7; *Connacht Tribune*, 22 January 1921, 5; Weekly review of Irish conditions, 28 January 1921, TNA: PRO CO 904/168 (2). The commander of the Auxiliary detachment, Temporary District Inspector Lieutenant T. Simmonds DSO MC DCM, was awarded the Constabulary Medal for bravery during this ambush. 'Although suffering from very painful wounds in the back he organized his defence splendidly, drove off the attackers and then withdrew with all the wounded clear of the wood to a place of vantage, where a defence position was taken up until the arrival of reinforcements.' Constabulary Medal Citation, 25 May 1921, TNA: PRO HO 351/73.
70. Military Court of Inquiry (Thomas Collins), 20 January 1921, TNA: PRO WO 35/147A; *Connacht Tribune*, 22 January 1921, 5.
71. *Manchester Guardian*, 20 January 1921, 7; *Connacht Tribune*, 22 January 1921, 5; Summary of Police Reports, received 2 February 1921, TNA: PRO CO 904/144. According to police reports, the arson was committed by 'non Sinn Feiners', 'loyal people', and 'law abiding people'.

72. *Connacht Tribune*, 29 January 1921, 5; RIC County Inspector's Monthly Report, West Galway, January 1921, TNA: PRO CO 904/114.
73. RIC County Inspector's Monthly Report, West Galway, January 1921, TNA: PRO CO 904/114.
74. RIC County Inspector's Monthly Report, West Galway, January 1921, TNA: PRO CO 904/114; cf. *Connacht Tribune*, 29 January 1921, 5.
75. Summary of Police Reports, 14 February 1921, TNA: PRO CO 904/144; *Connacht Tribune*, 19 February 1921, 5 ('The raiders stated they were looking for the murderers of police.'); *Manchester Guardian*, 19 February 1921, 11.
76. Summary of Police Reports, 14 February 1921, TNA: PRO CO 904/144. The report in the local press makes no mention of flogging: instead, it says the local men were forced to strip naked; after their clothes were piled and burned, they were forced to march down the road a distance and sing 'God Save the King' before they were let go (*Connacht Tribune*, 19 February 1921, 5). Cf. Witness Statement of Michael Hynes, NA BMH WS 1173, 13.
77. *The Times*, 21 February 1921, 12; Summary of Police Reports, 22 February 1921, TNA: PRO CO 904/144; *Manchester Guardian*, 26 February 1921, 11.
78. *Connacht Tribune*, 26 February 1921, 5; cf. Witness Statement of Michéal Ó Droighneáin, NA BMH WS 1718, 28–30.
79. *Manchester Guardian*, 5 March 1921, 6; Summary of Police Reports, 7 March 1921, TNA: PRO CO 904/144.
80. RIC County Inspector's Monthly Report, West Galway, February 1921, TNA: PRO CO 904/114.
81. Summary of Police Reports, 1 March 1921, TNA: PRO CO 904/144.
82. Summary of Police Reports, 4 March 1921, TNA: PRO CO 904/144; *Manchester Guardian*, 5 March 1921, 6; *Connacht Tribune*, 12 March 1921, 5.
83. *Manchester Guardian*, 5 March 1921, 6.
84. Summary of Police Reports, 18 March 1921, TNA: PRO CO 904/144; *The Times*, 18 March 1921, 14; *Manchester Guardian*, 19 March 1921, 9; *Connacht Tribune*, 19 March 1921, 5; *Manchester Guardian*, 20 March 1921, 7; *Connacht Tribune*, 26 March 1921, 5; *Connacht Tribune*, 26 March 1921, 8; *Connacht Tribune*, 2 April 1921, 5; *Connacht Tribune*, 2 April 1921, 8; Abbott, *Police Casualties*, 209; Witness Statement of John C. King, NA BMH WS 1731, 17; Witness Statement of William King, NA BMH WS 1381, 10–11.

    The reprisals at Clifden were carried out with the full approval of the local district commissioner, despite the fact that, even had County Galway been under martial law, official punishments could only be authorized by the local Army brigade commander: Townshend, *British Campaign in Ireland*, 166.
85. Summary of Police Reports, 25 March 1921, TNA: PRO CO 904/144; *Manchester Guardian*, 26 March 1921, 4; *Connacht Tribune*, 2 April 1921, 5.
86. RIC County Inspector's Monthly Report, West Galway, March 1921, TNA: PRO CO 904/114.

87. *Connacht Tribune*, 2 April 1921, 5. Constable Stephens did not recover: Abbott, *Police Casualties*, 216.
88. Summary of Police Reports, 7 April 1921, TNA: PRO CO 904/144; *Connacht Tribune*, 9 April 1921, 5; *Manchester Guardian*, 9 April 1921, 6; Witness Statement of George Staunton, NA BMH WS 453, 14–15; Witness Statement of John C. King, NA BMH WS 1731, 18; Witness Statement of William King, NA BMH WS 1381, 11–12.
89. Abbott, *Police Casualties*, 219.
90. *Connacht Tribune*, 30 April 1921, 5.
91. Summary of Police Reports, 24 April 1921, TNA: PRO CO 904/144; Summary of Police Reports, 25 April 1921, TNA: PRO CO 904/144; *Manchester Guardian*, 25 April 1921, 7; *Connacht Tribune*, 30 April 1921, 5–6; Peter J. McDonnell, 'Action by West Connemara Column at Mounterown: West Connemara Brigade, 23 April 1921', in *With the IRA in the Fight for Freedom* (Tralee, 1945), 204–209; Witness Statement of John C. King, NA BMH WS 1731, 21–28; Witness Statement of William King, NA BMH WS 1381, 12–16.
92. Summary of Police Reports, 1 May 1921, TNA: PRO CO 904/144; *Connacht Tribune*, 7 May 1921, 5.
93. *Connacht Tribune*, 9 April 1921, 5; *Manchester Guardian*, 9 April 1921, 6; RIC Inspector General's Monthly Report, April 1921, TNA: PRO CO 904/115; RIC County Inspector's Monthly Report, West Galway, April 1921, TNA: PRO CO 904/115; Witness Statement of Michael Hynes, NA BMH WS 1173, 9.
94. *Connacht Tribune*, 9 April 1921, 5.
95. *Connacht Tribune*, 9 April 1921, 5; *Manchester Guardian*, 9 April 1921, 6; RIC Inspector General's Monthly Report, April 1921, TNA: PRO CO 904/115; RIC County Inspector's Monthly Report, West Galway, April 1921, TNA: PRO CO 904/115.
96. RIC County Inspector's Monthly Report, West Galway, April 1921, TNA: PRO CO 904/115.
97. Military Court of Inquiry (Patrick Cloonan), 8 April 1920, TNA: PRO WO 35/146A; DAG GHQ Ireland to HQ Galway Brigade, 2 May 1921, TNA: PRO WO 35/146A; DI Galway to CI Galway, 10 May 1921, TNA: PRO WO 35/146A; Minute by RO, 22 May 1921, TNA: PRO WO 35/146A.
98. Summary of Police Reports, 28 April 1921, TNA: PRO CO 904/144 ('Card with inscription "Convicted Spy. Executed by I.R.A. Others beware" pinned on breast'); *Manchester Guardian*, 30 April 1921, 6; RIC Inspector General's Monthly Report, April 1921, TNA: PRO CO 904/115; RIC County Inspector's Monthly Report, West Galway, April 1921, TNA: PRO CO 904/115.
99. Summary of Police Reports, 1 May 1921, TNA: PRO CO 904/144; *Connacht Tribune*, 7 May 1921, 5. One witness at the inquiry testified that he found a note pinned to Molloy's body: it read, 'Reported informer. Convicted spy. Others beware. I.R.A.' While it is certainly possible that Molloy was executed by the IRA, the timing of this attack, combined with the rather odd wording of

the death notice, and their recent attempt to blame Cloonan's death on the insurgents, makes me wonder whether the police killed Molloy under a false flag. When John Geoghegan had been killed in February, witnesses reported finding a card pinned to the inside of his coat that read: 'Yours faithfully, M. Collins.'

100. RIC County Inspector's Monthly Report, West Galway, April 1921, TNA: PRO CO 904/115.
101. Summary of Police Reports, 12 May 1921, TNA: PRO CO 904/144; *Manchester Guardian*, 12 May 1920, 7; *Connacht Tribune*, 14 May 1920, 5.
102. Summary of Police Reports, 15 May 1921, TNA: PRO CO 904/144; *Connacht Tribune*, 21 May 1921, 5; *Manchester Guardian*, 21 May 1921, 4; Witness Statement of Michéal Ó Droighneáin, NA BMH WS 1718, 30–35.
103. Attempted murder and assault on John P. Green, Gerald Hanley, and James Egan, TNA: PRO CO 904/44; Summary of Police Reports, 14 May 1921, TNA: PRO CO 904/144; *Manchester Guardian*, 20 May 1921, 9; *Connacht Tribune*, 21 May 1921, 6.
104. Statement of 1st witness (Mrs Lily Margaret Gregory), Military Court of Inquiry (District Inspector Blake), TNA: PRO HO 351/77; *Connacht Tribune*, 21 May 1921, 5, 8; Ormonde Winter, *Winter's Tale* (London, 1955), 312–15.
105. Statement of 4th witness (John Christopher Bagot J. P. Esq.), Military Court of Inquiry (District Inspector Blake), TNA: PRO HO 351/77; *Connacht Tribune*, 21 May 1921, 8.
106. Statement of 3rd witness (Miss May Bagot), Military Court of Inquiry (District Inspector Blake), TNA: PRO HO 351/77; *Connacht Tribune*, 21 May 1921, 8. For more on the Ballyturin House ambush, see the remaining documents in Military Court of Inquiry (District Inspector Blake), TNA: PRO HO 351/77; *Manchester Guardian*, 17 May 1921, 5; *Manchester Guardian*, 18 May 1921, 9; *Connacht Tribune*, 21 May 1921, 5, 8; *Connacht Tribune*, 28 May 1921, 6; Witness Statement of Patrick Glynn, NA BMH WS 1033, 15–18. Lady Gregory was in England at the time, and heard the news of her daughter-in-law's brush with death from George Bernard Shaw: *Lady Gregory's Journals*, I, 256.
107. *Connacht Tribune*, 28 May 1921, 6. *Manchester Guardian*, 28 May 1921, 11; Abbott, *Police Casualties*, 242.
108. *Manchester Guardian*, 20 May 1921, 9; *Connacht Tribune*, 21 May 1921, 5, 8.
109. Summary of Police Reports, 21 May 1921, TNA: PRO CO 904/144; *Connacht Tribune*, 28 May 1921, 5.
110. RIC County Inspector's Monthly Report, West Galway, May 1921, TNA: PRO CO 904/115. Once again, the Deputy Inspector General did not repeat his county inspector's accusations. Walsh mentioned the shootings in his report, but his only comment was: 'These outrages took place in Galway town': RIC Inspector General's Monthly Report, May 1921, TNA: PRO CO 904/115. Sean Broderick later mentioned that 'matters were somewhat

interrupted' at this time, 'as Hugh Tully was my contact at the railway station': Witness Statement of Sean Broderick, NA BMH WS 1677.

111. RIC County Inspector's Monthly Report, West Galway, June 1921, TNA: PRO CO 904/115.
112. *Connacht Tribune*, 14 May 1921, 5.
113. Abbott, *Police Casualties*, 237–42.
114. Townshend, *British Campaign in Ireland*, 181–90; Boyce, *Englishmen and Irish Troubles*, 133–36.
115. *Parliamentary Debates*, Lords, 5th ser., vol. 44, cols. 690, 695–96.
116. On the origins of this speech, see Boyce, *Englishmen and Irish Troubles*, 137; Jones, *Whitehall Diary*, III, 77–78, 247–48.
117. Jones, *Whitehall Diary*, III, 79.
118. Austen Chamberlain to Hilda, 26 June 1921, quoted in D. G. Boyce, 'How to Settle the Irish Question: Lloyd George and Ireland 1916–21', in A. J. P. Taylor (ed.), *Lloyd George: Twelve Essays* (Aldershot, 1994), 156.
119. Townshend, *British Campaign in Ireland*, 191; Boyce, *Englishmen and Irish Troubles*, 138–40; Jones, *Whitehall Diary*, III, 79–81.
120. Michael Hopkinson, *The Irish War of Independence* (Montreal & Kingston, 2002), 201.
121. Hart, *The I.R.A. and Its Enemies*, 96.
122. Hart, *The I.R.A. and Its Enemies*, 17–18.

CHAPTER 3

1. Piaras Béaslai, *Michael Collins and the Making of a New Ireland*, II (New York, 1926), 24.
2. Dorothy Macardle, *The Irish Republic* (New York, 1965), 340.
3. Constables 73602 to 75027, RIC General Register, TNA: PRO HO 184/38–39. As these numbers imply, 272 of the men in the register have been excluded from the sample, either for being Irish or, more commonly, for being temporary constables.
4. Fitzpatrick, *Politics and Irish Life 1913–1921*, 23.
5. 'Ordinary Candidates must be at least 5 feet 8 inches in height, unmarried, and between 19 and 27 years of age. . . . Men who have served in His Majesty's Forces who do not come up to this standard, or who are married, will receive special consideration if strong and suitable.' RIC Constabulary List, January 1921, TNA: PRO HO 184/104.
6. See *Lady Gregory's Journals*, I, 210, for a Peeler's complaints about these 'little chaps'.
7. Constable 73746, RIC General Register, TNA: PRO HO 184/38.
8. Constable 74255, RIC General Register, TNA: PRO HO 184/38.
9. Testimony of John Caddan, *Evidence on Conditions in Ireland*, 414.
10. Brewer, *Royal Irish Constabulary*, 100, 105.

11. RIC Allocations Record, 1902–1921, Garda Siochana Museum, M.239. Of the remaining eleven, four had served in the Navy (including one in the Royal Naval Division), three in the cavalry, two in the Flying Corps, one in the Engineers, and one in the Machine-Gun Corps.
12. 'VACANCIES for PERMANENT CONSTABLE in the ROYAL IRISH CONSTABULARY are offered to ex-servicemen of good character and physique. Candidates should apply to the nearest Army Recruiting Office, where they will be dealt with, and should bring with them private references and a Birth Certificate.

    'If living in or near London, apply personally or by letter to the R.I.C. Recruiting Office, Army Recruiting Office, Gt. Scotland Yard, London, and if by letter state age, height, Regiment, Regimental Number and Record Office.': *Daily Mail*, 3 July 1920, 2. Note that Black and Tans were permanent members of the RIC, not part of the temporary forces. David Fitzpatrick has referred to the Black and Tans as temporary constables (e.g. *The Two Irelands*, 90, 268), but the 'Temporaries' were a separate and distinctive (and much less numerous) body of policemen.
13. *General Annual Report on the British Army for the Year Ending 30th September 1921*, Cmd. 1941 (1923) [henceforward *Army Report (1921)*], 6.
14. Four Black and Tans enlisted in Sheffield; one enlisted in Northumberland, possibly in Newcastle.
15. Constable 74133, RIC General Register, TNA: PRO HO 184/38. Wilkinson's conversion may have been related to the fact that he married a woman from County Antrim on 6 May 1921.
16. These proportions were almost identical to those in the pre-war Army: cf. Edward Spiers, *The Army and Society, 1815–1914* (London, 1980), 51.
17. *General Annual Report on the British Army for the Year Ending 30th September 1924*, Cmd. 2342 (1925), 71. The Royal Irish Regiment, the Connaught Rangers, the Prince of Wales's Leinster Regiment, the Royal Munster Fusiliers, and the Royal Dublin Fusiliers were disbanded in 1922. The Irish Guards and the Royal Irish Rifles remained, though the latter became the Royal Ulster Rifles.
18. Constable 74462, RIC General Register, TNA: PRO HO 184/38.
19. Constables 73607 and 74781, RIC General Register, TNA: PRO HO 184/38.
20. Fitzpatrick, *Politics and Irish Life*, 21.
21. Fitzpatrick, *Politics and Irish Life*, 22.
22. Training and Resettlement of Ex-Servicemen, f. 344.
23. Training and Resettlement of Ex-Servicemen, f. 345.
24. Testimony of John Caddan, *Evidence on Conditions in Ireland*, 419–20.
25. Brewer, *Royal Irish Constabulary*, 101.
26. W. R. Garside, *The Measure of Unemployment: Methods and Sources in Great Britain 1850–1979* (Oxford: Basil Blackwell, 1980), 47.
27. *Manchester Guardian*, 13 October 1920, 9.

28. Royal Irish Constabulary List, January 1921, TNA: PRO HO 184/104, 235–36; Brewer, *Royal Irish Constabulary*, 57; Abbott, *Police Casualties*, 132.
29. Brewer, *Royal Irish Constabulary*, 57.
30. Nevil Macready, *Annals of an Active Life*, vol. II (London: Hutchinson, 1924), 481.
31. Constable William Gibson, Petition to the Lord Lieutenant, 24 March 1921, TNA: PRO HO 351/69.
32. Douglas V. Duff, *Sword for Hire: Saga of a Modern Free Companion* (London, 1934), 55.
33. Duff, *Sword for Hire*, 59.
34. Duff, *Sword for Hire*, 60–61.
35. Constable 80263, RIC General Register, TNA: PRO HO 184/41.
36. Duff, *Sword for Hire*, 62.
37. Abott, *Police Casualties*, 244.
38. In addition, there is a serious discrepancy between Duff's description of the ambush at Mounterowen and the accounts of IRA Volunteers who fought on the other side. Duff claims that he was part of a detachment of 16 police in two Crossley tenders that went out in the morning to rescue the survivors of the ambushed cycle patrol, but wound up pinned down alongside them instead, for hours. Finally, after Duff had used up most of his ammunition, both parties of police were saved by the arrival of Auxiliaries with an armoured car: Duff, *Sword for Hire*, 72–75. The Volunteers who fought at Mounterowen, by contrast, make no mention of Duff's police detachment—only the armoured car and the Auxiliaries: McDonnell, 'West Connemara Column', 204–209; Witness Statement of John C. King, NA BMH WS 1731, 21–28.
39. Brewer, *Royal Irish Constabulary*, 54.
40. Allocations were not recorded in every case: 66 of the men in the sample either left the force in 1921 or were demobilised in 1922, but we do not know when they completed their training, nor where they served.
41. *Manchester Guardian*, 13 October 1920, 9; *Daily News*, 13 October 1920, 3.
42. Brewer, *Royal Irish Constabulary*, 107–108.
43. *Manchester Guardian*, 13 October 1920, 9.
44. *Memoirs of Constable Jeremiah Mee*, 83.
45. Testimony of John Tangney, *Evidence on Conditions in Ireland*, 395.
46. *Manchester Guardian*, 13 October 1920, 9.
47. Duff, *Sword for Hire*, 59.
48. O'Mahony to Goulden, 12 April 1967, Trinity College Dublin Archives [henceforward TCD], Goulden Papers 7382A/81.
49. Brewer, *Royal Irish Constabulary*, 102.
50. Three of these deaths are not recorded in the RIC's General Register: Abbott, *Police Casualties*, 188–89, 227, 232. Once again, the proportions of deaths per province correspond roughly to the proportions of violence per province: Munster 13, Leinster 4, Ulster 3, Connaught 1. In addition, the insurgents

killed three Irish recruits who enlisted in October 1920, and a fourth Irish recruit was accidentally shot dead.

51. Brian Griffin, 'The Irish Police, 1836–1914: A Social History' (Loyola University of Chicago, PhD, 1991), 524; *Army Report (1921)*, 61–63.
52. British Recruits Disbandment Register (Miscellaneous), TNA: PRO HO 184/167.
53. Witness Statement of John Duffy, NA BMH WS 580, 21–23; Register of Crime, TNA: PRO CO 904/45, 281; Constable 74213, RIC General Register, TNA: PRO HO 184/38.
54. RIC County Inspector's Monthly Report, Wexford, November 1920, TNA: PRO CO 904/113.
55. Constables 74334 and 75000, RIC General Register, TNA: PRO HO 184/38. Despite his very Irish surname, Constable O'Hara's home is listed as Rhodesia.
56. Constables 73878, 74684, and 74695, RIC General Register, TNA: PRO HO 184/38; this case is fully described in TNA: PRO HO 351/69.
57. RIC County Inspector's Monthly Report, Clare, December 1920, TNA: PRO CO 904/113; Constable 73615, RIC General Register, TNA: PRO HO 184/138.
58. Constable 73848, RIC General Register, TNA: PRO HO 184/38.
59. Bank raid by six RIC constables, TNA: PRO HO 351/69.
60. The ninth and tenth men were thirty-nine and twenty years old respectively. Charles Riley was dismissed on 22 October 1920 for larceny committed at the depot, and Jack Austin was dismissed on 27 January 1921 after being convicted by court martial of an undisclosed offence: Constables 73849 and 74337, RIC General Register, TNA: PRO HO 184/38.
61. Piaras Béaslai, 'The Anglo-Irish War', in *With the IRA in the Fight for Freedom: 1919 to the Truce* (Tralee, 1950), 6–9.
62. Donal O'Kelly, 'The Dublin Scene: War amid the Outward Trappings of Peace', in *With the IRA in the Fight for Freedom*, 26.
63. Florence O'Donoghue, 'The Sacking of Cork City by the British', in *With the IRA in the Fight for Freedom*, 130. One former Volunteer later recalled how one of his comrades had answered a woman who had asked them about the Black and Tans and Auxiliaries. 'The Black and Tans and Auxiliaries,' he said, 'are the scum of the British prisons and armies, and are sent over to this country, getting seven pounds per week, to shoot down men, women, and children, and destroy our homes, and get as much loot as they can possibly attend to.' (Witness Statement of John C. King, NA BMH WS 1731, 9.)
64. 'David Hogan' (pseud. Frank Gallagher), *The Four Glorious Years* (Dublin, 1953), 103.
65. Testimony of Francis Hackett, *Evidence on Conditions in Ireland*, 163.
66. Testimony of Mary MacSwiney, *Evidence on Conditions in Ireland*, 250.
67. Pat Mahon to J. R. W. Goulden, 13 February 1960, TCD, Goulden Papers 7382A/153.

68. Sample attestation papers of RIC recruits, TNA: PRO HO 184/237.
69. Notes on newspaper cutting (*Freeman's Journal*, 4 November 1920) preserved in TNA: PRO CO 904/168.
70. Newspaper cutting (*Freeman's Journal*, 4 November 1920) preserved in TNA: PRO CO 904/168.
71. Calendar of Prisoners (London, 1919), TNA: PRO HO 140/354; Calendar of Prisoners (London, 1920), TNA: PRO HO 140/361.
72. Constable 73629, RIC General Register, TNA: PRO HO 184/38.
73. Testimony of Ellen Wilkinson, *Evidence on Conditions in Ireland*, 599.
74. Bennett, *The Black and Tans*, 38.
75. Charles Townshend, 'The Irish Insurgency, 1918–21: The Military Problem', in *Regular Armies and Insurgency*, ed. Ronald Haycock (London: Croom Helm, 1979), 35; Martin Seedorf, 'Defending Reprisals: Sir Hamar Greenwood and the "Troubles", 1920–21', *Eire-Ireland* 25, no. 4 (1990), 83.
76. F. S. L. Lyons, *Ireland Since the Famine*, new ed. (Glasgow, 1973), 415. Lyons also wrote that the Black and Tans 'were not, as the contemporary legend had it, the sweepings of English jails, sadists and perverts let loose upon an innocent countryside'. Other historians have also written against this 'contemporary legend', but no one seems to have investigated the matter, and their remarks have made no impression on the popular memory of the Black and Tans. It is also worth noting that Lyons may have been mistaken about the Congo mercenaries as well as the Black and Tans. Though the Katangese Gendarmerie included a number of European freebooters (including a few former Waffen SS fighters and OAS terrorists), it seems that most of the gendarmes were in fact young South Africans and Rhodesians, many without previous military experience: see Anthony Mockler, *The Mercenaries* (New York, 1970).
77. *Report of the Commissioners of Prisons and the Directors of Convict Prisons with Appendices for the Year ended 31st March 1920*, Cmd. 972 (1920), 6; *Report of the Commissioners of Prisons and the Directors of Convict Prisons with Appendices for the Year ended 31st March 1921*, Cmd. 1523 (1921), 6. The figures in these reports were obtained by counting the numbers of prisoners received each year. These numbers were drastically reduced by the operation of the Criminal Justice Administration Act, 1914, which allowed more time for the payment of fines: the 1920 report calls this a 'very beneficent Act'. Nonetheless, both reports emphasise that the number of persons imprisoned without the option of a fine had also fallen sharply, from over 89,000 in 1909–10 to 26,136 in 1919–20. The commissioners were struck especially by the persistence of this trend in 1920–1, a period of severe economic depression: the number imprisoned without the option of a fine in 1920–1 was 30,512, still far below pre-war levels. The commissioners credited this 'principally to the effect of Unemployment Pay, which has prevented acute distress'.
78. Britain's pre-war Army was practically wiped out in the first year of the Great War. During its 1915 offensives the British First Army on the Western Front lost

5,927 officers and 134,579 other ranks, which was more than the full complement of the British Expeditionary Force in the summer of 1914: J E. Edmonds, *Military Operations, France and Belgium, 1915*, vol. 2 (London, 1928), 391–93.

79. Constable 75016, RIC General Register, TNA: PRO HO 184/39. Smith resigned the day after he was appointed. His fourteen years' military service is mentioned in a newspaper cutting (*Freeman's Journal*, 4 November 1920) preserved in TNA: PRO CO 904/168.
80. J. Anthony Gaughan, *Memoirs of Constable Jeremiah Mee, R.I.C.* (Dublin, 1975), 105fn.
81. Constable 77598, RIC General Register, TNA: PRO HO 184/41; Man shot dead by RIC constable, TNA: PRO HO 351/85.
82. Statement of Constable Hogan, RIC, 22 January 1921, TNA: PRO HO 351/85. Note the lapse into the passive voice.
83. Statement of Private Smith, Royal Scots Fusiliers, 22 January 1921, TNA: PRO HO 351/85. This was corroborated by Private McCowlett.
84. William Wilton, Petition to the Lord Lieutenant, 21 June 1921, TNA: PRO HO 351/85. Wilton had married a woman from Lancashire on 20 June 1915.
85. William Wilton, Petition to the Lord Lieutenant, 31 October 1921, TNA: PRO HO 351/85.
86. Thomas Chester, Petition to the Lord Lieutenant, 23 March 1921, TNA: PRO HO 351/69.
87. William Gibson, Petition to the Lord Lieutenant, 24 March 1921, TNA: PRO HO 351/69.
88. Edwin Hollins, Petition to the Lord Lieutenant, 22 March 1921, TNA: PRO HO 351/69; Harvey Skinner, Petition to the Lord Lieutenant, 23 March 1921, TNA: PRO HO 351/69.
89. *Report of the Labour Commission to Ireland* (London: The Labour Party, 1921), 7.
90. Spiers, *Army and Society*, 45–46.
91. Gareth Stedman Jones, *Outcast London* (Oxford, 1971; Toronto, 1992), 79.
92. Stephen Graubard, 'Military Demobilization in Great Britain following the First World War', *Journal of Modern History* 19 (1947), 304.
93. Constable John Norris of Middlesex continued to serve with the RIC in County Longford until he was demobilised on 2 February 1922. Constable Albert Smith of London continued to serve with the RIC until he was accidentally shot and killed on 9 April 1921: Constables 71895 and 72213, RIC General Register, TNA: PRO HO 184/37.
94. Tom Chester was a very untypical Black and Tan. Born 12 December 1891, over 5 feet 10 inches tall, he was a Roman Catholic from Berkshire who married an Irishwoman from County Kildare on 18 April 1916. He seems to have been residing in Ireland after the war: he joined the RIC in Dublin on 16 February 1920 and was recommended by a RIC district inspector rather than by a recruiting officer in Great Britain: Constable 70318, RIC General Register, TNA: PRO HO 184/36.

95. Opinions of Chief Crown Solicitor in cases of Tom Chester, William Gibson, Harry Skinner, and Edwin Hollins, 16 February 1922, TNA: PRO HO 351/69; Opinion of Chief Crown Solicitor in case of William Wilton, 6 March 1922, TNA: PRO HO 351/85. The first four men had the remainder of their sentences remitted on 18 February 1922. Wilton had the remainder of his sentence remitted on 9 March 1922.
96. RIC Returns by County, 1921, TNA: PRO HO 184/62; Outrage Reports, TNA: PRO CO 904/149; British Recruits Disbandment Register (by county), TNA: PRO HO 184/129–67.
97. RIC Returns by County 1921, TNA: PRO HO 184/62.
98. Dublin Castle weekly press releases, 18 February–30 June 1921, TNA: PRO CO 904/168; see also C. J. C. Street, *Ireland in 1921* (London: Philip Allan & Co., 1922), 35.

CHAPTER 4

1. Tudor to Under Secretary, 6 July 1920, TNA: PRO HO 351/63.
2. According to Brigadier Crozier, Tudor told the Commandant of the Auxiliary Division that his men were soldiers 'camouflaged' as police: Crozier, *Impressions and Recollections*, 251.
3. Winter to Under Secretary, 11 July 1920, TNA: PRO HO 351/63.
4. Speech of Police Adviser, Cabinet Conference, 23 July 1920, TNA: PRO CAB 24/109, CP 1693.
5. Tudor to Under Secretary, 28 July 1920, TNA: PRO HO 45/20096.
6. 'The R.I.C. County Inspector is nominally over the local Auxiliary commander for tactics, but for nothing else': F. P. Crozier, 'The R.I.C. and the Auxiliaries: Their Organisation and Discipline', *Manchester Guardian*, 28 March 1921, 7.
7. This was done to increase the number of companies available: Crozier, 'The R.I.C. and the Auxiliaries', 7.
8. Tudor to Under Secretary, 11 August 1920, TNA: PRO HO 45/20096.
9. Crozier, 'The R.I.C. and the Auxiliaries', 7.
10. Tudor to Under Secretary, 18 August 1920, TNA: PRO HO 45/20096. 'About August 20 I was sent for by General Tudor and asked to take over command of the new force': Crozier, 'The R.I.C. and the Auxiliaries', 7.
11. Tudor to Under Secretary, 8 September 1920, and Tudor to Under Secretary, 29 October 1920, TNA: PRO HO 45/20096. Later, it was explained that an intelligence officer was added to the headquarters staff to 'relieve the Adjutant of the duties of dealing with the reports of the Company Intelligence Officers': Whiskard to Treasury, Assistant Secretary, 3 December 1920, TNA: PRO 45/20096.
12. Statement of District Inspector Latimer, OC K Company ADRIC, undated, TNA: PRO WO 35/88A. In the autumn of 1921 Michael Collins wrote to the Intelligence Officer of the IRA's Sligo Brigade to inform him that P Company

ADRIC, stationed at Tubbercurry, had a strength of 68 temporary cadets and 13 temporary constables: Director of Intelligence to I/O Sligo Brigade, 31 October 1921, MA, Collins Papers A/0747/XXXV.

13. Tudor to Under Secretary, 10 August 1920, TNA: PRO HO 351/63.
14. Cope to Police Adviser, 16 August 1920, TNA: PRO HO 351/63. Despite Cope's intervention, a Temporary Cadet's conditions of service included the following promise: 'Preferential selections for permanent Cadetships will be given to suitable Temporary cadets as vacancies occur': *Auxiliary Division: Outline of Terms*, 7.
15. Cope to Treasury, Assistant Secretary, 13 August 1920; Waterfield to Under Secretary, 23 August 1920, TNA: PRO HO 351/63.
16. Tudor to Under Secretary, 6 November 1920, TNA: PRO HO 351/63.
17. The Division had moved its depot from the Curragh to Beggars Bush in the first week of September: Crozier, 'The R.I.C. and the Auxiliaries', 7.
18. Crozier, 'The R.I.C. and the Auxiliaries', 7. This formation is rather mysterious: though referred to as a 'Division', it was counted among the ADRIC's 19 companies; its duties are unclear.
19. E.g. Bennett, *The Black and Tans*, 77.
20. The earliest reference to blue uniforms seems to be Béaslai, *Michael Collins*, II, 28: according to Béaslai, the Auxiliaries 'wore khaki uniforms at first, but were afterwards supplied with special blue uniforms'.
21. *Auxiliary Division: Outline of Terms*, 7.
22. Statement of deficiencies in stores of Auxiliary Division RIC, 30 June 1921, TNA: PRO HO 45/20096. In his report to the court of inquiry, the commander of K Company mentioned that his Auxiliaries wore service dress (i.e. military khaki) with green tam-o'-shanters, while his Temporaries wore service dress with service caps: Statement of District Inspector Latimer, OC K Company ADRIC, undated, TNA: PRO WO 35/88A.
23. David Neligan, *The Spy in the Castle* (London, 1968), 87.
24. Neligan, *Spy in the Castle*, 86.
25. Bill Munro, 'The Auxiliary's Story', in James Gleeson, *Bloody Sunday* (London, 1963), 63–64.
26. Munro, 'The Auxiliary's Story', 63.
27. Testimony of Denis Morgan, *Evidence on Conditions in Ireland*, 42.
28. Brennan, *The War in Clare*, 87–91.
29. Brennan, *The War in Clare*, 91. Brennan explained that: 'I wore a gray-green coat cut like a military tunic, khaki breeches, collar and shirt, brown boots and leggings, Sam Brown belt and holstered revolver, field glasses slung over my shoulder, and no head gear. The only difference in our dress was that the Auxiliary tunic was khaki and this would not be very noticeable in moonlight.'
30. Ernie O'Malley, *Raids and Rallies* (Dublin, 1982), 143–47, 154–55.
31. Brewer, *Royal Irish Constabulary*, 116.
32. Munro, 'Auxiliary's Story', 64.
33. Roddy Doyle, *A Star Called Henry* (Toronto, 2000), 262.

34. A. D. Harvey, 'Who Were the Auxiliaries?', *Historical Journal* 35, no. 3 (1992), 665–69.
35. ADRIC Registers Nos. 1 and 2; ADRIC Journals Nos. 1 and 2, TNA: PRO HO 184/50–52.
36. Harvey, 'Who Were the Auxiliaries?', 666.
37. Harvey, 'Who Were the Auxiliaries?', 666.
38. Harvey, 'Who Were the Auxiliaries?', 667.
39. Cadets 647 to 920, ADRIC Register no. 1, TNA: PRO HO 184/50.
40. Temporary Cadets 734/79098, 732/79082, 916/79239, and 658/79038, ADRIC Register No. 1, TNA: PRO HO 184/50; RIC General Register, TNA: PRO HO 184/42.
41. Temporary Cadets 898/79229 and 749/79122, ADRIC Register No. 1, TNA: PRO HO 184/50; RIC General Register, TNA: PRO HO 184/42.
42. Temporary Cadets 670, 833/79155, and 890/79187, ADRIC Register No. 1, TNA: PRO HO 184/50; RIC General Register, TNA: PRO HO 184/42.
43. Harvey, 'Who Were the Auxiliaries?', 666; Frank Pakenham, *Peace by Ordeal* (London: Sidgwick & Jackson, 1972), 42.
44. On page 1 of a list of 'Auxiliary Division Deficiencies' submitted to the Treasury in the winter of 1922, TNA: PRO HO 351/123.
45. Harvey, 'Who Were the Auxiliaries?', 666.
46. Lieutenant D. Wainwright, RN (Temporary Cadet 809) was awarded the Albert Medal, while Captain C. de P. D. Swain (Temporary Cadet 654/79026) and Captain H. F. Littledale (Temporary Cadet 883/79198) were awarded Royal Humane Society Medals: ADRIC Register No. 1, TNA: PRO HO 184/50; RIC General Register, TNA: PRO HO 184/42.
47. Harvey, 'Who Were the Auxiliaries?', 666; Temporary Cadets 839/79250, 758/79130, 826/79176, and 834/79055, ADRIC Register No. 1, TNA: PRO HO 184/50; RIC General Register, TNA: PRO HO 184/42.
48. Indeed, six men in the sample came from the most prestigious regiments in the Army: the Foot Guards, the Household Cavalry, and the Rifle Brigade. Only seven men in the sample came from the Army's least prestigious elements: the Service Corps, the Ordnance Corps, and the Labour Corps. On the Army's regimental pecking order, see Keith Simpson, 'The Officers', in *A Nation in Arms: A Social Study of the British Army in the First World War*, eds. Ian Beckett and Keith Simpson (Manchester, 1985), 66.
49. To be fair to Harvey, he was aware of this latter possibility: 'few of the Auxiliaries are shown as having been officers in Irish regiments, and some of those so listed were probably English in any case'. Harvey, 'Who Were the Auxiliaries?', 667.
50. Temporary Cadet 727/79097 (A/Lt. T. F. P. Briggs, Royal Naval Reserve), ADRIC Register No. 1, TNA: PRO HO 184/50; RIC General Register, TNA: PRO HO 184/42.
51. *Parliamentary Debates*, Commons, 5th ser., vol. 136, col. 1,292.

52. RIC Officer's Register, TNA: PRO HO 184/47–8.
53. Temporary Cadet 815, ADRIC Register No. 1, TNA: PRO HO 184/50.
54. Temporary Cadet 864, ADRIC Register No. 1, TNA: PRO HO 184/50.
55. This was the aforementioned 2nd Lieutenant N. P. Wood, RAF, OC Q Company. Temporary Cadet 741/79123, ADRIC Register No. 1, TNA: PRO HO 184/50; RIC General Register, TNA: PRO HO 184/42.
56. Captain C. de P. D. Swain, TNA: PRO WO 374/66559 (Temporary Cadet 654/79026, ADRIC Register No. 1, TNA: PRO HO 184/50; RIC General Register, TNA: PRO HO 184/42). A Roman Catholic priest attested to Swain's good moral character when he applied for commission in the Territorial Force in 1912.
57. Lieutenant Colonel F. H. W. Guard, WO 339/37494 (Temporary Cadet 864, ADRIC Register No. 1, TNA: PRO HO 184/50).
58. Captain W. F. Russell-Jones, TNA: PRO 374/59847 (Temporary Cadet 697/79062, ADRIC Register No. 1, TNA: PRO HO 184/50; RIC General Register, TNA: PRO HO 184/42).
59. 2nd Lieutenant H. Crossley, TNA: PRO AIR 76/115 (Temporary Cadet 783/79172, ADRIC Register No. 1, TNA: PRO HO 184/50; RIC General Register, TNA: PRO HO 184/42).
60. 2nd Lieutenant A. J. Evans, TNA: PRO AIR 76/153–4 (Temporary Cadet 876/79173, ADRIC Register No. 1, TNA: PRO HO 184/50; RIC General Register, TNA: PRO HO 184/42).
61. 2nd Lieutenant H. J. Jacoby, TNA: PROWO 374/36889 (Temporary Cadet 781/79133, ADRIC Register No. 1, TNA: PRO HO 184/50; RIC General Register, TNA: PRO HO 184/42).
62. Lieutenant F. Fitch, TNA: PRO WO 374/24490 (Temporary Cadet 791/79150, ADRIC Register No. 1, TNA: PRO HO 184/50; RIC General Register, TNA: PRO HO 184/42).
63. 2nd Lieutenant A. F. Fletcher, TNA: PRO WO 374/2465 (Temporary Cadet 890/79187, ADRIC Register No. 1, TNA: PRO HO 184/50; RIC General Register, TNA: PRO HO 184/42).
64. Lieutenant C. T. Joslin, TNA: PRO WO 374/38649 (Temporary Cadet 762/79111, ADRIC Register No. 1, TNA: PRO HO 184/50; RIC General Register, TNA: PRO HO 184/42).
65. 2nd Lieutenant C. Taverner, TNA: PRO WO 374/67090 (Temporary Cadet 733/79100, ADRIC Register No. 1, TNA: PRO HO 184/50; RIC General Register, TNA: PRO HO 184/42).
66. 2nd Lieutenant G. E. Lissenden, TNA: PRO WO 374/42351 (Temporary Cadet 797/79162, ADRIC Register No. 1, TNA: PRO HO 184/50; RIC General Register, TNA: PRO HO 184/42).
67. Lieutenant S. T. Dawson, TNA: PRO WO 374/18783 (Temporary Cadet 657/79035, ADRIC Register No. 1, TNA: PRO HO 184/50; RIC General Register, TNA: PRO HO 184/42).

68. Lieutenant R. B. Pawle, TNA: PRO WO 374/52874 (Temporary Cadet 647/79039, ADRIC Register No. 1, TNA: PRO HO 184/50; RIC General Register, TNA: PRO HO 184/42).
69. Lieutenant R. L. Worsley, TNA: PRO WO 374/76913 (Temporary Cadet 770/79136, ADRIC Register No. 1, TNA: PRO HO 184/50; RIC General Register, TNA: PRO HO 184/42).
70. 2nd Lieutenant B. H. Emery, TNA: PRO WO 374/22472 (Temporary Cadet 699/79089, ADRIC Register No. 1, TNA: PRO HO 184/50; RIC General Register, TNA: PRO HO 184/42).
71. Captain W. G. Price, TNA: PRO WO 374/55242 (Temporary Cadet 769/79142, ADRIC Register No. 1, TNA: PRO HO 184/50; RIC General Register, TNA: PRO HO 184/42).
72. Lieutenant A. H. Waugh, TNA: PRO WO 374/72565 (Temporary Cadet 711/79149, ADRIC Register No. 1, TNA: PRO HO 184/50; RIC General Register, TNA: PRO HO 184/42). Waugh enlisted in the Division on 13 October 1920: a little more than a month later, on 17 November 1920, he was dismissed for drunkenness and threatening to shoot a civilian: Captain 1st DI Macfie, Adjutant ADRIC to Chief Recruiting Officer RIC, 18 November 1920, TNA: PRO WO 374/72565.
73. 2nd Lieutenant P. G. Wiles MM, TNA: PRO WO 374/74351 (Temporary Cadet 747/79117, ADRIC Register No. 1, TNA: PRO HO 184/50; RIC General Register, TNA: PRO HO 184/42).
74. Lieutenant P. J. Grundlingh, TNA: PRO WO 374/29668 (Temporary Cadet 728/79105, ADRIC Register No. 1, TNA: PRO HO 184/50; RIC General Register, TNA: PRO HO 184/42).
75. 2nd Lieutenant E. J. Shields, WO 374/62064 (Temporary Cadet 698/79086, ADRIC Register No. 1, TNA: PRO HO 184/50; RIC General Register, TNA: PRO HO 184/42).
76. Richard Bennett, 'Portrait of a Killer', *New Statesman*, 24 March 1961, 471.
77. Fred Copeman, *Reason in Revolt* (1948), 82.
78. Bennett, 'Portrait of a Killer', 471.
79. Harvey, 'Who Were the Auxiliaries?', 669.
80. *The Times*, 27 September 1920, 3.
81. Lieutenant P. J. Grundlingh, TNA: PRO WO 374/29668 (Temporary Cadet 728/79105, ADRIC Register No. 1, TNA: PRO HO 184/50; RIC General Register, TNA: PRO HO 184/42).
82. Munro, 'Auxiliary's Story', 63.
83. Wood to the Secretary, War Office, 3 June 1920; Military Secretary to Wood, 8 June 1920; Macready to Chetwode, 23 September 1920; Military Secretary to Wood, 2 October 1920, TNA: PRO CAB 134/2803. On 22 March 1921, after Wood became Commandant of the ADRIC, Chetwode finally wrote back to inform him that 'it is regretted that there is no prospect of offering you employment in Persia': Military Secretary to Wood, 22 March 1921, TNA: PRO CAB 134/2803.

84. 2nd Lieutenant B. H. Emery, TNA: PRO WO 374/22472 (Temporary Cadet 699/79089, ADRIC Register No. 1, TNA: PRO HO 184/50; RIC General Register, TNA: PRO HO 184/42).
85. Fleming to Inspector General, 12 September 1920, TNA: PRO HO 45/20096.
86. Cope to Treasury, Assistant Secretary, 31 August 1920, TNA: PRO HO 45/20096.
87. Munro, 'Auxiliary's Story', 63. See also V. H. Scott to Goulden, undated but probably February 1967, TCD, Goulden Papers 7382a/66.
88. Munro, 'Auxiliary's Story', 67.
89. *Labour Commission Report*, 7.
90. Macready, *Annals of an Active Life*, II, 483. See also Macready, *Annals of an Active Life*, II, 521–22. For an even more negative view, see the memoirs of Major-General Douglas Wimberley, Vol. I, IWM, PP/MCR/182, 153 (reproduced in Sheehan, *British Voices from the Irish War of Independence*, 187–88). Wimberley was stationed in County Cork, and served as adjutant of the 2nd Cameron Highlanders.
91. Supplementary Routine Orders No 392 Part II, Auxiliary Division RIC, Beggars Bush Barracks, 9 December 1921, TNA: PRO HO 351/187. Five pounds was not even the maximum possible fine: company commanders had the power to fine Temporary cadets five days' pay (£5 5s.), while the Commandant had the power to fine them seven days' pay (£7 7s.): Crozier, 'The R.I.C. and the Auxiliaries', 7.
92. Weekly Survey, 11 March 1921, TNA: PRO CO 904/168 (2).
93. RIC County Inspector's Monthly Report, Dublin, March 1921, TNA: PRO CO 904/114.
94. Weekly Review, 28 April 1921, TNA: PRO CO 904/168 (2).
95. Weekly Review, 30 June 1921, TNA: PRO CO 904/168 (2).
96. Coogan, *Politics and War in Meath 1913–1923*, 152–56; Townshend, *British Campaign in Ireland*, 163–64; Crozier, *Ireland For Ever*, 129–34.
97. In addition, Bruce suffered from 'loss of power and sensibility of the entire left leg with some wasting of the calf muscles' due to injuries received in a motor accident some time in 1920. It is not clear, however, whether he had his accident before or after he joined the Auxiliary Division: Report of the Medical Officer, Mountjoy gaol, 15 February 1921, TNA: PRO HO 351/127.
98. Bruce boasted that 'with my own revolver at 25 yards I have taken the five "pips" out of the five of diamonds with five shots': Major E. C. Bruce, Petition to be re-tried by court martial, 14 February 1921, TNA: PRO HO 351/127.
99. Crozier, *Ireland For Ever*, 96.
100. Documents relating to Major E. C. Bruce's petition to be re-tried by court martial, TNA: PRO HO 351/127.

101. 'Major Macfie' is probably Captain T. G. Macfie DSO MC, Adjutant ADRIC: he later resigned along with Commandant F. P. Crozier, in the wake of the Robinstown looting affair.
102. Documents relating to Major E. C. Bruce's petition to be re-tried by court martial, TNA: PRO HO 351/127.
103. As Crozier mentioned, the Auxiliary Division at first had no name, but then was briefly known as the Auxiliary Force (AFRIC), before it settled on Auxiliary Division (ADRIC). Bruce's use of the first acronym reflects his early enlistment and dismissal from the Division.
104. Major E. C. Bruce, Petition to be re-tried by court martial, 14 February 1921, TNA: PRO HO 351/127.
105. Tottenham was the Auxiliary Division's Chief Intelligence Officer at the time.
106. Major E. C. Bruce, Petition to be re-tried by Court Martial, 10 March 1921, TNA: PRO HO 351/127.
107. Crozier, *Ireland For Ever*, 97–99.
108. According to Crozier, Bruce's conviction had a salutary effect on the discipline of A Company in County Kilkenny. 'Only in Kilkenny under Captain Webb did sanity and honour appear to hold sway,' he wrote, 'and that because the commander was sound and the men had been taught a lesson over Bruce and the post office robbery that eventually killed Colonel Kirkwood.' Crozier, *Ireland For Ever*, 127.
109. Major Bruce appears to have protested his innocence to the end: see his fruitless petitions and appeals in TNA: PRO HO 351/127.
110. Copy of unsigned letter to Treasury Assistant Secretary, March 1922, TNA: PRO HO 351/123.
111. Martin Petter, '"Temporary Gentlemen" in the Aftermath of the Great War: Rank, Status, and the Ex-Officer Problem', *Historical Journal* 37, no. 1 (1994), 134.
112. T. I. 230/21, 26 February 1921, and unsigned letter to Treasury Assistant Secretary, May 1921, TNA: PRO HO 351/63. Recall that Tudor had originally sold the ADRIC as a means of quickly reinforcing the Royal Irish Constabulary.
113. See Chapter Three for a discussion of the allowances paid to Black and Tans.
114. Cope to Treasury, Assistant Secretary, 28 August 1920, TNA: PRO HO 351/63.
115. Waterfield to Under Secretary, 17 September 1920, TNA: PRO HO 351/63. Temporary constables were paid boot, rent, and separation allowances as well: *Parliamentary Debates*, Commons, 5th ser., vol. 136, col. 1,292.
116. Cope to Treasury, Assistant Secretary, October 1920, TNA: PRO HO 351/63.
117. Crozier to Inspector General, 17 September 1920; Assistant Inspector General to Under Secretary, 20 September 1920; Cope to Police Adviser, 21 September 1920; Tudor to Under Secretary, 26 September 1920; Cope to Inspector General, 28 September 1920, TNA: PRO HO 351/63.

118. Crozier to Police Adviser, 19 September 1920, TNA: PRO HO 45/20096.
119. Tudor to Assistant Under Secretary, 20 September 1920; Cope to Treasury, Assistant Secretary, 30 September 1920; Waterfield to Under Secretary, 8 October 1920, TNA: PRO HO 45/20096. To understand the need for stealth in this case, we must refer to the Treasury's minute of 23 August 1920, which states: 'My Lords assume that, inasmuch as these men have been recruited for the special purpose of taking duty in disturbed areas, they will not be regarded as eligible for the special service allowance which was recently sanctioned for ordinary R.I.C. personnel serving in those areas': Waterfield to Under Secretary, 23 August 1920, TNA: PRO HO 351/63.
120. Cope to Treasury, Assistant Secretary 7 February 1921, TNA: PRO HO 45/20096.
121. Waterfield to Under Secretary, 12 February 1921, TNA: PRO HO 45/20096.
122. Cope's marginal comments on Waterfield to Under Secretary, 12 February 1921, TNA: PRO HO 45/20096. These comments were later embodied in Cope to Treasury, Assistant Secretary, 22 February 1921, TNA: PRO HO 45/20096.
123. T.1. 230/21, 26 February 1921, TNA: PRO HO 351/63. See above for the Irish government's eventual reply (in May 1921) to the Treasury's plan to reduce the base pay of Temporary cadets.
124. Waterfield to Under Secretary, 8 March 1921, TNA: PRO HO 45/20096.
125. There is no record of the Treasury ever receiving the information it requested: see correspondence in TNA: PRO HO 351/63.
126. Report of Lieutenant Colonel Hemming, OC G Company ADRIC, 27 March 1921, TNA: PRO HO 351/122.
127. Sturgis to Treasury, Assistant Secretary, 18 February 1922, TNA: PRO HO 351/122.
128. What Cope is referring to here is unclear, but the Lakeside Hotel was the headquarters of G Company, ADRIC in Killaloe, County Clare.
129. Cope to Umfreville, 15 April 1921, TNA: PRO HO 351/122. Andrews had resigned just twelve days before, on 3 April 1921. In his reply, Umfreville said: 'Colonel Andrews I should very much like to find myself, but I believe that he heard something was in the air, and immediately vanished into the blue, and you and I will see him no more. It is a pity in one way, yet I cannot but consider him a good riddance': Umfreville to Cope, 20 April 1921, TNA: PRO HO 351/122.
130. Statement of deficiencies in stores of Auxiliary Division R.I.C., 30 June 1921, TNA: PRO HO 45/20096.
131. Mark Sturgis to Treasury, Assistant Secretary, 16 December 1921, TNA: PRO HO 45/20096.
132. The documents describing this dispute are in TNA: PRO HO 45/20096.
133. Tom Barry, *Guerrilla Days in Ireland* (Dublin, 1981), 43–51; Hart, *The I.R.A. and Its Enemies*, 21–38; Meda Ryan, *Tom Barry: IRA Freedom Fighter* (Dublin, 2005), 36–42; Kautt, *Ambushes and Armour*, 99–117.

CHAPTER 5

1. See, for example: Barry, *Guerrilla Days in Ireland*; Dan Breen, *My Fight for Irish Freedom* (Dublin, 1924; revised ed., Tralee, 1964); Brennan, *The War in Clare*; *Dublin's Fighting Story 1916–1921* (Tralee, 1949); *Kerry's Fighting Story* (Tralee, 1949); *Limerick's Fighting Story* (Tralee, 1949); Sean O'Callaghan, *Execution* (London, 1974); O'Malley, *Army Without Banners*; Ernie O'Malley, *Raids and Rallies* (Dublin, 1982); and *With the IRA in the Fight for Freedom*.
2. Military Court of Inquiry (J. T. Miller), 15 November 1920, TNA: PRO CO 904/43, file 33191; statements of evidence, undated, TNA: PRO CO 904/43, file 33191.
3. *Daily Telegraph*, 15 November 1920, 10.
4. From the report of the Military Courts of Inquiry into the deaths of British officers and Auxiliary Cadets on 21 November 1920, TNA: PRO CO 904/189/2.
5. Summarized findings of Military Court of Inquiry, Dublin Castle, 9 June 1921, TNA: PRO CO 904/189/2.
6. Report of District Inspector J. D. Crowley RIC, 10 May 1921, TNA: PRO CO 904/44, file 40006.
7. Military Court of Inquiry (W. H. Taylor and E. Carter), 9 February 1921, TNA: PRO WO 35/160.
8. Statement of 1st Witness [Constable Patrick Bergin RIC], undated, TNA: PRO CO 904/43, file 41664.
9. Witness Statement of Seamus Conway, NA BMH WS 440.
10. Statements of evidence, 3 February 1921, TNA: PRO HO 351/142. For more on the Clonfin ambush, see Kautt, *Ambushes and Armour*, 167–70; Marie Coleman, *County Longford and the Irish Revolution*, 126–27; Witness Statement of Sean MacEoin, NA BMH WS 1716 (Part 1), 148–55.
11. 'Murder of Police at Tullow' [Statement by Sergeant W. H. Warrington RIC], undated, TNA: PRO CO 904/43, file 39379; statements of evidence, undated, TNA: PRO CO 904/43, file 39379. Cf. Witness Statement of Daniel Byrne, NA BMH WS 1440; Witness Statement of Michael Fitzpatrick, NA BMH WS 1443.
12. Statement of Constable Thomas P. Byrne RIC, 10 April 1920, enclosed in Outrage Reports, 11 April 1920, TNA: PRO CO 904/148.
13. Military Court of Inquiry (W. H. Taylor and E. Carter), 9 February 1921, TNA: PRO WO 35/160.
14. For an account of the Castlemaine ambush from the guerrilla perspective, see Edward Gallagher, 'Unlikely Ambush Position was Deliberately Chosen near Castlemaine', *With the IRA in the Fight for Freedom*, 223–28; see also Abbott, *Police Casualties*, 248–49.

15. Statements of evidence, undated, TNA: PRO CO 904/42, file 39749. Cf. Witness Statement of Sean Glancy, NA BMH WS 964.
16. Outrage Reports, April 1920–December 1921, TNA: PRO CO 904/148-50.
17. The British Armies in France lost 510,821 killed and 1,523,332 wounded: Ian Beckett, 'The British Army 1914–18: The Illusion of Change', in John Turner, ed., *Britain and the First World War* (London, 1988), 111.
18. 105 killed and 131 wounded: Peter Hart, *The I.R.A. and Its Enemies*, 87.
19. Defence of Barracks: RIC Circular D 182/1920, 26 January 1920, TNA: PRO HO 184/124, f. 263.
20. Defence of Barracks: RIC Circular, 13 March 1920, TNA: PRO HO 184/124, f. 299.
21. Defence of Barracks: RIC Circular D 442/1920, 8 November 1920, TNA: PRO HO 184/125, f. 146.
22. Breen, *My Fight for Irish Freedom*, 107, and O'Malley, *Raids and Rallies*, 13–14, confirm this. The IRA attacked Hollyford RIC barracks unsuccessfully on the night of 11/12 May 1920: Breen, *My Fight for Irish Freedom*, 106–10, and O'Malley, *Raids and Rallies*, 11–26, describe the battle from the IRA viewpoint; see also the brief contemporary account by Sean Treácy in 'Report of Offensive Action', Vice Commandant, South Tipperary Brigade to Adjutant General, undated, MA, Collins Papers, A/0504/XVIII.
23. Defence of Barracks: RIC Circular, 13 March 1920, TNA: PRO HO 184/124, f. 299.
24. The RIC station at Schull, county Cork, was captured by surprise on the night of 4 October 1920: 15 constables were taken prisoner without a shot being fired. For a contemporary account, see *Manchester Guardian*, 6 October 1920, 7.
25. Defence of Barracks: RIC Circular D442/1920, 8 November 1920, TNA: PRO HO 184/125, f. 146.
26. Report of District Inspector Egan, 28 May 1920, enclosed in Outrage Reports, 30 May 1920, TNA: PRO CO 904/148. For an account of the attack on Kilmallock Barracks from the rebel viewpoint, see 'Fenian', 'Destruction of Kilmallock R.I.C. Barracks', *Limerick's Fighting Story*, 74–81; for an eyewitness account, see Brennan, *The War in Clare*, 49–52.
27. Brennan, *The War in Clare*, 50.
28. *Memoirs of Constable Jeremiah Mee*, 87–88.
29. Summarized findings of Military Court of Inquiry, Dublin Castle, 29 April 1921, TNA: PRO CO 904/189/2; see also Abbott, *Police Casualties*, 216–17.
30. Townshend, *The British Campaign in Ireland*, 214.
31. Moran, 'A Force Beleaguered', 118.
32. *The Rebellion in Ireland: Important Episodes, Outrages, Operations, and Encounters between Crown Forces and Rebels in 6th Divisional Area, April 1920—July 11th, 1921. Compiled by General Staff, 6th Division,* IWM, General Sir Peter Strickland Papers, P363.

33. Statements of evidence, 17 January 1921, TNA: PRO CO 904/43, file 39324. Cf. Witness Statement of Seamus Conway, NA BMH WS 440, 19.
34. Kautt, *Ambushes and Armour*, 205–10; Phil Quinn, 'Battle of Brunswick Street', in *Dublin's Fighting Story*, 159–61.
35. Summary of evidence in the case of Thomas Traynor: TNA: PRO CO 904/43, file 38887.
36. Roger Noble, 'Raising the White Flag: The Surrender of Australian Soldiers on the Western Front', *Revue Internationale d'Histoire Militaire* 72 (1990), 49.
37. Noble, 'Raising the White Flag', 63–65.
38. Noble, 'Raising the White Flag', 73–74.
39. Noble, 'Raising the White Flag', 72–73.
40. Sean Treácy, 'Report on Offensive Action', Vice Commandant, South Tipperary Brigade to Adjutant General, no date, MA, Collins Papers, A/0504/XVIII.
41. O'Malley, *Raids and Rallies*, 23.
42. O'Malley, *Raids and Rallies*, 37–38; Sean Treácy, 'Report on Offensive Action', Vice Commandant, South Tipperary Brigade to Adjutant General, no date, MA, Collins Papers, A/0504/XVIII.
43. Statements of evidence, 3 February 1921, TNA: PRO HO 351/42. Temporary Cadet J. S. W. Smith also testified that once the Auxiliaries had surrendered at Clonfin, 'I asked the leader of the rebels what he proposed to do with us, and if [he] would let us keep one of our tenders to take our wounded away in. He said "You may go free." Several of the others did their best to persuade him to kill us in cold blood, but he refused to allow this.' Military Court of Inquiry (District Inspector Craven, T/Cadet Houghton, and T/Cadet Bush), 4 February 1921, TNA: PRO WO 35/148.
44. Dwyer, *Tans, Terror and Troubles*, 229–30, 239. Constable William Muir committed suicide at Ballylongford RIC barracks, county Kerry, on 27 December 1920. 'Muir, about a month previously, had been kidnapped by Sinn Feiners and held by them for three days. He was, on his return, in a nervous and shaky condition, he became silent and would only speak when spoken to.' Summarized findings of Military Court of Inquiry (William Muir), January 1921, TNA: PRO CO 904/189.
45. Dwyer, *Tans, Terror, and Troubles*, 227. Cf. Bennett, *The Black and Tans*, 114, and Abbott, *Police Casualties*, 312–13.
46. Thomas Evans to Irish Minister for Defence, 20 January 1922, MA, Collins Papers A/0535/Item 13.
47. Minister for Defence to Thomas Evans, 23 January 1922; Minister for Defence to Adjutant General, 23 January 19222; Adjutant General to OC 3rd Western Division, 24 January 1922, MA, Collins Papers A/0535/Item 13.
48. OC 3rd Western Division to Adjutant General, undated, MA, Collins Papers A/0535/Item 13.
49. Adjutant General to Minister for Defence, 30 January 1922; Minister for Defence to Thomas Evans, 2 February 1922, MA, Collins Papers A/0535/Item 13.

50. Witness Statement of Thomas Brady, NA BMH WS 1008.
51. Witness Statement of Luke Duffy, NA BMH WS 661, 22; Witness statement of Sean Leavy, NA BMH WS 954, 18; Witness Statement of Martin Fallon, NA BMH WS 1121, 15–16.
52. Witness Statement of Luke Duffy, NA BMH WS 661, 23; Witness statement of Sean Leavy, NA BMH WS 954, 18–19; Witness Statement of Martin Fallon, NA BMH WS 1121, 17–18; Witness Statement of Frank Simons, NA BMH WS 770, 25.
53. Witness Statement of Frank Simons, NA BMH WS 770, 25.
54. Witness Statement of Martin Fallon, NA BMH WS 1121, 18. It seems the Roscommon Volunteers had a penchant for drowning their prisoners: in his Witness Statement, Fallon describes how he later succeeded in drowning another captured RIC constable in the Shannon (21); see also Witness Statement of Thomas Crawley, NA BMH WS 718, which describes the drowning of a spy in the Suck (11).
55. Julia Eichenberg, 'The Dark Side of Independence: Paramilitary Violence in Ireland and Poland after the First World War', *Contemporary European History* vol. 19, special issue no. 3(2010): 239. See also 'Ambush at Dromkeen', a five-part amateur web documentary by Australian broadcaster Phil Cleary that includes interviews with local historian Tom Toomey and others: www.youtube.com/watch?v=iN33MPq-Slw&feature=related (9 August 2009).
56. Summarized findings of Military Court of Inquiry, Dublin Castle, March 1921, TNA: PRO CO 904/189/2; for an account of the Dromkeen ambush from the IRA perspective, see J. M. McCarthy, 'Dromkeen Ambush Restored the Morale of the Local I. R. A. and People', in *With the IRA in the Fight for Freedom* (Tralee, 1945), 154–60. McCarthy makes no mention of police being shot after they surrendered.
57. Military Court of Inquiry (Auxiliaries killed in Kilmichael ambush), 30 November 1920, TNA: PRO WO 35/152. The bodies of the dead Auxiliaries may have been trampled by cattle in the aftermath of the engagement: see Kautt, *Ambushes and Armour*, 115.
58. Two Auxiliaries survived the ambush, though one of them did not survive for long. Cadet C. J. Guthrie managed to escape, but was later captured by local Volunteers and executed, partly to delay news of the ambush reaching the security forces, and partly as punishment for the killing of a civilian: Meda Ryan, *Tom Barry: IRA Freedom Fighter*, 47; cf. Peter Hart, *The I.R.A. and Its Enemies*, 35, 37. Cadet H. F. Forde, by contrast, was left for dead at the ambush scene, but was later found alive: he recovered from his wounds, but 'remained paralysed with brain damage for the remainder of his life': Hart, *The I.R.A. and Its Enemies*, 35; cf. Meda Ryan, *Tom Barry: IRA Freedom Fighter*, 47.
59. Tom Barry, *Guerrilla Days in Ireland*, 44–45.
60. Hart, *The I.R.A. and Its Enemies*, 21–38.
61. Ryan, *Tom Barry: IRA Freedom Fighter*, 49–67.

62. Barry, *Guerrilla Days in Ireland*, 45. In an interview 20 years later Barry admitted to saying 'Don't take any surrender.' See 'IRA Kilmichael Ambush', www.youtube.com/watch?v=x998_xo7e9s (9 August 2009). Although his defenders place great faith in Barry's account of the ambush, the version he presented in his memoirs includes at least two serious mistakes: he says that 'Of the eighteen Auxiliaries, sixteen were dead, one reported missing (after he had been shot, he crawled to the bog hole near the side of the road, where he died and his body sank out of sight) and one dying of wounds. The last-mentioned never regained consciousness before he died.' (51) Instead, as we now know, the first escaped, and was later captured and executed, while the other was rescued and later recovered from his wounds. Thus, we need not conclude that Barry was lying, as Peter Hart did, in order to wonder about the accuracy and completeness of Barry's recollections.
63. Meda Ryan, 'Tom Barry and the Kilmichael Ambush', *History Ireland* 13, no. 5 (2005): 18. Ryan says that the Bureau of Military History collection 'contains the contribution of five Kilmichael ambush participants. None of them explicitly mentioned a surrender, false or otherwise.'
64. Meda Ryan, 'Tom Barry and the Kilmichael Ambush', 18.
65. Witness Statement of Sean MacEoin, NA BMH WS 1716 (Part 1), 152.
66. For a good general discussion of surrender in battle, see Richard Holmes, *Firing Line* (London: Jonathan cape, 1985), 376–93.
67. Recommendation of RIC Sergeant John Hopley (68519) for Constabulary Medal, TNA: PRO HO 351/73. Cf. Abbott, *Police Casualties*, 119.
68. C. E. W. Bean, *Official History of the War of 1914–18*, IV: *The AIF in France 1917* (Sydney: Angus & Robertson, 1936), 772. This incident is so well-known that it was dramatised in an episode of an Australian television miniseries, *Anzacs* (1985).
69. I was surprised to discover that William Kautt has not only come to similar conclusions but actually cites the very same incident at the Battle of Menin Road in 1917 in support of his argument: see *Ambushes and Armour*, 116–17.
70. Statement of Head Constable J. Treanor, 10 April 1920, enclosed in Outrage Reports, two weeks ended 11 April 1920, TNA: PRO CO 904/148.

CHAPTER 6

1. Michael Hopkinson, 'Negotiation: The Anglo-Irish War and the Irish Revolution', in Joost Augusteijn (ed.), *The Irish Revolution, 1913–1923* (London, 2002), 121.
2. See Chapter Two for details.
3. Register of Crime, TNA: PRO CO 904/45, 92.
4. Register of Crime, TNA: PRO CO 904/45, 100.
5. Register of Crime, TNA: PRO CO 904/45, 273.
6. Register of Crime, TNA: PRO CO 904/45, 278.

7. This follows Jeffrey Sluka's definition of mass murder, i.e. 'five or more homicides in a single event': Jeffrey A. Sluka, '"For God and Ulster": The Culture of Terror and Loyalist Death Squads in Northern Ireland', in Jeffrey A. Sluka (ed.), *Death Squad: The Anthropology of State Terror* (Philadelphia, 2000), 152, note 30.
8. *Report of the Labour Commission*, 15, 96.
9. Register of Crime, TNA: PRO CO 904/45, 331; *Manchester Guardian*, 2 October 1920, 9; *Manchester Guardian*, 4 October 1920, 7–8; *Manchester Guardian*, 7 October 1920, 8; *Daily News*, 4 October 1920, 1; *Daily News*, 8 October 1920, 1; Abbott, *Police Casualties*, 128–29.
10. Register of Crime, TNA: PRO CO 904/45, 336; *Manchester Guardian*, 1 November 1920, 5; Abbott, *Police Casualties*, 138–39.
11. Register of Crime, TNA: PRO CO 904/45, 338; *The Times*, 5 November 1920, 12; Abbott, *Police Casualties*, 148.
12. Even standing crops were burned in at least one case, at Moneygold on 25 October 1920: *Manchester Guardian*, 1 November 1920, 5.
13. *Report of the Labour Commission*, 13–16, 90–98. The Commission itself investigated seven of these cases.
14. Register of Crime, TNA: PRO CO 904/45, 78.
15. Register of Crime, TNA: PRO CO 904/45, 79.
16. Testimony of Thomas Nolan, *Evidence on Conditions in Ireland*, 856, 858–59; cf. *Lady Gregory's Journals*, I, 187.
17. Register of Crime, TNA: PRO CO 904/45, 289.
18. Register of Crime, TNA: PRO CO 904/45, 346.
19. Register of Crime, TNA: PRO CO 904/45, 342.
20. Register of Crime, TNA: PRO CO 904/45, 100. See Chapter Two for more details.
21. *Irish Press*, 20 November 1920, 5.
22. Register of Crime, TNA: PRO CO 904/45, 95.
23. Register of Crime, TNA: PRO CO 904/45, 96. These two cases, along with several others, were later the subjects of an inconclusive government investigation after they were mentioned in a report published by the *Chicago Herald & Examiner*, dated 15 May 1921; see documents in TNA: PRO HO 351/136.
24. DC Cruise to Most Rev. Dr O'Dea, 26 November 1920, TNA: PRO HO 351/136.
25. *The Times*, 11 November 1920, 11.
26. *Report of the Labour Commission*, 27.
27. Constable Michael Foley was killed when an RIC bicycle patrol was ambushed at Oranmore on 21 August 1920; see Chapter Two.
28. *Manchester Guardian*, 22 October 1920, 9; *The Times*, 22 October 1920, 12.
29. Register of Crime, TNA: PRO CO 904/45, 86. Despite this remark, the report was not classified as an agrarian crime.
30. Register of Crime, TNA: PRO CO 904/45, 287.

31. Register of Crime, TNA: PRO CO 904/45, 76.
32. Register of Crime, TNA: PRO CO 904/45, 87.
33. Quoted in Street, *The Administration of Ireland*, 215. Cf. *Manchester Guardian*, 8 October 1920, 8.
34. For the initial press reports on this incident, see *Manchester Guardian*, 4 October 1920, 7–8, and *Daily News*, 4 October 1920, 1; for the District Inspector's report, see *Manchester Guardian*, 8 October 1920, 8; *Daily News*, 8 October 1920, 1.
35. RIC County Inspector's Monthly Report, North Tipperary, August 1920, TNA: PRO CO 904/112; *Manchester Guardian*, 18 August 1920, 7; *Daily News*, 18 August 1920, 3; *The Times*, 18 August 1920, 12; Abbott, *Police Casualties*, 111.
36. See Chapter One.
37. *Daily News*, 6 November 1920, 1, 3; *Manchester Guardian*, 5 November 1920, 9; *The Times*, 6 November 1920, 12; *Manchester Guardian*, 6 November 1920, 11.
38. *Manchester Guardian*, 5 November 1920, 9.
39. Register of Crime, TNA: PRO CO 904/45, 338; RIC County Inspector's Monthly Report, Sligo, November 1920, TNA: PRO CO 904/113; *The Times*, 5 November 1920, 12; Abbott, *Police Casualties*, 148.
40. See Chapter Two.
41. *Manchester Guardian*, 23 September 1920, 7; *Manchester Guardian*, 24 September 1920, 7; *Manchester Guardian*, 27 September 1920, 7; *Daily News*, 24 September 1920, 1; *The Times*, 24 September 1920, 10; *Daily Telegraph*, 24 September 1920, 9. Also, see Abbott, *Police Casualties*, 123–26, and Kautt, *Ambushes and Armour*, 91–95.
42. Register of Crime, TNA: PRO CO 904/45, 336; Abbott, *Police Casualties*, 138–39.
43. *Daily Telegraph*, 2 November 1920, 11; *Daily Telegraph*, 3 November 1920, 11; Abbott, *Police Casualties*, 140–41, 311–12. For a detailed account of the Tralee Blockade, see Dwyer, *Tans, Terror, and Troubles*, 228–53.
44. *Daily Telegraph*, 15 November 1920, 10; *Manchester Guardian*, 18 November 1920, 7; *Daily News*, 18 November 1920, 3; RIC Inspector General's Monthly Report, November 1920, TNA: PRO CO 904/113. See also Chapter Five.
45. Abbott, *Police Casualties*, 164.
46. Abbott, *Police Casualties*, 51–52.
47. Testimony of Denis Morgan, *Evidence on Conditions in Ireland*, 14–15.
48. *Manchester Guardian*, 28 September 1920, 9; *Daily News*, 28 September 1920, 1; *The Times*, 28 September 1920, 10; *Daily Telegraph*, 28 September 1920, 11; *Morning Post*, 28 September 1920, 7; Seamus Finn, 'Inside Information Acted on Efficiently led to the Fall of Trim Barrack, September 30, 1920,' in *With the I.R.A. in the Fight for Freedom*, 89–90; Coogan, *Politics and War in Meath*, 128–32.
49. See Chapter Five.
50. *Manchester Guardian*, 3 November 1920, 7; *Daily News*, 3 November 1920, 1; *Daily Telegraph*, 3 November 1920, 11.

51. *Daily Telegraph*, 3 November 1920, 11; *The Times*, 5 November 1920, 12; *Manchester Guardian*, 5 November 1920, 9; *Daily News*, 5 November 1920, 3; *Daily Telegraph*, 5 November 1920, 14.
52. *Report of the Labour Commission*, 33.
53. See Chapter Two.
54. RIC County Inspector's Monthly Report, Sligo, October 1920, TNA: PRO CO 904/113.
55. 'Inform all available Auxiliary force to proceed at once to Ballymote, where a Sergeant has been shot.' Telegram, District Inspector Sligo to Head Constable Constabulary Ballaghadereen, 3 November 1920, 4:28 p.m., reproduced in *Report of the Labour Commission*, 14.
56. Statement of District Inspector 1st Class O. W. Latimer, 16 December 1920, TNA: PRO WO 35/88A, Part 3, 13.
57. Abbott, *Police Casualties*, 35–40.
58. *Manchester Guardian*, 5 November 1920, 9.
59. *Manchester Guardian*, 4 October 1920, 8; *Daily News*, 4 October 1920, 1.
60. *Report of the Labour Commission*, 17; Testimony of John Derham, *Evidence on Conditions in Ireland*, 111–12.
61. Bennett, *The Black and Tans*, 141; Testimony of Donal O'Callaghan, *Evidence on Conditions in Ireland*, 828–33; Hopkinson, *Irish War of Independence*, 83; Townshend, *British Campaign*, 138–39; Martin Seedorf, 'The Lloyd George Government and the Strickland Report on the Burning of Cork, 1920', *Albion* 4, no. 2 (1972), 60–61.
62. *Manchester Guardian*, 21 April 1921, 7; *The Times*, 21 April 1921, 10.
63. Testimony of John Derham, *Evidence on Conditions in Ireland*, 102–104, 107–109, 117.
64. *Manchester Guardian*, 2 November 1920, 7. According to the *Guardian*'s correspondent, 'There is a persistent boycott of the police, and every day armed uniformed men enter the shops demanding supplies at the revolver point.'
65. Testimony of Denis Morgan, *Evidence on Conditions in Ireland*, 17.
66. *The Times*, 28 September 1920, 10; *Morning Post*, 28 September 1920, 7.
67. *Manchester Guardian*, 8 October 1920, 8; *Daily News*, 8 October 1920, 1.
68. *Manchester Guardian*, 5 November 1920, 9.
69. *Manchester Guardian*, 6 November 1920, 11.
70. *The Times*, 5 November 1920, 12; *Daily Telegraph*, 5 November 1920, 14.
71. *Manchester Guardian*, 15 October 1920, 10. This article was reprinted from the *Irish Bulletin*. 'Much of what is published in the "Irish Bulletin" is of a propagandist character,' says the *Guardian*, 'but these documents appear to us to bear the clear impress of truth, and we think it right that they should be given publicity.'
72. See Chapter Two.
73. Testimony of John Derham, *Evidence on Conditions in Ireland*, 102.
74. *Manchester Guardian*, 15 October 1920, 10.

75. See Chapter Two.
76. *Report of the Labour Commission*, 40.
77. *Manchester Guardian*, 27 September 1920, 7.
78. *Manchester Guardian*, 5 November, 9. According to *The Times*, the Black and Tans 'returned to their lorries, yelling as they went' after burning two last houses: *The Times*, 6 November 1920, 12.
79. *Manchester Guardian*, 24 September 1920, 7.
80. *The Times*, 28 September 1920, 10; *Morning Post*, 28 September 1920, 7.
81. See Chapter Two.
82. *Report of the Labour Commission*, 84–85.
83. Testimony of John Derham, *Evidence on Conditions in Ireland*, 105–107; *Manchester Guardian*, 23 September 1920, 7. Sergeant Patrick Finnerty had been shot and fatally wounded in Balbriggan on 14 April 1920, dying two days later: Abbott, *Police Casualties*, 69–70. The proceedings of the Military Court of Inquiry on the deaths of the two men is not among those available at the National Archives of the UK, but on 1 October 1920 Mark Sturgis recorded the following in his diary: 'The Military Court sitting in place of Inquest on the two SF's killed at Balbriggan has brought in a verdict that they were stabbed not by bayonets but by some sharp instrument like a knife by unknown members of the Police—this is pretty nasty. I wonder if it will be made public.' Hopkinson, *The Last Days of Dublin Castle*, 50.
84. *Manchester Guardian*, 27 September 1920, 7.
85. *Daily News*, 30 October 1920, 3; *Manchester Guardian*, 30 October 1920, 11.
86. *Manchester Guardian*, 30 October 1920, 11.
87. See Chapter Two.
88. *Daily News*, 30 October 1920, 3; Louise Ryan, '"Drunken Tans": Representations of Sex and Violence in the Anglo-Irish War (1919–21)', *Feminist Review* no. 66 (Autumn 2000), 79. Cf. *Manchester Guardian*, 30 October 1920, 11.
89. Quoted in Ryan, "Drunken Tans", 80.
90. Robinson to Dickson, 14 May 1921, TNA: PRO HO 351/167. In addition, Dickson told a witness that she was going to marry Bill Robinson: evidence of Charles Fyfe, 1 June 1921, TNA: PRO HO 351/167.
91. Evidence of Constable Henry Boyle, 1 June 1921, TNA: PRO HO 351/167; evidence of Charles Fyfe, 1 June 1921, TNA: PRO HO 351/167.
92. Evidence of Constable William Robinson, Military Court of Inquiry (Anne Dickson), 26 May 1921, TNA: PRO HO 351/167. There is a large question mark in the margin of this document, next to the final quoted sentence. General Macready reviewed this case, and made the following comment: 'I presume he will be tried. The excuse for taking the revolver out of his pocket is evidently a lie.' Deputy Adjutant General to Under Secretary, 31 May 1921.
93. Findings, Military Court of Inquiry (Anne Dickson), 26 May 1921, TNA: PRO HO 351/167.

94. Evidence of Sarah Kells, Military Court of Inquiry (Anne Dickson), 26 May 1921, TNA: PRO HO 351/167.
95. Documents in TNA: PRO HO 351/167. Robinson was sentenced to one year's imprisonment without hard labour. The remainder of his sentence was remitted on 14 February 1922.
96. Testimony of Ellen Wilkinson, *Evidence on Conditions in Ireland*, 600. Hanna Sheehy Skeffington (1877–1946) was an Irish republican propagandist (author of *British Militarism as I Have Known It* (1917)) and a former suffragette. A British officer had murdered her pacifist husband Francis in Dublin during the Rebellion of 1916.
97. Testimony of Donal O'Callaghan, *Evidence on Conditions in Ireland*, 750–51.
98. Testimony of Caroline Townshend, *Evidence on Conditions in Ireland*, 1,040.
99. *Report of the Labour Commission*, 29.
100. *Lady Gregory's Journals*, I, 202.
101. Cf. Ryan, "Drunken Tans". For some possible reasons why the police would show such comparative restraint toward women, see Chapter Seven.
102. *Manchester Guardian*, 21 October 1920, 9; *The Times*, 21 October 1920, 10; *Daily News*, 21 October 1920, 3.
103. *The Times*, 21 October 1920, 10; *Daily News*, 21 October 1920, 3.
104. Hugh Martin, *Ireland in Insurrection* (London, 1921), 115.
105. *Lady Gregory's Journals*, I, 206.
106. Testimony of Nellie Craven, *Evidence on Conditions in Ireland*, 507–508.
107. For example, Agnes King told the Commission that she was awakened in her Limerick hotel room by cries of 'Halt', 'Hands up', and 'Fire' from a man in the room next door. 'Never mind,' she was told. 'That is a man who was on the run, and he was caught and escaped. His mind is a little shattered now, and he is resting in the next room. He does that now all through the night.' Testimony of Agnes King, *Evidence on Conditions in Ireland*, 135.
108. Evidence of seventh witness, Military Court of Inquiry (Thomas Lawlor), 8 January 1921, TNA: PRO WO 35/153A.
109. Evidence of fourth witness, Military Court of Inquiry (Thomas Lawlor), 8 January 1921, TNA: PRO WO 35/153A.
110. Evidence of second witness (Dr Timothy Buckley), Military Court of Inquiry (Thomas Lawlor), 8 January 192, TNA: PRO WO 35/153A; evidence of third witness (Captain G. S. Livingstone, RAMC), Military Court of Inquiry (Thomas Lawlor), 8 January 1921, TNA: PRO WO 35/153A. The sergeant in charge of the police patrol testified that Lawlor had been detained and searched, and was then told to go home. 'I saw no blow struck,' he said: evidence of tenth witness (Sergeant Watson, RIC), Military Court of Inquiry (Thomas Lawlor), 8 January 192, TNA: PRO WO 35/153A.
111. Military Court of Inquiry (Joseph Taylor), 14 March 1921, TNA: PRO WO 35/160.

112. 3rd Evidence (District Inspector Captain Henry Gallogly), Military Court of Inquiry (Thomas Walsh), TNA: PRO WO 35/160.
113. 4th Evidence (Constable A), Military Court of Inquiry (Thomas Walsh), TNA: PRO WO 35/160.
114. 6th Evidence (Constable C), Military Court of Inquiry (Thomas Walsh), TNA: PRO WO 35/160.
115. Constable B was asked whether he knew that Walsh was an 'extreme' republican: 'I had heard he was a Sinn Feiner,' Constable B replied, 'but I had not heard that he had taken part in any murders': 5th Evidence (Constable B), Military Court of Inquiry (Thomas Walsh), TNA: PRO WO 35/160.
116. See Chapter Two.
117. Evidence of Temporary Cadet Lowe, Military Court of Inquiry (Louis D'Arcy), 26 March 1921, TNA: PRO WO 35/148.
118. General Sir Nevil Macready, note on Military Court of Inquiry (Louis D'Arcy), 26 March 1921, TNA: PRO WO 35/148.
119. General Sir Nevil Macready, note on Military Court of Inquiry (William McCarthy), 28 March 1921, TNA: PRO WO 35/148.
120. Handcuffs for Prisoners: RIC Circular C.562/1921, 30 March 1921, TNA: PRO HO 184/125, f. 235.
121. Testimony of Sergeant Keeney, Military Court of Inquiry (Thomas Collins), 20 January 1921, TNA: PRO WO 35/147A.
122. The loin is 'the part of the body on both sides of the spine between the false ribs and the hip bones'. Della Thompson (ed.), *The Concise Oxford Dictionary of Current English*, 9th ed. (Oxford: Clarendon, 1995), 802. Thus, the bullet in question must have gone through Collins's body from front to back.
123. Testimony of RAMC officer, Military Court of Inquiry (Thomas Collins), 20 January 1921, TNA: PRO WO 35/147A.
124. 2nd Witness (Section Leader C. Sutton, ADRIC), Military Court of Inquiry (Andrew Moynihan), 24 December 1920, TNA: PRO WO 35/155A. Sutton's evidence was corroborated by one of his men: 1st Witness (Temporary Cadet J. H. Jennings), Military Court of Inquiry (Andrew Moynihan), 24 December 1920, TNA: PRO WO 35/155A.
125. 3rd Witness (Dr A. A. Hargrave), Military Court of Inquiry (Andrew Moynihan), 24 December 1920, TNA: PRO WO 35/155A.
126. Adjutant North Mayo to Adjutant General, 12 October 1921, Collins Papers, MA, A/0749/XIV.
127. *Manchester Guardian*, 11 February 1921, 9; *The Times*, 11 February 1921, 11; *Manchester Guardian*, 13 February 1921, 6.
128. *Parliamentary Debates*, Commons, 5th ser., vol. 138, cols. 662–63.
129. Hopkinson (ed.), *The Last Days of Dublin Castle*, 124–26.
130. Hopkinson (ed.), *The Last Days of Dublin Castle*, 125. Basil Thomson was head of Special Branch at Scotland Yard. Captain Jocelyn Hardy was Thomson's liaison officer in Dublin Castle.

131. Macready to Anderson, 15 February 1921, Anderson Papers, TNA: PRO CO 904/188.
132. *Manchester Guardian*, 13 April 1921, 7; *Daily News*, 13 April 1921, 3.
133. *Manchester Guardian*, 14 April 1921, 7; *Daily News*, 14 April 1921, 1. It is likely that the defence argued successfully that any statement made by James Murphy to this police witness was hearsay rather than a dying declaration. 'In a trial for murder or manslaughter a declaration by the person killed as to the cause of his death, or as to any of the circumstances of the transaction which resulted in his death, is admissible as evidence. But this exception is very strictly construed. It must be proved that the declarant, at the time of making the declaration, was in actual danger of death, and had given up all hope of recovery.' 'Evidence', *Encyclopaedia Britannica* 11th ed., vol. X (Cambridge, 1910), 17.
134. *Manchester Guardian*, 15 April 1921, 9; *Daily News*, 15 April 1921, 5; *Manchester Guardian*, 16 April 1921, 10; *Daily News*, 16 April 1921, 3.
135. Cadet Welsh was acquitted on 13 April 1921, having been identified by just one witness.
136. Evidence of Sergeant Patrick Brown, RIC, Military Court of Inquiry (Patrick Ryan), 9 June 1921, TNA: PRO WO 35/157B.
137. Evidence of James Ryan, Military Court of Inquiry (Patrick Ryan), 9 June 1921, TNA: PRO WO 35/157B.
138. Evidence of Ellen Ryan, Military Court of Inquiry (Patrick Ryan), 9 June 1921, TNA: PRO WO 35/157B; evidence of Margaret Ryan, Military Court of Inquiry (Patrick Ryan), 9 June 1921, TNA: PRO WO 35/157B.
139. Evidence of Mrs M. M. Coleman, Military Court of Inquiry (James Coleman), 19 & 22 November 1920, TNA: PRO WO 35/147A; *Manchester Guardian*, 19 November 1920, 9; *Daily News*, 19 November 1920, 3; Hart, *The I.R.A. and Its Enemies*, 7–8.
140. Evidence of Mary Horan, Military Court of Inquiry (Tom Horan), 9 March 1921, TNA: PRO WO 35/152; evidence of Dr Edward Murphy, Military Court of Inquiry (Tom Horan), 9 March 1921, TNA: PRO WO 35/152.
141. Evidence of 3rd Witness (Miss Alice Kerr), Military Court of Inquiry (William Kerr), 13 June 1921, TNA: PRO WO 35/153A. A number of Auxiliaries were seconded to the USC to serve as platoon commanders.
142. William Kerr's wife was also present and corroborated her sister-in-law's evidence on events that night: evidence of 2nd Witness (Mrs William Kerr), Military Court of Inquiry (William Kerr), 13 June 1921, TNA: PRO WO 35/153A.
143. Evidence of 3rd Witness (Miss Alice Kerr), Military Court of Inquiry (William Kerr), 13 June 1921, TNA: PRO WO 35/153A. Another Belfast man, Malachy Halfpenny, was murdered on the same night, possibly by the same death squad: see Military Court of Inquiry (Malachy Halfpenny), 13 June 1921, TNA: PRO WO 35/151A.

144. Testimony of Susanna Walsh, *Evidence on Conditions in Ireland*, 634. Cf. Inquest on Thomas MacCurtáin, TNA: PRO CO 904/47B; see also Witness Statement of Michael J. Feeley, NA BMH WS 68.
145. *Manchester Guardian*, 29 March 1920, 9; *The Times*, 29 March 1920, 16; *Manchester Guardian*, 14 April 1920, 9.
146. *Manchester Guardian*, 30 March 1920, 9; *The Times*, 30 March 1920, 14; *Manchester Guardian*, 16 April 1920, 9.
147. *Manchester Guardian*, 19 November 1920, 9; *Daily News*, 19 November 1920, 3; Hart, *The I.R.A. and Its Enemies*, 7–8.
148. *Manchester Guardian*, 10 February 1921, 7; *The Times*, 10 February 1921, 11; Military Court of Inquiry (Thomas Halpin), 9 February 1921, TNA: PRO WO 35/151A; Military Court of Inquiry (James Moran), 10 February 1921, TNA: PRO W.O 35/155A; *Manchester Guardian*, 17 March 1921, 8.
149. A third man, Volunteer Joseph O'Donoghue, was killed as well. *Manchester Guardian*, 8 March 1921, p. 9; *The Times*, 8 March 1921, 12; Military Court of Inquiry (George Clancy, Michael O'Callaghan, and Joseph O'Donoghue), TNA: PRO WO 35/147A; Mrs Clancy, Mrs O'Callaghan, et al., 'The Limerick City Curfew Murders of March 7th 1921', in *Limerick's Fighting Story* (Tralee, 1949), 115–39.
150. Bennett, 'Portrait of a Killer', 471.
151. Bennett, 'Portrait of a Killer', 472.
152. Nathan's entry in the Register does not mention any special duty, but it does say that he reverted to the rank of temporary cadet from that of section leader on 15 December 1920; this may have been when he was recruited for intelligence work. Temporary Cadet 785/79173, ADRIC Register No. 1, TNA: PRO HO 184/50.
153. Bennett, 'Portrait of a Killer', 471.
154. Bennett, 'Portrait of a Killer', 472.
155. *Manchester Guardian*, 26 July 1920, 7.
156. *Manchester Guardian*, 30 July 1920, 7; Abbott, *Police Casualties*, 105.
157. *Manchester Guardian*, 20 November 1920, 13.
158. *Manchester Guardian*, 22 November 1920, 7; *Daily Telegraph*, 22 November 1920, 13; *The Times*, 22 November 1920, 12; RIC County Inspector's Monthly Report, Limerick, November 1920, TNA: PRO, CO 904/113; Patrick Maloney, 'With the Mid-Limerick Brigade Second Battalion', in *Limerick's Fighting Story 1916–21* (Tralee, 1949), 180–81.

CHAPTER 7

1. Hart, *The I.R.A. and Its Enemies*, 82.
2. *Dáil Debates* I (10 April 1919), 63.
3. Erskine Childers, *Military Rule in Ireland* (Dublin, 1920), 39.
4. Testimony of Mary MacSwiney, *Evidence on Conditions in Ireland*, 262.

5. Hart, *The I.R.A. and Its Enemies*, 6–8.
6. *Parliamentary Debates*, Commons, 5th ser., vol. 133, cols. 1,015–16, 1,019.
7. *Report of the Labour Commission*, 56.
8. Martin, *Ireland in Insurrection*, 60–61.
9. *Daily News*, 1 October 1920, 3.
10. *Manchester Guardian*, 13 October 1920, 9.
11. Testimony of John Caddan, *Evidence on Conditions in Ireland*, 415; *Manchester Guardian Weekly Edition*, 17 September 1920, 238.
12. *Manchester Guardian*, 7 October 1920, 8.
13. *Manchester Guardian*, 5 November 1920, 9.
14. Hopkinson (ed.), *The Last Days of Dublin Castle*, 46; *Daily News*, 10 November 1920, 3.
15. V. H. Scott to J. R. W. Goulden, 21 February 1967, TCD, Goulden Papers 7382A/68.
16. *Manchester Guardian*, 28 October 1920, 7; *Daily News*, 28 October 1920, 3.
17. *Daily News*, 28 October 1920, 3.
18. *Manchester Guardian*, 30 October 1920, 11.
19. *Report of the Labour Commission*, 26.
20. *Manchester Guardian*, 11 December 1920, 15; *Daily News*, 11 December 1920, 1.
21. *The Memoirs of John M. Regan: A Catholic Officer in the RIC and RUC, 1909–1948*, ed. Joost Augusteijn (Dublin, 2007), 139. Regan served as the RIC's County Inspector for Limerick in 1920–21.
22. *Parliamentary Debates*, Commons, 5th ser., vol. 133, cols. 994–95.
23. See Chapter Three.
24. Witness Statement of John Duffy, NA BMH WS 580, 21–22.
25. Hart, *The I.R.A. and Its Enemies*, 308–15.
26. Hart, *The I.R.A. and Its Enemies*, 311.
27. Hart, *The I.R.A. and Its Enemies*, 308. Cf. John Borgonovo, *Spies, Informers and the 'Anti-Sinn Féin Society': The Intelligence War in Cork City, 1920–1921* (Dublin and Portland, OR: Irish Academic Press, 2007), 91: 'Faced with numerous cases of complicity with the local Crown forces, the city's IRA leadership probably found it easiest to assassinate isolated men of low social standing, rather than prominent pillars of the community, close associates, or members of Republican families.'
28. RIC County Inspector's Monthly Report, Wicklow, February 1921, TNA: PRO CO 904/114.
29. RIC County Inspector's Monthly Report, Wicklow, February 1921, TNA: PRO CO 904/114; *Manchester Guardian*, 8 June 1921, 9; *The Times*, 8 June 1921, 14.
30. RIC County Inspector's Monthly Report, Queen's County, TNA: PRO 904/113.
31. Evidence of Dr Nicholas Maher, Military Court of Inquiry (James Whelan), TNA: PRO WO 35/159B.

32. Reive is referred to as 'Reeves' throughout the proceedings of the Military Court of Inquiry.
33. Evidence of Head Constable Michael Flynn RIC, Military Court of Inquiry (James Whelan), TNA PRO: WO 35/159B.
34. Findings, Military Court of Inquiry (James Whelan), TNA PRO: WO 35/159B.
35. Remarks by GOC 5th Division, Military Court of Inquiry (James Whelan), TNA PRO: WO 35/159B.
36. Rev. J. C. Johnston to Home Secretary, 2 January 1922, TNA PRO: HO 144/1761/429569.
37. Statement of John P. Green, 15 May 1921, TNA: PRO CO 904/44.
38. Report of Outrage, County Galway West Riding, District of Galway, Sub-District of Salthill, 15 May 1921, TNA: PRO CO 904/44; Galway District Inspector to West Galway County Inspector, 15 May 1921, TNA: PRO CO 904/44. Murphy and Orford had the remainder of their sentences remitted on 14 March 1922 and were released from prison on 17 March: Irish Secretary to Under Secretary, Home Office, 14 March 1922, TNA: PRO CO 904/44; Under Secretary of State, Home Office to Irish Secretary, 28 March 1922, TNA: PRO CO 904/44.
39. Galway District Inspector to West Galway County Inspector, 15 May 1921, TNA: PRO CO 904/44.
40. Harvey Skinner, Petition to the Lord Lieutenant, 28 November 1921, TNA: PRO HO 351/69.
41. Opinion of Chief Crown Solicitor on the case of Tom Chester, 16 February 1922, TNA: PRO HO 351/69.
42. Michel Foucault, *Discipline and Punish: The Birth of the Prison*, trans. Alan Sheridan (New York, 1995), 82–83.
43. Jonathan Shay, *Achilles in Vietnam: Combat Trauma and the Undoing of Character* (New York, 1994), 81.
44. 'Volunteer', 'The IRA Campaign in West Limerick', in *Limerick's Fighting Story*, 167; Abbott, *Police Casualties*, 253–54.
45. *Manchester Guardian*, 16 December 1920, 9; *Daily News*, 16 December 1920, 1; *Daily News*, 17 December 1920, 1, 3; *The Times*, 17 December 1920, 13; *Manchester Guardian*, 20 December 1920, 10.
46. *Parliamentary Debates*, Commons, 5th ser., vol. 138, cols. 244–46.
47. *Manchester Guardian*, 8 October 1920, 8.
48. *Manchester Guardian*, 5 October 1920, 5; *Daily News*, 6 October 1920, 1, 3; Martin, *Ireland in Insurrection*, 106–15.
49. Martin, *Ireland in Insurrection*, 115.
50. Martin, *Ireland in Insurrection*, 107.
51. Brewer, *Oral History*, 72.
52. Brewer, *Oral History*, 75.
53. On the Panopticon and 'panopticism' see Michel Foucault, *Discipline and Punish: The Birth of the Prison*, trans. Alan Sheridan (New York, 1995), 200–209. Charles

Townshend has described the 'intelligence gap' in Ireland as 'a two-way mirror behind which the rebels moved with almost complete assurance' (Townshend, *British Campaign in Ireland*, 125).

54. Application for a bonus for District Inspectors: DI Ryan, Lurgan, County Armagh, 13 January 1921, TNA: PRO HO 351/81.
55. Abbott, *Police Casualties*, passim.
56. Abbott, *Police Casualties*, 233.
57. Townshend, *British Campaign in Ireland*, 166–68; Abbott, *Police Casualties*, 317–19.
58. Outrage Reports, May 1921, TNA: PRO CO 904/150.
59. See Chapter Five.
60. Summarised findings of Military Court of Inquiry (John MacDonald), 28 May 1921, TNA: PRO CO 904/189/2; Abbott, *Police Casualties*, 222. For another example, see summary of police report on the death of Wilfred Jones, 22 April 1921, TNA: PRO CO 904/189/2; Abbott, *Police Casualties*, 222.
61. Dwyer, *Tans, Terror, and Troubles*, 302–304; Abbott, *Police Casualties*, 221–22; 'Fianna', 'The Fatal Challenge of Major McKinnon', in *Kerry's Fighting Story*, 142–46; see also documents in TNA: PRO T 192/155, in which one official comments: 'The fact is that the Auxiliaries are serving under war conditions, & it is a breach of discipline on their part to expose themselves to danger wilfully to amuse themselves.' (unsigned, 6 July 1921).
62. Abbott, *Police Casualties*, 259; Military Court of Inquiry (William F. Hunt), TNA: PRO WO 35/152; documents in TNA: PRO T 192/155; correspondence in TNA: PRO T 164/13/15.
63. Abbott, *Police Casualties*, 227. See General Macready's angry comments on Military Court of Inquiry (William Smith and John Webb), TNA: PRO WO 35/159A.
64. Abbott, *Police Casualties*, 227–28; Military Court of Inquiry (George Cuthberton and William Shaw), TNA: PRO WO 35/147B.
65. *Manchester Guardian*, 22 September 1920, 7.
66. *Daily News*, 6 November 1920, 1, 3; *The Times*, 6 November 1920, 12; *Manchester Guardian*, 6 November 1920, 11.
67. Brewer, *Oral History*, 63, 103, 113, 114.
68. 'Q. So their life consisted of doing their duty on the streets of the city and spending their spare time in the liquor store in the barracks and in bed? A. Yes, and in bed.' Testimony of John Caddan, *Evidence on Conditions in Ireland*, 416.
69. David Neligan, *The Spy in the Castle* (London, 1968), 88.
70. Crozier, *Ireland For Ever*, 107, 198–99.
71. Cross-examination of 6th witness (Constable A. E. Wood, RIC), Military Court of Inquiry (Dennis O'Donnell), 26 November 1920, TNA: PRO WO 35/157B.
72. Cross-examination of 7th witness (Constable S. W. Coe, RIC), Military Court of Inquiry (Dennis O'Donnell), 26 November 1920, TNA: PRO WO 35/157B.

73. Cross-examination of 8th witness (Constable A. Gray), Military Court of Inquiry (Dennis O'Donnell), 26 November 1920, TNA: PRO WO 35/157B.
74. Outrage Reports, week ending 25 July 1920, TNA: PRO CO 904/149.
75. Summary of Police Reports, 22 September 1920, TNA: PRO CO 904/142.
76. Summary of Police Reports, 23 September 1920, TNA: PRO CO 904/142.
77. *Manchester Guardian*, 5 November 1920, 9.
78. RIC Inspector General's Monthly Report, IG, November 1920, TNA: PRO CO 904/113.
79. *Manchester Guardian*, 4 October 1920, 8.
80. RIC County Inspector's Monthly Report, Roscommon, October 1920, TNA: PRO CO 904/113.
81. Testimony of Mary MacSwiney, *Evidence on Conditions in Ireland*, 256.
82. See Giovanni Costigan, 'The Anglo-Irish Conflict, 1919–1922: A War of Independence or Systematized Murder', *University Review* 5, no. 1 (1968), 64–86, for an Irish republican apologia. To be fair, the British refusal to treat captured rebels as prisoners of war did not encourage the guerrillas to follow these rules.
83. *Weekly Summary*, 3 December 1920, 1, TNA: PRO CO 906/38.
84. *Weekly Summary*, 13 August 1920, 1, TNA: PRO CO 906/38.
85. Report re Sergeant Restrick, Abbeydorney, 31 May 1920, MA, Collins Papers, A/0494/VIII/14.
86. Affidavit of James Murphy, *Evidence on Conditions in Ireland*, 779.
87. *Weekly Summary*, 3 June 1921, 1, TNA: PRO CO 906/38.
88. *Weekly Summary*, 11 March 1921, 1, TNA: PRO CO 906/38.
89. *Weekly Summary*, 8 October 1920, 1, TNA: PRO CO 906/38.
90. *Weekly Summary*, 1 October 1920, 2, TNA: PRO CO 906/38.
91. *Weekly Summary*, 8 October 1920, 2, TNA: PRO CO 906/38.
92. *Weekly Summary*, 8 October 1920, 2, TNA: PRO CO 906/38. Cf. *Weekly Summary*, 12 November 1920, 2, TNA: PRO CO 906/38; *Weekly Summary*, 12 November 1920, 2, TNA: PRO CO 906/38; *Weekly Summary*, 12 November 1920, 3, TNA: PRO CO 906/38. For an especially vivid and imaginative example, see 'The First Reprisal', *Weekly Summary*, 29 October 1920, 1, TNA: PRO CO 906/38, parts of which are quoted in Bennett, *The Black and Tans*, 101.
93. *Weekly Summary*, 26 November 1920, 1, TNA: PRO CO 906/38; see also *Weekly Summary*, 3 December 1920, 2, TNA: PRO CO 906/38.
94. *Weekly Summary*, 1 October 1920, 1, TNA: PRO CO 906/38.
95. *Weekly Summary*, 12 November 1920, 1, TNA: PRO CO 906/38.
96. *Weekly Summary*, 18 February 1921, 1, TNA: PRO CO 906/38. This editorial also describes a policeman's duty as 'a full-size man's job', which calls for 'all that is best in big-hearted men'.
97. 'This paper has been called a "weekly hate sheet." It is. It hates murder': *Weekly Summary*, 19 November 1920, 1, TNA: PRO CO 906/38.

98. Shay, *Achilles in Vietnam*, 3–37.
99. *Morning Post*, 22 July 1920, 7.
100. Hart, *The I.R.A. and Its Enemies*, 78–79.
101. *Manchester Guardian*, 19 April 1920, 8. The subheadings of this article are worth quoting here: 'Suspicion of a Counter-Vendetta—The Drift to Lynch Law—Vicious Circle of Violence'.
102. Martin, *Ireland in Insurrection*, 60.
103. RIC County Inspector's Monthly Report, Leitrim, June 1921, TNA: PRO CO 904/115.
104. RIC County Inspector's Monthly Report, Mayo, October 1920, TNA: PRO CO 904/113.
105. Hopkinson (ed.), *The Last Days of Dublin Castle*, 28.
106. RIC County Inspector's Monthly Report, Longford, November 1920, TNA: PRO CO 904/113.
107. *Daily News*, 6 November 1920, 1, 3; *The Times*, 6 November 1920, 12; *Manchester Guardian*, 6 November 1920, 11. The County Inspector's version was accepted and passed on to the British Cabinet by the RIC's Deputy Inspector General: RIC Inspector General's Monthly Report, November 1920, TNA: PRO CO 904/113.
108. Hopkinson (ed.), *The Last Days of Dublin Castle*, 136.
109. *Manchester Guardian*, 18 March 1921, 9; *Manchester Guardian*, 19 March 1921, 9; *Manchester Guardian*, 28 March 1921, 6; *Daily News*, 28 March 1921, 1; *The Times*, 28 March 1921, 8; Hopkinson (ed.), *The Last Days of Dublin Castle*, 150; Macready to Anderson, 28 March 1921, Anderson Papers, TNA: PRO CO 904/188; Macready to Anderson, 29 March 1921, Anderson Papers, TNA: PRO CO 904/188; Townshend, *British Campaign in Ireland*, 166. According to Castle gossip, Divisional Commissioner Cruise was an ambitious officer who was hoping to become the RIC's Inspector General: Hopkinson (ed.), *The Last Days of Dublin Castle*, 122.
110. See Chapter Two.
111. Discipline: RIC Circular D.446/1920, 12 November 1920, TNA: PRO HO 184/125, f. 149. The Deputy Inspector General had written a similar message six weeks before: Alleged Acts of Reprisal by Police and Soldiers: RIC Circular D.403/1920, 28 September 1920, PRO HO 184/125, f. 118.
112. Hopkinson (ed.), *The Last Days of Dublin Castle*, 110.
113. Hopkinson (ed.), *The Last Days of Dublin Castle*, 95.
114. Douglas Wimberley MS, vol. I, IWM, PP/MCR/182, 149; E. M. Ransford MS, IWM, 80/29/1; Townshend, *British Campaign in Ireland*, 205.
115. In his analysis of the findings of these courts of inquiry, Townshend notes that 'the tendency to exculpate Crown Forces for deaths caused "in the execution of their duty" is, as one would expect, clear, and the finding that victims "attempted to escape" or "failed to halt" often covered culpable laxity in the use of weapons': Townshend, *British Campaign in Ireland*, 107. In addition, the

course of military justice seems to have been easy to pervert. In his memoirs Douglas Wimberley describes how, as adjutant for the 2nd Cameron Highlanders, he held an inquest into the killing of a Cork man and returned a verdict of murder by persons unknown. Years later, he was informed that the victim had in fact been killed by a soldier in his own regiment: Douglas Wimberley MS, vol. I, IWM, PP/MCR/182, 153.

116. RIC Inspector General's Monthly Report, IG, December 1920, TNA: PRO CO 904/113.
117. Evidence of 1st Witness (Major J. A. Mackinnon, OC H. Coy Auxiliary Division RIC), Military Court of Inquiry (John Lean and Maurice Reidy), 27 December 1920, TNA: PRO WO 35/153A.
118. Evidence of 2nd Witness (Captain H. Wilkinson), 3rd Witness (DI 3 G. Livingston Shaw) and 4th Witness (DI 3 R. B. Robb), Military Court of Inquiry (John Lean and Maurice Reidy), 27 December 1920, TNA: PRO WO 35/153A. All three of these men said they were the first into the house after they heard shots fired. Robb, for example, said he followed Mackinnon into the room, saw Reidy draw his revolver and point it at the major, heard two shots, and saw Lean fall. He then went further into the room, where he saw Reidy dead in the chair. Only then did Wilkinson come in, he said.
119. Findings, Military Court of Inquiry (John Lean and Maurice Reidy), 27 December 1920, TNA: PRO WO 35/153A. Brigadier General Cumming concurred on 4 January 1921; Major General Strickland concurred on 9 January 1921.
120. Military Court of Inquiry (Tom Horan), 9 March 1921; DAG to Under Secretary, 26 March 1921; Jeudwine to GHQ Ireland, 7 April 1921; Military Court of Inquiry (Tom Horan), 19 April 1921, TNA: PRO WO 35/152.
121. Evidence of 5th witness (Head Constable John Clarke RIC, Strokestown), Military Court of Inquiry (Michael Mulloolly), 28 March 1921, TNA: PRO WO 35/155A.
122. Opinion, Military Court of Inquiry (Michael Mulloolly), 28 March 1921, TNA: PRO WO 35/155A.
123. Major General H. S. Jeudwine to GHQ Ireland, 7 April 1921, Military Court of Inquiry (Michael Mulloolly), 28 March 1921, TNA: PRO WO 35/155A.
124. Evidence of 6th Witness (anonymous, E. Coy ADRIC), 9 April 1921, TNA: PRO WO 35/155A. Another Auxiliary testified as well, but was unable to corroborate the first cadet's evidence: he did not see the shooting. Nonetheless, the court amended its findings to read: 'Michael Mulloolly 25 male was shot by a member of the Auxiliary Division in the execution of his duty on March 24th 1921 at Kiltrustan.'
125. O. Dalrymple to GOC, 20 April 1921, TNA: PRO WO 35/155A.
126. This fear cut both ways: many police would not identify republican suspects either. Police witnesses at courts of inquiry were often anonymous, and in his

memoirs Wimberley mentions taking elaborate precautions to protect the identities of police witnesses at identification parades: Wimberley MS, I, 149.

127. Proceedings of Military Court of Inquiry (Thomas Halpin and James Moran), 10 February 1921, and related correspondence, TNA: PRO WO 35/155A. After the Limerick curfew murders of March 1921, the Mayor of Drogheda sent a letter to the editor of the *Drogheda Independent*, accusing the authorities of covering up the murders of Halpin and Moran: see *Manchester Guardian*, 17 March 1921, 8. Most of the paperwork relating to this case was generated in response to the mayor's letter.
128. See correspondence in TNA: PRO WO 35/88/4.
129. GOC 6th Division to GHQ, 30 June 1921, TNA: PRO WO 35/88/4.
130. Hopkinson (ed.), *The Last Days of Dublin Castle*, 49–50.
131. D. G. Boyce, *Englishmen and Irish Troubles*, 55–56; Townshend, *British Campaign in Ireland*, 120.
132. Hopkinson (ed.), *The Last Days of Dublin Castle*, 52; cf. Townshend, *British Campaign in Ireland*, 82, 100, 163–64, 184; Hopkinson, *Irish War of Independence*, 79, 82.
133. For a recent example, see John Borgonovo and Gabriel Doherty, 'Smoking Gun? RIC Reprisals, Summer 1920', *History Ireland* 17, no. 2 (2009), 36–39.
134. *Parliamentary Debates*, Commons, 5th ser., vol. 138, cols. 647–48.
135. Quoted in Graham Bower, 'The Laws of War: Prisoners of War and Reprisals', *Problems of the War* 1 (1915), 27.
136. *Parliamentary Debates*, Commons, 5th ser., vol. 138, col. 1,997.
137. *Parliamentary Debates*, Commons, 5th ser., vol. 139, col. 439.
138. Witness statement of Seán MacEoin, NA BMH WS1716 (Part 1), 153.
139. Witness Statement of Thomas Costello, NA BMH WS 1296, 20. Costello technically disobeyed this order: 'There were a number of small places owned by Protestants in the area,' he recalled, 'but I did not consider it fair to burn those people's houses for something which was not their fault.' In the end, he decided to burn Moydrum Castle, the residence of Lord Castlemaine (20–22).
140. Witness Statement of Sean Leavy, NA BMH WS 954, 22.
141. The British legal scholar Hugh H. L. Bellot, who was against reprisals in principle, made a few exceptions in practice: 'I am even ready,' he said, 'to condone the refusal of quarter to a treacherous foe. When, for instance, the enemy are found to make an habitual practice of shamming dead, or of treacherous request for quarter, and then of firing upon their captors when their backs are turned, no troops can be expected to give quarter. Reprisals under such circumstances and in the heat of battle may be justified.' Hugh H. L. Bellot, 'War Crimes: Their Prevention and Punishment', *Problems of the War* 2 (1916), 50.

CONCLUSION

1. Huggins, Haritos-Fatouros, and Zimbardo, *Violence Workers*, 240.
2. Huggins, Haritos-Fatouros, and Zimbardo, *Violence Workers*, 244.
3. *Weekly Summary*, 12 November 1920, 1, TNA: PRO CO 906/38.
4. Huggins, Haritos-Fatouros, and Zimbardo, *Violence Workers*, 248.
5. Huggins, Haritos-Fatouros, and Zimbardo, *Violence Workers*, 257.
6. Huggins, Haritos-Fatouros, and Zimbardo, *Violence Workers*, 258–59.
7. Craig Haney, Curtis Banks, and Philip Zimbardo, 'Interpersonal Dynamics in a Simulated Prison', *International Journal of Criminology and Penology* no. 1 (1973), 90. See also the fuller and more recent account of this experiment in Philip Zimbardo, *The Lucifer Effect: Understanding How Good People Turn Evil* (New York: Random House, 2007).
8. Haney, Banks, and Zimbardo, 'Interpersonal Dynamics in a Simulated Prison', 92.

Bibliography

I. MANUSCRIPT COLLECTIONS

London

Imperial War Museum Joy Cave MS, 'A Gallant Gunner General'
E. M. Ransford MS
Sir Peter Strickland Papers
P. J. Swindlehurst Diary
H. N. G. Watson Papers
Douglas Wimberley MS
The National Archives of the UK

CABINET OFFICE
CAB 23 (Minutes and Conclusions)
CAB 24 (Cabinet Papers)

COLONIAL OFFICE
CO 904 (Chief Secretary's Office Records; RIC Records; Sir John Anderson Papers)
CO 906 (*The Weekly Summary*)

HOME OFFICE
HO 45 (ADRIC Records)
HO 267 (ADRIC Records)
HO 140 (Calendar of Prisoners)
HO 184 (RIC Records; ADRIC Records)
HO 351 (Miscellaneous Records)

TREASURY
T 164 (Pension Claims)
T 192 (Pension Claims)

WAR OFFICE
WO 35 (Military Courts of Inquiry; Raids Completed [F Company ADRIC]; Ambushes, Raids, Reprisals, and Casualties)

Dublin

Garda Siochana Museum RIC Allocations Record
Military Archives of Ireland Collins Papers

National Archives of Ireland Bureau of Military History witness statements
Trinity College Archives Goulden Papers

2. GOVERNMENT PUBLICATIONS

United Kingdom

Parliamentary Debates, Commons.

Parliamentary Debates, Lords.

Appendix to the Report of the Committee of Inquiry into the Royal Irish Constabulary and the Dublin Metropolitan Police. Cd. 7637 (1914).

Committee on Re-Employment of Ex-Service Men. Interim Report. Cmd. 951 (12 August 1920).

Return showing the number of serious outrages in Ireland reported by the Royal Irish Constabulary and the Dublin Metropolitan Police for the Months of May and June, 1920. Cmd. 859 (1920).

Return showing the number of serious outrages in Ireland reported by the Royal Irish Constabulary and the Dublin Metropolitan Police for the Months of July, August, and September, 1920. Cmd. 1025 (1920).

Census of England and Wales. 1921. Preliminary Report including Tables of the Population enumerated in England and Wales (Administrative and Parliamentary Areas) and in Scotland, the Isle of Man and the Channel islands on 19/20th June Cmd. 1485 (1921).

General Annual Reports on the British Army (Including the Territorial Force from the Date of Embodiment) for the Period from 1st October, 1913, to 30th September, 1919. Cmd. 1193 (1921).

Report of Mallow Court of Inquiry. Cmd. 1220 (1921).

Return of the Areas, Population & Valuation of Counties, Burghs & Parishes in Scotland. Cmd. 1376 (1921).

Report of the Commissioners of Prisons and the Directors of Convict Prisons with Appendices. (For the Year ended 31st March 1920). Cmd. 972 (1920).

Report of the Commissioners of Prisons and the Directors of Convict Prisons with Appendices. (For the Year ended 31st March 1921). Cmd. 1523 (1921).

Royal Irish Constabulary. Terms of Disbandment. Cmd. 1618A (1922).

Royal Irish Constabulary. Revised Terms of Disbandment. Cmd. 1673 (1922).

Royal Irish Constabulary Auxiliary Division. Outline of Terms on which Cadets were engaged and of Conditions on which at various times it was open to Cadets to re-engage for further Periods of Service. Cmd. 1618 (1922).

Royal Irish Constabulary. Return Showing Rates of Pay and Maximum and Minimum Compensation Allowances Payable on Disbandment. Cmd. 1719 (1922).

General Annual Report on the British Army for the Year Ending 30th September 1921. Cmd. 1941 (1923).

3. NEWSPAPERS AND JOURNALS

Connacht Tribune
Daily Chronicle
Daily Express
Daily Herald
Daily Mail
Daily News
Daily Telegraph
Freeman's Journal
Glasgow Herald
Globe and Mail
Irish Bulletin
Irish Press
Irish Times
Leeds Mercury
Manchester Guardian
Morning Post
New York Times
Pall Mall Gazette
The Times

4. BOOKS AND ARTICLES

Abbott, Richard, *Police Casualties in Ireland 1919–1922* (Dublin, 2000).

Allen, Mary, *The Pioneer Policewoman* (London, 1925).

Augusteijn, Joost, *From Public Defiance to Guerrilla Warfare: The Experience of Ordinary Volunteers in the Irish War of Independence 1916–1921* (Dublin, 1996).

Augusteijn, Joost (ed.), *The Irish Revolution 1913–1923* (London, 2002).

——*The Memoirs of John M. Regan: A Catholic Officer in the RIC and RUC, 1909–1948* (Dublin, 2007).

Barry, Tom, *Guerrilla Days in Ireland* (Dublin, 1981).

Béaslai, Piaras, *Michael Collins and the Making of a New Ireland* (New York, 1926).

—— 'The Anglo-Irish War', in *With the IRA in the Fight for Freedom: 1919 to the Truce* (Tralee, 1950).

Bean, C. E. W., *Official History of the War of 1914–18*, IV: *The AIF in France 1917* (Sydney: Angus & Robertson, 1936)

Beckett, Ian, 'The British Army 1914–18: The Illusion of Change', in J. Turner (ed.), *Britain and the First World War* (London, 1988).

Bennett, Richard, *The Black and Tans* (London, 1959; new edition, New York, 1995).

——'Portrait of a Killer', *New Statesman* (24 March 1961).

Borgonovo, John, *Spies, Informers, and the 'Anti-Sinn Féin Society': The Intelligence War in Cork City, 1920–1921* (Dublin, 2007).

—— and Gabriel Dohety, 'Smoking Gun? RIC Reprisals, Summer 1920', *History Ireland* (2009).

Bowden, Tom, *The Breakdown of Public Security: The Case of Ireland 1916–1921 and Palestine 1936–1939* (London, 1977).

Boyce, D. G., 'How to Settle the Irish Question: Lloyd George and Ireland 1916–21', in A. J. P. Taylor (ed.), *Lloyd George: Twelve Essays* (Aldershot, 1994).

—— *Englishmen and Irish Troubles: British Public Opinion and the Making of Irish Policy 1918–22* (London, 1972).

Breen, Dan, *My Fight for Irish Freedom* (Tralee, 1964).

Brennan, Michael, *The War in Clare 1911–1921* (Dublin, 1980).

Brewer, John D., *The Royal Irish Constabulary: An Oral History* (Belfast, 1990).

Campbell, Fergus, *Land and Revolution: Nationalist Politics in the West of Ireland, 1891–1921* (Oxford, 2005).

Carey, Tim and Marcus de Burca, 'Bloody Sunday: New Evidence', *History Ireland* (Summer 2003).

Carroll, F. M., '"All Standards of Human Conduct": The American Commission on Conditions in Ireland, 1920–21', *Éire-Ireland* (1981).

Childers, Erskine, *Military Rule in Ireland* (Dublin, 1920).

Coleman, Marie, *County Longford and the Irish Revolution 1910–1923* (Dublin & Portland, 2006).

Coogan, Oliver, *Politics and War in Meath, 1913–23* (Dublin, 1983).

Costigan, Giovanni, 'The Anglo-Irish Conflict, 1919–1922: A War of Independence or Systematized Murder', *University Review* (1968).

Crozier, F. P., *Impressions and Recollections* (London, 1930).

——*Ireland For Ever* (London, 1932).

Desmond, Shaw, *The Drama of Sinn Fein* (New York, 1923).

Doyle, Roddy, *A Star Called Henry* (Toronto, 2000).

Dublin's Fighting Story 1916–1921 (Tralee, 1949).

Duff, Douglas v., *Sword for Hire: The Saga of a Modern Free Companion* (London, 1934).

Dwyer, T. Ryle, *Tans, Terror, and Troubles: Kerry's Real Fighting Story 1913–1923* (Dublin, 2001).

Evidence on Conditions in Ireland: Comprising the Complete Testimony, Affidavits and Exhibits Presented before the American Commission on Conditions in Ireland, transcribed and annotated by Albert Coyle, Official Reporter to the Commission (Washington, 1921).

Fitzpatrick, David, 'The Geography of Irish Nationalism', *Past & Present* (February 1978).

——*Politics and Irish Life 1913–1921: Provincial Experience of War and Revolution*, 2nd edition (Cork, 1998).

—— *The Two Irelands 1912–1939* (Oxford, 1998).

Foster, Roy, *Modern Ireland 1600–1972* (London, 1989).
Foucault, Michel, *Discipline and Punish: The Birth of the Prison*, trans. Alan Sheridan (New York, 1995).
Foy, Michael T., *Michael Collins's Intelligence War: The Struggle between the British and the IRA 1919–1921* (Stroud, Gloucestershire, 2008).
'Galway', *Encyclopaedia Britannica*, 11th Edition, vol. X (Cambridge, 1910).
Garside, W. R., *The Measure of Unemployment: Methods and Sources in Great Britain 1850–1979* (Oxford, 1980).
Gaughan, J. Anthony (ed.), *Memoirs of Constable Jeremiah Mee, R.I.C.* (Dublin, 1975).
Gilbert, Martin, *Winston S. Churchill*, vol. IV: *The Stricken World, 1916–1922* (Boston, 1975).
Gleeson, James, *Bloody Sunday* (London, 1963).
Graubard, Stephen Richards, 'Military Demobilization in Great Britain following the First World War', *Journal of Modern History* (1947).
Haney, Craig, Curtis Banks, and Philip Zimbardo, 'Interpersonal Dynamics in a Simulated Prison', *International Journal of Criminology and Penology* (1973).
Hart, Peter, 'The Geography of Revolution in Ireland 1917–1923', *Past and Present* (May 1997).
——*The I.R.A. and Its Enemies: Violence and Community in Cork 1916–1923* (Oxford, 1998).
——,'The Social Structure of the Irish Republican Army, 1916–1923', *Historical Journal* (1999).
Harvey, A. D., 'Who Were the Auxiliaries?', *Historical Journal* (1992).
Hawkins, Richard, 'Dublin Castle and the Royal Irish Constabulary (1916–1922)', in Desmond Williams (ed.), *The Irish Struggle 1916–1926* (London, 1966).
Hennessey, Thomas, *Dividing Ireland: World War I and Partition* (New York, 1998).
Herlihy, Jim, *The Royal Irish Constabulary: A Short History and Genealogical Guide* (Dublin, 1997).
'Hogan, David' [pseud. Frank Gallagher], *The Four Glorious Years* (Dublin, 1953).
Holmes, Richard, *Firing Line* (London, 1985).
Holt, Edgar, *Protest in Arms: The Irish Troubles 1916–1923* (London, 1960).
Hopkinson, Michael (ed.), *The Last Days of Dublin Castle: The Diaries of Mark Sturgis* (Dublin, 1999).
—— *The Irish War of Independence* (Montreal & Kingston, 2002).
Huggins, Martha K., Mika Haritos-Fatouros, and Philip G. Zimbardo, *Violence Workers: Police Torturers and Murderers Reconstruct Brazilian Atrocities* (Berkeley, 2002).
Jones, Gareth Stedman, *Outcast London* (Toronto, 1992).
Jones, Thomas, *Whitehall Diary*, ed. Keith Middlemas (London, 1971).
Kautt, William H., *Ambushes and Armour: The Irish Rebellion, 1919–1921* (Dublin & Portland, 2010).
Kee, Robet, *The Green Flag: A History of Irish Nationalism* (London, 1972).

Kerry's Fighting Story (Tralee, 1949).
Limerick's Fighting Story 1916–1921 (Tralee, 1949).
Low, David, *Low's Autobiography* (London, 1956).
Lowe, W. J., 'The War against the R.I.C., 1919–21', *Éire-Ireland* (Fall/Winter 2002).
——, 'Who Were the Black-and-Tans?', *History Ireland* (Autumn 2004).
——. and E. L. Malcolm, 'The Domestication of the Royal Irish Constabulary, 1836–1922', *Irish Economic and Social History* (1992).
Lyons, F. S. L., *Ireland Since the Famine* (Glasgow, 1973).
Macardle, Doothy, *The Irish Republic* (New York, 1965).
Macready, Nevil, *Annals of an Active Life* (London, 1924).
Malcolm, Elizabeth, *The Irish Policeman, 1822–1922: A Life* (Dublin, 2006).
Martin, Hugh, *Ireland in Insurrection* (London, 1921).
Mcbride, Lawrence, *The Greening of Dublin Castle: The Transformation of Bureaucratic and Judicial Personnel in Ireland, 1892–1922* (Washington, 1991).
McColgan, John, *British Policy and the Irish Administration 1920–22* (London, 1983).
Murphy, Daniel J. (ed.), *Lady Gregory's Journals*, vol. I (New York, 1978).
Neligan, David, *The Spy in the Castle* (London, 1968).
O'Callaghan, Sean, *Execution* (London, 1974).
O'Halpin, Eunan, *The Decline of the Union: British Government in Ireland 1892–1920* (Dublin, 1987).
O'Malley, Ernie, *Army Without Banners: Adventures of an Irish Volunteer* (Boston, 1937).
—— *Raids and Rallies* (Dublin, 1982).
Parkinson, Alan F., *Belfast's Unholy War: The Troubles of the 1920s* (Dublin, 2004).
'Periscope' [pseud. G. C. Duggan], 'The Last Days of Dublin Castle', *Blackwood's Magazine* (August 1922).
Petter, Martin, '"Temporary Gentlemen" in the Aftermath of the Great War: Rank, Status, and the Ex-Officer Problem', *Historical Journal* (1994).
Report of the Labour Commission to Ireland (London, 1921).
Ryan, Louise, '"Drunken Tans": Representations of Sex and Violence in the Anglo-Irish War (1919–21)', *Feminist Review* (Autumn 2000).
Ryan, Meda, *Tom Barry: IRA Freedom Fighter* (Dublin, 2005).
——'Tom Barry and the Kilmichael Ambush', *History Ireland* (2005).
Seedorf, Martin, 'Defending Reprisals: Sir Hamar Greenwood and the "Troubles", 1920–21', *Eire-Ireland* (1990).
Shay, Jonathan, *Achilles in Vietnam: Combat Trauma and the Undoing of Character* (New York, 1994).
Sheehan, William, *British Voices from the Irish War of Independence 1918–1921* (Cork, 2005).
Simpson, Keith, 'The Officers', in I. F. W. Beckett and K. Simpson (eds.), *A Nation in Arms: A Social Study of the British Army in the First World War* (Manchester, 1985).

Sluka, Jeffrey A. (ed.), *Death Squad: The Anthropology of State Terror* (Philadelphia, 2000).

Spires, Edward, *The Army and Society, 1815–1914* (London, 1980).

Stewart, A. T. Q., *The Ulster Crisis: Resistance to Home Rule, 1912–1914* (London, 1967).

Street, C. J. C., *The Administration of Ireland, 1920* (London, 1921).

——*Ireland in 1921* (London, 1922).

Townshend, Charles, *The British Campaign in Ireland, 1919–1921: The Development of Political and Military Policies* (London, 1979).

—— 'The Irish Insurgency, 1918–21: The Military Problem', in Ronald Haycock (ed.), *Regular Armies and Insurgency* (London, 1979).

Travers, Tim, *The Killing Ground: The British Army, the Western Front, and the Emergence of Modern Warfare 1900–1918* (London, 1987).

Winter, Ormonde, *Winter's Tale: An Autobiography* (London, 1955).

With the IRA in the Fight for Freedom (Tralee, 1950).

'A Woman of No Importance' [pseud. Mrs. C. Stuart-Menzies], *As Others See Us* (London, 1924).

Zimbardo, Philip, *The Lucifer Effect: Understanding How Good People Turn Evil* (New York, 2007).

5. UNPUBLISHED THESES

Griffin, Brian, 'The Irish Police, 1836–1914: A Social History' (Loyola University of Chicago, PhD, 1991).

Moran, Mary Denise, 'A Force Beleaguered: The Royal Irish Constabulary, 1900–1922' (University College Galway, MA, 1989).

Seedorf, Martin, 'The Lloyd George Government and the Anglo-Irish War, 1919–1921' (University of Washington, PhD, 1974).

Index